Marketing
on the Internet

Marketing on the Internet

Principles of Online Marketing

Judy Strauss
University of Nevada, Reno

Raymond Frost
Ohio University

PRENTICE HALL
Upper Saddle River, NJ

Acquisitions Editor: Whitney Blake
Editorial Assistant: Michelle Foresta
Editor-in-Chief: Natalie Anderson
Marketing Manager: Shannon Moore
Associate Managing Editor: John Roberts
Permissions Coordinator: Monica Stipanov
Manufacturing Supervisor: Arnold Vila
Manufacturing Manager: Vincent Scelta
Design Manager: Patricia Smythe
Cover Design: Eve Adams

Library of Congress Cataloging-in-Publication Data
Strauss, Judy.
   Marketing on the Internet : principles of online marketing / Judy
   Strauss, Raymond D. Frost.
      p.   cm.
   Includes bibliographical references and index.
   ISBN 0-13-010585-6
   1. Internet marketing. I. Frost, Raymond D., [date]- .
II. Title.
HF5415.1265.S774 1999
658.8'00285'4678—dc21   98-56092
                                                           CIP

Prentice-Hall International (UK) Limited, London
Prentice-Hall of Australia Pte. Limited, Sydney
Prentice-Hall Canada, Inc., Toronto
Prentice-Hall Hispanoamericana, S.A., Mexico
Prentice-Hall of India Private Limited, New Dehli
Prentice-Hall of Japan, Inc., Tokyo
Pearson Education Asia Private Limited, Singapore
Editora Prentice-Hall do Brasil, Ltda., Rio de Janeiro

Printed in the United States of America

10   9   8   7   6   5   4   3   2

Dedicated to Cyndi, Malia, María-Teresa, and David

Contents

Part II Internet Marketing Strategies

CHAPTER **4** PRODUCT AND PRICING ON THE NET

CHAPTER 5   THE NET AS DISTRIBUTION CHANNEL

Part III   The Internet Marketing Plan

CHAPTER **8** THE INTERNET MARKETING PLAN

Preface

The Internet is the first exciting, significant marketing tool to emerge in many years. New opportunities create lots of questions, however. How can firms leverage new technologies to maximum benefit? How much commitment should marketers make to Internet programs? Is our market online? In this book, we attempt to answer these and many other questions—some developing even as we wrote the text!

We believe that the Internet is emerging both as an extremely useful tool for business planning and also as part of a company's marketing mix. As planning tool, the Internet search and resource sites can aid any discipline by opening a high-speed gateway to a wealth of information. In addition, the Net is a vehicle for marketing research. The Net also assists with text-based communication: one-to-one e-mail conversation and e-mail conferencing via newsgroups and mailing lists. In the marketing discipline, the Internet serves as distribution channel, communication medium, and fertile ground for new products. It has also lowered marketing costs and put tremendous downward price pressure on products sold online. Marketers use the Net for direct distribution of digital products (e.g., news stories and live radio) and for electronic retailing. The Net marketing communication function includes advertising to the tune of over $1 billion in 1998, public relations, and sales promotion (e.g., coupons and sweepstakes). Finally, Internet technologies have created the opportunity for a variety of innovative products for creating, delivering, and reading messages as well as services such as search engines, stock trading, and interactive games. What's next?

Several popular books exist to shed light on the problems, opportunities, and techniques of marketing online, and we have used them in our classes with some success. This textbook is different in five important ways.

- First, we explain Internet marketing not as a list of ideas and techniques, but as part of a larger set of concepts and theories in the marketing discipline. The Internet is, after all, just one of many tools marketers use. To this end, readers will find marketing concept reviews with Internet examples throughout. We strongly believe that Internet strategies are more likely to succeed if selected using the marketing planning process, especially as the Internet grows to maturity and competition intensifies. After the shakeout there will only be room for the best.

- Second, we highly recommend that marketers learn a bit about the technology behind the Internet, something most of us are not drawn to naturally. While it is not necessary to be able to set up commerce servers, knowledge of the possibilities for their use will give savvy marketers an advantage in the marketplace. This book attempts to educate marketers gently in important technology issues, showing the relevance of each concept.

- Next, this book does not cover Web site design. This is a topic we love to teach, our students enjoy learning, and one that is included in many Marketing on the Internet courses. We did not include it in this book both because we felt it important to focus on marketing concepts, and because there are many excellent books about how to build a Web site. We recommend using Andrew Sather et al., *Creating Killer Interactive Web Sites* (Hayden Books, 1997) as a companion book for those wanting to learn Web site design and implementation.

- The Web site that accompanies this text is an important part of the work. Designed as an instructor's manual, it contains important information updates to the material. Especially important is a section on Internet exercises for student application of the concepts. We've included exercises in the hard copy edition; however, we make periodic changes and additions as the Internet landscape moves.

- Finally, as teachers, we present Internet marketing in a format that we believe will enhance learning. We organize chapters to parallel principles of marketing texts and provide learning tools such as chapter objectives, summaries, and exercises. We have used this format successfully for 3 years in our Marketing in Cyberspace classes, and we hope it will work well for you too.

A MOVING TARGET

We might as well raise a flag from the start and mention that this book is a snapshot of the Internet from June to October 1998. The Net is a rapidly changing medium, and thus many things in this book will be out of date before it is off the press. This is especially true for the screen captures we used: several firms were completely redoing their sites as we submitted the text! Acknowledging the fluidity of the topic, we anchor concepts in classic marketing theory and constantly remind readers that cutting-edge material may be different when they read the words. We encourage readers to explore on their own, checking out the veracity of our remarks in the light of a moving target. To assist in this process, we give reference to Web sites throughout, and we will maintain a Web site containing updates to the book. We encourage all readers to contribute to its content (www.prenhall.com/frost).

AUDIENCE

We wrote this book to assist every student of marketing on the Internet who wants to learn this topic one step at a time. This primarily includes graduate and undergraduate university students, but the book also will aid other individuals who want to learn more about marketing online. Helpful background includes basic marketing and computer knowledge, although we provide short explanations of terminology and concepts to be sure all readers are up to speed. Various sections of the book should appeal to those with differing levels of Internet experience. For example, the chapter body starts at the beginning of a topic and builds, eventually integrating sophisticated concepts. Leveraging Technology sections and Ethics and Law pieces at the end of each chapter are quite challenging, presenting cutting-edge topics.

BOOK ORGANIZATION

This book elaborates on Internet planning and marketing mix topics from a strategic perspective. Marketing plan implementation issues are incorporated throughout the book; however, the final chapter puts it all together by demonstrating the pieces to an Internet marketing plan. The following table displays the book's organization, and the next paragraphs expand on each major section.

Part I: Online Marketing Prelude	Part II: Internet Marketing Strategies	Part III: Internet Marketing Plan
1. Introduction to the Internet	4. Product and Pricing on the Net	8. The Internet Marketing Plan
2. Internet User Characteristics and Behavior	5. The Net as Distribution Channel	
3. Online Research	6. Marketing Communications on the Net	
	7. Relationship Marketing through Online Strategies	

Part I: Online Marketing Prelude

Chapter 1: Introduction to the Internet

Marketers do not usually develop products and ads in the absence of strategic planning. Occasionally someone has a great idea at the right time and gets lucky, but usually marketing success requires homework before investment. There are lots of questions about the Internet's future profitability for businesses. The infrastructure companies such as ISPs, cable companies, and computer firms are growing wildly and many are profitable, but others are still dedicating huge amounts of money in hope of future profits. Innovative new products on the Web are attracting very large audiences but most are not yet profitable. These firms, as well as future contenders and other large corporations, are doing a lot of homework as the basis for financial forecasts. Chapter 1 assists by explaining the Net's context and by getting readers up to speed on basic concepts. Also in this chapter are explanations of current business models that firms are banking on for profits now and down the road.

Chapter 2: Internet User Characteristics and Behavior

Market segmentation is the cornerstone of marketing. Businesses identify and describe segments, scouring for those with the highest potential. Chapter 2 reviews segmentation bases and strategies, then seeks to answer the question, "Who is out there, all glassy-eyed behind computer terminals?" In order to initiate a solid Internet marketing plan, firms must have a good understanding of Net user characteristics and growth trends. This chapter provides current statistics, but more important, shows readers how to find the most up-to-date material online.

Chapter 3: Online Research

Like the library, the Internet is a tremendous source of secondary data for marketing planning. Chapter 3 reviews environmental scan factors of competition, political and legal environments, social and cultural trends, economies, technology, and resources, and it suggests ways to collect information about these factors on the Internet. Another important benefit of the Net is the ability to conduct primary market research online, both through e-mail and Web surveys. To round out part I, we describe how to collect online information about the firm's environment and market effectively and efficiently, discuss the strengths and limitations of these types of data, and provide ideas about evaluating the quality of online data.

Part II: Internet Marketing Strategies

Chapter 4: Product and Pricing on the Net

This begins the meat and potatoes of this book: strategies for online marketing. Chapter 4 is dedicated to product and pricing: it contains information about new Web products and current brands that were extended into Cyberspace, explaining what works online and what does not. The context of this discussion is marketing concepts such as new product strategies and branding strategies. Pricing discussions include cost differences for online marketers and pricing strategy differences between the online and offline environments. Light is shed on the pricing implications of online commerce.

Chapter 5: The Net as Distribution Channel

Distribution channels have changed significantly based on Internet technology. The Net evolved as a complete distribution channel itself as well as a forum for electronic commerce. Digital products such as electronic publishing, software, and digital audio and video are delivered right over the Net. Catalog companies such as L.L. Bean found it easy to adapt to electronic catalogs and order taking, but other retailers must make more substantial operational changes. Barnes and Noble (www.barnesandnoble.com), for example, entered Net marketing late in the game after Amazon.com had already gained an early share of Net users. Many firms are betting on the future of electronic commerce, but few, including Amazon.com, are profitable. Electronic Data Interchange (EDI) is at the roots of business-to-business electronic commerce. Firms such as Wal-Mart gained tremendous competitive advantage by creating a paperless distribution channel, and now those lessons are easily transferred to the Internet. With all this positive potential, I-Malls do not look as promising. Internet marketers considering electronic commerce must understand the landscape before building a storefront. This chapter explores these ideas grounded in the concept of distribution channel functions.

Chapter 6: Marketing Communications on the Net

This chapter focuses on marketing communication online because this is where most of the action currently takes place in the consumer market. Chapter 6 considers the promotion mix elements and their electronic extension. Net advertising expenditures are rapidly growing and the type of ads online is evolving. From banners and buttons to interstitials and sponsorships: which to pick? This chapter discusses the features of interactive ads as well as sales promotions such as coupons and free product samples over the Net. Public relations permeates every Web site, and PR personnel must understand which tactics are particularly well suited for use on the Net. If an organization's target stakeholders are online, the Net provides many exciting and efficient venues for communication with them. This chapter also discusses media buying. Where does the Net stack up as compared to television, radio, newspapers, and magazines for advertisers? Media buyers are unsure about how to buy online advertising because of uncertainty about the medium's effect on consumers and the uncertain information about audience size and characteristics.

Chapter 7: Relationship Marketing through Online Strategies

Chapter 7 is devoted to relationship marketing. This is the strategy of building long-term customer relationships—through customer satisfaction—with individuals or organizations who will buy many products over time. Target marketing evolved from the mass marketing strategy of the early twentieth century to the later idea of building smaller customer segments that share characteristics and needs. Relationship marketing occupies the opposite end of the continuum from mass marketing because it can involve catering marketing mixes to target markets consisting of one person each. This is the marketing concept at its finest: giving individual consumers exactly what they want at the right time and place. Coincidental to this recent shift in marketing thinking to relationship marketing came the technology with which to achieve it efficiently: the Internet. Companies such as Expedia and Amazon are capitalizing on the Net's potential for building customer relationships, one at a time, and this discussion explains why and how they do it. Obviously, relationship marketing is not one of the four Ps, but its importance to Net marketers warrants special focus.

Part III: Internet Marketing Plan

Chapter 8: The Internet Marketing Plan

Here the book turns to implementation considerations. Although execution factors are scattered throughout part 2, this chapter is all about creating an Internet marketing program. It relies on the planning ideas from section 1 and the strategy information from section 2. Chapter 8 discusses Net presence planning issues: things like who is the firm's market and what are the Web site objectives? It takes the business models from chapter 1, adds the part 2 information about what works and what doesn't, and talks turkey: what does it cost and how does a firm start?

Important End-of-Chapter Stuff

A number of items have been included at the end of chapters to help bring to life important practitioner perspectives, technical issues, and issues in ethics and law. Also included are savvy Web sites for further research.

- Important people working in the business of Net marketing wrote **Practitioner Perspective** pieces. Most of these discuss issues important to those on the front line, and some take a stab at predicting the future of the Net.

- The **Leveraging Technology** pages explain important technical concepts that are critical for building an online marketing program. For example, one explains cookie files and how they can help marketers to build relationships with customers. These sections have the benefit of explaining technology in words marketers can understand, but more important, they create a springboard for creative Internet marketing ideas.

- **Ethics and Law** are short pieces on an ethical or legal issue relating to the chapter. For example, at the end of chapter 7 on relationship marketing there is a discussion of online privacy. The entire issue of privacy as it relates to electronic databases and online marketing creates an environment in which marketers want to be careful. If consumers feel that marketers are unethical, this feeling obviously is not good for the future of Net marketing. Ethics and Law sections were written by an attorney and computer scientist who wants to help marketers keep their noses clean.

- **Savvy Sites** are lists of Web sites that are important to marketers. Because this book will be quickly outdated in many areas, these Web sites will help readers do their own research and evaluate the current state of Net marketing.

Pedagogical Features

We included many features to enhance learning in *Marketing on the Internet*. Based on our cumulative 20 years of teaching experience, we've identified the best practices in university teaching and integrated items that work well for us.

- **Marketing concept focus:** In each chapter we review several marketing concepts and then tell how the Internet is related to the concept. This technique provides a bridge from marketing principles the student already knows and presents material in a framework for easier learning. In addition, as things change on the Net, students will understand new ideas based on underlying concepts.

- **Learning objectives:** Each chapter begins with a list of objectives that, after studying the chapter, students should be able to accomplish. Given our active learning preference, the objectives are behavioral in nature.

- **Cases that discuss real companies:** A case history starts each chapter. Most are original Web success stories obtained through personal interviews with business founders. Students will find these to be exciting introductions to the material. Each case is the story of an entrepreneur, usually under age 30, who opened shop on the Web and made it work.

- **Multiple screen shots in each chapter:** Wherever possible we show actual Web pages to provide an example of the concept under review. The Web site address is easily readable on the screen capture so students may explore the site on their own.

- **Parenthetical technical terms:** We slide many technical terms into the text as parenthetical comments so they will be less threatening to students.

- **Chapter summaries:** Each chapter ends with a summary of its contents. While these summaries capsulize the chapter guts, they were not created so that students can read them in lieu of the chapter content.

- **Key concepts and terms**: Also at the end of each chapter is a list of important terms and concepts in the chapter. This will assist the student in checking for understanding.

- **Review questions:** Questions at the chapter end are aimed at both knowledge level learning and higher levels of application, synthesis and evaluation. These end-of-chapter questions are divided into two groups: knowledge level and critical thinking.

- **Exercises:** When students become actively engaged in the material, learning is enhanced. To this end we include several activities at the end of each chapter and one comprehensive Internet exercise.

- **Practitioner perspectives:** At the end of each chapter is a short essay written by someone in the field. We asked CEOs and top-level managers to write about cutting-edge issues in Internet marketing, and the results are quite interesting and inspirational. These, when joined with the chapter introductory cases and current examples throughout the text, give the marketing concepts life.

- **Leveraging technology:** These sections present the more technical aspects of Net marketing, explaining their relevance to marketers. Topics such as cookies and collaborative software have revolutionized Internet commerce and we highly recommend that students read these sections.

- **Ethics focus:** The Internet is in many ways the "wild west" where anything goes. If marketers understand the important ethics issues such as privacy and spam, they will have less chance of upsetting consumers and inviting regulation. An attorney specializing in Net ethics wrote an essay at each chapter end, and we include two important Internet ethics codes in the Appendix.

- **Savvy sites:** In addition to the numerous Web site addresses included in the chapter body, we've provided a list of important sites for further research on chapter issues.

- **Glossary:** Most people don't brag about a glossary, but we were unable to find a comprehensive glossary focusing on Internet marketing, so we included one in this book. The Internet has spawned an incredible amount of new terminology and we want to help readers understand the landscape.

INSTRUCTOR SUPPORT MATERIALS

This is the first edition of a book about a moving target. No one has quite laid out the territory the way we have in *Marketing on the Internet*. Naturally there will be lots of changes and updates. Therefore, we hope to build community with the faculty who adopt this book so that together we can continually improve its value in the classroom. To that end we've designed several interactive supplements along with the more traditional test bank.

WEB SITE

www.prenhall.com/frost

1. **Web site:** A Web site will serve as instructor's manual and water cooler for sharing ideas about teaching marketing on the Internet classes (www.prenhall.com/frost). On the site are updates on important Net marketing issues, and ideas we receive from others. Also on the site are more traditional instructor's manual items.

2. **Suggested syllabus**: A sample syllabus for teaching this class is on the *Marketing on the Internet* Web site.

3. **E-mail the authors:** We encourage e-mail from faculty using this textbook. Send questions, suggestions for improving the text, and ideas about teaching the class.

4. **Test bank:** A test bank is available to faculty adopting this textbook. Question items focus on chapter learning objectives and other important material. They include items at all levels of learning from knowledge through application and evaluation.

ACKNOWLEDGEMENTS

The most pleasant task in this project is expressing our appreciation to the many individuals who helped us create this work. When we began we had no idea that the scope of the job would require us to request, plead, cajole, and charm a number of folks into helping us. Our gratitude is enormous.

First, we would like to thank our students over the years. We teach primarily because we love working with our students. They inspire us, teach us, and keep us on our toes.

Next we want to thank Prentice Hall for believing in us and giving us a place to showcase our ideas. Our editor, Whitney Blake, was very helpful in keeping us focused. We also appreciate the support of our institutions, Central Connecticut State University and the University of Nevada, Reno. Our deans, department chairs, colleagues, and secretaries put up with us while we bent their ears and became monomaniacal about the task at hand. Next, we appreciate the fine suggestions of our reviewers. They gave us an objective perspective that helped us both to improve the work and to see that we were doing something worthwhile:

- John Bennett, Stephens College
- Catherine A. Cambell, University of Maryland
- Richard Clodfelter, University of South Carolina
- Jack Cole, ERIS Enterprises, Inc.
- Steve Dinger, Mission College
- Mark Gillenson, University of Memphis
- Blaine Greenfield, Bucks County Community College
- Robert Minch, Boise State University
- Nina Ray, Boise State University
- Bette Ann Stead, University of Houston

There are some individuals who contributed significantly to this book's content or design. Brian O'Connell contributed the interesting and timely Ethics and Law sections at the end of each chapter. His perspective is a great contribution. Steve Barrante advised us with the page layout and design. Seven practitioners wrote essays on cutting-edge topics: Manish Bhatia (Nielsen Media Research), Rick Boyce (HotWired), Ted Hawthorne (Relevant Knowledge), Mary Ann Packo (Media Metrix), Kathryn Creech (Home Arts), Peter Clemente (Cyber Dialogue), and Matt Straznitskas (BrainBug). We appreciate the fact that they took time from their busy days to contribute to student education. Similarly, we thank the many businesspeople who took time to be interviewed for the introductory cases to each chapter.

Four students provided excellent assistance: Cyndi Jakus managed the incredibly difficult task of obtaining permissions for reprinting screen shots and other copyrighted work in the book. Aiman Noursoultanova assisted with the permissions and editing and dedicated some of her life to creating an excellent glossary. Craig Sadosky put the Savvy Site sections together for us and assisted with research tasks. WeiXing Xu assisted with the references.

Finally, the support and encouragement to accomplish a major piece of work comes from friends and family. To them we are indebted beyond words.

Judy Strauss: I want to thank my children, Cyndi and Malia, who not only listened endlessly to my daily struggles and accomplishments, but also give purpose to my life. My friends, especially Ellen Greene and Jarek Strzemien, gave me considerable support through this project.

Raymond Frost: I want to thank my lovely wife, María-Teresa, whose constant support, faith, and understanding kept me whole throughout this process.

ABOUT THE AUTHORS

Judy Strauss and Raymond Frost have collaborated on several Web-based projects. In 1995 they developed a Web server and site for the School of Business at Central Connecticut State University. As Web sites do, it expanded to many pages, including individual pages containing their course syllabi and related materials. They have published academic papers on issues of Web audience measurement, Internet survey research, consumer/company e-mail communication, and Internet pedagogy. Their book, *The Internet: A New Marketing Tool*, is in its third edition. In addition, they have developed Web training seminars for business clients. They also developed a new course in 1996, "Marketing in Cyberspace." This book developed from that course.

Judy Strauss is Assistant Professor of Marketing at the University of Nevada, Reno. She has published academic papers in Internet marketing, advertising, and marketing education. She has had many years of professional experience in marketing, serving as entrepreneur as well as marketing director of two firms. She currently teaches business on the Web, marketing communications, and principles of marketing courses. Strauss earned a doctorate in marketing at Southern Illinois University, and a finance MBA and marketing BBA at University of North Texas.

E-mail: jstrauss@unr.edu

Raymond Frost is Professor of Management Information Systems at Ohio University. He has published scholarly papers in the information systems field and is an associate editor of *The Journal of Database Management*. Frost has ten years of experience managing computer resources. He currently teaches marketing in cyberspace, database, and telecommunications courses. Frost earned a doctorate in business administration and an MS in computer science at the University of Miami, and received his BA in philosophy at Swarthmore College.

E-mail: frostr@ohiou.edu

Marketing on the Internet

Chapter 1

Introduction
to the Internet

*"It's like a sailing race. The guy in front
knows what's happening with the wind first
and can react quicker."*

—Jerry Yang, co-founder of Yahoo!

Chapter Outline

- The Yahoo Story
- A Variety of Perspectives
- What Is the Internet?
- What Is the Web? (A Business Perspective)
- Hierarchy-of-Effects Explanation
- Internet Business Models
- The Web as an Important Part of The Economy
- Organization of This Book

Practitioner Perspective
Convergence:
What It Is and What It Means
— Manish Bhatia, Vice President, Interactive Services, Nielsen Media Research

Leveraging Technology
Bandwidth and Market Opportunities

Ethics and Law
Codes of Conduct

Learning Objectives

- Marketing review
  - Explain the hierarchy of effect's importance to marketers
  - Describe the marketing planning process
- Compare and contrast many different perspectives for describing the Internet
- Tell why bits are critical building blocks for the Internet's future
- Explain why mass customization unleashes the Internet's incredible marketing power
- Understand six Net business models for marketing communication and four for revenue generation
- Estimate the Net's impact on the U.S. economy
- Describe the Net as marketing mix tool

The

Yahoo!

Story

Yahoo! (www.yahoo.com) embodies one of the best examples of meeting organizational goals while serving customer needs. This is a company that even *before* its inception focused on serving the customer. The two chief yahoos are Jerry Yang and Dave Filo. They were graduate students together at Stanford University before leaving their studies to found Yahoo! Jerry is the more vocal and outgoing of the two; Dave is the technical genius.

Yahoo! got its start as "Jerry's Guide to the World Wide Web." This was literally a home page that Jerry and Dave created on their university computer accounts to keep track of the cool links that were out on the Web. They began to share the address with others and the page rapidly increased in popularity. In the tradition of the Web gift culture, they updated and maintained the list for free. Stanford provided the servers, so there was no cost to the viewing public. From the beginning, users would e-mail them suggested sites for inclusion and suggestions for improving the site. Jerry and Dave incorporated these suggestions in order to improve their product. They even solicited suggestions for sites to include. They also began to introduce new product benefits such as "What's New" and "What's Cool." User feedback was such an important reward that Jerry said, "If there was no feedback…we wouldn't have done it."

Choosing a name for the site was a bit problematic. The name they liked was yacc, a name referring to a software tool on a Unix computer system. Following the yacc model, they wanted the name to start with YA. Consulting a dictionary, they went through a list of possibilities before settling on Yahoo! They added the exclamation point just to be different.

Yahoo! received its first big break when Netscape put a link to the site on the Navigator browser. This helped to generate traffic. But when Netscape later canceled the link, the traffic stayed and Yahoo! continued to flourish. Why? Yahoo! delivered something that was rare—an index compiled by humans. The other Web search engines used software robots to categorize their sites, and while this method helped generate a larger list of sites than Yahoo! they tended not to be as relevant. People like the intuitive feel of the Yahoo! index. And the index continues to grow. Each one of its army of classifiers is able to categorize about 100 sites *daily*! It now has hundreds of thousands of sites classified, potentially making Yahoo! impossible for other search engines to catch.

Jerry and Dave were at first reluctant to sell advertising for fear of being labeled sellouts. Nonetheless, they needed some source of revenue, so they accepted their first ad in August 1995. Since that time their ad revenues have grown to nearly $100 million. Yet only 14% of the available ad space on Yahoo! has been sold, so there is still great potential for growth.

Wall Street continues to put its faith and dollars behind Yahoo! Investors have bid up the Yahoo! stock from $13 to $172 per share from April 1996 to July 1998. The company's market capitalization has grown from $100 million to $8 billion. This leads some to question whether the company can possibly be worth that much. To put this in perspective imagine that the TV preview guide that lists what's on the cable channels were able to attract more in advertising revenue than the networks themselves. Then again maybe if there were millions of channels, and preview guides were as useful as Yahoo!, they would attract more traffic.

Yahoo!'s marketing department divides the Web community into three groups— current surfers, near-surfers, and nonsurfers. They run ad campaigns in traditional media to appeal primarily to the near-surfers. These are people who will be online shortly, and if they start at Yahoo! they'll be hooked for a long time.

Yahoo! is currently the most popular site on the Internet, with over 32 million unique page views monthly. Founder Jerry Yang would like that number to rise to 100 million. He continues to believe that focusing on customer needs is the key to future success and the way to stay a step ahead of the competition. To this end Yahoo! has introduced a variety of free services: directories, news and reference, interactive and customizable pages, commerce and shopping, editorial, and many others.

Under Jerry and Dave's leadership, Yahoo! has progressed from a hub to a destination and media property. Jerry's goal is to create a "lifestyle medium," which means among other things building community online. He wants users to view Yahoo! not as a destination but rather as a tool. At a keynote address to Internet World in March 1998, he left the audience with this thought: "Think about what you do on the Web. Put more into it than you get out of it." Sitting atop an $8 billion company, he and Dave are living proof that this can be a formula for success.

A Variety of Perspectives

How should the Internet be understood? As a technological innovation? As a new form of publishing? As a new advertising medium? As a new form of electronic commerce? Is there any single best perspective for marketers?

Here it will be argued that there is not. In this chapter and those that follow, the Internet is explained from a variety of viewpoints. Multiple perspectives help bring out the richness of business opportunity in this exciting new medium. Innovative new businesses emerge every day online. Unimagined opportunities are on tomorrow's horizon.

Chapter 1 begins this text by hinting at the Internet's importance to marketers. It does so by suggesting several answers to the question: What is the Internet?

- It is a technology, a social space, and a marketing tool.
- The Web is a place for information publishing, transactions, and mass customization.
- The Net's marketing use is explained by the hierarchy-of-effects model.
- Its business potential is described by popular Net business models.
- The Net has an economic, social, and political context.

▪ It is part of the marketing planning process and indeed the marketing mix itself.

These definitions of the Internet help to explain its current impact and business potential. They set the stage for understanding how marketers can take full advantage of this new tool. Throughout, the reader is invited to share the spirit of adventure with which this text explores marketing on the Internet.

We now begin this exciting story by examining the Internet from many viewpoints.

What Is the Internet?

The Internet ("Net") is a network of computers reaching every country in the world. It is similar in some ways to the telephone system. Just as calls can be made anywhere in the world, so too can a computer contact any other computer connected to the Net. The World Wide Web ("Web") actually began as a very small part of the Internet. It was an experimental child of the Internet which grew up quickly to overtake its parent. The Web is that part of the Internet that can be surfed by following hyperlinks, the underlined text that takes a user from site to site with a click of the mouse. The interconnections between Web pages evoke the image of a spider web—hence the name. The Web has had such tremendous appeal that in a few short years it grew to be far and away the dominant part of the Internet. The Web launched the commercial success of the Internet: it attracted the commercial investment that fueled its growth. Most people who refer to the Internet are referring to the Web.

So what part of the Internet is separate from the Web? The biggest item is electronic mail. Electronic mail travels over the Internet but it is not part of the World Wide Web. Another item not part of the Web is Usenet. Usenet consists of over 50,000 discussion groups arranged hierarchically by topic. Users post messages under a discussion topic (technical term: thread) which other users can read and then post their responses. Both e-mail and Usenet predate the Web.

THE INTERNET AS TECHNOLOGY

One way to understand the Internet is to look at the technology that supports it. The details of that technology are incredibly complex but the concepts behind it are quite simple. To paraphrase Negroponte (1995), the Internet is all about moving bits from one place to another. Bits are the essential building blocks of digital information much as atoms are the building blocks of molecules. A bit can be either a zero or a one. Grouping bits forms more complex information such as letters, words, graphics, sound, or video. From the Internet's perspective a bit is a bit is a bit. The Internet does not distinguish between bits that carry text, graphics, sound, or video. From this humble beginning comes a new marketing landscape: things such as electronic commerce and banner advertising.

If the major task is to move bits from one location to another, then two key subtasks are critical to the Internet's success. First, the infrastructure must move those bits as quickly as possible. Speed is important and will be a repeated theme throughout this text. The Internet is currently too slow (see the leveraging technology sidebar at the end of this chapter to find out why). Slow speeds mean loss of business opportunities. For example, reliably carrying phone calls and music over the Internet requires lots of speed. The Holy Grail of the Internet architecture is video on demand and for that the speed is nowhere near adequate.

Second, making it easy for users to exchange bits is the basis for the World Wide Web. The Web was created to link all the bits together with a point and click graphical interface. In addition to pictures and sound, users want tools such as search engines to find quickly the bits they need. Tomorrow's users may well demand an intelligent interface that understands speech. For their part, marketers are finding tremendous opportunities based on Internet technologies—we have not seen this number of successful new products since the early 1970s. Marketers can also reach target markets more effectively with tools that track which bits the users are viewing. For more on the history and technology of the Net please see Appendix A.

THE INTERNET AS SOCIAL SPACE

The Internet is more than computers and their contents: it is a social space where users communicate with each other via e-mail, Usenet, and the Web. It is this feature, as well as the fact that there is no governing body, that allows the Net to be shaped by its users. The Net is truly a grassroots development, and marketers who reflect this philosophy in their Internet programs gain user approval.

"It's like going to a party without leaving home." So begins the confession of a teenage chat-room addict. The Internet is full of social spaces. Users can interact in real time via chat rooms, video conferencing, Internet phone, or interactive games. These products create marketing opportunities. For example, Yahoo! sponsors a free interactive games site. Users can play a variety of board games such as chess, checkers, poker, and the like against players from all over the world in real time. They can even chat by exchanging messages while playing. Why does Yahoo! offer this free service? Because it drives traffic to their site, builds brand loyalty, and serves as a forum for selling ads.

Web sites such as GeoCities create social spaces based on user interests. It has 2 million "homesteaders" populating its GeoAvenues with free Web pages. Users hang their Web sites out on avenues such as pets, careers, romance, women's issues, and sports. They interact in chat rooms and they draw friends to their Web sites. The effect is that marketers have easy access to self-formulated psychographic market segments.

THE INTERNET AS MARKETING TOOL

In the early 1950s marketers discovered something innovative: If you give customers what they want, and do it better than the competition, sales will grow. Furthermore, if a firm can do this while making a profit, life is sweet indeed. These ideas gave birth to the marketing concept: An organization exists to satisfy customer wants and needs while meeting organizational objectives. The Yahoo! case study, which opens this chapter, is an excellent example of how an organization employs the marketing concept. With the introduction of the Internet, marketers have the technology to mass customize communication and products to increasingly smaller targets: taken to its natural extension, a target market can now be one person. For example, PointCast sends news and sports information to users based on their individual needs, and at the Dell Computer Web site a customer can enter the exact specifications for a new computer and Dell will ship it within five days. The question in everyone's mind is, "Is this profitable?" And if not, what are the profitable uses of this new medium? In other words, are organizational needs being met as well as customer needs? The answer to this question has important implications for the future of electronic commerce, customer service, advertising, electronic publishing, and other marketing uses of the Internet.

The Internet is firmly established as a new marketing tool. Marketers use the Internet to gather data for marketing planning. The Net has become an integral piece of the marketing mix, spawning new products and serving as both a digital distribution channel and an electronic storefront. The Net is also a strong medium for communication with target audiences. In this function it is similar to a magazine or television except that the Net allows two-way communication. People are connecting to the Net at a phenomenal rate, and the number of unique Web pages now numbers 320 million. No medium in history, including television, has reached the 50 million user mark as fast as the Internet. The Web passed the 50 million user mark in 4 years; it took television 13 years to do the same. The Internet is a medium for communication and electronic commerce whose time has come.

What Is the Web? (A Business Perspective)

Following the 1991 National Science Foundation decision allowing commercial use of the Net, businesses and other organizations quickly moved into the Web and rapidly built it. This commercialization proceeded in three stages as follows. While these stages apply to the Web as a whole, interestingly, many online companies also repeat these stages. Nonprofit organizations and individuals publishing Web sites generally stick with the first stage, information publishing. This section examines the Web from a business perspective.

1. Information publishing
2. Transaction-based systems
3. Mass customization

INFORMATION PUBLISHING

Most businesses began by creating an informational home page. This is a low-risk and low-budget operation that creates a Web presence. Unfortunately, these pages often resembled an annual report: very linear and text heavy. This format was fine if the target audience was investors, but in most cases investors were not the target.

These initial attempts earned the name of *brochureware*. Truth be told most corporations did not give a great deal of thought to their early Web pages. Often it was left to technical people to implement without much input from marketing. This system has changed a great deal in a few short years.

Many businesses today realize that the Internet is an important marketing communications medium. This means that even an informational Web page must be a part of an organization's unified message. Brochureware is still a very valid use of the Web when implemented after careful planning.

Information publishing can be considerably more than self-promotion. Many businesses, including magazines and newspapers, specialize in the delivery of content. Indeed content providers are one of the key players in the online community. A great deal of focus will be given to content providers in the chapters that follow. Content providers tend to give much thought to their target audience and are able to help identify that target audience for their advertisers. Publishing content is a major function of the Web, and viewing content for research is the number one activity online. Selling ads and sponsorships to support that content is an increasingly important key driver of the success of the Web.

Web portals are a stunning example of effective content providers. These portals act as entry points to the Web — generally the first place that a user starts when she fires up her browser. Portals index and retrieve information from other content providers. The larger portals have done an amazing job at amalgamating content — from TV guides, to weather maps, to street maps, to phone book listings, to entertainment listings, and so on. The more content they can provide, the more they are likely to become the starting point for an online session. The largest of these portals, Yahoo!, has been incredibly successful, rising very quickly from a project of grad school students to become an $8 billion company.

TRANSACTION-BASED SYSTEMS

Transaction-based online systems allow organizations not only to communicate with the consumer but to sell online as well. These systems are considerably more difficult to implement than simple information publishing and often require the services of a professional programmer. Online storefronts fall into this category, as does business-to-business commerce. In both cases the Web page must link to backend computer systems (called backend because the user never interacts with them directly) to validate transactions and manage inventories. Transaction-based systems will continue to grow as organizations turn to the Web as a complementary distribution channel. These systems are studied carefully in chapter 5.

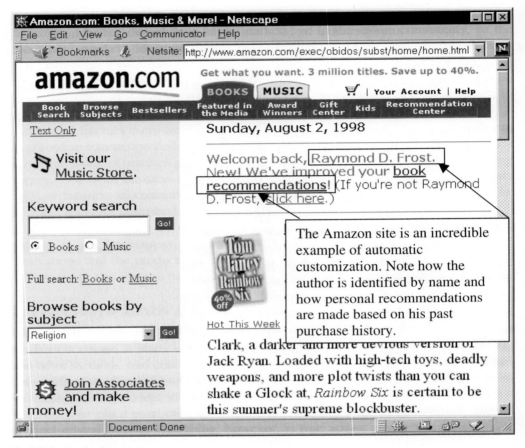

Exhibit 1 - 1 Amazon.com

MASS CUSTOMIZATION (PERSONALIZATION)

The really mind-boggling juncture of information technology and marketing is in the area of mass customization. Mass customization refers to creating systems that can personalize messages to a target audience of one. There are two forms of mass customization—automatic and manual. Under *automatic customization*, clever software tailors the content presented to the user based upon information known about the user and the user's historical surfing behavior. The products that perform automatic customization tend to be technically very sophisticated and ethically somewhat controversial. Some users do not like to be observed online even if the observation is performed by computer software. On the other hand, automatic customization has the potential to deliver tremendous benefits to the user by filtering undesired content. *Manual customization* relies on explicit a priori instructions from the user to determine preferred content categories.

Automatic Customization

A great example of automatic customization is Amazon. Amazon uses historical purchase information to predict which titles might be of interest to a returning customer. The Amazon home page is shown in Exhibit 1 - 1.

The Amazon site will be referred to at various points in the text. This site was conceived with a careful marketing plan by someone who thoroughly studied both Net users and the book industry. It is now the largest online retailer of books in the world. Part of Amazon's success is its continued focus on the customer's needs.

Even more incredible software has been developed which allows Web sites to communicate with one another in tracking a user's behavior online. One product by Aptex software (www.aptex.com) called SelectCast follows the model that "you are what you view." By examining the content that users view, SelectCast is able to target ads to that viewer. And what's more, the targeting can follow that user from site to site!

Manual Customization

Manual customization requires that users specify in advance what content they wish to view. Typically this is done with check boxes or pull-down menu items. One heavy use of manual customization is in the delivery of news services. The user is able to determine which sections of the newspaper he receives or indeed even which stories he wants to receive based upon keyword search terms. *The New York Times* (www.nytimes.com) offers this service as part of its *New York Times* Direct service. Exhibit 1 - 2 shows how the service is configured. Still other examples of manual customization include the following:

- Customized banking interfaces such as that offered by Bank of America's "Build Your Own Bank" (www.bofa.com). Bank of America presents customers with "Money Tips" geared to their interests, informs them of special offers via e-mail, and even assists with loan applications by transferring stored profile data to the application with the touch of a button.

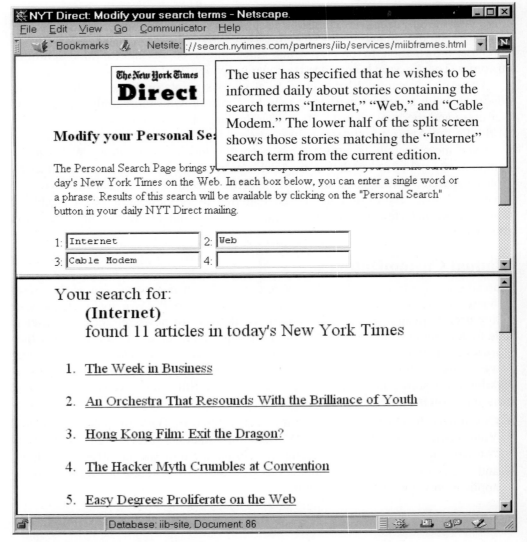

Exhibit 1 - 2 NY Times Direct

Source: www.nytimes.com. © 1998 The New York Times Company. Reprinted by permission.

- Customized CDs such as those offered by Cductive (www.cductive.com). Users pay $4.99 for the first track and $0.99 for each additional track up to 72 minutes of music.

- Customized computers such as those offered by Dell (www.dell.com). Dell allows users to configure their custom computer using drop-down menus. Price trade-offs are explicitly listed (e.g., add $149 for a 17" monitor).

- Customized catalogs such as those offered by Cisco (www.cisco.com). These catalogs contain negotiated prices and may list only the products that businesses want their employees to purchase. Furthermore, customers can go straight from the catalog to an online ordering process.

Hierarchy-of-Effects Explanation

Marketers' use of the Net for information publishing, transaction systems, mass customization, and other uses can be understood in light of the "think, feel, do" hierarchy-of-effects model. This model suggests that consumers first become aware of and learn about a new product (think), then develop a positive or negative attitude about it (feel), and ultimately move to purchasing it (do) (Ray 1973). The thinking, or cognitive, steps are awareness and knowledge. The feeling, or attitude, steps are liking and preference. The doing, or behavioral, steps are conviction and purchase. This model is well accepted for high-involvement product decisions (those that are perceived as being high financial, emotional, or social risk). This is so because consumers spend some amount of time gathering information and considering alternatives prior to purchase. Conversely, for low-involvement decisions, consumers often just hear about a product, give it a try, and then decide if they like it. Exhibit 1 - 3 presents this classic model and its low-involvement adaptation.

If a firm wants to build brands and inform, it will operate at cognitive and attitude levels of the hierarchy of effects, perhaps utilizing information publishing, Web advertising, and other promotional techniques. If a firm desires online transactions (behavior), the communication messages will be more persuasive and include ways to actually complete the transaction on the Web site. Finally, firms wanting to build relationships with customers will utilize mass customization. Relationship building using online strategies occurs at all hierarchy levels. These ideas are used throughout this book. Almost every Internet marketing strategy has at its roots objectives formulated from a hierarchy-of-effects model. This is so because, above all, the Net is a way to communicate with stakeholders (those having an interest in the firm).

In the next section, we describe the hottest Internet "business models." These are organized according to hierarchy-of-effects steps as a way to understand the marketing objectives behind each model.

High Involvement		Low Involvement	
Awareness	Cognitive	Awareness	Cognitive
Knowledge	(think)	Knowledge	(think)
Liking	Attitude	Purchase	Behavior
Preference	(feel)	Conviction	(do)
Conviction	Behavior	Liking	Attitude
Purchase	(do)	Preference	(feel)

Exhibit 1 - 3 Traditional Media Hierarchy-of-Effects for High- and Low-Involvement Product Decisions

Internet Business Models

The hierarchy is a good context in which to discuss the question posed earlier in this chapter: "What are some profitable uses of the Internet?" At the November 1997 AdWeek (www.adweek.com) conference at Internet World (www.iw.com), many Internet practitioners described the Net in terms of business models. By this they meant the ways in which firms can use the Net profitably. One speaker said the Net is a medium for customer service, relationship building, and branding: that is, extensions of a firm's current marketing communication program. Another claimed that revenues on the Net can be achieved through advertising, commerce, and subscriptions to online publications. These practitioners were describing current uses of the Net and were also predicting important future uses. Analyzing all of this talk as well as current writing about profitable uses of the Net led to a short list of very strong ways to reach and interact with customers or potential customers and to generate revenues. These business models are presented in Exhibit 1 - 4. The number in parentheses indicates which chapter in this book has the most information on the model.

If Internet companies want to create awareness, knowledge, or positive brand attitudes, they might choose one of the models in row one of Exhibit 1 - 4. Most of these models also have the power to build stakeholder relationships. The models begin with pure marketing communication techniques such as advertising, sales promotion, and public relations without seeking immediate transaction. Firms can implement their strategies through any Internet format: the Web, e-mail, or the Usenet. It is important to remember, however, that the user has control of the mouse and can click away at any point, forming an individual clickstream of information. Therefore, stakeholder communication and branding strategies must be different from those used in traditional media (i.e., individualized, global, and quickly enticing).

- **Stakeholder communication** refers to information, persuasive or not, about the company and its brands. Stockholders, consumers, employees, the media, suppliers, and the government are all examples of stakeholder groups. McDonald's Corporation (www.mcdonalds.com) has a series of Web pages for stockholders, and Media Metrix (www.mediametrix.com) has pages for the media ("press room"). Many firms have Web pages for employee viewing only: These are often placed on Intranets. When firms put pure information on their Web sites, it is called brochureware.

Hierarchy of Effects	Business Model
Cognitive and Attitude	Stakeholder communication (6) Branding (6) Sales promotion incentives (6) Lead generation (6) Customer service (6) E-mail databases (6)

Transactive Behavior (revenue generating)	Sell product (4 & 5)
	 Electronic publishing
	   1. Sell content (4 & 5)
	   2. Sell ads (4 & 6)
	 Agent services (5)

Exhibit 1 - 4 Internet Business Models

- **Branding** is a process of selecting brand names (e.g., McDonald's) or brand marks (e.g., the golden arches) and supporting them with marketing communications. A firm wants the public to recognize its brand name and to feel positively about it; thus brand advertising does not attempt to sell product as a direct and immediate effect. The Internet has not been nearly as strong as television for brand advertising, but the Net is gaining in use for branding. Forrester Research predicts that $4.1 billion will be spent on Web brand advertising in 2000.

- **Sales promotion incentives** are offers of cash or free product to build short-term sales. J. Crew sends coupons by e-mail and www.hotcoupons.com offers coupons for most U.S. cities. EudoraPro offers a 30-day trial of its software for users who register, and MusicBoulevard offers free audio clips of its CDs. This technique is called sampling. Many other online sales promotion tactics are described in Chapter 6.

- **Lead generation** occurs when a company uses e-mail or its Web site to gather names of potential customers. The folks at www.hermanmiller.com, an office furniture supplier, entice users to complete a form requesting a salesperson to contact them at a later date.

- **Customer service** is extremely important for creating customer satisfaction and building business revenues. Happy customers have positive attitudes and often tell their friends about their experiences. A good example of customer service occurs on the Rollerblade site (www.rollerblade.com). This site includes a retail finder so that users may locate product near their homes. Feedback mechanisms on Web sites, availability of foreign language versions, and customer satisfaction surveys are also good examples of customer service. An important customer service tool is outgoing e-mail from a company to a user.

- **E-mail databases** are used increasingly by organizations wanting to build relationships and turn prospective customers into clients. When organizations keep in touch about relevant and useful information and answer e-mail promptly and appropriately, customers are happy. Of course if e-mail communication turns into spam (unsolicited and unwanted e-mail), it has the opposite effect. E-mail databases are often used for customer service, but this is a growing model and deserves special attention.

Chapters 4 and 5 are devoted to transaction-based business models. Chapter 4 discusses many new types of products and services that exist because of new technology as well as current products that extended their lines for online customers. Chapter 5 focuses upon the distribution channel, describing new opportunities for digital distribution and online storefronts. All the models previously described lead users through the hierarchy of effects, but transaction models actually generate revenue.

Sell product refers to actual online transactions by companies that sell their own products or resell products they purchased elsewhere (i.e., retailers). Approximately two-thirds of all revenue generated through product transactions occur in the business-to-business market, but there is much promise of a robust consumer marketing in the future. Many obstacles such as perceived transaction security must be overcome first, however. There are many ways to create digital value, and lots of firms are trying to understand how to become profitable or save expenses using this model.

Electronic publishing is actually a subset of selling product. Media create online versions of their publications and generate revenue in one of two ways: (1) they sell subscriptions (e.g., *The Wall Street Journal*), and/or (2) they sell advertising space. Generally online media are categorized by news. business, personal finance, entertainment, or health and family. While this information is outstanding for users, they have not been quick to pay for it. Thus the advertising model is winning out so far.

Agent services occur when firms serve as middlemen but do not take possession of the product. A good example of this is a travel agent such as www.travelocity.com. Many new agents appear online every week. One group are product aggregators, selling advertising or natural gas during online auctions. Another group are intermediaries in the distribution channel that assist users in finding product. Shopping agents will search the Web to find the best prices for specified products. Finally is an innovative new development called *syndicated selling*. This occurs when a Web site offers other Web sites a commission for referring customers. Amazon has tens of thousands of affiliates (i.e., agents), who put the Amazon logo on their site and receive up to 15% of the dollars spent by referred customers.

There are several additional things to consider when using these models. First, the Internet is a global medium. This means that marketers must consider their target markets as compared to the Net's audience. For example, a U.S. pharmaceutical company Web site once offered free samples of one of its products and it received requests from all over Africa that it had to politely decline. Second, a common thread running through all models is the idea that communications and product offerings can be individualized to a target market of one. Finally, one might wonder why firms choose cognitive and attitude objectives and not just go for the sale. Recall that consumers move through the steps of the hierarchy, usually one at a time, and they must be made aware of a product before they can buy it. Naturally some marketing communication seeks to accomplish the entire hierarchy in one piece: for example, one ad might introduce a new product and entice consumers to buy it.

Having touched upon users and Web business models, we may now turn to macroeconomic issues. What is the economic potential of this powerful new medium?

The Web as an Important Part of the Economy

Imagine for a minute that one day the price of gasoline dropped to 10¢ per gallon. This would create enormous wealth in the U.S. economy. All businesses would see their overhead costs decline for heating, air-conditioning, machinery, lights, and so on. These savings could be passed on to consumers in the form of lower prices. Also, Americans would have more money in their pockets that they were not spending on gasoline. Something like this is happening as a result of the Internet.

The "gasoline" in an information economy is information. And the cost of information is falling dramatically as a consequence of the Internet. The savings are not only on the costs of research but also on the transfer of information. For example, a customer's order is information which must be entered into the supplier's computer system. If suppliers have to enter the information manually, then they incur a labor cost. On the other hand, if customers enter their orders on a Web site, the supplier incurs no labor cost. A significant savings? Some put the savings at 30%. The overhead savings can be returned to the customer in the form of lower prices or to the stockholders as more profits. Take as another example the distribution of a newspaper. It costs money to print and distribute a newspaper (30% to 40% more). If the distribution cost can be reduced dramatically by distributing online, then the savings can be returned to the customer by eliminating the subscription fee entirely! By continually reducing the distance between people and the information that they need, the Internet makes that information cheaper. As a result, people can afford more and higher-quality information at decreasing costs.

There is no question that the Internet has had an effect on U.S. and world economies. The size of that effect is somewhat difficult to measure, because the Internet is lumped into the same category with the rest of information technology in government reporting. Yet interestingly, it is the U.S. government that makes the greatest claims about the Internet's economic worth. The basis of these claims is explored in the following sections on the stock market, new media revenues, reduced inflation, efficiency and effectiveness, and jobs.

INTERNET STOCKS ARE UP

First Internet stocks have attracted tremendous investment dollars. This trend is somewhat surprising because at the end of the first quarter of 1998, most of the highly valued Internet companies were operating in the red. The combined value of these top companies was over $35 billion. There is a certain hysteria surrounding Internet stocks that has some investors scratching their heads. By any traditional measure most of the Internet stocks are overvalued, and yet as investment dollars continue to pour in, the value of those stocks continues to increase by the law of supply and demand. At the time of this writing, the market was experiencing a correction downward. Other analysts see a very bright future for Internet stocks. The bullish analysts view buying Internet stocks like buying stock in NBC at the time of the creation of television. NBC may not have made great financial sense at the time but its future was beyond anyone's expectations.

Stock trading online has become big business. Charles Schwab, one of the larger online trading companies, has 1.4 million online accounts representing $103 billion. These accounts were all created over a period of 18 months. Will online stock trading eventually make brokers obsolete? In the 1980s when the London Stock Exchange went online, brokers disappeared from the trading floor almost overnight. Already in the United States, the NASDAQ exchange operates as an association of dealers without a trading floor and the NYSE and ASE have been able to handle increased trading volume through online technology. What further changes will be driven by Internet stock trading?

One very nontraditional measure of Internet stocks is Mecklermedia's Web Site Value Index. This index takes the total worth of a company (market capitalization) and divides it by the number of monthly users. By this measure Yahoo!, with a value of $8 billion divided by 32.9 million unique monthly users, has a value per user of $243. The next closest site is Microsoft with a $93 value per user. Is this a meaningful measure? It's tough to tell. Most of these measures are useful primarily for comparing companies.

NEW MEDIA REVENUES

The new media industry "combines elements of computing technology, telecommunications, and content to create products and services which can be used interactively by consumers and business users" (Coopers & Lybrand 1997, p. 16). Some of the businesses in the new media industry include content design and development, content packaging and marketing, content distribution and transport, electronic commerce as a primary business channel, software development, content creation tools, and other services to aid new media companies. When taken as a whole, Pricewaterhouse & Coopers LLP (formerly Coopers & Lybrand) predicts that new media revenues in the United States will exceed those of recorded music and most traditional media (**Exhibit 1 - 5**). In New York City alone, new media industry revenues topped $2.8 billion in 1997, a 59% increase from the previous year. At this point it is difficult to know how much of new media revenue growth comes at the expense of traditional media revenues, but one thing is clear: There is more money being pumped into the economy because of the Internet.

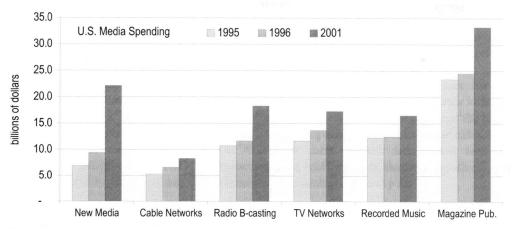

Exhibit 1 - 5 U.S. Media Spending
Source: Coopers & Lybrand L.L.P (1997), "2nd New York New Media Industry Survey: Opportunities and Challenges of New York's Emerging Cyber-Industry," Industry report sponsored by New York New Media Association and NYC Economic Development Corporation.

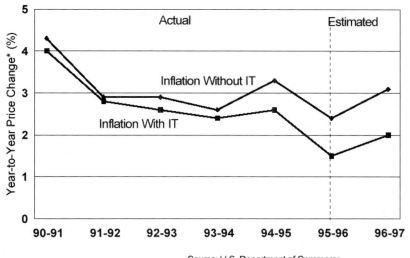

*As measured by the Gross Domestic Income Implicit Price Deflator

Source: U.S. Department of Commerce Economics and Statistics Administration Estimates based on Bureau of Economic Analysis and Census data

Exhibit 1 - 6 Information Technology Lowers Inflation

REDUCED INFLATION

According to a report released by the Commerce Department (www.ecommerce.gov) in April 1998 entitled, "The Emerging Digital Economy," information technology has even helped to keep inflation in check (from 3.1% down to 2%). This amazing feat is shown in Exhibit 1 - 6.

But how much of the deflationary effect is due to the downward pressure on prices created by online selling? How much is the result of the lowered cost of information? How much is simply the result of rapidly falling computer prices and cheap imports? What is surprising is that if cheap information returns dollars to the pockets of consumers, then increased inflation should be expected as those consumers bid up the price of goods and services.

EFFICIENCY AND EFFECTIVENESS

Cheap information allows businesses to become more efficient by reducing the costs of doing business and more effective by opening up strategic opportunities. Effectiveness refers to choosing the right thing to do in order to maximize a company's competitive advantage. Efficiency refers to doing it with the minimum expense of resources (inputs to outputs). Both concepts at the macro level have an effect on the economy overall. If businesses become more efficient (save money) as a result of the Internet, then they are able to improve their competitive position and lower prices for the consumer. If businesses become more effective (choose good business opportunities), then they are also able to improve their competitive position and introduce more value for the consumer and shareholder.

The Internet allows gains in efficiency and effectiveness as measured from the standpoint of different business value chain functions.

Gains in Efficiency

- **Purchasing:** Automation leads to elimination of jobs, which lowers labor costs. Online bidding attracts more bids, which creates a downward pressure on prices.
- **Inventory management:** Businesses pay interest on inventories. Reducing inventories through Just-In-Time and electronic delivery systems saves money.
- **Cycle times:** Two developments allow automotive manufacturers to reduce cycle times from 4-6 years to 2.5 years. First, by direct connection with their suppliers they are able to verify a design's compatibility with existing parts. Second, by placing design teams around the globe they are able to design 24 hours a day as the teams pass work off to one another.
- **Customer service:** Systems that allow users to self-diagnose and solve problems at a Web site save corporations from fielding expensive (labor cost) calls.
- **Sales and marketing:** Entering orders online saves labor costs in rekeying orders.

Gains in Effectiveness

- **Purchasing:** Online searching helps to locate hard-to-find components. It is especially effective during a strike by a product supplier.

- **Inventory management:** Reduced inventories also allow corporations such as Dell to incorporate the latest technology in their products rather than stale components off the shelf.

- **Cycle times:** Reducing cycle times allows the manufacturers to respond more quickly to changes in the marketplace.

- **Customer service:** Better customer service leads to improved customer satisfaction and greater likelihood of repeat purchases.

- **Sales and marketing:** Automatic configuration agents can verify the integrity of an order immediately rather than kicking it back weeks into the process. Doing this leads to greater customer satisfaction.

JOBS

The Internet has also helped to create high-paying jobs for the techno savvy. This is always a concern for students of marketing on the Internet. Using the New York City market as a proxy for the United States gives some indication of employment opportunities in new media (Coopers & Lybrand 1997). The figures below are comparisons from a 1995/1996 survey to a follow-up study ending mid-1997.

- For the 18 months ended mid-1997, dollars spent on new media payroll increased to $2.73 billion (93%).

- During that same period, the total number of new media companies grew by 16% and the average number of employees per firm grew by 31%.

- By the year 2000, New York new media companies project a 79% increase in the number of industry jobs. Of these, 87% will be full-time, 87% will be part-time, and 50% are for freelancers.

- Marketing and sales positions in new media have quintupled during the 18 months ending in mid-1997.

- Thirty-one percent of new media managers own equity in the business.

New media companies represent the largest and fastest growing U.S. industry sector in 20 years. This text will argue that the most valuable person in this economy understands both technology and marketing. The aim of this book is to help educate that person.

Organization of This Book

The marketing process forms a framework for organizing information about Internet marketing in this book. While the hierarchy of effects helps guide objectives, it is the marketing mix strategies that create the desired effect in target markets. Next is a review of the marketing planning process, followed by the specific application to *Marketing on the Internet* chapters.

MARKETING PLAN TASKS

Marketing is the process of planning and executing the conception, distribution, promotion, and pricing of ideas, goods, and services to create exchanges that satisfy individual and organizational objectives. In plain English, this means that marketers plan marketing mixes (4 Ps) to meet the needs of customers, and then carry out those plans. Specific tasks involved in this process are outlined in Exhibit 1 - 7 and summarized below.

- *Situation Analysis*
  - *Environmental factors.* Marketers collect and analyze information about the environment that is external to the organization. Topics of an environmental scan include economic analysis, social and demographic trends, and more. Environmental scanning is a continual task, permeating the entire process.
  - *Market opportunity analysis.* This entails a demand-and-supply analysis: identifying and describing potential market segments (demand), and identifying key competitors in these potential segments (supply). The MOA often also includes a SWOT analysis (strengths, weaknesses, opportunities, threats): an analysis of the firm's strengths and weaknesses to deploy against opportunities and threats found in the environment. Much of this information comes from the environmental scan.
- *Selecting target market(s).* At this stage, marketers analyze many market segments using several criteria including profit potential, and eventually select one or more targets. Because the Net is a communication medium, at this stage firms may select other stakeholders as well (e.g., employees, suppliers).
- *Setting objectives.* On the basis of the firm's mission and resources, marketers set overall market share and other goals, and also set objectives for each target market.
- *Designing marketing mix strategies.* This entails developing the marketing mix strategies of product, pricing, distribution, and promotion to accomplish set objectives.
- *Action plan.* Armed with marketing strategies, planners outline specific tactics for plan implementation.
- *Budget.* At this stage a budget to cover the planned strategies is set, and the plan is implemented.
- *Evaluation plan.* The plan results must be evaluated continuously to see if the objectives are being realized.

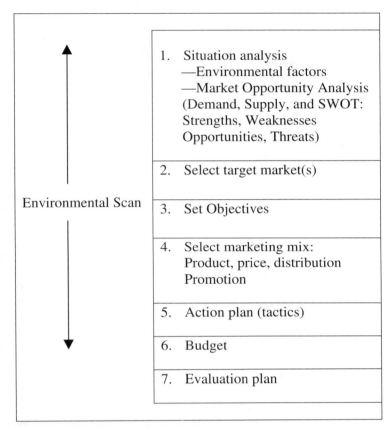

Environmental Scan

1. Situation analysis
   —Environmental factors
   —Market Opportunity Analysis
   (Demand, Supply, and SWOT:
   Strengths, Weaknesses
   Opportunities, Threats)

2. Select target market(s)

3. Set Objectives

4. Select marketing mix:
   Product, price, distribution
   Promotion

5. Action plan (tactics)

6. Budget

7. Evaluation plan

Exhibit 1 - 7 Marketing Plan Tasks

Where does the Internet fit in this process? It is a research tool for planning and evaluating, and it is a part of the marketing mix itself. Marketers attempt to move users through the hierarchy of effects, from product awareness through purchase, and attempt to build relationships with users through marketing mix tools. Many innovative new *products* emerged because of the Internet, and firms often extend current product lines to take advantage of new technology. Electronic commerce has *pricing* implications because consumers can easily and quickly search the Web for the lowest priced products, and businesses can easily watch competitive price levels. The Internet's biggest marketing applications are in the area of product distribution and promotion. The Net itself is a *distribution channel* for digital products such as radio broadcasts, software, and publications, and it also serves as retail storefront for companies selling online. *Marketing communication* (promotion) about the other three Ps is enhanced by electronic forums such as e-mail, bulletin boards, and the Web. Dollars spent on Net advertising are increasing, sales promotions such as coupons and free samples are abundant, and public relations tactics permeate most Web sites and many e-mail communication programs.

PART 1: ONLINE MARKETING PRELUDE	PART 2: INTERNET MARKETING STRATEGIES	PART 3: INTERNET MARKETING PLAN
1. Introduction to the Internet 2. Internet User Characteristics and Behavior 3. Online Research	4. Product and Pricing on the Net 5. The Net as Distribution Channel 6. Marketing Communications on the Net 7. Relationship Marketing through Online Strategies	8. The Internet Marketing Plan

Exhibit 1 - 8 Organization of Book

MARKETING PROCESS APPLIED TO THIS BOOK

This book elaborates on planning and marketing mix topics from a strategic perspective. Marketing plan implementation issues are incorporated throughout the book; however the final chapter shows how these strategies combine to build an Internet marketing plan. Exhibit 1 - 8 displays the book's organization.

S u m m a r y

This chapter explains why the Internet is important to marketers by looking at a variety of perspectives.

Organizations utilize the marketing concept to satisfy customer needs while furthering organizational goals. By use of mass customization, the marketing concept can be applied to micromarkets and even individual customers.

The World Wide Web ushered in the birth of the Internet as a commercial success. The NSF approval of the Web for commercial uses, when combined with easy hyperlink surfing, opened up this vast resource to nontechnical people for the first time. And the medium continues to grow at an unprecedented rate (faster even than TV) and with boundless optimism.

Right now the Internet is slow. As bandwidth increases in the years to come, fascinating business opportunities will develop—especially those that rely on multimedia applications.

The Internet is social space where communities of users gather around shared interests in chat rooms, board games, and videoconferencing. Businesses that can cater to these communities will realize tremendous marketing opportunities.

Business use of the Web has evolved in stages from information publishing to transaction-based systems to mass customization. All three stages are in heavy use today. Content providers publish information, storefronts conduct online transactions, and marketers customize marketing communications to increasingly small segments. Successful businesses will ensure that effective use of the Internet follows an overall marketing communication plan.

The hierarchy-of-effects model provides a theoretical framework with which to view this new medium. As in the brick and mortar world, consumers often progress through cognitive, attitude, and behavior stages. Furthermore, interaction helps Web sites build relationships with customers and prospective customers.

The business community has been grappling to build models that help us understand and exploit this new medium. Practitioners suggest a number of models, each of which brushes a piece of the canvas. These models range from stakeholder communication to branding to sales promotion and finally the ultimate transaction. Placing these models in relationship to the hierarchy-of-effects model helps us to understand the complete picture.

Few would dispute that the Internet has had an effect on the economy. However, the direction and magnitude of that effect is a subject of debate. Internet stock prices are astronomical. All bets are on future success as current losses are overlooked. New media industries that support the Web are raking in revenue, and the job outlook for graduates entering this field looks bright indeed.

The remainder of the book elaborates on planning and marketing mix topics from a strategic perspective. Much traditional marketing theory will be cast in the light of the Internet. It is an exciting time to study a new medium and the authors hope that the reader will share their sense of adventure.

Key Concepts and Terms

1. The marketing concept states that an organization exists to satisfy customer wants and needs while meeting organizational objectives.

2. The Internet provides an unprecedented opportunity to tailor the marketing concept to individual customers through mass customization.

3. What really launched the popularity of the Web was the ability to incorporate graphics.

4. More bandwidth will enable many more business opportunities, especially those that depend on multimedia—such as online video on demand.

5. Interaction helps to build customer relationships.

6. Most business models for the Internet relate to the hierarchy of effects.

7. The Internet has injected wealth into the economy by reducing the cost of information.

8. Cheap information allows businesses to become more efficient by reducing the costs of doing business and more effective by opening up strategic opportunities.

- Agent service
- Automatic customization
- Bandwidth
- Business-to-business commerce
- Chat room
- Effectiveness
- Efficiency
- Electronic commerce
- Environmental scan

- Hierarchy-of-effects
- Hyperlink
- Information publishing
- Intranet
- Manual customization
- Market opportunity analysis
- Marketing concept
- Mass customization
- Transaction-based systems
- Usenet

Exercises

REVIEW QUESTIONS FOR KNOWLEDGE TESTING

1. Give examples of agent services.
2. What is the difference between efficiency and effectiveness? How can the Internet further both of these goals?
3. What are the stages in the hierarchy-of-effects model?
4. What is bandwidth? Why is it important?
5. Name several Internet business models to affect consumer awareness and attitudes.
6. Name several Internet business models that generate revenue.
7. In what way is an online order form an example of the reduced cost of information?

DISCUSSION QUESTIONS FOR CRITICAL THINKING

1. How can cheaper information lead to increased wealth?
2. How strong can an online community be if the members never meet face to face?
3. Why does automatic mass customization raise ethical issues not raised by manual mass customization?
4. The telephone became a popular medium once it entered the home. Is entering the home critical for the Internet as well? Why or why not?
5. What is the current stock price of Yahoo!? Would you invest in Yahoo!? Why or why not?
6. Why does the environmental scan permeate the entire marketing plan process?

7.   What is the most important use of the Internet for marketers?

ACTIVITIES

1.   Gather in groups of four. For five minutes quietly brainstorm businesses, such as video stores, that might be affected by increased bandwidth on the Internet. Share your ideas in a round robin fashion without interrupting the speaker. When everyone has shared, try to reach a consensus.

2.   Watch an hour of television including the commercials. Write down each mention of a web site and in what context the mention appeared. What conclusions can you draw about cross promotion?

3.   Visit www.yahoo.com and search for "Internet Marketing." Make note of several banner ads that appear, and for each one tell at which stage of the hierarchy of effects you think it is directed.

INTERNET EXERCISE: THE MARKETING CONCEPT

(Note: The Internet exercises in this text were first developed by the authors for Kotler/Armstrong, Principles of Marketing, *8th ed. (Upper Saddle River, NJ: Prentice Hall, 1998) and are reprinted here by permission of Prentice Hall.)*

Web sites can demonstrate the marketing concept by exhibiting a company's special features to customers and prospects. Many sites target customer segments by language, gender, and age. Web users want to know about product benefits and where products can be purchased. However, sites that give surfers something of interest beyond product descriptions create additional value. Web sites, particularly e-mail, provide a convenient way for customers to communicate with the company. E-mail is a good example of Web-based customer orientation. Complete the following chart to indicate which benefits are supported on the Web sites of two athletic shoe companies. Then decide which firm is more customer oriented.

Benefit	Nike www.nike.com	New Balance www.newbalance.com
Product benefits		
Retail locator		
Non-product information		
Multiple languages		
Multiple targets: gender		
Multiple targets: age		
Multiple targets: different sports		
Customer feedback		
Fun to surf?		

For Discussion

1. Of the benefits listed above, which three do you think are the most important? Why?

2. Overall which site better embodies the marketing concept? Why?

3. Suggest one or more customer benefits not listed above that the "better" site contains.

INTERNET EXERCISE: CITIZEN-ACTION PUBLICS

Many different publics form a company's marketing environment. One public gaining power as a result of the Internet is the citizen-action public. A group can organize a boycott of a company's products simply by posting messages to newsgroups and chat rooms or by designing its own Web page. Others target direct marketing in general and even offer services to eliminate unwanted "junk" postal mail and junk e-mail. Visit Yahoo at www.yahoo.com and look under Business and Economy: Consumer Economy: Consumer Opinion: Boycotts: Use the information you find there to complete the following chart.

Company	Boycott	Reason for Boycott

For Discussion

1. What strategy should a company use to respond to its boycotted site?

2. Visit the Web pages of the companies you have listed. What type of action, if any, have they taken to respond to the charges precipitating the boycott?

3. There are companies that will monitor what is being said about your company on the Internet so as to give you an opportunity to respond quickly to rumors before they become major media events. How much would you be willing to spend for such a service? Why?

Practitioner   Perspective

CONVERGENCE: WHAT IT IS AND WHAT IT MEANS

Manish Bhatia, Vice President, Interactive Services, joined Nielsen Media Research in 1989. Since 1995, Manish has worked on developing Nielsen Media's Interactive Business including surveys, site tracking, and panel-based research services. The following is an excerpt from a paper which outlines the future of TV with a focus on convergence and the resulting implications for all traditional media players, including advertisers, advertising agencies, content producers, and research companies.

The future of television: The television as we know it is poised to go through a major transformation. The pressure to change is coming from two major directions: Digital TV (DTV) and the Internet. The Federal Communications Commission has outlined a timetable for broadcasters to convert to digital TV, with the first transmission scheduled to begin in 1998. Digital TV, as the name implies, means that instead of using frequencies and waveforms to transmit TV signals, the information would now go digitally—in bits and bytes.

To handle digital signals, reception devices need to have the necessary components to receive and display this information. These include a processor, an operating system, storage, and a display device. A collection of these elements, in essence, represents a PC. The predominant means to access the Internet currently is the PC. Approximately 40% to 45% of U.S. homes have one. About 50% of the PC homes have access to the Internet at home. While looking to expand that user base, the computer industry seems to have its eyes set on another device that is much more prevalent in U.S. households—the TV. The TV is by far the most popular electronic medium that exists. It is in 98% of U.S. households and is in use for more than 7 hours a day, every day of the year. It is extremely easy to use and appeals to people in virtually every social, economic, and demographic group.

Convergence — What is it? Consumers use the TV to get TV content and PCs to get Internet content. Numerous companies are working hard to change that. The TV and the Internet are colliding, and the result is the early emergence of a converged environment. The physical distinctions between TVs and PCs are beginning to blur, and either device will soon be able to receive and display Internet or TV information.

Numerous companies are working to make this happen: Intel's Intercast system is already delivering digital information along with analog TV on enabled PCs. WebTV allows TV viewers to surf the Internet on their TVs without needing a PC. WorldGate is working on delivering the Internet to the TV by encoding the Internet information on the Vertical Blanking Interval (VBI) of a traditional TV signal. They also offer the ability to link TV programs and commercials to related Web-based content with a technology called "Channel Hyperlinking." In the WorldGate model, Internet access would become an add-on to the cable service just as a pay network currently is. Windows 98 is designed with a built-in TV tuner that will allow the PC to receive TV content. This product allows PC users (who have a TV Tuner card) to watch television from their desktops. Soon PCs will come equipped with the TV Tuner card and the requisite software to enable watching TV on computers.

Convergence—What does it mean? All of this is happening today and it has serious implications for all players in the media industry (advertisers, advertising agencies, and content producers/broadcasters). The reasons that so many companies are working on making convergence a reality are clear.

The Internet has demonstrated a compelling advertising and direct marketing model for various companies.

Users have found value in the things that the Internet enables them to do. These include everything from getting personalized stock quotes to searching for product information to making travel reservations.

Connecting the two media (TV and Internet) offers the opportunity to combine the mass reach of TV with the power of interactivity offered by the Internet and the back-end efficiencies offered by Internet-based fulfillment systems. This allows advertisers to unleash the power of targeting and interactivity on a much larger scale than before.

The implications of such a transformation affect all players in the industry.

Advertisers will soon be able to "interact" with their viewers on a historically passive medium. Technology will allow for complete interactivity—from brand awareness to purchase—between the viewer and the marketer, all from one platform, all in a single session. A car manufacturer will be able to point a viewer to the nearest dealer or offer on-the-spot cash rebate for the purchase of the vehicle. McDonald's may be able to offer cents-off coupons redeemable within 24 hours to visit one of their stores. The possibilities and opportunities are endless.

For the reasons listed above, a lot of the traditional marketing functions will now be possible on the TV. Thus, media plans will become more and more integrated within the overall marketing plan. Also, as the marketing functions are enabled over the TV set, the share of the overall marketing budget assigned to media advertising will likely increase to reflect the expanding power of the TV as an overall marketing and fulfillment vehicle. This is probably the biggest opportunity TV has to assume a broader marketing role beyond being just one of the media vehicles used to fulfill part of a marketing plan's objectives.

L e v e r a g i n g   T e c h n o l o g y

BANDWIDTH AND MARKET OPPORTUNITIES

Incredibly complex infrastructure systems bring a variety of utilities to the consumer's home. These include the telephone, cable TV, water, and electric power. In most cases the consumer does not know or care how the infrastructure that delivers these systems works. What interests the consumer are benefits. For example, the consumer might be interested in receiving 25 more TV channels or being able to videoconference from home. To provide these additional services would require major infrastructure improvements behind the scenes.

Nonetheless, in this, and in other technology sidebars throughout this book, the authors are going to suggest that the marketing student does need a rudimentary understanding of information technology to identify and seize business opportunities on the Web. A good jumping off point for that understanding is an infrastructure issue into which many companies are pouring billions of dollars—that issue is bandwidth.

Bandwidth refers to the carrying capacity of an information channel—in other words, the amount of information that can squeeze through an information pipe. That pipe might be a telephone or cable TV wire. Greater bandwidth results in greater speed of delivery of information through that pipe. A lack of bandwidth leaves the consumers waiting at their terminal for Web content to download. Bandwidth is measured in bits per second. Modems are used to pump information over a telephone line. The fastest modems operate at about 50,000 bits per second. How much information does this represent? It takes about 10 bits to form one character such as the letter "A." So a channel carrying 50,000 bits per second (50 Kbps) could carry about 5,000 characters per second

$$\frac{50,000 \text{ bits}}{\text{second}} * \frac{1 \text{ character}}{10 \text{ bits}} = \frac{5,000 \text{ characters}}{\text{second}}$$

Text travels very efficiently over the Internet. The same is not true, however, for graphics. A photograph could easily require 500,000 bits. At 50,000 bits per second, the photograph would take 10 seconds to transmit

$$500,000 \text{ bits} * \frac{1 \text{ second}}{50,000 \text{ bits}} = 10 \text{ seconds}$$

Full motion video requires 32 frames per second, each one of which requires 500,000 bits. This means that full motion video is just not possible at telephone modem speeds.

Just how fast does transmission need to be to support various media types? What are the bandwidth requirements? Advances in compression methods change these numbers constantly but the following table serves as a rough guide:

Media Type	Minimum number of bits per second	Abbreviation
Text	25,000	25 Kbps
Graphics (pictures)	50,000	50 Kbps
Sound	100,000	100 Kbps
Video	1,000,000	1 Mbps

Why should marketers care? One reason marketers care is that one major marketing opportunity, developing low-involvement brands, is not possible without increases in bandwidth. Branding soap, for example, requires creating an emotional feel-good experience for the consumer. This atmosphere is best created by the multimedia sight and sound experience of television. High-quality multimedia on the Web just isn't there yet for lack of bandwidth. Here are some other marketing opportunities that would be made possible through greater bandwidth:

- Personal selling via the computer as a videoconferencing device
- Phone calls delivered over the Internet
- Delivery of music CDs over the Web
- Delivery of movies over the Web
- Real time virtual reality

Right now the Internet is in a very curious stage of development. The information channels that form the backbone of the Internet have amazing carrying capacities and are constantly being upgraded by firms such as Cisco, Sprint, MCI, AT&T, and UUNet. However, the last link along the path to the Internet, the telephone line to the consumer's home, is woefully outdated and is a bandwidth stranglehold. This is so because the phone line was never designed to carry anything other than voice communications. Voice communications do not require a tremendous amount of bandwidth. The latest round of 56K modems (56,000 bits per second) have just about squeezed as much information out of the phone line as is possible without major infrastructure changes. Those changes are finally on their way.

Digital Subscriber Line (DSL)

Digital Subscriber Line (DSL) technology refers to a family of methods for transmitting at speeds up to 8 Mbps (8 million bits per second) over a standard phone line. There are nine variations of DSL, a few of which are described here:

- Asymmetric Digital Subscriber Line (ADSL: The information coming to the user's home (technical term: downstream) is delivered faster than the information that the user sends back upstream. The differences in speed can be enormous, e.g., 8Mbps vs. 32Kbps (8 million vs. 32,000 bits per second).

- Symmetric Digital Subscriber Line (SDSL): The information is delivered at the same speed upstream or downstream.

- Rate Adaptive Digital Subscriber Line (RADSL): The information is sent at the maximum speed the line can handle under changing weather and interference conditions. This is similar to modems, which can adapt to different speeds depending on the quality of the phone line.

All of the major phone companies have deployed or are planning to deploy the infrastructure to support DSL technology on a trial basis. There are still some technical issues to be resolved. One of the more serious issues is that in many neighborhoods phone companies have tried to save money in the past by installing hardware that channels traffic from multiple homes onto a single line back to the phone company. This grouping is not compatible with DSL, which requires that each phone line from every home extend all the way back to the phone company's central office. Still there is optimism in the industry that the technical difficulties can be overcome. And the difficulties must be quickly overcome or the phone companies will lose the high-speed data market to the cable companies, who do already have their infrastructure widely disseminated.

Cable Modems

While the phone companies are sorting out the DSL issues, the cable companies have already gotten a head start with cable modems. The cable companies have banded together into two consortiums. The first consortium, called the @Home Network, was formed by Comcast Corporation, Cox Communications, Rogers Cablesystems Limited, Shaw Communications, Inc., and Tele-Communications, Inc. (TCI). Time Warner, Time Warner/Advance-Newhouse, and MediaOne Group Inc. formed a more recent consortium called Road Runner. These consortiums help to set standards and share development costs.

The consortiums have attracted venture capital. As an example, Compaq Computer and Microsoft have each invested $212.5 million in Road Runner. Clearly the personal computer industry has a stake in selling computer upgrades to consumers needing beefed-up machines to handle the additional bandwidth.

Cable modems allow transmission of Internet traffic over the cable TV wire connected to the home. The speed of transmission over a cable modem ranges between 500 Kbps and 2.5 Mbps. Cable companies do not face the same daunting infrastructure issues that the phone companies face. In fact the major problem cable companies may face is having too many subscribers! This is so because subscribers in a cable neighborhood share bandwidth. The more subscribers there are, the less bandwidth there will be to repartition. Therefore, if a neighborhood becomes saturated with subscribers, then each subscriber will experience delays. However, right now this is a problem the cable companies would love to have.

The big advantage that the cable companies have is early market penetration. In May 1998, the number of cable modem subscribers topped 200,000 for the United States and Canada. The infrastructure is already in place to support 11 million homes. Some 120,000 cable modems were installed this year vs. only 4,000 DSL modems in the same time frame (Forward Concepts **www.fwdconcepts.com**). The early adopters opted for cable modems because they were the first technology available. This early usage also gives cable modems the advantage of diffusion via word of mouth.

Another advantage that the cable companies have results from solving their infrastructure issues early on. They are now able to focus on establishing value-added services. These include:

- Video-on-demand
- CD-quality audio
- Online games available for download and purchase

Each value-added service provides a barrier to entry for the phone companies. Why purchase a service with fewer features? And because providing each service requires a learning curve, it will be hard for the phone companies to catch up. One way the phone companies could compete is through price. But, as the following table shows, so far they are unable or unwilling to do so.

Cost Comparison

	DSL	Cable Modem
Monthly charge	$60 to $100	$35 to $55
Installation fee	$300	$80 to $175
Bandwidth	32 Kbps to 8 Mbps	500 Kbps to 2.5 Mbps

While it looks like the cable companies have won the high-speed data access game, nonetheless the phone companies have deep pockets. The consumer can only benefit from the competition to bring high-speed bandwidth to the home. The best solution for the consumer will probably be based on availability, features, and cost.

Ethics and Law

CODES OF CONDUCT

Authors' Note: This is the first in a series of sidebars on ethics and law, which will appear at the end of each chapter. Dr. Brian O'Connell, a lawyer and computer science professor, writes these sidebars on ethics and law in the online world. In this first piece, Dr. O'Connell introduces the long history of self-regulation which has characterized professional communities throughout the ages — from the Hippocratic Oath of doctors to the Code of Ethics of the American Marketing Association. This piece is particularly timely since industry self-regulation helps to fend off government regulation and is good business. The message has not been lost on major Internet industry players. Jerry Yang, co-founder of Yahoo!, in his spring 1998 Internet World keynote address observed, "If we piss off our users by selling out on their privacy or intruding on their privacy then they'll never come back again."

The study of ethics has been in existence for over 2,500 years. Its central focus is the analysis and description of such basic concepts as what is right and wrong and how we go about judging the differences. An important dimension of this investigation concerns the types of conduct that comprise ethical behavior. These tasks necessarily involve the examination of responsibilities, rights, and obligations. Ethical inquiry is not limited to purely theoretical boundaries. Rather, questions are studied at all levels of human interaction and often appear as political, legal, and commercial issues.

A particularly important aspect of ethical inquiry involves the study of professional activities. Traditionally, groups of individuals possessing special skills or knowledge have established codes and systems of fair practice. A classical example is the Hippocratic Oath of physicians. Ethical standards work both externally and internally. They help to communicate consistency and trustworthiness to the community at large while also assisting in maintaining stability and integrity within the profession. In these ways, ethics are both pragmatic tools and essential elements of professional identity.

Documents such as the American Marketing Association's (AMA) Code of Ethics reflect the recognition of a commitment to the exercise of honesty, integrity, and fairness within all professional transactions (AMA 1996). The code appears in an appendix to this book. In addition to articulating overall values, professional codes such as that of the AMA provide members with guidelines that are specific to their pursuits. They are often products of the combined experiences of practitioners and scholars which are passed along to the entire membership and published to the public. Historically, codes have been interpreted or revised to respond to changed circumstances and new issues. In the past, these processes have been relatively gradual, with modifications often coming in conservative degrees. Today, this situation has been fundamentally transformed.

Modern technology presents a radical challenge to marketing ethics as well as to those of other professions. The extent of this demand is perhaps best reflected in the revolutionary features of the computer itself. When compared with other major technical advances such as the printing press, telephone, or automobile, digital media is arguably unique in its capacity for speed, ubiquity, and versatility. Computers serve as data collectors, compilers, and disseminators. They represent the fastest growing form of communication and, through the Internet and similar systems, forge global links of unprecedented proportion.

These factors have created vacuums in ethical policy. Although they do not directly challenge such general ideals as fairness or honesty, digital processes and potentialities are so new that ethics, like many other social endeavors, is only beginning to adapt itself to the Computer Revolution. Currently, a number of critical issues are confronting those who work within electronic environments. These include the ownership of intangible data, often termed "intellectual property", the role of privacy in a virtual world without walls, locks, or doors, the extent to which freedom of expression should be allowed, the uses of data, including methods of collection, and the special status of children who log into digital networks.

Easy solutions are seldom achieved within ethics, and in electronic contexts, progress is complicated by a lack of comparative historical situations. Likewise, the ability to analogize computers to objects or institutions with which society has had greater experience is often questionable. Is the computer network more like a broadcast station or a printing press or a public library? Our current lack of experience in these matters makes it difficult to say for certain. Finally, the fact that electronic spaces are global in nature accentuates the earlier observation that ethical positions are by no means agreed upon. What is accepted in Europe may be rejected in Asia or America.

The seemingly limitless opportunities afforded by computers also suggest the need for the constant assessment of ethical implications. Each participant in electronic marketing is given not only the responsibility to adhere to professional codes, but in a very real sense, the unique opportunity to contribute to these standards in a meaningful way.

S a v v y   S i t e s

Web Site and Address	Importance to Net Marketers
Computer Reseller News www.crn.com	This site often features stories on electronic commerce.
Cnet www.cnet.com	Cnet provides general information about computing and the Internet.
Cybersolve www.cybersolve.com	Cybersolve is a webzine that contains articles and online books about WWW marketing. It's a great academic source of information.
E-Commerce Today www.ectoday.com/	This is yet another source for current news stories on e-commerce. Registration is free for this site to access limited information.
InfoWorld—Electric Electronic Commerce www.infoworld.com	At this site is a special section of the publication InfoWorld devoted to electronic commerce.
Internetweek www.techweb.cmp.com	Internetweek features news stories about electronic commerce from a technical perspective. Great for techies.
Internet World (formerly WebWeek) www.internetworld.com	Internet World has articles on electronic commerce and marketing.
Jupiter Communications www.jup.com	Jupiter offers lots of interesting tidbits about the Net for commerce and advertising.
Mouse Tracks nsns.com/MouseTracks/	A service of New South Network Services, Mouse Tracks has lots of good information about the state of the Net. Of special interest are syllabi from university marketing courses and lists of Net marketing resources.
New York Times www.nytimes.com	This is a *New York Times* special section devoted to marketing and electronic commerce. Go to this web page to register. It's free!
The Tenagra Awards awards.tenagra.com	The Tenagra Awards have been given since 1994 to "recognize organizations and individuals whose achievements fundamentally impact the way marketing, public relations, and advertising are done on the Internet.
Wilson Internet Services www.wilsonweb.com/webmarket/	This is an excellent site to find articles on Internet marketing gathered from a variety of publications. A highly recommended bookmark

2

Internet User Characteristics and Behavior

"[In 1999] the media will stop hyping total Web user estimates. Why? We don't bother to count how many people use the telephone."

—Cyberdialogue/findsvp

Chapter Outline

- The GVU Story
- Internet Growth Rate
- Size of the Internet
- Market Segmentation
- Consumer Navigation Behavior

Leveraging Technology
Content Filtering

Ethics and Law
Copyright, Patent, and Trademark Law

Learning Objectives

- Marketing review
- Describe the diffusion process and adopter categories
- Tell why the product life cycle is important to marketers
- List several market segmentation bases and variables
- Explain several ways to measure the Internet's size
- Tell why it is hard to measure the number of online users
- Position Internet user growth on the Product Life-Cycle curve
- Discuss the importance of segmenting Net users by behavior
- Compare U.S. and global Internet user size and characteristics
- Explain three important consumer navigation behaviors
- List and describe several important Web sites that measure Net usage

The

GVU

Story

Back in the Internet's early days users wondered how many others were sitting behind their computers spending much too much time looking for cool stuff. At first it was mere curiosity, but as the Internet exploded from fun toy to commercial medium, counting eyeballs became critical. Recognizing this need, a graduate student at Georgia Tech's Graphic, Visualization, and Usability Center (GVU) stepped up to the plate. At age 24, Jim Pitkow pioneered use of the Web for survey research by posting _The First User Survey_ in January of 1994 on the GVU Web site. He did not want to clutter up the newsgroups, which in those days had no commercial messages, and he similarly felt that users would not want surveys appearing in their e-mail in-boxes. Pitkow and the GVU folks reasoned that the best approach was to advertise the Web site survey, invite users to stop by, and give them an easy point-and-click interface when they arrived.

This strategy worked well. _The First User Survey_ received over 4,500 responses and taught the Net community a lot about user characteristics and behavior. Since then, GVU posted surveys every six months and it continues to provide detailed data and analysis free to the Web community. Their work expanded from a general survey to a series of 15 to 20 specialized survey areas. The number of respondents grew from 23,000 (The Third User Survey) to 88,000 (The Seventh User Survey). Quite impressive!

How do they get such large numbers to fill out lengthy questionnaires? They announce the survey broadly both on the Internet and in traditional media. For their most recent survey they even announced it on WebTV. The following is taken from the methodology section of their _Eighth User Survey:_

The GVU Surveys employ nonprobabilistic sampling. Participants are solicited in the following manner:

- Announcements on Internet-related newsgroups
- Banners placed on specific pages on high-exposure sites (e.g., Yahoo!, Netscape)
- Banners randomly rotated through high-exposure sites (e.g., WebCrawler)
- Announcements made to the www-surveying mailing list, a list maintained by GVU's WWW User Surveys composed of people interested in the surveys
- Announcements made in the popular media (e.g., newspapers, trade magazines) (_source_: gvu.gatech.edu/user_surveys)

The GVU surveys do not attempt to count the number of Web users, but instead to describe them. The reason for this lies in the Web-based survey methodology itself. Everyone who fills out a survey is already a Web user and thus it is impossible to predict what proportion of the population are not Web users. Many other research companies attempt to count Internet users by using techniques such as random digit dialing telephone surveys. Calling people at random and asking them if they use the Internet or not will lead to more accurate user estimates. This chapter discusses user statistics generated by many different techniques, and each has its limitations. Users of the GVU data should realize that because respondents are not selected at random, but instead fill out the questionnaires because they are interested, therefore their answers do not necessarily parallel the answers that all Web users would give if polled. The GVU researchers are very helpful by trying to point out different areas of bias in their survey results.

If GVU surveys do not count eyeballs, then what do they measure? First is a general demographic section which asks respondents about their characteristics such as age, income, and profession. Also in this section are questions about Internet usage, and opinions about data privacy, censorship, and politics. Second are consumer surveys on the topics of transaction security, purchasing behavior, and information-gathering behavior on the Web. Finally are special sections for Webmasters, Internet Service Providers, and Web page designers. Following their early tradition, these data are free to everyone at www.gvu.gatech.edu/user_surveys.

As for Jim Pitkow, he is now Jim Pitkow, Doctor of Computer Science, and works with an impressive staff to continue the work he pioneered. Just goes to show what kind of opportunities exist for students in this exciting new medium called the Internet.

Internet Growth Rate

Internet usage is growing; of that there is little debate. The questions are, how big and how fast? The answers are critical for organizations using the Internet for business purposes such as electronic commerce and communication with various stakeholders. There are several reasons for this:

- The cost of building and maintaining an Internet program can be very expensive. For example, The American Honda Company spent $2 million creating a new Web site and promoting it online in 1997. Even smaller firms incur costs and training time by beginning slowly with an e-mail program to keep in touch with customers. It does not make sense for a firm to allocate funds for an Internet program if the market size does not grow large enough to sustain the Internet and yield an acceptable return on investment.

- Internet infrastructure companies invest millions researching new technologies to make the Internet faster and easier for users. For example, the cable companies, satellite sponsors, and telephone companies are all racing to create the fastest way to deliver content to users. There are big rewards for the winners, but only if the population of users increases enough to warrant the investment.

- Most firms are not able to change direction quickly but must plan strategy in advance. Retailers, for example, may consider selling product online: a move that takes lots of planning and coordinating both internally and in the distribution channel. Once they are committed to online retailing, it is nearly as costly and difficult to withdraw if there are not enough online buyers to justify this channel. For strategic planning purposes, Internet user predictions are extremely important.

Organizations also want to know the characteristics of Internet users so that they can determine whether or not their target markets are in the online community. In the consumer market, demographics, geographic area of residence, and user psychographics are all important descriptors. Also important is consumer online behavior. For example, businesses want to know what attracts users to particular Web sites, how they find sites, and how long they stay at a site. Advertisers want to know whether Web users give up some of their TV time to surf or not.

Not all Internet users are individuals; some represent businesses. Seventy percent of all online transaction dollars are generated in the business-to-business market such as online sales of natural gas. According to *Direct Magazine*'s online marketing survey, 77% of all business-to-business companies had a Web site in 1997 while only 59% of business-to-consumer firms had a Web site (www.computerworld.com). The business users are described by size, geography, product usage, and type.

This chapter starts by estimating the size of the market for Net consumers, putting it in the context of two important marketing concepts: diffusion of innovations and the product life cycle. Next, the focus shifts to user characteristics and behavior, focusing on the consumer market.

DIFFUSION OF INNOVATION AND ADOPTER CATEGORIES

Diffusion is the process by which new products are spread to members of the target market over time. It starts with communication from marketers through advertising and other methods, and continues with both marketing communication and consumer communication through word-of-mouth. As folks learn about the product, an increasing number adopt it through purchase. This process of communication and adoption take place over varying amounts of time, depending on many personal and product-related factors. One thing, however, is true across products and industries: Adopters at any particular stage tend to share common characteristics. Rogers (1962) studied over 500 product diffusions and concluded that there are five categories of adopters:

1. **Innovators** are the first 2.5% of consumers to purchase a product. They tend to be risk takers, be eager to try new products (especially high-tech products), and have higher levels of education and income. They are very self-reliant, gaining information from experts and the press rather than from peers. The first consumers to buy digital TVs are in this group.

2. **Early adopters** are the next 13.5% to purchase the product. These people are also eager to buy new products, but they are more community minded than innovators and thus tend to communicate with others about new products. For this reason, early adopters are often opinion leaders: people whom others seek for advice about products and other things. For example, a consumer will go to an opinion leader to ask her which Internet Service Provider she uses and recommends.

3. **The early majority** comprise the next 34%. These consumers do not rush to try new products but collect information first, perhaps talking to opinion leaders, and

purchase only after thoughtful consideration. For new products that are low involvement (i.e., low financial, social, technological risk and low emotional appeal and importance), the early majority may not give much thought before purchase, but they do watch to see others using the product before they purchase it. The consumers who are just beginning to surf the Net as of this writing in 1998 may be in this group.

4. **The late majority** consist of the next 34% to adopt. These folks are skeptical and generally purchase a product only after their friends already have done so. They adopt because of the desire to conform to group norms. These consumers rely more on word-of-mouth communication than on media advertising. These are the people who are cybercritics, calling the Internet a fad and saying it is a waste of time: "Give me a good old-fashioned letter over e-mail any time."

5. **Laggards** are the final 16%. They are very traditional and are generally of lower socioeconomic status. Often they adopt a product when newer products have already been introduced. For example, laggards might use the Internet via the telephone through an Internet Service Provider when most of the market has already moved to cable modems or some other new fast information delivery technology.

Nonadopters are not included in these five categories; however, there are some consumers who may never go on the Internet. It is important for Internet companies to define this group and avoid directing marketing resources toward them.

Various strategies are effective for different adopter categories. For example, an Internet company with a brand-new technology will want to use heavy public relations to spread the word to innovators. This might include press releases and lots of information on a Web site. In addition, the firm may use advertising by purchasing banner ads on other high-tech sites. This same advertising will make early adopters aware of the new product as well. Then the firm will want to give early adopters, especially opinion leaders, incentives to tell their friends about the product. These incentives might include ads that suggest the benefits of telling friends, or could be as direct as offering free product for referrals. More important, however, is that the early adopters have an excellent experience with the product—otherwise the word-of-mouth communication will not be positive. For later adopters, marketing communication that uses "bandwagon" appeals might work well. For example, the Web site and advertising can talk about how many other happy people are using the product, so why not give it a try? Also, recalling that early adopters tend to be from higher socioeconomic groups than later adopters helps Internet marketers to develop communication messages with appropriate appeals. For example, a hot, brand-new high-tech product can be presented as high status and something that people who are into technology will want to get before their friends.

PRODUCT ADOPTION AND THE PRODUCT LIFE CYCLE

The Product Life Cycle concept (PLC) suggests that products move through four stages from inception through obsolescence: introduction, growth, maturity, and decline. While this theory is difficult to apply and is criticized by many marketers, it is useful for conceptualizing the evolution of a product or industry over time. There are three important reasons that the PLC is a useful concept for marketers. First, promotion, pricing, and distribution strategies differ according to PLC stage. For example, a new product such as cable modems might be introduced at a high price level with a massive amount of consumer advertising. Second, the PLC stage indicates the type of competition that might be encountered. For example, when the Internet reaches the maturity stage, there will be lots of competition, resulting in industry consolidation. Third, marketers want to know how long it will take a product to move from introduction to decline. With a long cycle, marketers can justify larger investments than with a quick cycle such as that experienced with a fad product.

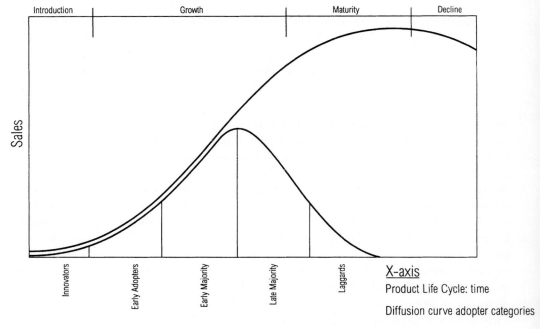

Exhibit 2 - 1 Product Life Cycle and Diffusion of Innovation Curves

For any new product, it is vital to understand whether it is being introduced in an industry that is brand new, or whether it is jumping in late, at a mature stage of the industry cycle. For example, the personal computer industry probably entered the maturity stage of the PLC during the late 1980s. Competition became fierce and many firms disappeared either through failure or purchase. A new brand would experience more difficulty gaining market share in that climate than early in the PC Product Life Cycle, when sales often topped 25% a year. Nevertheless, new product entries that meet the needs of consumers better than existing products can gain a foothold. Such was the case of Dell Computer. This firm offers mail order computers at low prices to businesses and individuals, all available from its Web site: clearly a competitive advantage.

Product adopter categories relate to the product life cycle (see Exhibit 2 - 1). Innovators and early adopters are the ones who buy products and fuel their expanding sales through the PLC introduction and growth stages. The majority buy products in the late growth stage, moving it into maturity. Laggards adopt in the maturity stage, and when the product enters decline, an increasing number of consumers stop using and purchasing the product.

These concepts are important to keep in mind during the following sections of this chapter. Internet marketers continually scan statistics revealing user adoption rates and characteristics in order to answer the questions of how big the Internet will get and how long it will take: typical PLC and adopter questions.

Size of the Internet

NUA Internet Surveys suggests that as of June 1998 there were 122 million Internet users in the entire world (www.nua.ie). Intelliquest found 62 million worldwide users in February 1998 (www.intelliquest.com). Is it possible that the Internet population nearly doubled in four months? To answer this question, one must examine the way these firms collect data and report their findings. In this case, the difference is at least partly based on the definition of a Net user. NUA's estimate includes all adults and children who accessed the Net during the three months prior to the survey. Intelliquest counted only adults 16 years of age and older. Since NUA used a broader definition of users, that could be one reason its number is higher than Intelliquest's. In late 1997, A. C. Nielsen estimated 8.9 million users aged 12 and over in Canada, and Cyberdialogue/findsvp claimed 31.3 million current Internet users 18 and older in North America (www.commercenet.com; www.cyberdialogue.com). While these figures are quite old, they serve to show that research firms use different definitions of online users. Cyberdialogue/findsvp's 31.3 million estimate, for example, is based on users who use one application in addition to e-mail (e.g., the Web). In this same 1997 American Internet User Survey, Cyberdialogue/findsvp estimated 40.6 million North American adults used the Net for some purpose in the past 12 months.

DEFINING "USER"

[cyber dialogue] Tom Miller of Cyberdialogue/findsvp developed a guide which helps to illustrate why Net population estimates vary so wildly. Exhibit 2 - 2 includes some of his ideas. In this table, *geography* refers to the Net user's area of residence categorized by country, region, or world such as United States, North America, or anywhere in the world. Research firms that count users in the North American region will produce bigger population estimates than those firms that count users in the United States only. Similarly, firms counting users in the entire world will produce larger estimates than those counting users in North America only. *Age* is an important variable because companies rarely target both adults and children with the same marketing mix, so they must be clear about what is being measured. *Recency of use* refers to the last time a user was on the Internet. This table measures recency of use in months, but some surveys use the even narrower category of the previous week, or further qualify the time frame by number of times online (e.g., once or twice in the time period, or daily). Most surveys do not qualify users by *application* that they use (e.g., Web browser, e-mail, FTP), but some do report number of e-mail users. Finally, *access* refers to how users get onto the Internet. The smallest measure is account holders at one Internet Service Provider (ISP) such as America Online (AOL), and a larger number includes those with an account at any ISP. The biggest measure includes users of subsidized accounts such as university students and residents using the Net at their library. As the Internet increases in size, these categories will expand to capture better information, similar to that in other media such as the Nielsen ratings.

Variable	Effect on Population Estimate		
	Big	**Bigger**	**Biggest**
Geography	Country	Region	World
Age	Adults 18+	Adults 16+	Adults and children
Recency of use	Last 3 months	Last 6 months	Last year
Application	Only e-mail	E-mail plus Web	Any application
Access	America Online	Any ISP account	Any access

Exhibit 2 - 2 Net User Definitions

The largest estimate of the Net population will be all the items in the rightmost column: adults and children in the entire world who used the Internet at least once in the past year for any purpose from e-mail and surfing the Web and perhaps using File Transfer Protocol (FTP) to move files. This is the definition used by NUA which resulted in the 122 million estimate. Conversely, A. C. Nielsen's estimate of 31.3 North American users 18 and older is narrower and thus smaller.

What does all this mean to marketers? They must be very careful to understand the definitions used by research firms before applying user estimates to strategic planning. Further, they must realize that size estimates are inexact, making adjustments for data limitations. Finally, because of the imprecision of user size surveys, they may be better used to measure trends than absolutes.

MEASURING THE INTERNET'S SIZE

Marketing research firms use surveys to count user eyeballs. Some firms, like GVU, put Web surveys on the Net and ask users to describe themselves. Others, like A. C. Nielsen, call people at random and ask them questions. The latter technique is a more scientific method, but all techniques have limitations. This topic is discussed in more detail in chapter 3, but at this point it should be noted that the numbers presented in this chapter are "inexact at best." To compensate, many Internet marketers review other types of data. Some of the following statistics help businesses understand the size and growth rate of this new medium:

- Number of computers connected to the Internet
- Sales of products and services directly related to Internet access
- Number of subscribers to Internet Service Provider firms
- Internet user growth trend compared with adoption of earlier media such as television

Some of these statistics are in this chapter and current at the time of this writing. The exercises at the end of this chapter provide an opportunity to update these figures for a more current analysis of the Internet's size. To put the following statistics in perspective, recall that there were 267 million people in the United States in 1997 and nearly 6 billion in the world.

Number of Users

 The people at NUA Internet Surveys keep track of the Internet's size by scanning reports of other marketing research firms (www.nua.ie). In June 1998, they posted a table (Exhibit 2 - 3) that includes various survey results over a 12-month period. Because the source surveys' methodologies varied, they took an "educated guess" at the real numbers. If there was more than one survey for an area, they took the mean user number unless one of the surveys stood out as being more reliable or comprehensive, in which case they quoted only that one. Recall that NUA's world figure includes both adults and children.

Because North America is currently the largest market, research firms spend more effort computing its size. Exhibit 2 - 4 is a list of estimates submitted by various research firms.

Region	Number of users
Africa	800,000
Asia/Pacific	19 million
Europe	24 million
Middle East	750,000
Canada and USA	70 million
South America	7.25 million
World Total	**122 million (approximate)**

Exhibit 2 - 3 Internet Users by Region
Source: www.nua.ie

Country	Date	Number	% of Total Population	Source
U.S.	February 1998	62 million[a]	30.0	Intelliquest
U.S.	November 1997	56 million[a]	22.0	Intelliquest
U.S.	June 1997	51 million[a]	19.17	Intelliquest
U.S.	April 1997	40-45 million[a]	16.16	Cyberdialogue/ findsvp
Canada	September 1997	8.9 million[b]	31.0	A. C. Nielsen
Canada	Spring 1997	8 million[b]	27.7	A. C. Nielsen

[a] includes adults 16 and over
[b] includes users 12 and older

Exhibit 2 - 4 Estimates of North American Internet Market by Firm

These figures are interesting but not too useful because they are only rough snapshots of the user population at a particular time. As was previously mentioned, it is perhaps more meaningful to look at these statistics over time, especially in light of varying methodologies and conflicting statistics. This way marketers can get a feel for the Internet's growth and make forecasts about the future, answering the questions of how big and how fast.

By the end of 2000, some analysts predict there will be 150 to 200 million users worldwide. Morgan Stanley bases its 157 million forecast on PC adoption rates and proportion of users connecting to the Internet (Meeker 1997):

- "Annual PC unit shipments may grow from 71MM in 1996 to 130MM in 2000.

- Actual PC users should also climb, from 167MM in 1996 to 269MM in 2000.

- We assume that 58% of PC users in 2000 will use the Internet, implying 157MM Internet users in 2000."

 **COMMERCENET** Nielsen Media Research and CommerceNet join forces to conduct annual user surveys using a random digit dialing telephone methodology. Because of their method, the statistics they report are among the most accurate available and are used widely by both industry and government agencies. This group forecasts 132.75 million worldwide Internet users in 2000. They further suggest that there will be 126 million Web users, indicating that, unlike the gap in 1995 and 1996, most people on the Net will also use the Web. People who use the Internet but don't use the Web are probably using e-mail. Exhibit 2 - 5 shows the number of North American users over the age of 16 from 1995 through 1998 based on solid research, with projections until 2000.

Do these curves resemble the product life cycle? Even though user size numbers vary from survey to survey, the direction is always the same: bigger. Looking at the numbers and shape of the curve, it seems that the Internet as an industry is still in the growth stage. It is interesting to note that many survey data indicate users now appear to be adopting the Internet at a faster rate outside of the United States than inside. It is also certain that for the Internet in general, at least in the United States, innovators and the early adopters have probably all been online and now the early majority are trying it out. Naturally this information is very general, and Internet companies in particular areas will want to examine adoption curves for their own industries (e.g., ISPs, Web media publishers).

Number of Hosts

Another way to look at the Internet's size is to examine the number of host computers. A host is a computer system connected to the Internet with its own address. A host can be a desktop computer or a proxy server serving many users. In the latter case, many users are sharing the same Internet address via the proxy server and, unfortunately, are counted as one host. The ratio of desktops to proxy servers is not known. As a result, a count of hosts really gives no definite indication of the number of users. Nonetheless, the number is useful to show trends over time. The host count survey, conducted semiannually by Network Wizards (www.nw.com), sends a message (technical term: "pings") to every possible Internet address and counts those that respond. Their statistics, then, represent the minimum verifiable number of computers with Internet access. To measure user size, one would have to multiply their numbers first by the number of computers utilizing each proxy server, and second by the number of users using each desktop computer.

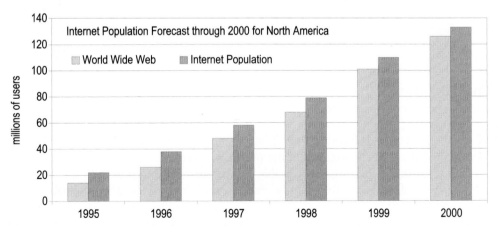

Exhibit 2 - 5 Internet Population Forecast through 2000 for North America
Note: 1998 numbers were measured in June 1998 and were expected to grow to 76.5 million for Web and 87.75 million for Net by year end.
Source: CommerceNet (www.commerce.net) and Nielsen Media Research (www.nielsenmedia.com)

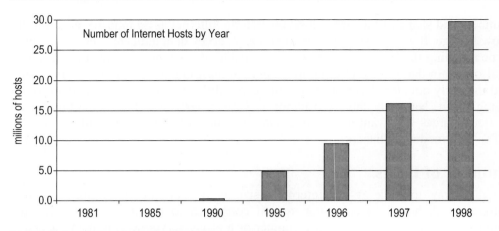

Exhibit 2 - 6 Number of Internet Hosts by Year
Source: Network Wizards (www.nw.com)

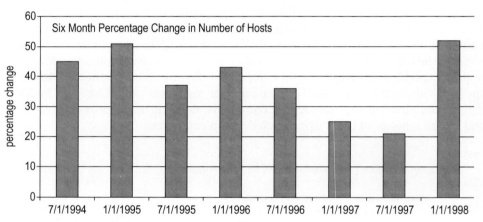

Exhibit 2 - 7 Six Month Percentage Change in Internet Hosts
Source: Network Wizards (www.nw.com)

Exhibit 2 - 6 and Exhibit 2 - 7 show how many hosts Network Wizards measured, and the percentage growth the numbers represent.

It is interesting to note that while the number of host computers in the Network Wizard survey increased substantially every year since 1994, the rate of growth slowed from January 1996 through July 1997. The incredible growth spike from July 1997 to January 1998 perhaps occurred because Network Wizard changed its survey methodology drastically. This new method more accurately measures hosts that were previously missed, but it does make it difficult to compare surveys. Discounting the last measure, one might conclude that the growth in number of hosts is slowing. Of course, one would want to know the number of users at each host before making generalizations about Net users from these numbers. These figures are included because they help to indicate trends and because they represent the only measure that extends longitudinally back to 1981.

Number of Products and Services

 One indicator of the Internet's size is sales of products related to its use. Dollars spent on Internet Service Provider subscriptions, modems, WebTV, e-mail software, and other hardware and software provide clues about the market size. Believing that these figures are leading indicators for the Information Technology market, International Data Corporation (IDC) (www.idc.com) tallied 1996 sales statistics and made projections of future sales in the year 2000 (as cited on www.cyberatlas.com in June 1998). For comparison purposes, they calculated the compound annual growth rate (CAGR) for each product area. Their findings appear in Exhibit 2 - 8. If IDC's projections are realized, the Internet is indeed still growing rapidly and there are many business opportunities (and jobs).

Product/Service	1996 $ (Millions) Actual	2000 $ (Millions) Forecast	1996 to 2000 CAGR percentage
Internet access	3,149	11,300	37.6
Personal computers	5,511	16,200	30.9
Network computers	706	15,440	116.3
Servers	2,247	13,150	55.5
Network equipment	3,500	10,300	31.1
Software	916	12,221	91.1
Services	2,477	13,770	53.6
Total	**18,506**	**92,381**	**49.5**

Exhibit 2 - 8 Dollars Spent for Internet-Related Products
Source: IDC (www.idc.com)

Comparing Internet Growth with Other Technologies and Media

A final indicator of the Internet's growth is how it compares with other similar product introductions. Has the Net grown faster or slower than TV or the telephone, for example? Exhibit 2 - 9 shows the amount of time it took several selected technologies to reach 10 million users. Exhibit 2 - 10 shows how long it took the Internet, the radio, network TV, and cable TV to reach 50 million households in the United States. Superimposing these growth lines on the product life cycle is quite illuminating. These figures show the Internet to be the fastest growing technology and communication medium: quite impressive!

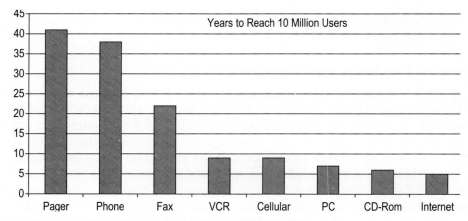

Exhibit 2 - 9 Adoption Rate for Selected Technologies

Source: Originally appeared on Mecklermedia Corporation's, "www.cyberatlas.com" Web site. Copyright © 1998 Mecklermedia Corporation 20 Ketchum Street, Westport, CT 06880; http://www.internet.com. All rights reserved. Reprinted with permission.

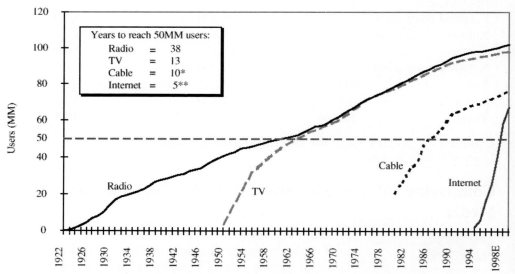

Source: Morgan Stanley Dean Witter Technology Research. E = Morgan Stanley Dean Witter Research Estimate

*We use the launch of HBO in 1976 as our estimate for the beginning of cable as an entertainment/advertising medium. Though cable technology was developed in the late 1940s, its initial use was primarily for the improvement of reception in remote areas. It was not until HBO began to distribute its pay TV movie service via satellite in 1976 that the medium became a distinct content and advertising alternative to broadcast television.

**Morgan Stanley Dean Witter Technology Research Estimate

Exhibit 2 - 10 Adoption Curves for Various Media

How Big and How Fast?

So, what do all these numbers and charts mean? The Internet was very small during the 1980s, experiencing a slow but steady growth until 1994 due to an increasing number of text-based users (e.g., e-mail and file transfer). Then, with the introduction of the World Wide Web and subsequent multimedia content expansion, the number of Net users exploded, doubling in size each year for three years (1995, 1996, and 1997). In fact, the Internet has grown much more quickly than any other medium in history.

Approximately 25% of the U.S. population now uses the Internet, and while the number is rapidly growing, the rate of growth has slowed. This is primarily a function of the math: It is easier to double small numbers than large ones. Conversely, the world adoption rate is increasing very rapidly now, with an estimated 122 million online. The largest Internet populations are concentrated in North America, but the adoption process is proceeding rapidly to other geographic regions.

Also slowing is the number of net surveys attempting to measure eyeballs in North America or the world. Researchers are focusing instead on defining and counting adopters in smaller user segments. The folks at Cyberdialogue/findsvp predict for 1999: "The media will stop hyping total Web user estimates. Why? We don't bother to count how many people use the telephone." The Internet is now large enough that its tremendous marketing potential is uncontested. To underscore this point, there is fierce competition among Net products that once were the only entry in an industry. For example, in the beginning there was Yahoo! However, users may now choose from among many search engines and directories. In this climate it is no longer possible to just put a product "out there" and see who buys, hoping that increased Net usage carries the sales. Now the task is to examine Net users by other characteristics such as age, income, shopping, and other Net behavior, and by local areas of residence. The question, "Who is out there?" is interesting, but more important, Internet marketers need to identify smaller segments of users and ask, "What are their needs and how can we profitably deliver them better than our competition via the Internet?"

Market Segmentation

Groups of people that share one or more characteristics and have common needs comprise a market segment. During the planning process, marketers aggregate consumers or businesses into several potentially profitable segments and then after careful analysis, select one or more target markets from among those segments. After setting objectives for each target, marketers develop marketing mixes and associated budgets to appeal to each group. We use the word "groups" loosely here. A market segment can actually be any size from one person to millions of people. This is important to remember when we discuss Internet marketing, because the technology allows easy market mix targeting to individuals.

For example, at a university, the admissions people probably examine the following segments of potential students in the consumer market: high school seniors, high school juniors, community college students, other university students (who might transfer), and adult learners wanting continuing education. Each of these segments is considered in terms of geographic area of residence as well: in-state or out-of-state, or within a 30-mile radius of campus and outside that radius, for example. These segments share certain demographics, geographics, and behavior with regard to education (some are in high school, some in college, some not attending school). All of the people in these segments will have a demand for higher education. In the business-to-business market, the university might develop segments of business to which they want to target the MBA program. These segments might consist of small, medium, and large companies either in or out of the city, or of particular industries that populate the area such as insurance and gaming.

The university will target one or more of these groups by developing different marketing mixes that will appeal to them. For the high school junior target, admissions folks know that students are making a list of schools based on academic program quality and availability of particular majors (e.g., marketing or MIS). Conversely, high school seniors are already armed with a short list of schools, and they select a "product" based on perceived quality of campus life. Since these two markets are fairly similar in terms of their product needs, the university will simply vary promotional appeals to each group. Adult learners, on the other hand, may require different majors and courses, necessitating product adaptation as well as promotional variation to meet their needs. In the business-to-business market, the university might develop courses to teach at the company and accompanying promotion for large firms.

Where does the Internet fit in this example? The university Web site will have different sets of pages for each target. Some pages show programs and majors (perhaps for juniors and adult learners), and some pages will show the campus, student organizations, and the Greek system (for seniors). In addition the university can describe various product benefits for each target: study skill programs and advising for high school students and after-hour registration for adult learners, for example. The university can also develop an e-mail list for communication with members of various targets. Internet marketing strategies will be described in part 2 of this book. For now, just remember that marketers develop different marketing mixes for various target groups based on their shared characteristics and needs.

MARKET SEGMENTATION BASES AND VARIABLES

There are four general bases for consumer market segmentation: demographics, geographic location, psychographics, and behavior with regard to the product. Within each basis, there are many segmentation variables. For example, McDonald's demographic segmentation focuses on the variables of age and family life cycle, targeting adults, children, senior citizens, and families. One way to look at this is that segmentation bases are a few general organizing categories, and segmentation variables include numerous subcategories.

To muddy the water a bit, companies often combine bases and focus on categories such as geodemographics (geography and demographics). Similarly, they can build segments using any combination of variables that makes sense for their industry. The important thing to remember is this: Marketers identify segments based on variables that can be used to identify and reach the right people at the right time.

After the targets are selected, they can be further described using many other variables. For example, it is much easier to build a list of high school juniors than it is to build a list of juniors who like to read classic literature. But, after the university has a list of juniors, it can use primary and secondary research to describe them by saying a certain percentage read classics and another percentage read popular novels. It is important to know which variables identify the target and which simply further describe it, because marketers use identification variables to enumerate and access the target.

SEGMENTATION COVERAGE STRATEGIES

A final point to recall about market segmentation is that a firm may choose from among three different market coverage strategies:

1. *Mass marketing*, also called *undifferentiated targeting*, exists where the firm offers one marketing mix for the entire market. Wrigley's gum uses this strategy. On the Internet, many firms use an undifferentiated strategy. For example, banner ads that appear on portal site home pages (e.g., Yahoo!) tend to appeal to the entire market.

2. *Niche marketing*, also called *concentrated targeting*, occurs when a firm selects one segment and develops one or more marketing mixes to meet the needs of that segment. Amazon adopted this strategy when it targeted Web users exclusively. Cyberdialogue/findsvp calls the Internet "a niche in time," indicating its ripeness for niche marketing (Clemente 1998). This strategy has real benefits but can be risky because competitors are often drawn into lucrative markets.

3. *Multisegment targeting*, also called *differentiated targeting*, exists when a firm carefully selects two or more segments and designs marketing mix strategies for each. Most firms today use a multisegment strategy.

One type of multisegment targeting is micromarketing. Taken to its extreme, this can be a target market of one person. The Internet's big promise, one that is currently being realized by some firms, is this individualized targeting. Amazon, for example, builds a profile of each user who browses or buys books at its site. They keep track of the books that their customers read and they make recommendations based on past purchases. Amazon also sends e-mail notification about products that might interest particular individuals. This is the marketing concept at its finest: giving individual consumers exactly what they want at the right time and place.

INTERNET USER CHARACTERISTICS AND BEHAVIOR

In this section, user characteristics and Net behavior are examined according to some of the common segmentation bases and variables previously discussed. The first section describes user demographics; the second, geographic area of Net use; the third, user psychographics; and the fourth, user behavior on the Net. Within each section are estimates of the proportion of users in various segments as well as user profiles.

Demographic Segments

In the Internet's early years, the typical user was a young male, college educated, and realizing a high income: except for gender, the description of a typical innovator. As the Net population increases, the demographics of U.S. users begin to look more like the mainstream population. Peter Clemente of Cyberdialogue/findsvp, agrees that U.S. Net users are looking more like the U.S. population in general: Internet users in 1997 were older, were more likely female, had lower incomes, and were less educated than in 1994. Exhibit 2 - 11 is adapted from his book, *The State of the Net: The New Frontier.*

Demographics	1994 Internet Users	1997 Internet Users	All U.S. Adults
Total Adults	3.5 million	36.3 million	
Age			
18-29	42%	30%	22%
30-49	45%	54%	42%
50 and over	13%	16%	36%
Gender			
Male	78%	61%	48%
Female	22%	39%	52%
Household income			
Average income	$66,300	$51,900	$44,900
Median income	$64,000	$44,200	$34,000
Education			
College graduate	51%	42%	21%
Not college graduate	49%	58%	79%

Exhibit 2 - 11 U.S. Internet Users
Source: Clemente, Peter, Thomas Miller, Andrew Richardson, and Craig Gugel (1998), "Consumer Online Commerce," Private Report. New York: Cyber Dialogue and Organic.

Cyberdialogue/findsvp projects that the segment of children under the age of 18 will grow rapidly in the future. They count 9.8 million children online in the United States during 1997, with 13.8 million projected in 1998, and 26.7 million in the year 2000. Capitalizing on the child market, McDonald's created part of its Web site for children. Right on the home page consumers can choose to click on the icon of either jumping children or happy adults. The children's pages are full of cool stuff for kids. Incidentally, the government closely regulates advertising to children, and there is a current controversy about how much information Web marketers can solicit from children.

The GVU surveys contain information on all Net users in the world (versus U.S. only). For comparison purposes Exhibit 2 - 12 shows demographic trends of the respondents to GVU's Web surveys. For each table the figures are taken from the fall survey, except for the final data point, which represents January 1998 numbers. World trends parallel U.S. trends, with Net users becoming older, more likely female, and having lower incomes and education levels. Interestingly, Europeans answering GVU's 1998 questions were younger (averaging 30 years old), more highly educated, and with lower incomes (averaging $48,000) than their U.S. counterparts.

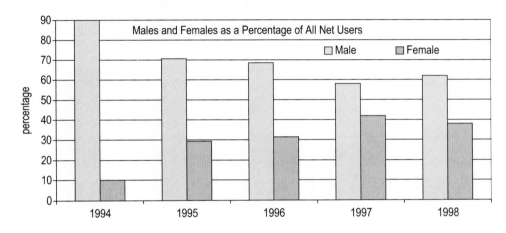

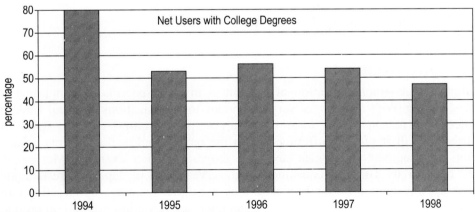

Exhibit 2 - 12 Trends in Net Demographics

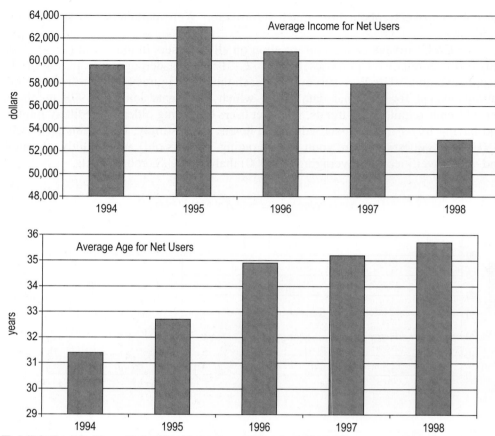

Exhibit 2 - 12 Trends in Net Demographics (continued)
Source: www.gvu.gatech.edu/user_surveys

Geographic Segments

Although the geographic location of computers in cyberspace is not important to users accessing Web sites, it is very important to organizations with an Internet presence. The reason is that most firms target specific cities, regions, states, or countries with their product offerings. Even the largest multinational firms usually develop multisegment strategies based on geographics. For example, McDonalds serves beer to its German consumers and serves sake in Japanese restaurants. Conversely, a restaurant in San Francisco may use a niche strategy by targeting only local residents. An important reason for geographic segmentation is based on product distribution strategy: a consumer goods company such as General Foods will want to reach only customers in countries to which it distributes products. Before an organization decides to serve the Web community, it must examine the proportion of Net users in its selected geographic targets. With this idea in mind, the next section discusses number of users for each of the U.S. states and then gives user statistics for other selected countries.

United States

In the United States at least 46 million (24%) adults over the age of 18 and another 13.8 million children are online (Clemente 1998). This figure is too broad for companies with limited distribution, however. The *Hartford Courant* newspaper needs to learn how many Connecticut residents are online before it invests many resources in a Web site. There are an increasing number of local and regional companies with Web sites, and another group of firms such as Sidewalk and CitiSearch that specialize in aggregating local businesses onto one broader site. The growth in local Web sites occurred because residents of local areas want online information about sports, weather, news, and local restaurants and other businesses. Businesses as well as educational and other organizations need statistics on the proportion and characteristics of wired residents by state, region, or even county and city.

Other Countries

One quarter of U.S. adults are online, but what about the rest of the world? Exhibit 2 - 13 presents the number of computer systems (hosts) in the top 18 wired countries other than the United States according to Net Wizards (www.nw.com). In the table are growth rates from 1997 to 1998. Recall that Net Wizards measures only host computers, so these figures represent the absolute minimum number of users on the Net. The actual number for each country depends on how many computers are linked to each host and how many users access each computer.

According to these numbers, Taiwan experienced the largest growth in the past year, followed by Spain, the United Kingdom, and New Zealand. These countries, plus the top five in terms of numbers, represent outstanding potential target markets for Internet companies.

The Internet, as an innovation, grew quite rapidly in the United States, making it in absolute numbers the most wired country in the world. Other English-speaking countries such as the United Kingdom, Canada, and Australia, and some fully industrialized nations such as Japan and Germany, are also experiencing high penetration rates. Like wildfire, Internet connectivity is spreading to users in other countries worldwide. The Organization for Economic Cooperation and Development released a study in 1997 explaining that high access costs, not language differences are what dictate country usage ("High Access Charges" 1997). For example, in Mexico and Ireland consumers pay over $90 a month for 20 hours of Internet use (including telephone bills). Unlike in the United States, phone companies in many countries levy a per minute charge for *local* calls. This is in addition to the ISP charges for Internet access. Other events that slow Internet adoption worldwide include infrastructure problems and government censorship and regulation. Nevertheless, the benefits of worldwide connectivity to multinational businesses, when coupled with what appears to be intense consumer demand, make it only a matter of time before we are truly a global community connected by the Internet.

Rank	Country	1997 Hosts	1998 Hosts	% Growth
1	Japan	734,406	1,181,991	60.9%
2	Germany	721,847	1,099,050	52.3%
3	United Kingdom	591,624	1,226,568	107.3%
4	Canada	603,325	1,000,468	65.8%
5	Australia	514,760	742,064	44.2%
6	Finland	283,526	460,574	62.4%
7	Netherlands	270,521	389,713	44.1%
8	France	245,501	406,798	65.7%
9	Sweden	232,955	328,039	40.8%
10	Norway	171,686	292,068	70.1%
11	Italy	149,595	257,921	72.4%
12	Taiwan	34,650	178,914	416.3%
13	New Zealand	84,532	174,406	106.3%
14	Spain	110,041	238,195	116.5%
15	Denmark	106,476	170,635	60.3%
16	South Africa	99,284	194,883	96.3%
17	Korea	66,262	127,903	93.0%
18	Brazil	77,148	122,814	59.2%
Total		**5,098,139**	**8,593,004**	**68.6%**

Exhibit 2 - 13 Growth in Host Computer Systems by Country
Source: www.nw.com

Psychographic Segments

User psychographics include personality, values, lifestyle, activities, interests, and opinions (AIO). *Personality* characteristics are traits such as other-oriented versus self-oriented, and habits such as procrastination. *Values* are deeply held convictions such as religious beliefs. *Lifestyles* and *activities* as psychographics refer to non-product related behavior such as playing sports or eating out. For example, Web users say that surfing takes their time away from these other activities: reading (39%), sleeping (23%), socializing (14%), and working (12%) (www.intelliquest.com). *Interests* and *opinions* are attitudes and beliefs people hold. These can relate to the product: For example, some people believe that the Web is a waste of time and others think they could not exist without e-mail.

There are two things that may be a bit confusing here: First is the difference between attitudes and behavior. Attitudes are internal thoughts about people, products, and other objects. They can be either positive or negative, but the whole thing happens inside a person's head. Behavior is a person's physically doing something. Examples of behaviors include talking, eating, watching an infomercial on television, writing for a free videotape, calling a 1-800 number to order, shopping, or purchasing a product. The second confusing item is that marketers do not include product-related behaviors in psychographic segmentation. This is so because product behaviors are such an extremely important segment descriptor that they get a category all by themselves (see the next section). So, when marketers discuss psychographics, they mean the general ways that consumers spend time. Frankly, this is a bit arbitrary, and in the "real world" some of these distinctions may not be made, but for learning purposes, this approach makes for better understanding of consumers.

Psychographic information about consumers assists in defining and describing market segments, so that Internet companies can better meet consumer needs. It is especially important for Web page design. For example, Japanese users do not like the flippant and irreverent tone at some U.S. sites. Japan's Web sites are more serious and do not include things such as political satire. Information like this, which describes attitudes, is increasingly available about Web users.

VALS^tm Typology

SRI Consulting introduced the Values and Lifestyles Program (VALS) in 1978 (VALS^tm is a trademark of SRI International). Many marketers who wish to understand the psychographics of both existing and potential customers use the VALS program. SRI categorizes people by two dimensions: self-identity and resources. The philosophy is that consumers purchase products that shape their identities using psychological, physical, demographic, and material resources. SRI developed a series of questionnaires to measure these attributes and then placed respondents in lifestyle groups. Of special interest to Net marketers is iVALS, a survey developed especially for Net users. Because SRI does not present statistics for the iVALS survey, this chapter focuses on VALS. Web users can actually take the surveys at SRI's site and find out what type they are. Exhibit 2 - 14 is a graphic depiction of the VALS typology (www.future.sri.com):

Exhibit 2 - 15 contains brief descriptions of various categories from SRI's Web site, along with the proportion of U.S. residents in each type.

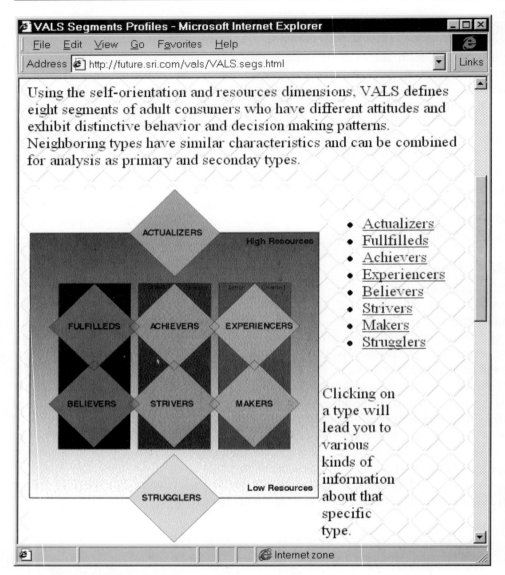

Exhibit 2 - 14 VALS Segments

Type	Description
Actualizers **11.4%**	Actualizers are successful, sophisticated, active, "take-charge" people with high self-esteem and abundant resources. They are interested in growth and seek to develop, explore, and express themselves in a variety of ways—sometimes guided by principle, and sometimes by a desire to have an effect, to make a change.
Fulfilleds **10.4%**	Fulfilleds are mature, satisfied, comfortable, reflective people who value order, knowledge, and responsibility. Most are well educated and in (or recently retired from) professional occupations.
Achievers **14.4%**	Achievers are successful career and work-oriented people who like to, and generally do, feel in control of their lives. They value consensus, predictability, and stability over risk, intimacy and self-discovery. They are deeply committed to work and family.
Experiencers **12.9%**	Experiencers are young, vital, enthusiastic, impulsive, and rebellious. They seek variety and excitement, savoring the new, the offbeat, and the risky. Experiencers combine an abstract disdain for conformity with an outsider's awe of others' wealth, prestige, and power.
Believers **16.9%**	Believers are conservative, conventional people with concrete beliefs based on traditional, established codes: family, church, community, and the nation. They follow established routines, organized in large part around home, family, and social or religious organizations to which they belong.
Strivers 12.1%	Strivers seek motivation, self-definition, and approval from the world around them. They are striving to find a secure place in life. Unsure of themselves and low on economic, social, and psychological resources, Strivers are concerned about the opinions and approval of others.
Makers **12.4%**	Makers are practical people who have constructive skills and value self-sufficiency. They live within a traditional context of family, practical work, and physical recreation and have little interest in what lies outside that context. Makers experience the world by working on it—building a house, raising children, fixing a car, or canning vegetables—and have enough skill, income, and energy to carry out their projects successfully.
Strugglers **9.6%**	Strugglers' lives are constricted. Chronically poor, ill-educated, low-skilled, without strong social bonds, elderly, and concerned about their health, they are often resigned and passive. Their chief concerns are for security and safety.

Exhibit 2 - 15 Descriptions of VALS Categories

Source: www.future.sri.com. © 1998 SRI consulting. All rights reserved. Unauthorized reproduction prohibited.

Which VALS^tm types are Web users? According to Bill Guns at SRI, Actualizers represent more than 30% of Netizens. The next three largest groups are Achievers, Fulfilleds, and Experiencers. These groups probably represent early adopter categories. There are very few Net users in the Believer or Struggler groups. This information is very useful because SRI can provide lists of consumers by type to assist marketers who are trying to reach their targets.

Behavior Segments

There are two commonly used behavioral segmentation variables: benefits sought and product usage. Marketers using *benefit segmentation* often form groups of consumers based on the benefits they desire from the product. For example, from the iVALS categories at www.future.sri.com, it would be easy to form one segment of Internet users who are techno-savvy, trying new Web sites and experimenting with new things such as downloading new software from a site and figuring out how it works. The second segment are users who feel frustrated by computers and use search engines and other Web sites that make things easier to use and understand. In the first segment, users benefit from the challenge, and in the second from ease of operation. *Product usage* is operationalized in many ways. Marketers often segment by light, medium, and heavy product usage. Heavy Internet users might be those who go online daily, medium users those who get on once every few days, and light users those who connect only once every week or two. These numbers are arbitrary: it takes research to decide how to split surfers into appropriate user categories. Another schema by product usage categorizes consumers as brand loyal, loyal to the competitive product, switchers (don't care which brand they use), and nonusers of the product.

Benefit Segmentation

The Internet has over 320 million unique pages of content (Lawrence and Giles 1998). There is something for everyone here: information, entertainment, news, social meeting places, and more. If marketers can form user segments based on the benefits sought, they can design products to meet those needs. In many ways doing this makes more sense than simply making demographic segments and trying to figure out what, say, professional women in Iowa want from the Web. In fact, marketers will use all segmentation bases to define, measure, and identify target markets, but benefits sought is the key driver of marketing mix strategy.

What better way to determine benefits sought than to look at what people actually do online? A Business Week/Harris Poll asked Web users how often they do particular activities online. The responses are in Exhibit 2 - 16. Combining that with the Price Waterhouse's findings (Exhibit 2 - 17) about how much time users spend in online activities gives us a single answer: the largest benefit segment is research. If "research" includes searching the Web, then statistics from Web user surveys validate these findings. Relevant Knowledge measures the surfing patterns of a large sample of Web users and reports the top sites on a monthly basis. According to the May 31, 1998 survey, Yahoo! was the most visited brand, with 31.4 million people over age 12 stopping by within the month, and Excite was third with 19.4 million visitors.

It may be discouraging to marketers to see that only 1% of users spend only 1% of their online time shopping, but perhaps some of the research time is spent getting product information. For example, the 13% who are getting information about computers may be interested in eventual purchase. According to J. D. Power and Associates, 16% of new-car buyers last year gathered information on the Web. Online banking and investing might be considered shopping as well. According to BancAmerica Corp., the average transaction revenue per user in 1997 was $24.00, up from $16.19 in 1996 (www.computerworld.com). Perhaps consumers are averse to claiming that they shop online, or maybe they have different definitions of what it means to shop. Segmentation has a lot to do with defining and measuring categories meticulously.

Primary Activity	Percent Who Do It Often
Research	50%
Education	37%
Entertainment	31%
News	30%
Hobbies	18%
Gameplaying	14%
Obtaining information on computers and software	13%
Socializing	13%
Investing	12%
Shopping	1%

Exhibit 2 - 16 Most Common Online Activities
Source: Originally appeared on Mecklermedia Corporation's, "www.cyberatlas.com" Web site. Copyright © 1998 Mecklermedia Corporation 20 Ketchum Street, Westport, CT 06880; http://www.internet.com. All rights reserved. Reprinted with permission.

Activity	Time Spent
Research	43%
E-mail	34%
Game Playing	9%
Online Magazines or news	5%
Online banking	2%
Two-way voice	1%
Online shopping	1%

Exhibit 2 - 17 Proportion of Online Time Spent in Various Activities
Source: Originally appeared on Mecklermedia Corporation's, "www.cyberatlas.com" Web site. Copyright © 1998 Mecklermedia Corporation 20 Ketchum Street, Westport, CT 06880; http://www.internet.com. All rights reserved. Reprinted with permission. Approximate figures do not total to 100%.

Another way to look at Web benefits is to view them in light of online social activities. Users join chat rooms of interest, visit Web sites such as GeoCities that are arranged by "neighborhoods" of people sharing common interests, and post to the over 15,000 special interest newsgroups called the Usenet (which is accessible at www.dejanews.com). They connect with others in these social spaces as well as through e-mail. GVU's *Eighth User Survey* examined "community" membership and found that survey respondents join communities to feel connected with others who have the following common interests: 44.8% with folks who share their hobbies; 31.5% with other professionals; 27.2% with family members; 15.7% in support groups; 9.5% chatting about politics; and 6.9% in religious groups. Some of the Web sites that appeal to virtual communities are Women's Wire (discussing women's issues), Talk City (for pure chat), Tripod (hangout for twenty-somethings with free resume posting), and Utne Online (chat on New Age issues).

How can marketers use this information? After defining segments, they select target markets based on user needs and other planning issues such as competitive products, and then design marketing strategies to appeal to selected targets. For example, because 50% conduct research online, marketers could delve deeper and find out what types of research users do online; for example, do they research for work, product information, school, or personal reasons such as health? Armed with a slew of research benefit segments, marketers can design content channels to meet user needs better than competition does.

User Segments

An important way to segment Netizens is by how they access the Internet. Exhibit 2 - 18 indicates the U.S. trend in home users versus work users from 1996 with projections into 2000: a healthy market in each segment. Home users often have slower connection speeds than do those who enter the Net from work, making large graphics and other files difficult to read in the rumored 3 seconds a user will await page download. It is also likely that each segment has different needs on the Web. Peter Zandan, former CEO of IntelliQuest, believing the Net user segments are not that simple, coined the term WOHO to describe users who access both at <u>WO</u>rk and at <u>HO</u>me (www.intelliquest.com). He maintains that this segment encompasses 27 million Americans, representing 41% of all U.S. computer users.

Year	Home	Work	Total
1996	13 million	15 million	28 million
1997	20 million	20 million	40 million
1998	27 million	30 million	57 million
2000 projection	42 million	60 million	102 million

Exhibit 2 - 18 Estimated U.S. Web Users by Access Location
Source: BancAmerica Robertson, Stephens report (reprinted in Emmerce at www.computerworld.com)

Clemente (1998) of Cyberdialogue/findsvp stepped up the level of sophistication when he first split Net users into two groups: those who personally pay for their own Internet access (63% of all adults), and those for whom access is subsidized by their company or academic institution. This sounds a bit like "home" versus "work" use, but he didn't stop there. He formed four segments based on both payment for access and primary reason for using the Net (personal, business, or academic):

- Personal Interest Consumers (46%) pay for their own access and go online for personal reasons such as entertainment, sports, and local information. This has been the largest and fastest growing segment since 1995, with 16.7 million current users. Their average age is 40, their average income is $54,300, and most tend to be married with children under 18.

- Occupational Consumers (17%) also pay their own way, but they use the Net mostly for business such as accessing business news and product information, doing research, and conducting online banking and investing. Their average age is 41, 74% are male, their income is $65,500, and 62% are college graduates.

- Corporate Users (31%) go online at work to get business-related news and research and to download software. Their average age is 35, income is $53,000, and 44% are female.

- Academic Users (6%) use the Internet at school or other academic institution and conduct online research or access adult education and training. Their average age is 28, income is $38,600, and they are 43% female. Students are in this segment.

Using the fine research at Cyberdialogue/findsvp, Clemente further defines each segment by usage pattern in terms of access method, speed of access, frequency of Web use, and online shopping. Because we suggested heavy, medium, and light usage rates earlier, there are now real data to find the size of each segment. As can be seen from Exhibit 2 - 19, heavy users do indeed frequent the Web daily: from 43% to 61% in each segment. Medium users access weekly, from 29% to 47% per segment, and light users visit the Web less than weekly. Note that these statistics measure Web use only and do not include other Net use such as e-mail.

Consumer Navigation Behavior

Before exiting the topic of Net users, we need to mention the study of consumer navigation behavior. A large amount of research is being conducted in the communications discipline about computer mediated communication: how people interact with computers. Some of this is available online at the Journal of Computer Mediated Communications (www.ascusc.org/jcmc/). Marketers use this information to design Web sites that draw their target markets, entice them to stay awhile, and encourage them to return soon. In this section are three important areas from this research.

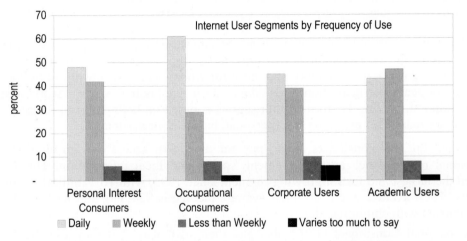

Exhibit 2 - 19 Internet User Segments by Frequency of Web Use
Note: Numbers do not add to 100% because of a small percent responding, "varies too much to say"
Source: Clemente, Peter, Thomas Miller, Andrew Richardson, and Craig Gugel (1998), "Consumer Online Commerce," Private Report. New York: Cyber Dialogue and Organic.

ATTENTION

Some researchers believe that consumers pay more focused attention to Web sites than to the content in any other medium. When in front of a television, the folks on the couch are easily distracted by other people or activities in the environment. The same holds true for the passivity of radio listening. The audience seems to pay more attention to print media but still flips pages hastily. Hoffman and Novak at Vanderbilt University applied the concept of flow from psychology to Web navigation behavior (www2000.ogsm.vanderbilt.edu). They define flow as:

the state occurring during network navigation which is: (1) characterized by a seamless sequence of responses facilitated by machine interactivity, (2) intrinsically enjoyable, (3) accompanied by a loss of self-consciousness, and (4) self-reinforcing.

Does this sound familiar? What it means is that when consumers are online, they are 100% involved, and not easily distracted. They are very experimental with their navigation and have a good time doing it. What it means to marketers is that once they can capture a pair of consumer eyeballs, they can make a big impression in a short time as long as the Web site is enjoyable, self-reinforcing, and even a bit challenging. Recall that what is enjoyable for one segment may be different for another, however. This is good news for marketers trying to capture audience attention through the clutter of commercial messages on traditional media.

PRIVACY

Internet users guard their privacy online. According to Hoffman, Novak, and Peralta, 94% of Web users have refused to provide information at a Web site and 40% have given false information (www2000.ogsm.vanderbilt.edu). In GVU's *Eighth User Survey,* 30.5% of respondents said that the most important issue facing the Internet today is privacy. This may be one reason that site registration schemes did not go over well with users, and that many consumers are reluctant to send credit card and other information over the Internet. This need for privacy affects marketer use of e-mail databases and information collection via Web sites. If privacy is important to Netizens, marketers must give it to them, or assure them of the benefits of providing information.

USER CONTROL OF MESSAGE

With television, even though the audience can switch channels, it must take the entire broadcast package: program, advertisements, and even interruptions for special announcements. Conversely, Web sites are not yet packaged nicely into channels and broadcast to user homes where viewers passively watch sent content. On the Web, users have micro control of what they view. A typical "clickstream" pattern for a consumer who wants to order flowers online for a friend's birthday might go like this: go to Yahoo! to look up flowers; click on the first site on the list; decide that's not very good and hit the "back" button to return to Yahoo!; click on the 1-800 Flowers site; see a cool banner ad for flower postcards and click on it; visit the postcard site and send a free virtual flower bouquet instead.

Users can also create actual Web page content at corporate sites. For example, at www.nbc.com users can put themselves in a *Homicide* story line or send in jokes for the *Tonight Show* page. Since viewers decide whether or not they want to view ads, and because Web content is broken into very small discrete segments (versus 30-minute TV shows or several-page magazine articles), each user quickly constructs a message that appeals to him: micromarketing at its best. In this environment, the burden is on marketers to entice consumers who are now actively involved in their own message construction.

Summary

The Internet's growth rate can be understood in light of two marketing concepts—diffusion of innovation and the product life cycle. Diffusion of innovation explains how innovators and early adopters have helped to lead the way for the early majority—the group just beginning to surf the net. The product life cycle (PLC) explains why the Internet will continue to grow rapidly. It has passed its introduction and moved into an early growth stage. The next few years will witness the mid and late growth stages as the Internet approaches maturity.

The size of the Internet has been a controversial number because of differing definitions of what constitutes an Internet user and inherent limitations of different measuring techniques. Size can be measured directly by the number of users or indirectly by the number of hosts or number of related products and services. By any measure, the Internet is growing faster than any other medium in history. Nonetheless, absolute size of the Internet used to be a more important question than it is today, since very few dispute that there are market opportunities. Of more interest today are the market opportunities in particular market segments.

Market segmentation describes groups of people that share one or more characteristics and have common needs. Segmentation analysis is critical in order to identify target markets and then to develop a marketing mix to reach those markets. Market segmentation can be understood in terms of segmentation bases and variables. Bases form the major categories and segment identifiers, and variables describe the detail within those categories. The four classic bases are demographics, geographic location, psychographics, and behavior with regard to the product. Behavioral segmentation looks at benefits sought by consumers, thus helping marketers to design products to meet user needs. One way to determine benefits sought is to look at what consumers do online, both when surfing solo and when inhabiting online social spaces. Another type of behavioral segmentation groups users by how they access the Internet.

No matter what segment users fall into, they seem to share one common characteristic: intense involvement in the media. The term *flow* has been used to describe this highly involved experience. Internet users tend to jealously guard their privacy and will quickly click to what they want to view.

Key Concepts and Terms

1. Probabilistic sampling is more accurate than nonprobabilistic sampling.

2. Determining the absolute size of the Internet has decreased in importance.

3. Diffusion of innovation and the PLC help explain the rapid growth of the Internet.

4. Varying strategies are effective for different adopter categories and for different segments in general.

5. The different definitions of Net users profoundly influence size projections.

6. Number of users cannot be inferred from number of hosts.

7. Segmentation always precedes developing the marketing mix.

8. The Internet allows micromarketing to the individual.

9. While the Internet is global, firms often target locally. This situation creates a potential problem.

10. The psychographics of the population and of Internet users are not the same. Internet users are almost three times as likely to be Actualizers.

11. The most important segmentation variable may be benefits sought.

12. Users pay more attention online than they do in any other medium.

13. Internet users are concerned about their privacy

- Achievers
- Activities, Interests, and Opinions (AOI)
- Actualizers
- Adoption curves
- Attitudes
- Believers
- Benefit segmentation
- Compound annual growth rate (CAGR)
- Concentrated targeting
- Demographics
- Differentiated targeting
- Diffusion of innovations
- Early adopters
- Early majority
- Experiencers
- Flow
- Fulfilleds
- Geodemographics

- Geographics
- Innovators
- Internet Service Provider (ISP)
- Laggards
- Late majority
- Makers
- Micromarketing
- Multisegment targeting
- Nonprobabilistic sampling
- Personal Interest Consumers
- Product Life Cycle (PLC)
- Proxy server
- Psychographics
- Random digit dialing
- Strivers
- Strugglers
- Switchers
- Undifferentiated targeting

Exercises

REVIEW QUESTIONS FOR KNOWLEDGE TESTING

1. Complete the following matrix:

Category	Percentage of Population	On Net Now (yes/no)
Innovators		
Early adopters		
The early majority		
The late majority		
Laggards		

2. Define diffusion of innovation.
3. What is the most inclusive definition of a Net user? The most exclusive definition?
4. What is benefit segmentation?
5. Define flow.

DISCUSSION QUESTIONS FOR CRITICAL THINKING

1. In what way are the PLC and diffusion of innovation similar?
2. Where does the Internet fit in the Product Life Cycle? Use evidence to support your claim.
3. What marketing strategies would you use to appeal to Actualizers?
4. Why has determining the absolute size of the Internet decreased in importance?
5. Why can't the number of Net users be inferred from the number of hosts?
6. Describe some potential problems created by a global Internet for firms attempting regional targeting.
7. What products would appeal to the largest online psychographic group?
8. What are the implications of flow for advertisers?
9. What are the implications of micromarketing?

ACTIVITIES

1. Watch a friend surf for 10 minutes and record the clickstream. (Netscape records sites visited in its history list; Internet Explorer records sites visited using the drop-down arrow by the back button.) List each site, page within, and how long

she spends on each page. Note whether or not she clicked on a banner ad. What conclusions can you make from this experiment?

2. Conduct a survey in your class to determine how many students fall into various benefit segments. Tally your answers and see if they match statistics in this chapter.

3. Select three user estimates displayed in chapter exhibits, visit the source Web site, and then update the numbers. Explain the differences.

4. Visit Cyberatlas.com and GVU's site and determine current user demographics. What is the profile of a current Web user?

5. Locate information about the number of users by country. Which ten countries have the highest number of users, and how many users are in each of those countries?

INTERNET EXERCISE: AGE SEGMENTATION

Marketers use consumer age as a basis for demographic segmentation. They use terms such as *kids*, *teens*, *Generation X*, *baby boomers*, *and mature adults*. A marketing mix can be designed to appeal to any of these groups. Before designing a marketing mix, marketers should know the size of the target segment. For this exercise, visit the U.S. Census site (www.census.gov), follow "topics A-Z," and then click on links to age data, yearly estimates, at the national level. The resulting table shows ages by five-year categories over time. Combining categories, complete the following table. Note: Be careful, the numbers are truncated. Next, visit GVU and complete the cells based on Net users answering their Web surveys.

U.S. Population			
Age Segment	Number in 1990	Number in Mid-decade	Most Current Year
Under 10			
10-19			
20-29			
30-39			
40-49			
50-59			
60-69			
70-79			
Over 79			
Total Population			

GVU Web Survey Respondents		
Age Segment	**Number in Mid-decade**	**Most Current Year**
Under 10		
10-19		
20-29		
30-39		
40-49		
50-59		
60-69		
70-79		
Over 79		
Total		

For Discussion

1. Which U.S. and GVU segments are currently the largest? Which ones have grown the most? Which will be the largest in five years?

2. How can you explain the differences between U.S. and GVU figures from question 1?

3. What ages are Generation Xers? How many are there in the GVU sample compared with population?

4. What ages are Baby Boomers? How many are there in the GVU sample compared with population?

5. If you were a marketing consultant for Mazda, which segment would you recommend targeting? Why?

6. Is this segment well represented in the online market according to GVU's data?

Leveraging Technology

CONTENT FILTERING

One growing segment of Web users is children under the age of 18. Many families are concerned that their children will be exposed to pornography, violence, or other unwanted material online. Even children not seeking material perceived as objectionable may be exposed to it by the results of an innocent search. For example, a search using one of the top search engines for "fun for girls" resulted in 13 of the first 20 pages linking to sex sites—including www.asiansex.com, www.lovestar.com, www.picturepost.com, www.amsterdam4sex.com, and www.cybersextalk.com. The descriptions of those sites that appear right on the search engine's listings could not be reprinted here.

There are many solutions to serve the needs of user segments that do not want exposure to this type of material. One group of solutions aims to curb exposure to offensive material through education and/or legislation. Another group of solutions aims to limit exposure by use of technology.

Education- and Legislation-Based Solutions

1. Educate children not to pursue offensive online material.
2. Create an outright ban on offensive material through legislative means.
3. Require/encourage providers of offensive material to put age warnings on their sites (i.e., "if you are under 18 do not enter here").
4. Require/encourage providers of offensive material to run an age verification system. Such systems require users to purchase a password using a credit card. The presumption is that minors do not have access to credit cards.
5. Require/encourage providers of offensive material to rate their material using industry-standard ratings similar to those used by the film industry.

Technology-Based Solutions

6. Ask the Internet service provider to filter the content coming to the user.
7. Filter the content right on the user's own computer.

All of these solutions have their merits and drawbacks and can be the topic of a rather lively debate. Elements of this debate are discussed elsewhere in this text. However, this piece will sidestep the debate and focus instead on the solutions that are technologically based—those that monitor and filter content using computer software.

Content can be filtered by software running on any computer along the path from the user's computer to the Internet. In the corporate world employees are typically barred from objectionable sites by software running on a corporate computer which serves as the gateway to the Internet. This computer is called a proxy server. All communication to and from any corporate computer to the Internet passes through the proxy server. The solution is very efficient and even allows employers to record attempted accesses to objectionable sites—taking disciplinary action when desired.

The home user typically does not have access to a similar service, because Internet Service Providers (ISPs) are reluctant to filter content on their site since many users want to access this type of material. Notable exceptions to this reluctance include America Online (AOL) and Prodigy Internet, which provide families with multiple passwords. The children can then be restricted to a kid's area of the service. Some countries, such as China and Vietnam, go one step further by filtering content at the ISP level for everyone (adults as well as children). Incidentally, censorship is at the heart of the ethics debate on this issue.

In the United States, the home user must install software on her own computer to filter content. There are a number of products that perform this task. Popular products include NetNanny, CyberSitter, Cyber Patrol, Cyber Snoop, SurfWatch, and Rated-PG. As the names indicate, these products are intended to impede children's access to the questionable sites. Many provide password overrides so that, if they wish, other household members have full Internet access. Most products provide free updates as the list of objectionable sites grows, and many are customizable so users may add or remove items from the list.

One way the products operate is by maintaining "can go" and "can't go" lists. Under the "can't go" scenario, the products maintain a list of banned sites. This list can easily exceed 25,000 sites. Each time the child attempts to access a site, the software checks the site address against the list of banned sites. If there is a match, then the software can take one of the following actions:

1. Make a silent record of the access for the parent to see later but do nothing else.

2. Mask out objectionable words or images from the accessed site.

3. Block any access to the banned site.

4. Shut down the browser completely.

Under the "can go" scenario, the child can visit only sites that are on an approved list and nothing else. These might include such G-rated sites as www.disney.com. The parents can always add to this list according to requests from the children. Again, the same series of actions would be available should a child try to access a site not on the "can go" list.

Vendors update the "can't go" lists periodically and then allow users to download the updated lists from their Web site. Updates are a major concern—especially for the "can't go" list, since new adult sites are constantly coming online. These sites can still be blocked according to the words in the site name (e.g., www.cybersextalk.com) or the words in the Web page itself (e.g., "this site contains graphic sex"). Even incoming e-mail or MS-Word documents can be scanned. In all cases the same list of action options above is available.

The products can even monitor outgoing e-mail messages to make sure that children are not giving away private information such as their name, phone number, or address to a cyber pedophile. To accomplish this, the software is programmed to recognize the name, phone number, and address of members of the household and then scan for these in any outgoing message.

While all this may sound pretty impressive, how good are these products, really? A recent *Consumer Reports* review notes that none of the products is completely effective. The reason? Web sites change too quickly. Nonetheless, the products have improved since the *Consumer Reports* review. Some of the products now update their lists automatically. Many feel that these content-filtering products do provide the level of protection that families need. These products are an example of a unique marketing mix that is tailored to a target market based both on demographics (age) and psychographics (beliefs).

Ethics and Law

COPYRIGHT, PATENT, AND TRADEMARK LAW

Law is similar to ethics in the sense that it too is an ancient expression of values. Unlike ethics, though, it is always intended to apply to entire nations or states. In the Anglo-American tradition, law is made by legislatures such as Congress, enforced by agencies such as the police or regulatory bodies, and interpreted by the courts. In all of these instances, it is a public endeavor. This is reflected in the fact that law is often a result of political and social compromise. Additionally, law attempts to be consistent in both time and place so that citizens will be familiar with their rights and obligations.

A primary function of law is to define ownership, and here the goal of consistency is currently being challenged by digital technology. Traditionally, the law has protected intangible or intellectual property through three basic mechanisms. *Copyright* addresses the realm of ideas—specifically, the right to publish or duplicate the expressions of these ideas. *Patent* law is centered upon inventions and the ability to reproduce or manufacture an inventor's product. *Trademark* is concerned with images, symbols, words, or other indicators that are registered with the government and have become positively associated with a product's identity in the market. It is important to note that these categories have never been inflexible; often the boundaries between them have been modified by legislation and the courts.

Computer-based communication has posed particularly difficult problems for intellectual property. For instance, the electronic media by which messages are carried can properly be thought of as inventions which would classically be protected by patent law. On the other hand, the messages are also expressions of ideas—the subject of copyright law. Similarly, graphical objects are both inventive creations and expressive; they may also reasonably be deemed to be associated with a commercial entity, and trademark becomes a consideration.

The current law of intellectual property is understandably in flux. At this early stage, it appears that copyright has been established as the primary means of protecting most written material on the Internet, including text and other data. In 1997, President Clinton signed the No Electronic Theft Act. The NET Act confers copyright protection for computer content when appropriation is done for commercial or private financial gain. Punishment under this provision may include criminal prosecution.

In addition to legislation, the World Intellectual Property Organization (WIPO) has enacted two treaties which conform international copyright law to digital contexts. These agreements have to be ratified by the U.S. Senate in order to be applicable to American law.

Trademark law has been applied in the protection of domain names. These Internet devices are unique configurations of letters or numbers which are used to route data among users: for example, www.companyname.com. The extent to which trademark will be used to decide domain cases is not clear; however, some prominent corporations have asserted this protection for their Internet addresses. Another area where trademark may become involved is the "look and feel" of screen images. If certain presentations can be demonstrated to achieve an identifiable impression and meaning, trademark may be applied to prevent others from duplication.

The use of patent law in computing is uncertain. Normally, patents are granted for inventive processes or steps, and the law itself is tailored toward industrial or mechanical concerns. There is currently no consensus as to whether programs or software presentations behave in these ways. Most likely, patent law will have to be revised in a manner similar to copyright if it is to be effective.

A final major area of intellectual property protection involves the use of licenses. These instruments involve contractual agreements made between consumers and software producers which allow the buyer to use the product but restricts duplication or distribution. While they are common to business situations, the extent to which the courts will enforce licenses with noncommercial purchasers is not clear—primarily because of the lack of bargaining which takes place between the user and the seller. Normally, a contract requires that an agreement can be shown, and it is not certain that average buyers agree with or even read the fine print that appears on their diskettes, boxes, or software manuals.

The desire for certainty in electronic transactions is providing a great motivation for the production of laws that are specific to digital environments. No doubt, legislatures and international bodies will be swiftly enacting greater protections. In this process, it is important to consider that while intellectual property laws can act as incentives to create useful material, they can also work to restrict the data exchange which has contributed to the Internet's popularity. The achieving of a balance between both concerns will be an important and continuing task for digital law and ethics.

S a v v y   S i t e s

Web Site and Address	Importance to Net Marketers
Commercenet www.commerce.net	Commercenet, in conjunction with Nielsen Media Research, provides excellent Net user demographic information with insightful graphs and charts.
Computerworld's Emmerce www.computerworld.com	This site features cutting-edge news stories about issues affecting electronic commerce.
Cyberdialogue/findsvp www.cyberdialogue.com/isg	FIND/SVP's Emerging Technologies Research Group is now Cyberdialogue/findsvp. The result? A site with samples of current facts about Net users and electronic commerce from a team that sells research to businesses.

Forrester Research www.forrester.com	Some free information about information technology issues can be found here.
International Data Corporation (IDC) www.idcresearch.com	Some very useful and free information can be found at this site. The topics include information technology and data analysis, in addition to a global perspective on IT trends.
Morgan Stanley www.ms.com	At this site Morgan Stanley offers the "Internet Quarterly," a report that features updated information and graphic highlights regarding Internet business.
A. C. Nielsen Media Research www.nielsenmedia.com/	Nielsen and I/PRO have teamed up to conduct Internet demographic surveys. Some of the results can be found at this site.
NUA Internet Surveys www.nua.ie	This is a good source of international information about the Internet. NUA also reprints results of other research about Net users and electronic commerce.
Project 2000 at Vanderbilt University www2000.ogsm.vanderbilt.edu	Project 2000 is produced by the Owen School of Management at Vanderbilt University. The site is devoted to topics about marketing on the Internet. There are plenty of excellent scholarly publications to be found here, and a nice assortment of relevant links with descriptions.

Chapter **3**

Online
Research

"I do not seek, I find."

—Pablo Picasso

Chapter Outline

- The RelevantKnowledge Story
- Marketing Information via the Internet
- Secondary Data via the Internet
- Primary Data through Online Research

Practitioner Perspective

Building a Panel to Project the Behavior of the Web-Using Universe: The "Magic of Random Probability Sampling"
— Ted Hawthorne, Vice President, Research and Client Information, RelevantKnowledge

Leveraging Technology

Site Rating Services

Ethics and Law

Jurisdiction

Learning Objectives

- Marketing review
  - Differentiate secondary and primary data
  - Define marketing information system
  - Describe several types of information needed in an environmental scan
  - Identify the steps in a primary marketing research project
- List several online sources of publicly and privately generated secondary data important to marketing managers
- Explain several ways to check the quality of secondary data gathered online
- Describe an effective process for searching the Web
- Compare and contrast open-text and subject tree searches
- Tell how the Internet is used as a contact method for four primary research approaches
- Identify the strengths and weaknesses of the Internet for primary data collection

The

Relevant Knowledge

Story

A sign at the fall 1997 Internet World conference in New York read, "RELEVANT KNOWLEDGE IS LOCATED IN MEETING ROOM 45." The uninitiated observer might have taken this to mean that something worthwhile could be learned at the indicated location— and they would be right. Those better versed would recognize RelevantKnowledge as the clever name of an Internet startup firm. It seems unlikely that two attorneys would end up founding a company to measure Web traffic—less likely still that they would be wet-behind-the-ears college graduates. But then this is the Internet and anything goes! Jeff Levy (Harvard BA, JD) and Tim Cobb (UNC Chapel Hill BS, U. Penn. JD) formed RelevantKnowledge in 1997 to become the Nielsen Ratings of the Web. Levy describes RelevantKnowledge as an upbeat and trendy company. Its employees tend to be in their mid 20s, and the atmosphere is very informal. It is a blue jeans crowd which makes its home in a renovated old factory. While they were late to enter the Web measurement market, they believe that their superior methodology will give them "second mover advantages" to propel them beyond the other heavy hitter— Media Metrix (www.mediametrix.com).

Both Levy and Cobb developed their careers at Turner Broadcasting—Levy rose to become an entertainment attorney and Cobb advanced to business ventures vice president. Why did they leave these exciting, secure positions to become entrepreneurs on the Web? There were two reasons. First they both had an entrepreneurial bug, and second they had seen the power of relevant information for TV advertising. They developed a business plan and then went shopping for venture capital, since "You don't want to lose your mom's money." The venture capitalists were polite but declined to help two lawyers with no background in starting a business. After many such strikeouts, Mom's money started looking more and more attractive. Reluctantly, they turned to their family and friends to put together about $500,000. More money was later raised from a group of local businessmen. Finally, when the business was up and running, the venture capitalists began to invest.

There are three ways to measure traffic on the Web:

1. Survey the users to find what they remember from their surfing experiences. This strategy is followed by @Plan in Stamford, CT.

2. Analyze the log file of each client's Web site. I/Pro (www.ipro.com) measures activity at their clients' Web sites using this strategy.

3. Form a representative panel of thousands of viewers, then observe what each of them does on her computer. RelevantKnowledge and Media Metrix both follow this strategy. This is the same type of strategy that the Nielsen Ratings use for TV.

The representative panel approach has pluses and minuses. On the plus side:

1. It bypasses the problem of proxy server caching (see chapter 6, Leveraging Technology). Users accessing copies of Web sites are still all counted.

2. It bypasses the problem of false visits from search engines and other agents. There are no search engines on the panel—only people.

3. It solves the problem of counting unique rather than repeat visitors. This is hard and in some cases impossible to do through other techniques.

On the minus side:

1. Putting together a panel that is representative of the general population is very difficult.

2. While it is easier to get home users to participate, businesses often refuse to let their employees install monitoring software on their work computers—especially software that will communicate outside of the corporate firewall with the monitoring company.

3. Personal agents that run on the PC can record false visits to sites. Examples include shopping agents as well as browser caching agents.

4. Multiple users in a household or business setting might use the same PC. Sorting out who did what requires cooperation from panel members.

Of these minuses, the biggest concern is whether the panel is representative of the general population. To be representative, every member of the population has to have an equal chance of being selected and the selected have to agree to participate. The selection process is best handled by random digit dialing, since almost everyone owns a telephone. Participation is a different story. At $50 a year no one will do it for the money, but many users are thrilled to be chosen. Since RelevantKnowledge used only random digit dialing, Levy claims that his panel is more representative than the Media Metrix panel. And he's betting the future of the company on providing superior data.

RelevantKnowledge uses a panel of 7,200 users (6,400 home users and 800 business users). Its competitor, Media Metrix, has a larger panel at 11,700 home and 1,500 business users. Is panel size an issue? It depends. To make statements about the 1,000 most highly trafficked Web sites, RelevantKnowledge claims that its panel size is adequate. If so, then its panel size is certainly adequate to track the top 200 sites, which represent 95% of the ad spending. Panel size becomes an issue only for statements about sites not in the top 1,000—and these companies would not be RelevantKnowledge customers. Nonetheless, Levy acknowledges that advertisers would prefer a 10,000-member panel, and he plans to expand in this direction. This expansion may not seem significant, but advertisers pay for space based on site traffic, so lots of dollars rest on the accuracy of these numbers.

RelevantKnowledge can produce highly targeted reports with its data. For example, it produces an Internet Commerce Report that can compare the travel section of a general information site with a site dedicated entirely to travel. This is much more relevant information than comparing the travel site to the entire general information site. As another example, the individual site report separates a given site into content sections (technical term: baskets) and then produces usage statistics for each section. These numbers help advertisers decide which page to buy.

Who buys these reports at about $50,000 a pop? RelevantKnowledge's clients include J. Walter Thompson, Netscape, Infoseek, GeoCities, CNN, BBD&O, Modem Media, Organic Online, and Left Field. RelevantKnowledge has about 100 clients, compared with 150+ for Media Metrix. However when RelevantKnowledge began, Media Metrix already had 125 clients, so one could argue that RelevantKnowledge is catching up fast. Among those willing to invest are the sites themselves, ad agencies, and the financial sector looking for more information to value stocks on the market. For now these players are willing to purchase reports from multiple companies since they don't know who has the best numbers. Currently there are three companies besides RelevantKnowledge providing sample-based Web measurement: Media Metrix, Net Ratings, and Nielsen Media. However, if TV is any guide then eventually this industry will shake out to one player—the one who can provide the most relevant knowledge.

Note: As this book went to press in November of 1998, RelevantKnowledge and Media Metrix announced that they would merge under the Media Metrix name. Levy and Cobb will remain in Atlanta as vice chairmen of the new company.

Marketing Information via the Internet

Marketers use data to assist in decisionmaking, and the Internet has facilitated this process tremendously. Data help marketers understand competitors, consumers, the economic environment, political and legal factors, technological forces, and other factors in the macroenvironment affecting an organization. Secondary data on the Net are often more current than data published in hard copy, and they are easy, inexpensive, and quick to access. Marketing planners also use the Net to collect primary data about consumers. Through online e-mail and Web surveys, online experiments, focus groups, and observation of Net user discussions, marketers learn about both current and prospective customers.

A good way to think of the role of data in marketing decisionmaking is by understanding the marketing information system (MIS). The MIS is a system of assessing information needs, gathering information, analyzing it, and disseminating it to marketing decisionmakers. The process begins when marketing managers have a problem that needs data prior to solution. The next step is to gather those data from internal sources, through secondary sources, or by conducting primary marketing research. Finally, the process ends when the same managers receive this information in a timely and usable form. For example, Web advertisers need audience statistics prior to deciding where to purchase banner ad space (the problem). They want to know how many eyeballs view various Web sites to evaluate the value of Web ads versus TV and other media ads, and they need to know whether or not an ad on a particular Web site will reach their target market (information need). The best way to get this information is through secondary sources such as RelevantKnowledge or Media Metrix. As was explained in the introductory case, these firms use large panels of consumers to create Web site ratings. Web advertisers use the data to make effective and efficient Web media buys.

This chapter discusses the Internet as a means of gathering information used in a marketing information system. It does not focus on the information particular to Internet marketing, but rather describes the Internet as a tool for researching all of the firm's marketing information needs. The first topic is secondary data available online. These are data that have been gathered for some other purpose but are useful for the current problem. This part deals with types of secondary data that are available online and suggests ways to evaluate the quality of these data. The second topic is primary data collection online. This part describes the marketing research process, discusses online methodologies, and enumerates the strengths and weaknesses of the Net for primary data collection.

Secondary Data via the Internet

When faced with an information need, the marketing decisionmaker first looks for secondary data. The reason is that this information can be collected more quickly and less expensively than primary data. Nowhere is this truer than on the Internet: up-to-date information from over 194 countries is available 24 hours a day, 7 days a week, from home or work, delivered in a matter of seconds.

On the other hand the major weakness of secondary data is a mismatch between these data and the marketer's information needs. This is so because the data are usually gathered for a different purpose than the one at hand. Another common problem is the quality of secondary data. Because marketers have no control over data collection procedures, they should always evaluate its quality. Finally, secondary data are often out of date. The U.S. Census provides lots of population statistics, its heavy data collection periods occur only every 10 years, and results do not appear until a year or two later. A marketer using data at www.census.gov must read the fine print to see if the statistics are from the 1990 population census or from a more current update survey.

SCANNING THE MACROENVIRONMENT

Marketers continually scan the firm's macroenvironment for threats and opportunities. What type of information do marketing managers need? An environmental scan seeks market information about the following:

- demographic trends
- competitors
- technological forces
- natural resources

- social and cultural trends
- world and local economies
- legal and political environments

Firms focus on factors important to their industry, and they continually collect information. One of the Internet's major benefits is access to secondary data about environmental factors and trends. The following sections present examples of public and private sources of data about the firm's macroenvironment. Extensive lists are located at your nearest search engine.

Publicly Generated Data

Most U.S. agencies provide online information in their respective areas. Do you have a cool new product idea and want to know about patents? Visit the U.S. Patent Office home page to get a list of application procedures and to scope out the competition of pending patents (www.uspto.gov). Many global organizations, such as the World Trade Organization (www.wto.org) and International Monetary Fund (www.imf.org), are also good sources of data for environmental scans involving countries other than the United States. In the not-for-profit category, most universities provide extensive information through their libraries, and many faculty post their research results online. For example, Tom Novak and Donna Hoffman of Vanderbilt University share their important electronic commerce research at the Project 2000 site (www2000.ogsm.vanderbilt.edu). Finally industry- or profession-specific information is available at the sites of professional associations such as the American Marketing Association (www.ama.org). All of this information is free and available to all Internet users: an incredible cost- and time-saving feature for marketing managers. A sampling of important public sites is displayed in Exhibit 3 - 1 (the complete list is nearly endless).

Privately Generated Data

Many firms and individuals put timely information on Web sites. This makes the Web especially useful for monitoring the competitive environment. Firms will not only learn about competitive marketing strategies, but can sometimes catch announcements of new products or price changes prior to the media's reporting on them. For example, Toyota will be introducing a low-price sub-compact automobile in January 1999 to replace its Tercel, and one can bet that Honda and Nissan dealers will get a first glimpse at www.toyota.com.

Another good resource is large research firms, such as Cyberdialogue/findsvp and Forrester Research, who put sample statistics on their sites as a way to entice users to purchase full research reports. RelevantKnowledge similarly posts the top twenty Web sites in a survey period. While incomplete, these tidbits of information are often quite helpful in an environmental scan and assist marketers who are deciding whether to purchase the full report.

Content providers deliver a plethora of information to the Net community. *American Demographics* is of special interest to marketers because it allows users free access to stories about U.S. population characteristics as well as social and cultural trends (www.demographics.com). The Commerce Business Daily is an important resource because it includes government requests for proposals online (www.cbd.savvy.com).

News aggregators are another important source of privately generated information: These are firms that monitor a number of media sources, presenting selected stories to users. Thanks to news aggregators, the Internet has made scanning the world for news less effort than clicking a mouse. Pointcast was one of the first to bring world news to every desktop in the form of continuous feed through the screen saver function (www.pointcast.com). Users simply select news categories of interest and Pointcast sends stories from over 200 sources. Many other Web sites offer individualized news stories by allowing users to customize pages at the firm's Web site (e.g., My Yahoo!). This is a good way to monitor competitive action and other environmental scan factors as well as to see what the media is saying about a firm and its products.

Factor	Web Site Example	Description
Demographic trends	www.census.gov	The mother lode of demographic data about U.S. residents is the U.S. Census
Competitors	www.sec.gov	Security and Exchange Commission (SEC) site contains all the financial report filings from public companies in its EDGAR database
Technological forces	mentor.lanl.gov	Physicists at Los Alamos laboratories operate a server with support of the Department of Energy that contains all academic papers describing physics discoveries
Natural resources	www.epa.gov	The Environmental Protection Agency reports on research about the natural environment
Social and cultural trends	www.odci.gov/cia	CIA Factbook contains economic and population information about foreign countries
World and local economies	www.stat-usa.gov (see Exhibit 3 - 2)	The U.S. Department of Commerce provides economic data published by the U.S. government as well as National Trade Data Bank information for importers and exporters
Legal and political environments	thomas.loc.gov/home /thomas2.html	Thomas is the official site for the U.S. Congress library; it contains up-to-the-minute text and news on current bills

Exhibit 3 - 1 Web Sites for Environmental Scanning

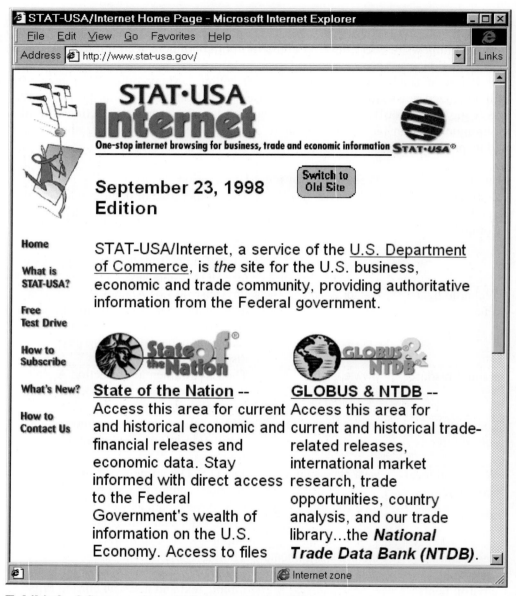

Exhibit 3 - 2 Stat-usa from U.S. Department of Commerce
Source: www.stat-usa.gov

Closely related to news aggregators are firms that gather outside data, often include their own information, and then produce category-specific Web sites, either for free or for fee. For example, Jupiter Communications offers current news and research findings about Web advertising (www.jup.com). CyberAtlas (www.cyberatlas.com) is a "reprint" service that scans the Web for current studies and press releases about Web user characteristics and behavior.

Rather than waiting for services or Web sites to deliver news of interest, some firms pay others to search the Net for news about the environment in a more proactive manner. In addition to searching news stories, these services search every digital word online: this includes individual Web sites, online bulletin boards, and consumer chat. These services can be compared to clipping services in traditional media that scan publications for stories about particular companies or issues; however, because of technology the online versions can perform this service much more accurately, extensively, and quickly.

Online Databases

Commercial online databases contain publicly available information that can be accessed via the Internet. There are thousands of databases on a great number of topics such as news, industry data, encyclopedias, airline routes and fares, yellow page directories, and e-mail addresses. Prior to the Internet, marketers could stop at their local library and review computer or CD-ROM databases such as ABI Inform, which includes published business news stories from periodicals. Thanks to the Internet, most of these databases and others are also available from any computer at a remote location.

Some databases are free to the Net community while others charge a fee. Travel agent Web sites such as Travelocity (www.travelocity.com) allow users to search for the best schedules and rates between two cities: ideal for an airline or travel firm wanting to monitor the competitive environment. Of special interest to marketers is online access to Dun & Bradstreet's business information of 11 million U.S. private and public companies and more than 50 million companies in 200 countries worldwide (www.dnb.com). D&B Internet Access(TM) provides free look-up of both private and public companies, free access to basic identification information, and the option to order and purchase from a select group of D&B reports and services using a credit card (Exhibit 3 - 3). Companies can also subscribe to D&B and make its information available to decisionmakers via its internal computer network (technical term: intranet).

Trailblazer Web sites, also called index pages, help marketers find relevant Web sites quickly. Trailblazer sites are those that contain long lists of links to outside sites on a particular topic. The University of Texas at Austin (advweb.cocomm.utexas.edu/world) is a good example of a public trailblazer site: It maintains a very useful page with links to advertising-related Web sites (Exhibit 3 - 4). The Savvy Sites listed at the end of each chapter in this text contain many trailblazer pages.

Scanning the Microenvironment

A firm's microenvironment includes factors within the company itself, internal stakeholders such as stockholders and employees, as well as its distribution partners and customers. The organization's marketing information system often includes mechanisms for collecting and sharing data through an Intranet. For example, if marketers want to compare customer profiles with population statistics, they can download census information from the Internet, save it in a spreadsheet, then merge it with proprietary demographic statistics about the firm's customers contained on its Intranet.

Database marketing involves building and maintaining an electronic list of customers and prospective customers, along with their addresses, phone numbers, and purchase behavior. Firms have used database marketing for many years, but new storage and retrieval technologies, and the availability of large amounts of secondary electronic information, have recently escalated its growth. For example, visitors to Expedia are asked to register in order to use its services. This firm has a large database which includes e-mail addresses, customer characteristics, and surfing and purchase behavior.

Back Web Technologies (www.backweb.com) provides software that automatically integrates data from both the firm's macroenvironment and its microenvironment. For example, a marketing manager can be working on a marketing plan, and when she saves the file it can be automatically put on the server for other managers to access. Internal data are seamlessly integrated with the firm's Web site, external Web sites, newsgroups, and databases—all with search capabilities.

With all that information in cyberspace, how can marketers find their way around in a timely manner? This is a huge problem for Internet researchers. Tim Berners-Lee, the Web's creator, recently suggested that one of the most important tasks ahead is organizing the Web's information into user-friendly information channels. Appendix B offers a brief discussion of basic searching procedures, the tools for searching the Web, and a few helpful techniques. To master Web searching, however, please consult the help feature on search sites or read books dedicated to this problem.

Information Quality

Both primary and secondary data are subject to many limitations; thus marketers should apply information with caution. It is advisable to be as objective as possible when reviewing data, and to keep a skeptical attitude prior to using information in decision making. Nowhere is this truer than on the Internet. Why? Because anyone can easily publish on the Web. There is no review process such as that provided by book or other media publishers. Furthermore, no one is "in charge" of the Internet's content, monitoring information accuracy or appropriateness. Special care should be taken with secondary data from foreign countries, because of cultural and data collection technique differences.

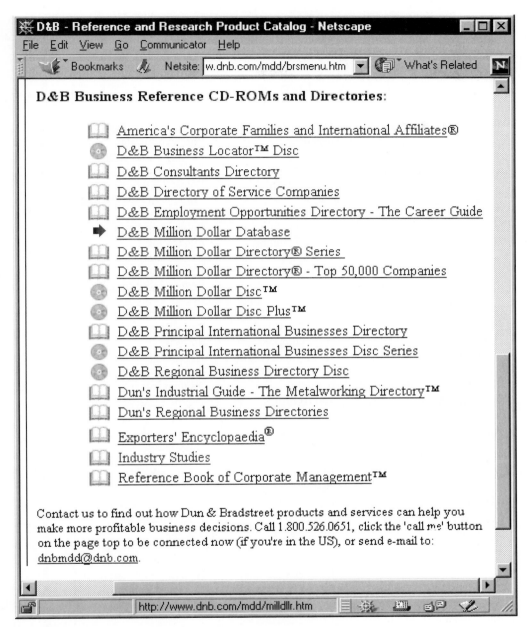

Exhibit 3 - 3 Dun and Bradstreet's Databases
Source: www.dnb.com

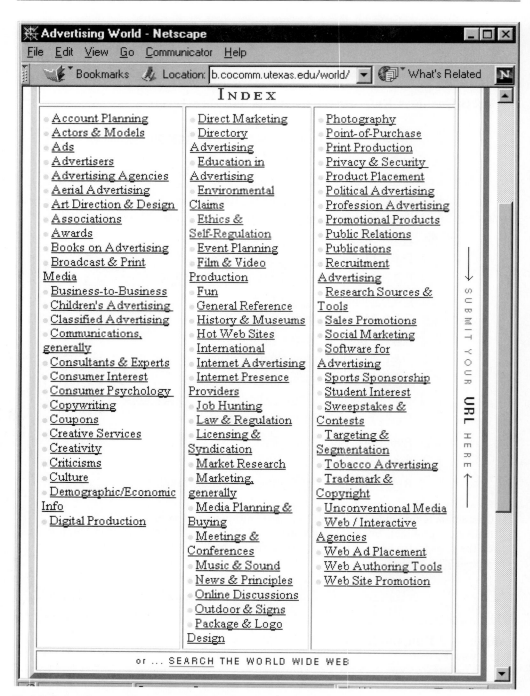

Exhibit 3 - 4 University of Texas Trailblazer Page
Source: advweb.cocomm.utexas.edu/world

It is important to remember not to be seduced by good design: The best-designed sites may not be the most accurate or credible, and vice versa. For example, the Securities and Exchange Commission publishes reports filed by public companies in simple text, spending no taxpayer money to make them pretty. The University at Albany, SUNY library (www.albany.edu/library/internet/addiction.html) created a page to show just how easy it is to get fooled. The following steps can be taken to evaluate the quality of secondary data collected online (some of this information is from the Albany site):

- Discover the Web site's author. A site published by a government agency or well-known corporation has more credibility than one published by an unknown author. Sometimes discerning the differnce is quite tricky: for example, there are usually several sites for the same musical group — some official and some published by individual fans. A search in AltaVista for "Rolling Stones" yielded over 67,000 results. Which of these are authorized by the group?

- Try to determine if the site author is an authority on the Web site topic. For example, an economist from Harvard University or Merrill Lynch, Pierce, Fenner, and Smith might have more credible information about interest rates than will a politician. Furthermore, the university Web site may have less bias than the financial firm's site.

- Check to see when the site was last updated. On average Web sites change every 75 days, but some have not been maintained for several years. Obviously, the more current, the better. Check the hyperlinks. Although most sites contain occasional broken links, a site with many inoperative links is a site that has not been updated recently.

- Determine how comprehensive the site is: Does it cover only one aspect of a topic, or does it consider the broader context?

- Try to validate the research data by finding similar information at other sources on the Internet or in hard copy at the library. If it is not possible to find the exact same statistics, look for other things. For example, one validation of the number of people with Internet service providers might be to check the number of people with computers: The latter should be larger. In general it is also a good idea to compare sites that cover the same topic.

- Check the site content for accuracy. If there are lots of errors or if numbers don't add properly, this is a sign that the data cannot be trusted.

- Don't rest easy when the first good site full of hyperlinks appears on the screen. Remember that this is only one site of many potential sources, and that the list of related hyperlinks are provided as a service and are not necessarily the best other sites for the topic.

Primary Data Through Online Research

When secondary data are not available to assist in marketing planning, marketing managers may decide to collect their own information. Primary data is information gathered for the first time to solve a particular problem. It is usually more expensive and time-consuming to gather than secondary data, but on the other hand the data are current and are generally more relevant to the marketer's specific problem. In addition, primary data have the benefit of being proprietary and thus unavailable to competitors.

PRIMARY RESEARCH STEPS

A primary data collection project includes many steps. Briefly, managers must decide the following things:

- What is the exact problem? As with secondary data, specificity is vital.
- What is the research plan?
  - *Research approach*. On the basis of the information need, researchers choose from among experiments, focus groups, observation techniques, and survey research.
  - *Sample design*. At this stage researchers select the sample source and number of desired respondents
  - *Contact method*. Ways to contact the sample include traditional methods such as the telephone, mail, and in-person as well as the Internet.
  - *Instrument design*. If a survey is planned, researchers develop a questionnaire. If the plan calls for an experiment or observations, they develop a protocol to guide the data collection.
  - *Data collection and analysis*. Researchers gather the information according to plan, then analyze the results in light of the original problem.
  - How will the data be distributed to decisionmakers? Research data might be placed in the MIS database or might be presented in written or oral form to marketing managers.

The ease and cost efficiency of reaching users via computer, as well as other factors, have resulted in much primary data being collected electronically via computer networks. Online research refers to marketing research that is conducted over a computer network. Internet contact methods include all electronic networking such as e-mail messaging either between individuals or *en masse* through mailing lists, e-mail conferencing on bulletin boards (Usenet), and the World Wide Web.

The Internet has been used as a contact method for each of the four research approaches (experiments, focus groups, observation, and surveys), with survey research being by far the most common type. Each method can provide important information but the limitations should be understood prior to decisionmaking. Remember that online research can collect information only from people who use the

Internet. This leaves out a huge portion of the U.S. population, and many more in other countries. The next sections describe peculiarities of each approach for online research, focusing on survey research.

ONLINE EXPERIMENTS

Experimental research is attempting to test cause-and-effect relationships. A researcher will select subjects, randomly put them into two or more groups, and then expose each group to different stimuli. The researcher then measures responses to the stimuli, usually in the form of a questionnaire, and then sees if there are differences among the groups. If the experiment has been carefully controlled such that only the experimental stimuli were varied, group differences can be attributed to the stimuli (cause and effect). Of course, these effects must be tested in other situations and with other subjects to discover their degree of generalizability.

On the Internet, two researchers conducted an experiment to test the effectiveness of banner advertising (Briggs and Hollis 1997). One measure of a banner ad's effectiveness is to see how many users click on it. But even if surfers don't click, the ad may still have increased their brand awareness or influenced their attitudes toward the product or company. Perhaps they didn't click because they were focused on a Web search for something else, but the ad still affected them. These researchers solicited a random sample of visitors to *HotWired's* Web site and asked them to complete a short questionnaire right at the site. After they finished, they were sent back to *HotWired's* home page and randomly shown one of three test banner ads for each of three products: men's apparel, ISP, and Web browser. The next day, the researchers sent these users a thank you e-mail and asked them to participate in a second survey: This one asked questions about the impact of the ad on their impressions of the brand. This is an example of a well-designed experiment using both e-mail and the Web. Incidentally, as a result of this experiment, the researchers concluded that banner ads work, "unequivocally." Advertising awareness for the brands tested increased from a low of 12% to a high of 200% for the various product ads tested, and brand loyalty increased from 5% to 50%—all based on one exposure to a banner ad.

ONLINE FOCUS GROUPS

Focus group research is a qualitative methodology that attempts to collect in-depth information from a small number of participants. Focus groups are often used to help marketers understand important feelings and behaviors prior to designing survey research.

Many advertising agencies and market research firms use the Internet to conduct online focus groups. The Chiat/Day agency conducted some of the first online focus groups in 1995. This contact method provides some advantages over traditional groups where all the participants are in one room together around a table. First, the Internet is good for bringing people together who do not live in the same geographic area. Imagine a focus group containing consumers from five different countries, all discussing online shopping experiences, for example. Second, since the participants type their answers at the same time, they do not depend as much on what the others say ("group think"). Finally, by using the Web, researchers can show participants animated ads, demonstrate software, or use other multimedia stimuli to prompt group discussion. On the other hand, online focus groups can accommodate only several participants at a time while traditional groups generally host 10 to 12. The reason is that it is difficult to manage simultaneous, overlapping conversation in cyberspace. Also, nonverbal communication is lost in cyberspace—in offline groups facial expressions can be very revealing in a way that typed smiley faces do not match (technical term: emoticons). Another disadvantage of online groups is the authenticity problem. Without seeing people in person, it is difficult to be sure they are who they say they are. For example, it is quite common for children to pose as adults online. This problem is discussed more thoroughly in the survey research section. Nevertheless, focus groups are quicker and less expensive to operate than offline versions.

King, Brown and Partners, a San Francisco research·firm, conducts online focus groups for its clients (www.kingbrown.com). This is their procedure:

- Contact potential participants via e-mail, asking them to go to a Web site and answer screening questions (for example, the market may be teenagers in Europe who buy Levi's).
- Send e-mail messages to qualified users, offering them money to participate in the group.
- Have clients and 4-8 participants appear at an online site at the appointed time and day, and have all greeted electronically by the moderator.
- Split the screen into two vertical portions: on the right, the moderator types questions and the participants type responses. Multimedia can also be presented on the right side. The left side is a "back room" where clients can communicate with each other and the moderator through their keyboards as the group progresses.

ONLINE OBSERVATIONS

Observation research monitors people's behavior by watching them in relevant situations. For example, retailers videotape shoppers to see the pattern they choose through the store and to monitor other shopping behaviors. Some researchers believe that actions speak louder than words, making customer observation stronger than surveys which record people's statements about what they believe and do. Of course, as a qualitative method, observations of a small number of people cannot be used to describe how all people might act.

The Internet is a perfect place to observe user behavior, because the technology automatically records actions in a format that can be easily, quickly, and mathematically manipulated for analysis. The most common form of observational research online is Web site firms' monitoring the surfing patterns of visitors. Web site log software, such as NetTracker, records user data for a Web server. Log software generates reports on numbers of users who view each page, location of site visited prior to the firm's site, and what users buy at a site. These statistics can be arranged by date, time, and user's geographic location and can be further manipulated to produce ratios such as pages viewed per sale or number of impressions for a banner ad. For example, because of its online registration requirement, Expedia can track visitors' ticket purchases, browsing patterns, and how often they visit the site. It uses the information to send special offers to users as well as to offer services such as the fare watcher. Amazon, through collaborative filtering software, keeps track of books ordered by customers and makes recommendations based on customer trends in its database. These observational data help firms improve online marketing strategies and produce more effective Web sites.

Another interesting form of observational research, available only on the Internet, is monitor consumer chatting and e-mail posting through chat rooms, bulletin boards, or mailing lists (technical term: LISTSERVs). The Usenet consists of over 50,000 newsgroups, each one a forum for public discussion on a specific topic. People post articles to newsgroups for others to read. Discussions range from the meaningful to the absurd, but marketing planners can learn about products and industries by monitoring discussions. There are even firms that, for a fee, monitor the Usenet and notify corporations of any bad rumors circulating about them. This information enables them to quickly post a response to dispel the rumor. A highly specialized search engine called DejaNews was developed to save and index all postings to the Usenet. So far, DejaNews has indexed over 100 million postings and provides a free service which allows users to scan through them. To get an idea of the value of consumer observation, see Exhibit 3 - 5 for one person's view of the Honda CR-V. This type of information is extremely important for both Honda and its competitors. Other ways to catch customer chat are to provide space on the firm's Web site or to subscribe to e-mail lists on product-related topics.

ONLINE SURVEY RESEARCH

Surveys are performed online by sending questionnaires to individuals via e-mail, or by posting a survey form on the Web or on an electronic bulletin board. The latter is not recommended unless the bulletin board is owned by the organization: Netizens do not take favorably to companies posting commercial messages on the Usenet. BizRate is a good example of a firm that has built its business using online survey research. The Leveraging Technology section at the end of this chapter describes how BizRate presents Web questionnaires to a random sample of shoppers at client sites for the purpose of helping the sites improve marketing efforts.

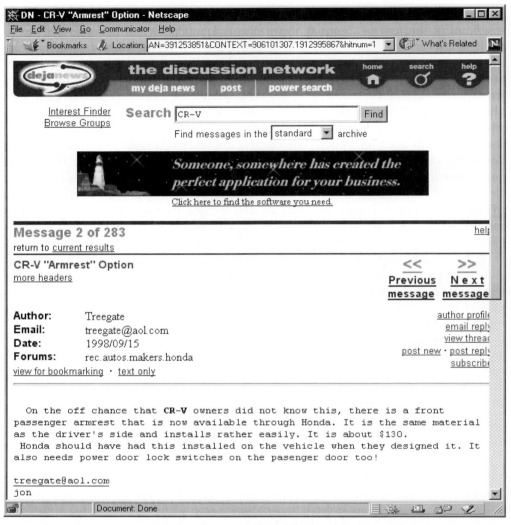

Exhibit 3 - 5 Consumers discussing product in the Usenet
Source: www.dejanews.com

E-mail Surveys

An organization can draw a sample of e-mail addresses from its database, purchase a list, or gather e-mail addresses from the Web or Usenet newsgroups. Using these methods, the firm will obtain e-mail addresses from a very specialized group of individuals and thus exercise control over who gets the electronic questionnaire. After sending a questionnaire, the researcher can easily and inexpensively send e-mail reminders to those respondents who have not yet returned it. Perhaps because of this capability, response rates are just as high for e-mail surveys as they are for traditional contact methods. As with all methodologies, the percentage of the sample responding is partially dependent upon their interest level in the survey topic.

One problem with e-mail survey research is that many consumers do not have the technical skill to put the incoming e-mail questionnaire into a "reply and edit" mode to type their answers in the appropriate places. Respondents who are able to do this are often sloppy, placing their answers in any location near the question, thus increasing the chance of tabulation error. In 1995 FIND/SVP, a large market research firm, tested a way to solve this problem by placing two asterisks (* *) after each question and asking respondents to place their responses between them. They developed computer software that would select responses in that location, thus minimizing time and tabulation error. In general, e-mail survey research is quite promising as a contact method and will continue to grow as e-mail reader software improves.

Web Surveys

Many companies post questions on their Web pages. Respondents type answers into automated response mechanisms in the form of radio buttons (users click to indicate the response), drop-down menus, or blank areas (see a page from the ninth GVU survey in Exhibit 3 - 7). Sometimes the purpose of these questionnaires is simply to gather statistics about visitors to a particular site (e.g., Web site registration), but sometimes it is more formal survey research. Chapter 2 discussed GVU and the surveys these researchers conduct every six months from the Georgia Tech Web site. Usually researchers will post a Web survey and then send e-mail and use other forms of publicity to direct respondents to the Web site.

Online survey research has many advantages and disadvantages over traditional contact methods: a few of them are discussed in the next paragraphs, and Exhibit 3 - 6 contains a summary table.

Online Survey Research Advantages

First of all, online survey research is fast and inexpensive, especially compared with traditional survey methodologies. Questionnaires are delivered nearly instantaneously worldwide over the Internet and there is no postage charge or interviewer salary to pay. Web surveys can easily be converted to HTML files and do not need lengthy printing, collating, and mailing time. Those who complete the questionnaires generally do so in the first three days, making the entire process very quick. Second, marketing researchers can reach a diverse, large group of people in 200 countries. It is not nearly so easy to conduct research from one country to another using traditional contact methods. Third, some researchers believe that Web surveys reduce errors. For example, the second GVU study (1994) introduced "adaptive" questions. These are contingency questions that the computer automatically presents depending upon responses to previous questions. For example, if a respondent answers "c" to question 9, the software can immediately skip three questions and present question 12. GVU researchers feel that this technique reduces the complexity and time involved for respondents. In addition, respondents' entering answers into the computer eliminates data entry errors found in traditional methods: Typing errors are made when another person must key in answers from a paper and pencil questionnaire. Fourth, some researchers have discovered that respondents will answer questions more honestly and openly on a computer than when an interviewer is present. In addition, respondents will answer very sensitive questions about private matters over the Net. The reason may be that the computer is impersonal and no one is there watching what the respondent types. Fifth, online questionnaires are a novelty and many people seem to enjoy completing them: GVU repeatedly attracts well over 10,000 respondents every six months to its five to seven lengthy Web questionnaires. As more researchers use the Net for survey research, however, the novelty effect may wear off. Finally, data entered into a computer are easy to tabulate with a statistical software package. In addition, results can be analyzed daily and sent to decisionmakers if desired.

Advantages	Disadvantages
Fast and inexpensive	Sample selection small
Diverse, large group of Net users worldwide	Generalizability questionable
Computer entry reduces errors	Self-selection bias
Honest responses to sensitive questions	Respondent authenticity uncertain
Novelty for respondents	Frivolous/dishonest responses
Electronic data are easy to tabulate	Duplicate submissions

Exhibit 3 - 6 Advantages and Disadvantages of Online Survey Research

Online Survey Research Disadvantages

The inability to draw a probability sample of Internet users is the biggest problem facing researchers using online methodologies. The reason a probability sample is currently impossible is that there exists no list of Internet users. Researchers employing in-person or mail contact methods do have population lists and thus can draw probability samples. There are no public lists of all telephone numbers either, but random digit dialing technology solved the problem for this contact method. Without the ability to draw a random sample, researchers cannot declare their results generalizable to the entire population of interest. What this means is that researchers can send e-mail questionnaires to samples of respondents or put a Web survey online, but they must be very careful when interpreting the results. What does it mean when 15,000 people click off the products they've shopped for online in the GVU survey in Exhibit 3 - 7? How does the result relate to all Web users? This is the generalizability problem. As Internet population characteristics become better defined, researchers can compensate for this problem because they can compare the survey respondent characteristics to those of the Net population and weight responses accordingly.

As if this weren't bad enough, the problem worsens with Web surveys and questionnaires posted on bulletin boards, because there is no control over who responds. Whereas the person receiving an e-mail generally keeps it private, responding personally, anyone can answer a Web survey. This possibility creates a self-selection bias that is difficult to measure. For example, the largest group of people answering early GVU surveys were computer professionals and college students—these were the users with the time, ability, and interest to spend hours answering online questionnaires.

A closely related concern is respondent authenticity. While this is a problem in any self-administered survey methodology, it seems particularly acute on the Internet. Surveys have found that anywhere from 20% to 50% of Web users have posed as the opposite sex on the Internet! In addition, children pose as adults online. This situation is not easy to correct and obviously biases survey results. Many researchers are attempting to screen out nonlegitimate, or flippant respondents. One way is to watch for frivolous results such as responses that form a pattern (e.g., each response is increased by one: 1, 2, 3, 4, and so on).

Closely related to this problem is that of duplicate responses to online surveys. GVU put e-mail address screening into their second user survey and found that 709 (3.8%) of their 18,503 completed questionnaires were multiple submissions from the same address (gvu.gatech.edu/user_surveys). Some respondents simply make a mistake and submit a questionnaire more than once, and perhaps others want their opinion counted heavily!

Solutions to Sampling Problems

In 1995 FIND/SVP attempted to minimize sample bias in two ways. First, they devised a method of gathering e-mail addresses from Usenet groups by using computer software that employs a system of nth skips through groups and posters to those groups. Their method selects unique addresses before counting for skips. They selected the Usenet because it represents the largest amount of activity on the Internet. Second, they ran parallel telephone surveys and compared the two for response and demographic differences.

```
╔══════════════════════════════════════════════════════════════════╗
║ ※ Internet Shopping (Part 1) Questionnaire - Netscape    _ □ ☒  ║
╠══════════════════════════════════════════════════════════════════╣
║  File   Edit   View   Go   Communicator   Help                   ║
╟──────────────────────────────────────────────────────────────────╢
║  ▼ ⚮ Bookmarks  ⚲ Location: http://www.gvu.gatech.edu/u ▼  ☐▼ What's Related  N ║
╚══════════════════════════════════════════════════════════════════╝
```

Not Answered ▼	**If you have done this type of browsing, how much**

Not Answered
I don't do this
Much less
Somewhat less
About the same
Somewhat more
Much more

ll be doing this in the next six months compared to

nths? ◄———————————————————— Drag-down | Drop-down |

**is type of browsing, please indicate the products
re browsed for (please check all that apply):**

ch browsing | Radio buttons |

☐ Computer hardware   ☑ Computer software/games   ☐ Wine

☐ Generic grocery items (e.g. milk, eggs)   ☐ Brand-name grocery items (e.g. soft drinks, cigarettes)   ☐ Recreational equipment (e.g. skis, bikes)

☐ Flowers   ☐ Magazines/newspapers   ☑ Books

☐ Video/Movies   ☑ Music CDs/Tapes/Albums   ☐ Concerts/Plays

☐ Travel Arrangements   ☐ Home electronics/appliances   ☐ Autos/Motorcycle

☐ Precious metals   ☐ Jewelry   ☐ Investment Choices (e.g., stocks)

☐ Stock market quotes   ☐ Banking/Financial Services   ☐ Insurance services

☐ Legal services   ☐ Clothing/Shoes   ☐ Real estate

| Type answer |

Please add any other products or services here.

```
┌─────────────────────────────────────────────┐ ▲
│ I have also looked at grad schools          │ ▒
│                                             │ ▒
│                                             │ ▼
└─────────────────────────────────────────────┘
```

Exhibit 3 - 7 GVU Web Survey
Source: www.gvu.gatech.edu

Another way to combat sampling problems is to use online panels, such as that used by RelevantKnowledge (see introductory case). Called single-source data systems, they include a panel of people who have agreed to be the subject of marketing research. Usually they are paid and they often receive free product for their time. People on a panel complete extensive questionnaires after being accepted, so that researchers have information about their characteristics and behavior. This way, when panel members are asked to test product, are given questionnaires to complete, or are sent coupons and other promotions, researchers can correlate results with already collected demographic data. NPD Group maintains a panel of 15,000 consumers who are recruited online and then subsequently called to verify that they are actually who they say they are (www.npd.com). NPD will post Web surveys for its clients and then send e-mail messages to this panel notifying them of the survey. NPD's surveys not only query users about their interactive attitudes and usage, but they also conduct general concept testing and customer satisfaction surveys.

Ethics of Online Research

With traditional research, respondents are often offered a nominal fee (e.g., $1.00) to complete a questionnaire, but it is not yet possible to send money online. Almost everyone conducting marketing research on the Web has considered its "gift culture," and thus researchers often give something to respondents. Some researchers draw names of those who submit responses, offering free products or cash. Others donate money to charities selected by respondents (e.g., $3.00 to one of three charities listed on the Web page for each questionnaire submitted). Many post the entire results in downloadable form (e.g., GVU), and most provide at least some results on the Web sites after the survey period is completed. These gifts increase response rates while accommodating the Net culture.

In addition to giving to the Net community, there are other ethical concerns regarding survey research on the Net:

1. With e-mail surveys, respondents may be upset at getting "junk" e-mail.

2. Some researchers "harvest" e-mail addresses from newsgroups without permission. Perhaps this practice is similar to gathering names from a telephone book, but some people object because consumers are not posting with the idea of being used by marketers.

3. Some companies conduct "surveys" for the purpose of building a database for later solicitation. Ethical marketers clearly mark the difference between marketing research and marketing promotion and do not sell under the guise of research (technical term: SUGging).

These and other concerns prompted ESOMAR®, the European Society for Opinion and Marketing Research, to write guidelines for Internet research (see Appendix C). ESOMAR has over 3800 members in 96 countries (www.esomar.nl).

In spite of serious shortcomings, the Net is a useful place to conduct a primary research project and will probably increasingly be used in the future. However, when using any primary or secondary data, marketers must evaluate its quality carefully and apply it accordingly.

Summary

Marketers use primary and secondary data in order to make informed marketing decisions. The firm itself collects primary data whereas secondary data is obtained from an outside organization. Both types of data can serve as input to a marketing information system—a system that stores and disseminates information to assist in decision making.

Secondary data are available from a number of government and private sources. The data are especially helpful to scan the firm's macroenvironment in search of threats and opportunities. But many firms also mine their internal data such as sales figures in order to scan the microenvironment. The best marketing information systems are able to smoothly integrate internal and external data to produce timely and informative reports.

Marketers need to know not only how to find relevant data but also how to judge the quality of that data. Search tools such as Yahoo! can help to locate the data, though well-planned searches are likely to yield superior results.

Information quality is more suspect on the Internet because there are fewer editorial controls. Virtually anyone can publish a Web page. Techniques such as discovering the Web site's author and trying to determine whether the author is an authority on the subject can help to avoid embarrassing and costly research mistakes.

Primary data are often gathered when secondary data sources are inadequate. While difficult, time-consuming, and expensive to collect, primary data also tend to be highly relevant to the research problem at hand. Primary data are gathered online through experiments, focus groups, observations, and surveys. Online surveys are a very attractive means of data collection. However, marketers need to keep in mind that creating a random sample is very difficult online. The best solution is to use random digit telephone dialing to select the sample—a technique used by market research firms such as RelevantKnowledge.

Finally, marketers should be aware that this powerful medium presents a real threat to consumer privacy and therefore should be judiciously employed. Ethical standards such as those set up by ESOMAR and the AMA help guide marketers as they conduct research.

Key Concepts and Terms

1. The best way to create a representative sample is to use random digit dialing.
2. Secondary data can be collected more quickly and less expensively than primary data.
3. A firm's macroenvironment consists of all stakeholders, organizations, and forces external to the organization.
4. A firm's microenvironment consists of stakeholders and forces internal to the organization.
5. The best marketing information systems are able to integrate data from the macro- and microenvironments and automatically push the distilled data out to corporate desktops via an intranet.
6. Trailblazer pages catalog a wealth of resources on a particular topic and can be a tremendous aid to marketing research.
7. Since there are no editorial controls for many sites online, the data tend to be more highly suspect.
8. Primary data can usually be collected less expensively on the Internet than via any other channel.
9. Surveys posted on Web pages and sent by e-mail are quite common in use but their results must be used judiciously.

- Adaptive questions
- Directory search
- Environmental scan
- Extranet
- Harvesting addresses
- Intranet
- Log file
- Macroenvironment
- Marketing information system
- Microenvironment
- Open text search
- Primary data
- Probability sample
- Proxy server caching
- Random digit dialing
- Secondary data
- Trailblazer page
- Usenet

Exercises

REVIEW QUESTIONS FOR KNOWLEDGE TESTING

1. List three ways to measure traffic on the Web.
2. List the advantages and disadvantages of constructing a representative panel.

3. What are the strengths and weaknesses of the Internet for primary data collection?

4. What are the strengths and weaknesses of the Internet for secondary data collection?

5. Define marketing information system.

6. List the types of data needed in an environmental scan.

7. Identify the steps in a primary marketing research project.

8. List several online sources of publicly and privately generated secondary data important to marketing managers.

9. Describe an effective process for searching the Web.

10. List the four marketing research approaches.

DISCUSSION QUESTIONS FOR CRITICAL THINKING

1. How can you protect yourself against bad data online?

2. How would you respond to the comment, "Ethics are nice, but this research report is due on Friday and I need quick and easy data"?

3. Which research method(s) would you use to test a new product concept? Why?

4. Which research method(s) would you use to test the brand image of an existing product? Why?

5. Marketers often distinguish between aided and unaided recall of brand. Do you think that both techniques could be supported in an online format? Why or why not?

6. Can you think of a marketing research technique that could not be supported online? If so, which one and why not?

7. Is it better to begin with an open text or a subject tree search? Justify your choice.

ACTIVITIES

1. You have been given the difficult task of researching online marketing communication practices in the soft drink industry. Do some online searching and list sources that you discover to help with this problem.

2. Toyota has asked you to test the effectiveness of its new banner ad using all four primary research techniques. Design these tests.

3. Find information on the U.S. Census and Nielsen TV ratings, either online or in the library. What methodology does each use? Evaluate their strengths and weaknesses based on what you've learned about research methods in this chapter.

INTERNET EXERCISE: RESEARCH METHODOLOGY

Several firms conduct research on the Net population: A. C. Nielsen, the Graphic Visualization Center at Georgia Tech, FIND/SVP, Cyber Dialogue, and others. The problem is that this research often yields conflicting results. This dissimilarity can be caused by different research methods used by the firm conducting the research. CyberAtlas provides a summary of research findings on Net users (www.cyberatlas.com). Visit the demographic page at CyberAtlas and follow the link to the latest GVU survey (www.cc.gatech.edu/gvu). Find one other current survey and complete the following table.

Study Findings	Recent GVU Study	Other (specify)
Net user ages: % over 18		
Net user income levels: % over $50,000		
Percent female users online		

Primary Data Collection Method		
Research approach		
Contact method (online, phone, other)		
Sampling method		
Number in sample		

For Discussion

1. What differences did you note in the findings from these two studies?
2. What are the strengths of GVU's methodology?
3. What are the limitations of GVU's methodology?
4. What differences are there in data collection methods?
5. Based on methodological differences, what explanation can you give for research finding differences? If you were unable to complete the data collection section for another survey, speculate on how differing methods might cause result differences.

INTERNET EXERCISE: SPAMMING

Spamming refers to the bulk distribution of unsolicited, and often unwanted, e-mail messages. Because e-mail carries no postage cost, this form of direct marketing has grown rapidly in the past few years. Used properly, online direct marketing can inform consumers of products or updates of interest to them. When abused, spamming becomes at best an annoyance to Internet users and at worst patently offensive: for example, adult sites that spam to underage users. As a reaction to these abuses, services have sprouted up to fight unwanted e-mail. Visit Yahoo! at www.yahoo.com and search for anti-direct marketing. Find Zero Junk Mail www.zerojunkmail.com and one other company that fights spamming. Complete the following table.

Benefits	Zero Junk Mail	Other (specify)
Stop direct mail		
Stop direct e-mail		
Others: (specify)		

For Discussion

1. What is the cost of the Zero Junk Mail service? Is it worth it?

2. Does Zero Junk Mail promise to stop direct marketing entirely or just filter it to the items that you want?

3. If marketers were doing their job correctly, would filtering be necessary? Explain why or why not.

4. A particularly venal form of spamming disguises the sender's e-mail address so as to make it impossible to respond requesting removal from the list. Do you believe that this practice should be allowed?

Practitioner Perspective

BUILDING A PANEL TO PROJECT THE BEHAVIOR OF THE WEB-USING UNIVERSE: THE "MAGIC OF RANDOM PROBABILITY SAMPLING"

Ted Hawthorne is Vice President, Research and Client Information at RelevantKnowledge. Ted created and formerly directed the research department at The Travel Channel, a 24-hour basic cable television service, where he was the primary contact with leading outside research firms. Ted attended Emory University and received his Bachelor of Arts from the University of Georgia's Henry W. Grady College of Journalism.

It is virtually impossible to measure the behavior of the entire U.S. print, radio, or television universe, because of the overwhelming size and the costs associated with trying to do so. To overcome this limitation, companies that buy and sell advertising to promote their products or themselves via these traditional media conduct their business transactions using powerful behavioral data derived from representative subsets, or samples, of these media populations.

Measuring Web activity continues to be a challenge for all concerned. Web sites, advertisers, and ad agencies are all waiting for the "one-to-one" marketing that eludes them in traditional mass media. Capturing the usage of everyone on the Web, particularly with its current rapid expansion, presents the same, if not greater, challenges facing the traditional media mentioned above. Server log analysis and cookie tracking both have serious limitations that prevent users from agreeing on the numbers, much less providing a real-time understanding of Web activity.

Just like companies in print, radio, and television, those conducting business on the Web need a proven and reliable method for understanding the characteristics, behavior patterns, and number of individuals in the universe to succeed. The basis for achieving this success on the Web is not new or unproven. It centers around the process of reliably projecting Web behavior from an equal-probability based sample derived from using four key steps: enumerating, sampling, recruiting, and weighting.

Therefore, the same sampling techniques used in traditional media can be used with similar accuracy on the Web. However, this does not mean that results from every sample can be used to reliably make inferences about the larger population. To ensure the accuracy of the projections based on a sample there are four critical steps:

1. Understanding the characteristics of the population you will be projecting to through the enumeration

2. Sampling potential panelists in such a way as to ensure everyone has an equal chance of being contacted

3. Recruiting panelists through methods that result in a statistically valid representation of this population

4. Accounting for known biases between the population and the panel through a process known as weighting

Server Side Analysis Has Serious Flaws

Server log analysis provides a picture of all personal computers coming to a particular site. Sessions can be tracked to determine actual pages transmitted by the server (though not necessarily seen by the user), advertisement banners requested, and session duration. Unfortunately, these log analyses have severe limitations:

- Server log analysis provides in-depth information on activity within a site. It does not allow accurate comparisons across sites. This is a small issue for a Webmaster trying to manage a site; however, it is a major challenge for advertisers making cross-site buying decisions.

- Server logs track personal computer sessions, not individuals. This includes traffic generated by spiders and Web crawlers trying to catalog the Web. In addition, individuals using multiple computers show up as multiple users, not one, while individuals sharing one computer look like one computer rather than several users.

- There is no way accurately to link demographic and non-Web behavioral information to site usage information collected in server logs. Is the user of a personal computer a 34-year-old male with two children, a retired woman of 65, or a 13-year-old boy? The log file cannot tell.

The use of cookies addresses the intrasite limitation by allowing those tracking a personal computer to understand everywhere the computer surfs on the Web. Unfortunately, cookies do not provide demographic or psychographic information. Because they track activity at the machine level, they also cannot track a unique Web user. In other words, unless each Web user surfs from a single dedicated personal computer, the mapping from computer to individual is impossible using cookies. Finally, cookies cannot track everyone accurately. Heavy users turn them off; cookies get replaced, thus limiting to a few months the historical information stored, and while cookies can help a site target ads to repeat visitors, they are not a technology that helps audit the individuals that are exposed to or respond to specific advertisements.

Representative Panels Provide a More Accurate Picture

Step 1: Enumerating the Population

Samples must be representative of the larger population. It is one thing to describe the observed characteristics and behaviors of a sample, but a very different thing to project that behavior to a larger population. To project the behavior of a representative subset to the larger population, the first step must be to understand the characteristics and composition of the entire population. Therefore, an enumeration study must be conducted to establish the characteristics of the target population before respondents are asked to participate in the panel.

When comparing services, one must ask, "How extensive is your enumeration and how often is it performed?"

Failure to survey the Web population as it changes from early adopters to a more heterogeneous population makes accurate projections impossible. With the Web growing at such high rates, even enumerating every six months makes for less accurate projections. To maintain an accurate assessment of the ever-changing Web population, RelevantKnowledge conducts its enumeration quarterly. RelevantKnowledge was the first Web measurement company to use enumeration techniques to define the Web-using universe and remains the only company to conduct a quarterly measurement of the domestic Web population.

Step 2: Generating a Representative Sample

As any seasoned researcher will tell you, there's the right way and the wrong way to ensure accurate audience projections. When considering the value and relevance of a sample, it's imperative to remember that bigger is not always better. For example, consider a research company that sets out to measure the number of people who drive Ford automobiles. If to do this, they stood outside a Chevrolet dealership and counted the make of the cars that drove by, the results would be invalid. It would not matter if the sample size given this technique were 50,500 or 50,000. As a result of the bias in the sampling technique, there is an inherent flaw in the sample selection process that size can never overcome.

As the above example indicates, the sampling method should be considered before the sample size. Conclusions drawn from samples are valid only if the sample used to obtain the information is representative of the entire population. Building the most representative sample possible requires that the sample selection method give everyone in the population an equal probability of being selected. Standing by a Chevy dealership gives Chevy owners a greater probability of being in the sample.

Once RelevantKnowledge understands the composition of the domestic Web universe via its enumeration process, it develops a panel that is an accurate reflection of that universe using the same stringent methods (random digit dialing, or RDD) it uses in the enumeration process. RDD refers to a process of recruiting households for a panel based on a random selection of phone numbers and is the method used by RelevantKnowledge to draw its sample of Web users. RDD includes people in the sample who may be excluded by other sampling techniques, meaning that once RelevantKnowledge controls for the number of phone lines, each household has the same chance of being selected into its panel. With this method, the only households that do not have an equal chance of being in the sample are households without a telephone. Since the task is to obtain a random selection of Web users, making the assumption that Web-using households have a telephone seems reasonable.

This method is the only way to ensure that the resulting samples are representative of the population from which they are drawn. The same is true of Web usage. Recruiting just online service (AOL, Compuserve, Prodigy, MSN) subscribers systematically excludes the 60%+ portion of the Web population that uses an ISP to access the Web. A panel comprised only of those persons will not deliver accurate projections of Web usage.

Step 3: Recruiting Sample to Maximize Survey Response Rates

After RelevantKnowledge contacts a random sample of the target population (in this case, Web users) the company must make sure that a random sample actually participates. Unfortunately, no sampling methodology yields a 100% response rate. Some individuals just refuse to participate in research studies. Since no research firm will ever know the behavior of the individual who refuses to cooperate in its surveys, this leads to nonresponse bias. The percentage of a survey sample that participates is known as response rate, and it is one measure of how well a sample reflects the population. The challenge for RelevantKnowledge and all other measurement companies is to maximize the response rate in order to minimize nonresponse bias.

Multiple attempts and recontacts maximize the benefits of random digit dialing. It has been observed that light Web users are less sophisticated and are reluctant to install new software on their personal computer. Thus they are less likely to participate in a sample like this. If RelevantKnowledge did not work to convince these individuals to participate, the panel would be biased against light Web users.

Calling individuals and describing the purpose of the survey increases the number of people willing to participate. Written material mailed to the potential participant reinforces the telephone recruitment call. For those who are willing to participate, a follow-up call can help maximize the response rate.

Step 4: Weighting the Panel

Weighting can correct for response bias. If characteristics in a sample are represented disproportionately when compared with the universe, one can mathematically correct for this disproportion. For example, suppose RelevantKnowledge knows that the population of Web users is 56% male, but its sample is 58% male. RelevantKnowledge knows that the panel, along with any projections based on it, will be skewed slightly toward male behavior unless the results are adjusted proportionately to match the population. In this example, the company knows the characteristic it is concerned about and has data about the behavior associated with that characteristic. RelevantKnowledge can therefore weight the data to account for the disproportionate sample.

Weighting cannot correct for characteristics that do not exist in the sample. Suppose, however, that a research firm uses ad banners on search engines to recruit its panel of users. Contrary to popular thinking, not everyone uses a search engine. Therefore, these people with definitively different behavior will not be in the sample. Because none of these people are in this sample, the panel represents none of their behavior; there is nothing to adjust. This means that inferences cannot be made about the total Web-using universe from this sample.

In addition, weighting cannot correct for nonresponse bias. As was mentioned, because surveys rarely, if ever, yield 100% response rates, the researcher can never know if the behavior of those who choose not to participate is like those who choose to participate. Again, weighting cannot "proportionately correct" the situation since nonrespondents are not in the sample at all.

RelevantKnowledge has a balanced sample. The home-only sample is balanced along geographic and demographic attributes before weighting. These attributes are within 2% of the universe enumeration conducted quarterly. The sample of business users as a percentage of the total sample is smaller than it should be according to the enumeration. Because RelevantKnowledge measures the business user sample every quarter, it weights this smaller sample to correct for this underrepresentation and makes projections accordingly.

Biases of Short-Cut Sample Methodologies

Other Web measurement companies use less stringent techniques, such as lists of addresses or self-selection, to build their panels. Unfortunately, these techniques systematically exclude portions of the population. Equal probability samples are not possible when significant portions of the population are knowingly omitted.

Targeted lists like recent personal computer purchasers systematically exclude Web users using Macintosh, UNIX, and older computer operating systems. If a recent computer buyer is a first-time buyer, his Web activity will be very different from that of more experienced Web users. Using such a targeted list will result in a panel biased toward mass users and away from early adopters with higher Web usage. Sampling via direct mail can result in an equal-probability sample only if the mail list provides a complete and accurate reflection of the universe.

Limited Response Rate of Other Recruiting Methods

If both RDD and recruiting by mail yielded the same response rate, then as a business RelevantKnowledge would be better off using the mail. But RDD generates a higher response rate than mail-based surveys. Those using the mail must hope this invitation stands out among the many unsolicited items people receive on a daily basis. Mail surveys typically yield a 2% response rate although that figure increases when respondents are interested in the topic. Even with an effective follow-up campaign via mail, there is a limit to the response rate that direct mail pieces will generate.

If the response rate is 2%, those using a mail-based recruiting method have no idea how the other 98% of the population behave. Since a research firm can make inferences only from a sample that reflects all characteristics of the population being measured, it cannot be confident that the behavior of the 98% who refuse to participate is reflected in the sample it has drawn. Similarly, if RDD yields a 40% response rate (a more typical response rate for media research using RDD), then nothing is known about how 60% of the population behaves. This problem is known as nonresponse bias and must be managed by the research firm. One way to reduce nonresponse error is to combine methods: for example, use a combination of RDD and mail methodologies.

Summary

Survey and media research only begins with an equal-probability sample. Since all surveys are subject to nonresponse bias, the "theory" has to be discussed within practical realities. The challenge is to minimize this bias. The higher the response rate, the less likely it is that a sample has omitted a characteristic of the population. Media, marketing, and survey researchers agree that random digit dialing with successful recontact efforts ensure that the response rate is high and the sample is balanced.

The RDD technique is more costly and time-consuming. RelevantKnowledge is the only Web measurement company 100% committed to this approach. RelevantKnowledge knows that it is the best approach to drawing a sample that most closely reflects the entire Web universe. Since RelevantKnowledge experiences a 40% cooperation rate, one can fairly state that nothing is known about how the 60% that does not participate behaves. While this cooperation rate also results in nonresponse bias, it is still 20 times better than direct mail and 40 times better than e-mail or banner ads. As a result, RelevantKnowledge has a more representative sample than its competitors.

When evaluating the usefulness of one sample versus another, ask these three questions:

1. Is the sample tied to a known, defined universe that is updated frequently?

2. Was the sample drawn against this known universe and in such a manner that every Web user has an equal chance of being selected? Asked another way: Does the approach systematically eliminate segments of the population being sampled?

3. Does the method of recruiting the sample produce the highest possible response rate, limit the effect of nonresponse bias, and represent the greatest portion of the population being measured?

Leveraging Technology

SITE RATING SERVICES

With over 300 million Web pages on the Internet and no foreseeable end to the growth, it will become increasingly difficult for consumers to distinguish between reputable and nonreputable sites. In the brick and mortar world, consumers use a number of techniques such as contacting the Better Business Bureau to gauge legitimate businesses, but only some of these techniques apply online. The online consumer needs to know two things:

1. Is this a legitimate business or a front for fraud?

2. Assuming that the business is legitimate, how good is it? Does it deliver quickly on promises? Does it get a lot of complaints? What will the shopping experience be like?

A lot of attention has focused on the first item—legitimizing businesses on the Net. This makes sense since it is the basis for making the Internet safe for electronic commerce. Not so much attention has focused on the second—the shopping experience. One notable exception, however, called the BizRate Guide (www.bizrate.com), will be described in detail later.

Before giving out credit card information, the consumer wants to be assured that the business on the other end is legitimate. How does the consumer know? Off of the Internet, consumers rely on the following resources to judge whether to conduct business with a particular company:

1. Their own assessment of the look and feel of the company

2. Referrals from other consumers by word of mouth

3. References from the Better Business Bureau

4. References from the local Chamber of Commerce

5. Newspapers and news magazine shows that highlight good businesses and expose some of the scams

6. The fact that licensing and law enforcement shut down illegitimate businesses

7. Surveys such as those conducted by J. D. Powers and Consumer's Union

8. Approvals from other trusted businesses—for example, the Good Housekeeping Seal of Approval or *Consumer Reports*

On the Web, many of these services do not exist. The last item—approvals from other trusted businesses—is a model gaining favor on the Web. As a result, a number of services have sprung up on the Web to help consumers gauge legitimate businesses. These include:

1. The Excite Guaranteed Logo (www.excite.com). All credit card purchases by law have a maximum $50 liability for fraudulent use. Excite will pick up the $50 liability if one of their "guaranteed" merchants turns out to be a fraud.

2. The Lycos Shopping Network Stores (www.lycos.com). All Lycos-affiliated merchants agree to use secure communications for electronic transactions.

3. The TRUSTe trustmark (www.truste.com), whose premier sponsor is AT&T. Merchants receiving the trustmark are periodically reviewed by the TRUSTe service. Among other things the merchant must have a published privacy policy—though it is free to decide what that policy should be.

All of these services involve voluntary compliance from vendors. Some charge a fee for listing the vendor. On all of the services, vendors not abiding by the rules are removed from the lists. Violators are identified both by excessive consumer complaints and by review—either formal or secret (i.e., posing as a consumer). These services are a good first start but often consumers want richer information about a vendor—something more than that the vendor supports secure ordering and does not get a lot of complaints.

Providing richer information requires both categorizing services offered by vendors and surveying consumers who interact with those vendors along a number of critical dimensions. Enter the BizRate Guide.

BizRate operates at two levels. First, BizRate reviewers visit each listed site to determine what benefits the site provides. These include:

- Secure ordering/payment system (SSL/SET)
- Online ordering shopping cart system
- Online order-tracking system
- Customer information privacy
- Gift wrapping
- Live customer support
- International shipping
- Product search

Second, merchants participating in the BizRate Guide agree to let BizRate survey their customers! There are two surveys. The prepurchase survey (so called because it surveys variables used in the purchase decision) is completed immediately after the purchase. After executing the purchase, the customer is transferred to the BizRate Web site to complete the prepurchase survey. It is similar in concept to the survey forms one fills out in hotels and restaurants immediately after experiencing the service. The customer receives a second, postpurchase survey via e-mail following the expected delivery date of the product. The following performance variables are surveyed by BizRate Guide and rated on a scale of 1 to 10. The performance variables are described on the BizRate site as follows:

Prepurchase:

Price Relative to the Competition:
Consider the price of products relative to other merchants' prices in this category.
Product Selection:
Consider the breadth of product selection that the merchant has made available, keeping in mind the merchant's stated area of focus.
Product Information:
Consider the quality, quantity, and relevance of information provided for making your purchase decision an informed one.
Web Site: Aesthetics:
Consider not just how attractive the site was, but how appropriately graphics were used to enhance your shopping experience, not only slow it down.
Web Site: Navigation:
Consider the overall layout/organization, movement around the site, and missing/nonfunctional links.

Postpurchase:

On-Time Delivery:
Consider timeliness in the context of the promised delivery date.
Customer Support:
Consider how available and effective the merchant was in resolving any questions/complaints or problems that you encountered. Also keep in mind steps the merchant took by itself to make sure that you were informed of your order status and were happy with the transaction.
Ease of Returns:
If you found it necessary to return/cancel any of the merchandise that you purchased, please rate how easy the return/cancellation process was.
Customer Loyalty:
The next time you are going to buy such products, what is the likelihood that you will purchase from this merchant again?
Product In-Stock:
Consider how many of the items that you wanted to order were immediately available. (Do not include items not yet released by the manufacturer.)

The cumulative average responses along the different dimensions are then published on the BizRate site for the entire world to see (Exhibit 3 - 8). At the time of this writing, CD Universe at 8.74 was the top-rated music site on the BizRate Guide. However, the other top sites were not far behind.

- CDnow   8.62
- Music Boulevard 8.53
- Tower Records   8.27
- CD World   8.23

This indicates a relatively small difference in customer perception among the top vendors—a sure sign of a very competitive marketplace. Incidentally, the rating dimensions would serve as a good guide for any business entering the Web for electronic commerce.

None of this costs the merchant or customer a penny. Furthermore, in order to maintain its impartiality, the BizRate Guide accepts no fees from vendors. Nor does it allow advertising on its site. So how does BizRate make money? By selling detailed reports back to the merchants. These reports contain the detail lost in the average ratings presented on the Web site. The reports help merchants tune their services to offer even better customer service. One of the more interesting reports shows a trend analysis of the performance variables. A sample copy of this report for a fictional merchant is presented in Exhibit 3 - 9.

Most consumer and media perceptions of online commerce put it on a par with the Wild West of the 1800s. It is therefore somewhat ironic that in this very free-wheeling atmosphere, consumers possess, perhaps for the the first time ever, detailed and timely information about the vendors with whom they do business. Each consumer benefits from the shopping experience of her online colleagues!

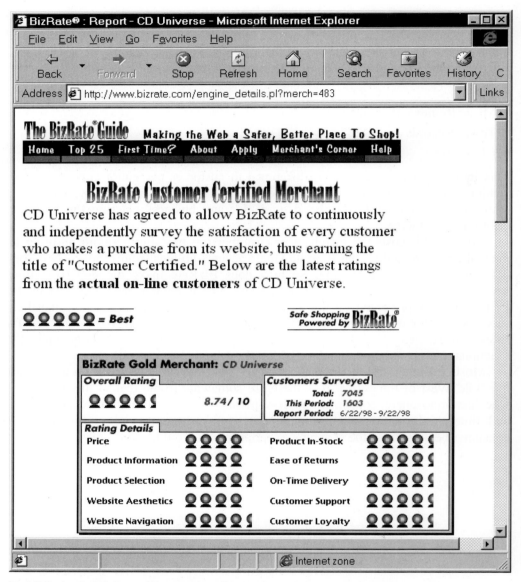

Exhibit 3 - 8 BizRate Results for CD Universe (www.cduniverse.com)
Source: www.bizrate.com

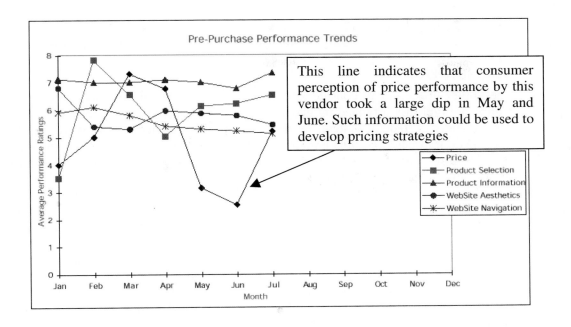

This line indicates that consumer perception of price performance by this vendor took a large dip in May and June. Such information could be used to develop pricing strategies

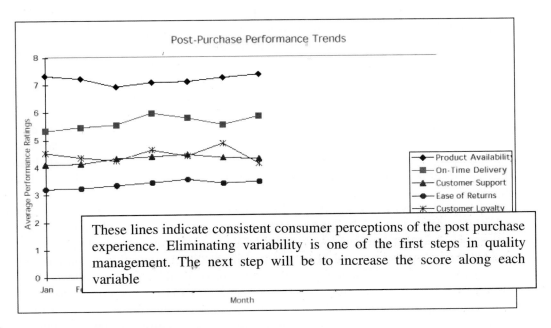

These lines indicate consistent consumer perceptions of the post purchase experience. Eliminating variability is one of the first steps in quality management. The next step will be to increase the score along each variable

Exhibit 3 - 9 BizRate Performance Trend Analysis
Source: www.bizrate.com

Ethics and Law

JURISDICTION

The ability of a court to consider and decide a case is based upon its jurisdiction. Courts are typically arranged by geographic boundaries, such as by states or, in the case of the U.S. federal system, by districts. In contrast, media such as the World Wide Web transcend physical borders. It is the popularity of borderless information flow that now challenges traditional concepts of jurisdiction. Simply put, courts must decide where a handshake occurs on the Internet.

In the most general terms, courts decide whether they have the right to hear a particular case by considering several factors. Through the years, physical location has been the touchstone for a decision-making process which breaks down into three general elements:

The first factor for consideration concerns whether a defendant who is being hailed into a court has purposely availed herself of the privilege of doing business within that court's state. This requirement is normally satisfied when a defendant has taken actions to create a substantial connection with the state. A second factor pertains to whether the cause of action arises from conduct that has occurred within the state. The actions must be related to the actual matter and not be merely incidental. Finally, a court will consider whether subjecting a defendant to its jurisdiction would be consistent with traditional notions of justice and fair play— normally a question that involves balancing the state's interest in the matter against the burdens placed upon the various parties to the controversy.

In the period between 1991 and 1994, a Texas programmer uploaded 32 programs to the CompuServe computer located in Ohio, under an agreement which stated that the programs would be marketed as a joint venture with CompuServe and governed by Ohio law. In the course of business, CompuServe filed a suit against the programmer in the federal district court of Ohio. The defendant contested this forum's right to hear the case, claiming, among other things, that he had never been to Ohio.

Inevitably, the matter was decided by a panel of federal circuit court judges, who noted that the exclusively electronic contacts with the state presented a unique matter for its consideration. Although this was the first time that the issue had been brought before the court, the tribunal affirmed that the traditional question to be answered was whether the circumstances of the defendant's conduct would allow him to reasonably anticipate liability to Ohio jurisdiction. In this regard, it noted that repeated communications were made with the state and that the fact of their digital nature did not alter the quality of the contact. Additionally, the panel found that product advertisements provided by CompuServe offered sufficient indication that an ongoing relationship with an Ohio company had been achieved. The opinion went on to explain, perhaps in anticipation of more global, Internet-based suits, that this particular matter involved a computer that was specifically located in a state and refused to hold the defendant liable to suits instituted in any location where his software had been downloaded (*CompuServe* v. *Patterson*, 89 F.3d 1257 (6th Cir.), 1996).

In *Minnesota v. Granite Gate Resorts* (1996 FED App. 0228P (6th Cir.) the appellate court of Minnesota examined the issue of Internet advertising. The matter involved the promotion of an online gambling service operated by a Nevada corporation which invited users to submit their names electronically to a mailing list in order to receive further information regarding *WagerNet*, a digital betting system. The *WagerNet* site was not located in Minnesota; *WagerNet* advised that all claims regarding its use had to be brought in a Belizian court and cautioned users to consult their individual state gambling laws.

An investigation into the business was conducted by the Minnesota Attorney General's office and a complaint was subsequently filed alleging deceptive trade practices, false advertising, and consumer fraud. The defendant filed for a dismissal of the action based upon a lack of jurisdiction. The court disagreed and found that the defendant had purposely availed itself of a Web site that could be reached by its state's residents. It also cited a finding that at least 248 state computers had accessed the location and consequently declared that the defendant had consciously decided to transmit information to all Internet users, knowing that such information would be received globally.

A recent decision by the Second Circuit Court illustrates another avenue of approach. In *Bensusan Restaurant* v. *King* (126 F.3d 25 (2d Cir.), 1997), the court reviewed a controversy arising between entrepreneurs operating very dissimilar establishments in New York and Missouri. The plaintiff, the New York proprietor of the famous Blue Note jazz club, sought to prevent a local Missouri establishment that was using the same name from advertising its venue on the Web.

In upholding the dismissal of the complaint for lack of jurisdiction, the court relied upon the relevant New York statute which required a physical presence for conferral of jurisdiction. As all of the activities had taken place within electronic environments, the court reasoned that it would be "impolitic" to confer jurisdiction.

Finally, in *Conseco, Inc., et al.* v. *Russ Hickerson*, (No. 29A04-9802-CV-85, 1998 Ind. App. Lexis 1328, Indiana Court of Appeals, August 14, 1998), the plaintiff, an Indiana corporation, filed a suit against the defendant, a resident of Texas, alleging that material contained within the defendant's Web site amounted to trademark dilution and infringement, commercial disparagement, defamation, and tortious interference with contractual relationships. The defendant had previously instituted a suit against a Conseco subsidiary, and his site contained a request that visitors e-mail to him any information concerning fraudulent or unfair activities by the company.

In dismissing the matter for lack of jurisdiction, the court stated that although the effects of the defendant's Web site were "felt" at the Conseco headquarters in Indiana, this fact was insufficient, in a medium of global reach, to apprise the defendant that his conduct would subject him to Indiana jurisdiction. Rather, the court noted in its determination, the court should look to "the level of interactivity of the site and commercial nature of the information exchange." It subsequently found that the defendant had not advertised in the state, had sent no e-mails, had made no phone calls, and had indeed not visited Indiana. Jurisdiction was therefore denied.

These conflicting cases are examples of the uncertainty that dominates current legal debates. The situation is, not surprisingly, no less complex on the international level. As the law develops, courts and those involved in the making of treaties will have to consider carefully how jurisdictions' fundamental concept of stability can be translated in an environment that never rests, even at geographic borders.

S a v v y   S i t e s

Web Site and Address	Importance to Net Marketers
American Demographics www.demographics.com	American Demographics is a monthly publication geared toward marketers. The online edition contains the full edition of this publication—and archive—that features articles, trends, and "marketing tools."
ANYwhere Online www.anywhereonline.com	ANYwhere Online is a market research center that specializes in providing market information on the Internet. There are some excellent links to find at this site such as Ad Age's Net Marketing.
Deja News www.dejanews.com	Deja News is a Web-based discussion forum where users can access discussion groups on literally any topic imaginable
Ecommerce www.ecommerce.gov	This site contains an online, downloadable report called "The Emerging Digital Economy," which is an impressive macroeconomic guide to electronic commerce. Best of all, it's free. The site also contains a link to "Business America," a government publication that covers international trade and electronic commerce. This is a great source of information for exporters using information technology to expand into new markets.
The Global Internet Project www.gip.org./	"The Global Internet Project is an international group of senior executives committed to spurring the growth of the Internet worldwide." The site focuses on the Internet's impact on society, globalization, laws, etc.
GPO Access www.access.gpo.gov/	GPO Access is a service of the U.S. Government Printing Office that provides free electronic access to a wealth of important information products produced by the federal government. This includes important business materials such as Commerce Business Daily (CBDNet).

The Market Research Center www.airsearch.com	At this site you will find a directory (http://www.asiresearch.com/bookem/intro.htm) that will link you to any product or service category you can think of, from snacks, to pets, to utilities. This is a smart place to visit for information about competitor sites.
The U.S. Census Report www.census.com	The U.S. government publishes all its demographic, social, and economic data at this site. Here you will find more statistics than you know what to do with.

4

Product and Pricing on the Net

"There are many choices for news, but the fact is, there really is only one Bugs Bunny. And when you have franchises like a Bugs Bunny or a Mickey Mouse, or the products that the networks have, there is only one place you can go to get that."

—Jim Moloshok, Warner Bros. Online

Chapter Outline

- The Datek Story
- Product
  - New Product Opportunities
  - New Product Strategies for Internet Marketing
  - Products that Use the Internet as a Distribution Channel
- Pricing
  - Factors Putting Downward Pressure on Internet Prices
  - Costs Putting Upward Pressure on Internet Prices
  - Online Pricing Strategies

Practitioner Perspective

Why Don't These Numbers Match?
—Bob Ivins, Senior Vice President, Media Metrix, Inc.

Leveraging Technology

Shopping Agents

Ethics and Law

Hyperlinks, Meta-Tags, and Framing

Learning Objectives

- Marketing review
  - Identify the characteristics of services that differentiate them from tangible products
  - Describe six new product strategies
  - Understand the importance of branding and positioning
- Explain what is meant by the "fourth channel"
- Discuss three areas of new product opportunity for moving messages on the Web and the hottest areas for new products unique to the Net
- Identify the best product opportunities for offline products using the Net as a distribution channel
- Give examples of online branding and positioning strategies
- Understand the factors putting downward pressure on Internet pricing
- Contrast online selling costs that have increased and decreased because of the Internet
- Explain three pricing strategies appropriate for products selling on the Net

The
Datek
Story

Imagine being Chairman, CEO, and president of the nation's third largest online trading company, owning a mansion on the Jersey shore, flying a private Gulfstream jet, and commanding a personal net worth of $100 million at the ripe old age of 27. Such is the life of Jeffrey Citron. Citron rose from a stock clerk at the age of 17 to his current dizzying height. He accomplished this by seizing technological opportunities to automate stock trading, thereby improving service, cutting costs, and lowering prices. Datek Online has earned a cult following, especially among very active (technical term: hyperactive) traders.

According to Morgan-Stanley, Internet business opportunities are greatest in "fragmented markets where selection, information, convenience, and price are especially critical shopper variables and where shoppers may prefer to do their own legwork if it's easy to do" (Meeker 1997). This description puts financial services at the top of the list as a Web retailing "sweet spot" and helps to explain why Datek and its competitors are enjoying such rapid growth. Online trading grew by 25.5% during the first quarter of 1998 and now averages 191,000 trades per day!

Datek enjoys 8% of this growing online trading market—a respectable showing in a fragmented market. At the time of this writing Datek had 80,000 customers with combined assets of $1.5 billion. Forrester projects that this market will grow in five years to more than 14 million investors with $688 billion worth of assets.

How good is Datek Online? Quite a few content providers in the financial sector develop ratings lists, with wildly varying methodology. Online investors at The Street.com (www.street.com) rated Datek number 1. Another financial content site, SmartMoney (www.smartmoney.com), rated Datek number 2. Barron's rated it the most cost-effective online broker. Gomez Wire (www.gomez.com) rated it in the top ten overall and in the top three for hyperactive traders. Datek is especially popular among hyperactive traders because of its price and the speed of its trade executions.

How does Datek Online price its services? Currently Datek charges $9.99 for an online trade, compared with $29.95 for Schwab. Some other online brokers match or slightly beat Datek's price but none offer Datek's speed of order execution. Orders that take more than 1 minute to execute are free. Real-time quotes are free, as are some other services. All of this leads to the obvious question: "People ask me how we can make money at $9.99. I like to turn the question around: How has everyone else gotten away with charging so much? Because we have a completely electronic model, we can make a profit at $9.99" (Alex Goor, Datek Executive Vice President as quoted in Yahoo! Internet Life). To put this in perspective, consider that Merrill Lynch has 46,000 brokers; Datek manages its operations with 100 staff members. Of course, Datek doesn't offer all the services provided by full-service brokers, but investment-savvy customers may not need or want to pay extra for things such as company and economic research analysis or Merrill Lynch branded mutual funds.

TECHNOLOGY AND POSITIONING ARE KEY

Technological innovation has been the key to Datek's success. Under Citron's leadership, first the internal operations and then the trading systems were computerized. At the time, these changes were revolutionary—attracting both extreme praise and bitter envy. Computerization allowed Datek to bring big investor services to the small investor at rock bottom prices. Datek was the largest user of NASDAQ's Small Order Execution System (SOES) when it was first developed, earning Datek traders the title of SOES Bandits. The company developed the Island Electronic Communications Network, an independent trading network which eliminates the middleman (technical term: market makers) in trading. Datek also makes money by leasing software it has developed to other companies.

Datek found its own "sweet spot" position by using "cool" Net lingo and creating a genX image: Traders are greeted with messages such as, "Hey, you bought 5 shares of Disney at...." The software programs Datek develops to conduct business have playful names such as The Island, Watcher, and Monster Key. Datek is also the exclusive sponsor of the Dilbert Financial Indices including the POINTY-HAIRED BOSS INDEX (TPHBX), the DOGBERT Index (DOGBX), and the DILBERT Index (DILBX). In addition, the company is one of the top five Internet advertisers. Recent initiatives include niche advertising, especially targeting female investors.

Product

A product is a bundle of benefits that satisfies the needs of organizations or consumers and for which they are willing to exchange money or other items of value. The word *product* includes items such as tangible goods, services, ideas, people, and places. All of these are marketed on the Internet. The bundle of benefits often includes color, taste, style, product guarantee, service warrantee, and package design and size. In addition, the brand name and its image are often part of the benefits a user desires. Along with Internet technology came a new set of desired benefits, including effective Web navigation, quick download speed, clear site organization, attractive and useful site design, secure transactions, user privacy, free information or services, and user-friendly Web browsing and e-mail reading. Thousands of new products were quickly created to fill these and many other user needs. As Internet technology evolves, the cycle continues.

Some new products such as search engines are unique to the Internet while other products such as books simply use the Internet as a new distribution channel. Both types of products will be discussed in this chapter. The chapter focuses upon new products, however, because Internet technologies created a wealth of opportunities (and continue to do so). In addition to categorizing new Net products by usage, the chapter suggests new-product strategies for Internet marketers.

New-Product Opportunities

New products include everything from an existing product that has been even slightly modified to a completely revolutionary item. On the Internet, New York Times

Direct is an example of the former, and Netscape Web browser of the latter. This section begins with a look at how new technologies create a context for new products. It continues with a discussion of new-product opportunities created by Internet technology, and then describes new-product and branding strategies to capitalize on these opportunities.

NEW TECHNOLOGIES SPAWN NEW PRODUCTS

Every new technology creates a proliferation of new products: For example, think of the automobile and the related products it created. Focusing on communications technology, consider the new companies and products that were introduced as a result of television and radio. Entire broadcast networks, infrastructure delivery systems, and many associated services were born. One forward-thinking firm even introduced a search directory for television: *TV Guide.*

The telephone was an important communications technology that profoundly affected commerce. Drawing out the parallels between the Internet and the telephone helps to develop an understanding of Internet-related products and services. Like the Internet, the telephone gave birth to a tremendous generation of business opportunity and wealth. At the time of its breakup in 1984, AT&T was the largest corporation on the planet. Similar to the Internet, telephone technologies created a new channel for transactions as well as generating a slew of new products. Each of these roles will now be discussed.

New Transactive Medium

Media are channels of communication, such as the television, radio, telephone, and Internet. Transactive media are interactive channels of communication that are capable of carrying product transactions. According to Mary Modahl of Forrester Research, there are only four ways to reach a customer that have interactive capabilities, thus allowing transactions to occur:

1. *In-person.* A salesperson communicates with a prospect in order to complete a transaction.
2. *Mail.* A firm sends offers through the mail with product sales as the objective.
3. *Telephone.* A telemarketer uses the telephone to sell product.
4. *Internet.* Firms create content that persuades and allows users to purchase online or offline.

Prior to the telephone, there were only two transactive media channels. After the telephone, it took about 100 years for the fourth channel to appear. Because of its role as transactive medium, the telephone, like the Internet, was a new product that greatly facilitated the introduction of other new products and increased sales of existing products.

	Telephone	**Internet**
Infrastructure Backbone	Circuit-switching equipment, PBX machines, fiber optic lines, call centers	Packet-switching equipment, satellite dish, Internet Service Providers (ISPs)
Tangible Products	Telephones, cordless phones, fax machines, cellular phones, answering machines, speakerphones, videophones	Video cameras, modems, cable modems, Internet ready keyboards, smart card readers, Web servers, ad servers, e-mail servers
Intangible Products and Services	Call waiting, caller ID, call blocking, speed dialing, three-way calling, wakeup calls, voice mail	Web authoring software, browsers, search engines, promotion agents, online communities, online games, online shopping, conferencing, shared whiteboards, music sampling, mapping, weather, classifieds, yellow pages, entertainment guides, ad management and tracking

Exhibit 4 - 1 A New Communications Channel Creates New Business Opportunities

New Technology, New Products

The telephone generated the introduction of a number of entirely new products, including the telephone instrument itself. Some new products formed the infrastructure backbone, which allowed voice communication to travel seamlessly from user to user. Other products were tangible goods: hardware used to code and decode voice transmissions. Still another group consisted of intangible products: software and services complementing the telephone's main purpose. Exhibit 4 - 1 compares products in each area that were developed for the telephone and the Internet. Note the variety of products on the Internet. This technology allows for a greater number of products than are possible with telephone technologies. In fact, the Internet can even carry live voice transmissions, thus replacing conversations by telephone.

The speed and sophistication of innovation in the Internet arena are breathtaking. There are at least four reasons for this. First, there is healthy competition in Internet industries. By contrast, through most of its history (until 1984) the telephone industry was a monopoly controlled by AT&T. Monopolies tend to stifle innovation. Second, most Internet products are software based. Software-based products can be built with a laptop computer in a cabin—they don't require an extensive manufacturing facility. By contrast, most telephone products are hardware based. In hardware-based systems, innovation is expensive as it requires manufacture and distribution of new products. Third, Internet products tend to be more sophisticated since the medium is richer. The Internet can transmit full multimedia content: text, graphics, audio, and video. By contrast, the telephone has one major purpose: to transmit voice. Even such a simple task as navigating through menu options is handled awkwardly by a touch tone phone. Fourth, the terminal device on the Internet is a programmable computer. A programmable device can be easily updated by downloading and installing the latest version of software. By contrast, consumers do not as a rule trade in their telephones just because a model with new features appears in the market.

Nonetheless, the infrastructure of U.S. phone companies is the best in the world. When is the last time you remember not receiving a dial tone? This reliability is due in large part to clear accountability. The local phone company is responsible for local calls and the long-distance provider is responsible for long-distance calls. Paying customers will let their dissatisfaction be known. The Internet, on the other hand, is a cooperative of providers all working together to carry each other's traffic. The cooperative is only as good as its weakest link. While infrastructure products and services have gotten much better recently, still they do not approach the reliability and service guarantees of the phone company.

NEW-PRODUCT OPPORTUNITIES ON THE INTERNET

In the same way that the telephone spawned the innovation of many products never seen before, so too have a number of products been invented for the Internet medium. These include products for creating, delivering, and reading messages. There are products to help content providers develop Web sites, infrastructure products to run the Internet itself, and end user products to connect to the Internet. In addition to software and hardware, new services such as search engines and Web development firms assist users and content providers in their tasks. In this section we discuss new products for creating, delivering, and reading Internet messages, and then describe general content and service areas that are ripe for commercialization on the Internet.

New Products for Creating, Delivering, and Reading Internet Messages

The communication process begins when a person decides to send a message to one or more other people. The sender encodes the message, he sends it through a medium, then the recipient receives and decodes the message. In the offline world, the sender might be a firm creating an ad (encoding) and placing it on television (medium) for a viewer to see (decode). On the Web, the sender is a content provider who composes multimedia messages that are digitally encoded, the medium is the Internet infrastructure, and the receivers are Web users. For example, senders encode messages in e-mail software and send them over the Internet to receivers, who decode the message using an e-mail client such as Eudora.

Product Type	Function		
	Content Provider: Encodes Message	**Internet Infrastructure: Delivers Message**	**End-User: Decodes Message**
Hardware (Tangible Product)	Modem, Web server, ad server	Packet-switching equipment, router, data line, satellite	Modem, PC
Software (Intangible Product)	Web authoring, encryption, database, audio/video digitizing	Protocols (TCP/IP): transmission control and Internet, Ethernet, search robots	Web browser, e-mail reader, decryption, audio/video playing
Services	Web development firm, Web designers and copywriters	Internet Service Providers (ISPs), equipment maintenance	

Exhibit 4 - 2 New-Product Opportunities for Encoding, Delivering, and Decoding the Message

New hardware, software, and support services have been, and are continuing to be, developed to assist content providers in encoding messages, the Internet infrastructure in delivering them, and the end user in decoding them. Exhibit 4 - 2 displays examples of new products in each area.

Content Provider Hardware and Software

Individuals and firms publishing content on the Web or composing e-mail need hardware and software to encode their messages. PCs and modems are the basics, but to host an in-house Web site a Web server is needed. This is a computer with Web server software that is dedicated to holding all the information for public viewing. In order to turn regular text and graphics into Web pages, content providers need software such as NetObjects Fusion or Microsoft FrontPage. If the content provider is selling product online, she will need a commerce server and encryption software for credit card security. These are industrial products because they are sold in the business-to-business market, as are the infrastructure products discussed in the next section.

One interesting new product was developed for Internet publishers who frequently change the content on their sites. StoryServer, produced by Vignette Corporation, solved a big problem associated with other Web authoring tools by providing templates that allow publishers to separate page design and other format coding from its content (Wingfield 1998). Editors can thus quickly write or edit a story and drop it into the Web page without having to reformat or reprogram the page. This product is especially good for news operations, where stressful deadlines prevail: StoryServer clients include ZDNet, Time Warner Inc., the Chicago Tribune, and CBS SportsLine. Interested in purchasing a copy? That will be $125,000, please.

Infrastructure Products

Infrastructure products permeate the nooks and crannies of the Internet. Most of it is transparent to the end user. Routers send data across the country over high-speed fiber optic lines, and phone lines carry the data the last leg of the journey to the home. Cable companies are making infrastructure improvements to their cable plants in order to offer Internet service to the home. Phone companies are beginning to upgrade their switching equipment and lines in order to offer high-speed Digital Subscriber Line (DSL) access to the home. Satellites provide high-speed Internet service to homes that can not be reached by cable or DSL.

The company that makes most of the Internet's switching equipment is Cisco Systems. Cisco Systems is the third largest company on the NASDAQ stock exchange and one of the top 40 companies in the world. It had revenues of $8.46 billion in 1998—pretty good for a company that shipped its first product in 1986. It is the worldwide leader in networking for the Internet and continues to offer higher and higher bandwidth at lower and lower prices. Cisco is just one of hundreds of companies that provide infrastructure products and services that form the backbone of the Internet. Internet service providers (ISPs) purchase Cisco's (and other vendors') equipment in order to offer Internet services to the home. Leading ISPs include America Online, MCI, and MindSpring.

End User Hardware and Software

In the consumer market, every personal computer needs some type of device in order to connect to the Internet. In the corporate or campus setting this tends to be a network card. From home most people use a modem. Companies such as US Robotics and Motorola produce the modems for home computers. Modems are typically bundled with personal computers at the time of purchase. The marketing of modems tends to emphasize their speed. The highest-speed modems operate at 56kbps.

The demand for even more speed has spawned the introduction of cable modems, DSL, and satellite dishes. Of the three, cable modems have the largest installed base. The cable companies see the introduction of high-speed Internet service as a great way to generate additional revenue while meeting customer needs. All three technologies were covered in more detail in the Leveraging Technology section in chapter 1.

Users need browser software in order to surf the Internet. Netscape produced the first commercial browser and holds a thin lead in this market, though Microsoft is catching up. Oddly enough both products are offered for free. There are two reasons for giving away the browser. First, the companies try to build brand recognition in order to market their encoding and infrastructure products such as Web authoring tools and Web server software. Second, when the browser launches, it goes to the respective company's home page, thus delivering audience, which can be sold to advertisers.

A number of third-party firms have produced add-on software for the major browsers called plug-ins. Plug-ins such as Macromedia's Shockwave and Flash add functionality such as animation to browsers. The plug-in is free since the real goal is to create demand for Macromedia's encoding software, for which they charge. Content providers are willing to buy the encoding software, since it helps them create higher-quality content. The content in turn attracts an audience which they can sell to advertisers. Other examples of free plug-ins include Real Networks G2 player, Adobe PDF reader, and Microsoft Media Player.

Users employ e-mail client software in order to send and receive e-mail messages. Some of the more popular e-mail clients are Netscape Messenger, Qualcomm Eudora, and Microsoft Outlook. Most e-mail clients, especially the "Lite" versions, are also offered for free for reasons similar to those listed above.

Internet Services to Facilitate Encoding, Delivering, and Decoding Messages

Marketers make a distinction between products and services principally because different marketing strategies are used for each one. The U.S. economy is primarily a service economy. As it turns out, much of what content providers offer over the Internet are services as well. Services have four characteristics which distinguish them from tangible products.

- *Inseparability*. They must be consumed where they are produced. Unlike a tangible product, such as a PC, a service cannot be shipped to another location.

- *Perishability*. If not consumed when it is produced, the service goes to waste. For example, if the airline takes off half full, revenue is lost.

- *Variability*. The quality is changeable from one use of the service to another. Unlike a box of cereal, the breakfast at a restaurant varies in quality from day to day. Variability occurs because people, not machines, deliver services.

- *Intangibility*. A service is a performance which cannot be seen, felt, or touched. The service provided by a dentist is a good example of this characteristic.

Many service firms sprang into existence just to assist content providers in building and maintaining their Web sites: ad agencies such as Adjacency and BrainBug, research firms to help measure Web traffic such as Media Metrix, and many others. Also in this category are site promotion services and firms that build databases. Infrastructure services exist to maintain satellites, switches, and other equipment that keeps messages moving over the Net. An entire industry of Internet service providers was born to provide message transmission services over the infrastructure. Each one of these services represents a new business opportunity unique to the Internet.

Content provider and infrastructure services just described fulfill the four service criteria. End user services are not as easy to classify. This point can be understood in light of a service example: the Yahoo! site. Yahoo! is definitely *intangible*, and if user visits fall below expectations the unused capacity goes to waste, especially if advertising dollars are lost (*perishable*). The user must be connected to the Yahoo! site in order to access its services. Therefore the service is *inseparable*; it must be consumed where it is produced. Yahoo! has designed its site to handle millions of visits each day. Here the Internet differs markedly from most services in the brick and mortar world. A query typed into Yahoo! will produce the same results every time. There is no variability since the service is actually provided by a computer program rather than an employee as in most service businesses. Unlike your hairdresser, who may be having a bad day, Yahoo! does not have bad days! Yahoo! and many other Internet services overcome variability through automation.

Most services are offered to the consumer free of charge. These services typically are ad supported or are provided by the sponsoring content provider as a way to draw traffic to the site. By contrast, services offered to businesses usually come with a fee. Ad management or Web site auditing, for example, can incur healthy fees.

Four Huge Opportunity Areas

There are tremendous new product opportunities in areas other than the purely technical message encoding, transmitting, decoding, and related services. These opportunities consider user needs for information, shopping, entertainment, and communication.   Walid Mougayar (1997) suggests four major areas for Net commercialization:

- *Communications and collaboration.* This includes gathering and processing information, communicating, collaborating, and publishing. All media that place their content online for subscription or as advertising sponsored fall into this category. Also, new ways of communicating online and useful information organization schemes for the Web are sure to meet with success.

- *Networked applications.* Included here are distributed Internet applications, linked corporate and legacy data, Web-enabled and live applications, and object-oriented applications. These are database applications and methods for sharing information within an organization.

- *Real-time multimedia.* Opportunities here are distance learning and education, virtual reality, entertainment, and video/audio conferencing. This includes live broadcasting from radio stations or online chatting and other real-time broadcasts. Web/TV convergence will reward content providers who are ready when the time comes.

- *Electronic commerce.* This includes buying/selling online, digital value creating, virtual marketplaces and storefronts, and new distribution channel intermediaries. Many people believe this to be the Internet's "killer application" in the future.

New-Product Strategies for Internet Marketing

Many new products, such as Netscape, Yahoo!, and Amazon were introduced by "one pony" firms. This means that the firm was built around the first successful product. Other firms, such as Microsoft, added Internet products to an already successful product mix. This section explores product mix strategies as well as branding and positioning strategies.

PRODUCT MIX STRATEGIES

How can marketers integrate these hot product ideas into current product mixes? There are actually six categories of new-product strategies from which to choose (Lamb, Hair, and McDaniel 1994). The first one, discontinuous innovation, is the highest-risk strategy, and the last is the least risky. Firms will select one or more of these strategies based on marketing objectives and other factors such as risk averseness, strength of current brand names, resource availability, and competitive entries. Of course, many of the Internet's successes were born from the good ideas and experimentation of entrepreneurs operating on a shoestring who got lucky by having the right idea at the right time.

- **Discontinuous innovations** are new-to-the-world products never seen before, such as were music CDs and the television at their introductions. On the Internet, the first Web authoring software, modem, shopping agent, and search engine fall into this category, as do most of the first entry products discussed in the previous sections. There are many discontinuous innovations yet to come on the Internet. As was previously mentioned, this strategy is quite risky, but the rewards for success are great indeed.

- **New product lines** are introduced when firms take an existing brand name and create new products in a completely different category. For example, General Foods applied the Jell-O brand name to pudding pops and other frozen delights. Microsoft created a new line when it introduced Internet Explorer, the Web browser; since Netscape had already been in the picture since April 1994, Microsoft's entry was not a discontinuous innovation.

- **Additions to existing product lines** occur when organizations add a new flavor, size, or other variation to a current product line. The New York Times Direct is a slightly different version of the hard copy edition, adapted for online delivery. It is yet another product in the New York Times line, which includes the daily paper, weekly book review, and others. GTE's SuperPages is an interactive line extension to its yellow page directories (superpages.gte.net). Many banks have begun offering banking over the Internet. Stockbrokers such as Schwab have also opened up Internet operations. Realtors now offer online listings for many communities throughout the United States.

- **Improvements or revisions of existing products** are introduced as "new and improved" and thus replace the old product. CyberAction improved on baseball cards by creating digital multimedia downloadable cards at its site (www.cyberaction.com). When users click on the card, they get animation, sound, and player statistics. On the Internet, firms are continually improving their brands to add value and remain competitive.

- **Repositioned products** are current products that are either targeted to different markets or promoted for new uses. Yahoo! began as a search directory on the Web and recently repositioned itself as a portal: an Internet entry point with many services. By so doing, Yahoo! positioned itself against the leader, America Online.

- **Lower-cost products** are introduced to compete with existing brands by offering a price advantage. When America Online and other ISPs were charging per hour rates for Internet access, several other providers introduced unlimited use at flat rate pricing for $19.95 per month. Firms such as EarthNet were able to grab significant share until America Online followed suit and won back customers. The Internet also spawned a series of free products with the idea of building market share so the firm would have a customer base for marketing other products owned by the firm. For example, Eudora Light, the e-mail reader software, and Netscape were two first entries with this strategy.

BRANDING STRATEGIES

A brand includes a name (McDonald's), a symbol (golden arches), or other identifying information. When a firm registers that information with the U.S. Patent office, it becomes a trademark and thus is legally protected from imitation. According to the U.S. government, "a trademark is either a word, phrase, symbol or design, or combination of words, phrases, symbols or designs, which identifies and distinguishes the source of the goods or services of one party from those of others" (source: www.uspto.gov). All of the new-product strategies listed in the previous section have branding implications. Companies creating new products face several branding decisions: what domain name to use for the site, whether to apply existing brand names or to create new brand names for new products, and whether or not to lend their brand name as a co-brand with other firms.

Internet Domain Names

Organizations spend a lot of time and money developing powerful, unique brand names (brand equity). Using the company trademark or one of its brand names in the Web address helps consumers quickly find the site. For example, www.coca-cola.com adds power to Coca-Cola brands. InternNIC, a division of Network Solutions, Inc., provides domain registering services for a mere $100 for two years per name (www.internic.net). One of the problems is that with more than 130,000 registered domain names, the name a firm desires may not be available. For example, DeltaComm, a software developer and ISP in North Carolina, was the first to register www.delta.com, preempting Delta Airlines (www.delta-air.com) and Delta Faucet (www.deltafaucet.com). What to do if the firm name is taken? One solution is to buy the name from the currently registered holder. Many creative Netizens registered lots of popular names and offer them for sale at prices of up to $50,000. A "whois" search at InterNIC's site reveals domain name owners. A second solution is to come up with a new or modified site name, as did Delta Airlines.

Incidentally, when registering a name, firms would be welladvised to also purchase related names to keep them out of the hands of others. For example, Compaq Computer Company paid $3 million for the AltaVista search engine site (www.altavista.com) only to find that www.alta-vista.com was already in operation as an adult site with sexual material. Similarly, the huge Amazon bookseller does not own www.amazon-book.com. Also, many individuals publish sites that are criticisms on a corporate site, calling them www.companyname.sucks.com. As a result, some companies have begun buying their own www.companyname.sucks.com to preempt their detractors.

Picking the right domain name can make a huge difference when trying to entice users to the site and building consistency in the firm's marketing communications. For example, Time Warner's Pathfinder is a Web site containing online versions of many successful magazines: *People*, *Time*, *Fortune*, *Money*, and *Entertainment Weekly*. Dan Okrent, editor of New Media for Pathfinder, claims that the biggest error the firm made with the online division was selecting the name "Pathfinder" for the site. Pathfinder does not have the name recognition of its well-established magazine brands and thus the firm failed to capitalize on the value of its brands. Furthermore, according to Okrent, "Pathfinder" has little meaning to users.

Using Existing Brand Names in Cyberspace

Firms can use existing brand names or create new brands for their new products. An existing brand name can be used for any new product, and doing this makes sense when the brand is well-known and has strong brand equity (value). For example, Amazon recently added music CDs to its product mix. It is beneficial for Amazon to use its well-established Web brand name for the CD offerings rather than begin a new electronic storefront with another name. Similarly, products with offline sales that introduce online extensions will most likely use the same brand name (e.g., New York Times).

Alternatively, some firms may not want to use the same brand name online for several reasons. First, if the new product or channel is risky, the firm does not want to jeopardize the brand's good name by associating with a product failure. Entering the online publishing business tentatively, *Sports Illustrated* did not want use its brand online and instead created an extension, naming it Thrive (www.thriveonline.com). The *Sports Illustrated* affiliation is not mentioned online. Second, a powerful Internet success might inadvertently reposition the offline brand. Most Internet products carry a high-tech, "cool," and young image, and this will carry over to offline branded products. For example, NBC on television serves an older market than does MSNBC online. Because the network hopes to bring younger viewers from MSNBC on the Internet to its television network, it made a decision to stick with the brand name—thus intending to reposition the offline brand image. Firms must be careful to be sure that online brand images will have a desired effect on the offline versions and that overextended product lines do not create fuzzy brand images. Third, sometimes the firm wants to change the name slightly for the new market or channel to differentiate it from the offline brand. For example, *Wired* magazine changed the name of its online version to HotWired to convey a high-tech image, and perhaps to position the two publications differently.

Creating New Brands for Internet Marketing

If an organization wants to create a new Internet brand, a good name is very important. Good brand names should suggest something about the product (e.g., www.WebPromote.com), should differentiate the product from competitors (e.g., www.WomensWire.com), and should be capable of legal protection. On the Internet, a brand name should be short, memorable, and easy to spell and should translate well into other languages. For example, Dell computer at www.dell.com is much easier than Hammacker Schlemmer (www.hammacker.com), the gift retailer. As an example, consider the appropriateness of these search tool names: Yahoo!, Excite, Lycos, AltaVista, InfoSeek, HotBot, WebCrawler, GoTo.com, and LookSmart. Which ones fit the above criteria?

Co-branding

Co-branding occurs when two different companies put their brand name on the same product. This practice is quite common on the Internet and is a good way for firms to build synergy through expertise and brand recognition. Yahoo! and *TV Guide* combined to provide television listings on the Yahoo! site. HeadHunter (www.headhunter.net) co-branded with GeoCities to provide free career services in GeoCities neighborhoods (www.geocities.com). With a longer-term commitment, EarthLink, the largest independent ISP, joined forces in early 1998 with Sprint, the telephone company. The two are creating a co-branded business with a new EarthLink–Sprint name and logo. They will use the co-brand to provide ISP services to the 130,000 Sprint ISP customers and to pursue AOL customers (source: www.spiderline.com).

ONLINE POSITIONING STRATEGIES

Position refers to a brand, company, or product image relative to the competition, all from the consumer's perspective. When a brand holds a unique position it is said to have a market niche. For example, Rollerblade has a cool Web site that is the place to go for information about in-line skating activities and news. The goal of most firms is to build a strong, defensible position on one or more bases that are important to consumers—and to do it better than competitors. The following are a few of the many possible bases of Web site positioning:

- *Attribute*. Home Arts allows users to build unique menus at its site using criteria such as ingredients and calorie counts (www.homearts.com).

- *Product user*. GeoCities hosts free Web pages for users that are placed into neighborhoods based on their specific interests. GeoCities is the place users can go to explore a particular interest.

- *Competitor.* Some firms are market leaders, some are followers, some are challengers, and some are market nichers. In the fight for hub status, America Online is the industry leader, Yahoo! is a challenger, and there are several followers. For example Aqueous (www.aqueous.com) is a search engine and directory dedicated entirely to sites with water-related content.

- *Scope.* On the Web, a firm can have a comprehensive site with a broad selection of information and offerings. For example, Digital City offers information, chat, and bulletin boards about 27 cities. Alternatively a site can be large and deep, with complete information and offerings in one category. Such is the case for Music Boulevard, Dell Computer, and Travelocity. Finally, a firm can sponsor a small site to introduce users to the product and direct them elsewhere: this is called a microsite. Examples include the separate Web sites that Levis has produced for its Dockers and Slates product lines. A comprehensive site obviously involves much more resource commitment than does a microsite.

- *Price leadership.* This strategy is discussed further in the pricing section later in this chapter.

Product Differentiation

Product categories exhibit varying amounts of differentiation among brand entries. On one extreme are commodity products: items such as fruits and vegetables, for which it is difficult to identify product differences, thus making positioning quite difficult. To most Web users, PC modems with a 56kbps capability are included in this category: They are all the same. Products that are unable to differentiate themselves based on benefits or perceptions of differences generally compete on price. On the other extreme are products with many features, either real or perceived, to make them different. For example, Web search tools offer various benefits: Some are directories and some are engines, and each offers unique benefits such as games or a dictionary. Other products falling into this category include clothing and gourmet foods. For these products, the firm has to do a good job differentiating the product in order to command a higher price. Some sites have gotten quite creative in this arena. The Gap, for example, allows customers to mix and match clothing online in order to build a wardrobe. Land Rover allows customers to build their Land Rover online and see the final product with all the accessories. The expectation is that customizable products such as clothing and automobiles will form an increasingly large component of online sales as sites become more sophisticated and bandwidth increases.

Products That Use the Internet as a Distribution Channel

Much of the excitement surrounding the Internet focuses on products that use the Internet as a new distribution channel. Chapter 5 discusses consumer shopping behavior as well as the distribution and retailing aspects of online selling. In this chapter we describe the types of products that Web users are buying online.

According to Clemente (1998) of Cyber Dialogue, in 1997 online sales represented $3.3 billion. Another $4.2 billion was spent offline after a product was researched online. Other estimates put the online sales figure as high as $17 billion. However big the figure, it pales in comparison with the $2.6 trillion spent each year offline in retail stores. Nonetheless, the sales figures represent a 153% increase over 1996. And it is the forecast of continued growth that excites marketers.

Products that represented the top online spending in 1997 are PCs and peripherals (20%), travel (16%), software (13%), books (8%), flowers and gifts (3%), and music (2%). Exhibit 4 - 3 displays these figures as well as projections for the year 2002. The "other" category includes clothing, cars, consumer electronics, and food; this category will grow as more firms offer their products online.

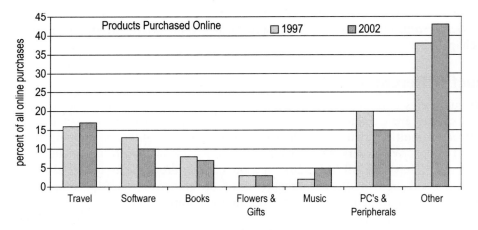

Exhibit 4 - 3 Products Purchased Online and 2002 Projection
Source: Adapted from Clemente, Peter, Thomas Miller, Andrew Richardson, and Craig Gugel (1998), "Consumer Online Commerce," Private Report. New York: Cyber Dialogue and Organic.

Clemente claims that products with successful online sales share attributes that make them particularly attractive for online sales.

1. *Nonperishable.* The items can be shipped by a common carrier without spoiling in transit. Books do not go bad, though it may be argued that Internet books like this one have a relatively short shelf life!

2. *High relative value.* The top items tend to be a bit pricey. A PC, for example, is a serious purchase. It is not likely that a consumer will buy low-involvement products such as light bulbs or razors online.

3. *Information intensive.* The items require research which can also be conducted online. For example, many consumers research extensively when planning for travel.

4.   *High-tech*. The Internet's current users have an interest in high-tech products.

Morgan Stanley Dean Witter research suggests that the following are Web "retailing sweet spots:" insurance and financial services, computer software and hardware, travel, books, magazines, music and video, flowers and gifts, automobiles, office products, and specialized sporting goods (Meeker 1997). Conversely, home furnishings, toys, tools and home repair, and apparel have low business opportunities in their thinking. Why? Because products that do well in online channels are those that consumers do not mind doing their own work to research and buy, and for which shoppers seek information, selection, convenience, and low price.

Pricing

Online pricing strategies parallel offline strategies. That is, firms set overall strategies based their marketing objectives and then fine-tune for individual products and markets. Many factors influence prices: marketing objectives, costs, product demand, competitive environment, and government influences. Businesses are still experimenting with pricing strategies on the Internet, but one thing is true about Internet pricing: There is tremendous downward pressure. This section describes factors putting downward pressure on pricing, suggests several areas of cost increases on the Internet channel, and concludes with three low price strategies appropriate for the current pricing environment.

Factors Putting Downward Pressure on Internet Prices

There are many forces driving prices down in the Internet channel. First, consumers can easily search nationwide or even worldwide for the lowest price on a given item. Shopping agents such as PriceScan (www.pricescan.com) facilitate these searches by displaying the results in a comparative format. See Exhibit 4 - 4. Since the results are listed in order with the lowest price first, outlets that are not price competitive risk being left off of the first screen and might as well be invisible. In an effort to stop the focus on low prices, at least one shopping agent, CNET Shopper, recently changed its default to list vendors in order by sponsor rather than by price. Second, all new Internet products are immediately visible to would-be competition. Because things move quickly on the Internet, the high pricing that often goes along with a first-entry advantage does not last very long. Third, since most online retailing takes place across state lines, there are often no taxes to pay on purchases. Eliminating the 5% to 8% sales tax reduces the consumer's out of pocket expenditure. Although states and foreign governments have challenged the Internet tax-free zone, the U.S. Government continues to support a moratorium on taxes for Internet purchases. Fourth, many Internet companies are financed through venture capital or stock issues. Many investors take a long-term view with Internet companies and are willing to sustain losses in the short term in order to let those companies grow. They understand that the most important goal is to establish brand equity and grab market share. Companies operating under this halo are willing to sustain losses for up to five years in order to promote their brand. Therefore, they can sell below fair market value since they do not have to show a profit on sales.

Finally, costs are often lower in this channel, and that can result in either higher profits or lower prices. Because of the reasons just identified, the current effect is to put downward pressure on Internet pricing. Following are some of the online cost savings:

- Since customers fill out their own order forms, firms save the expense of order entry personnel and paper processing. These expenses can be considerable. For example, American Airlines has thousands of order entry personnel on duty nationwide at any given time. The cost of producing and processing an invoice electronically is $10 on average, compared with $100 in offline transactions, and an average retail banking transaction costs $0.15 to $0.20 online versus $1.50 offline (Mougayar 1997). Cisco Systems, the world's largest manufacturer of networking equipment, allows Web-based orders from its customers. The paperwork reduction it reaps from this saves $270 million each year.

- Some firms do not even hold inventory, saving considerably on financing costs. Rather they acquire the inventory in response to the customer's order or have it drop-shipped from a business partner.

- Online storefronts are able to lower their overhead costs since they do not have to rent and staff expensive retail space. Amazon's warehouses are considerably less expensive to rent and staff than the retail space of a trendy shopping mall. Furthermore, these warehouses can be located in areas with low rents, low wages, low taxes, and quick access to shipping hubs.

- Successful firms are able to realize economies of scale in Cyberspace, just as in the brick and mortar world. For example, because of its enormous size, Amazon can negotiate discounts with its suppliers and with its shipping partners.

- Firms do not incur mail distribution and printing costs for their product catalogs. Once the catalog is placed online, there is little or no incremental cost for access.

- Customer service requests average $15 to $20 in an offline call center versus $3 to $5 when customers help themselves on the Internet (Mougayar 1997).

- Promotional printing and mailing expenses are saved when a firm promotes online via e-mail or the Web site.

Costs Putting Upward Pressure on Internet Prices

There are at least six factors that increase the costs of products sold online. Unless marketers can raise prices, these narrow the gap between costs and prices and lower profits. First, online retailers face hefty distribution costs for their products since each product must be shipped separately to its destination. This is similar to the catalog marketer's cost structure. Most retailers pass on this shipping cost to their customers and reveal it only at the conclusion of the order entry process. Hiding exorbitant shipping and handling costs until the last minute offends many customers. In some cases the shipping cost cancels out the cost savings. Second, many Web sites pay a commission on referrals through a process called syndicated selling. Syndicated selling rewards the referring Web site by paying a 7% to 15% commission on the sale. This commission, like all channel intermediary costs, has the effect of inflating the price of the item or lowering company profits. (For more on syndicated selling please see the distribution chapter.) Third, auctions have become a popular form of purchase online. Auctions pit consumers against one another to drive up the price of the auctioned item—in some cases above fair market value. Fourth, Web site development and maintenance is not cheap. Forrester research estimates the cost for a "conservative" site to be $10,000 to $100,000, while an "aggressive" site costs $1 million or more—and that is just to develop the site. Maintenance can be quite expensive, especially with hardware, software, and monthly Internet connection costs. Fifth, Internet users demand free product and samples at Web sites, thus driving costs up. Sixth, online marketing and advertising costs tend to be higher than their offline equivalents. A survey by the Boston Consulting Group found that 43% of online revenue goes to marketing and advertising whereas only 14.2% of revenue covers the same costs for offline department stores (Machlis 1998).

Downward price pressure paints a gloomy picture for marketers, unless costs are low enough to allow a decent profit. In balance, many factors such as lower distribution and communication costs ease the situation substantially, but the fact remains that few firms are profitable online. In the end, a marketer must create digital value for users and do it better than the competition in order to draw advertisers and sell product at profitable prices.

Online Pricing Strategies

In this climate of downward price pressure, three online strategies seem appropriate: penetration pricing, price leadership, and pricing promotions. Each is discussed below.

PENETRATION PRICING

Penetration pricing is the practice of charging a low price for a product for the purpose of gaining market share. This strategy is particularly effective in a price-sensitive market like the Internet. America Online adopted this strategy when it adopted the $19.95 monthly flat rate Internet access a couple years ago. An AOL spokesperson explained that the firm was trying to buy "real estate." AOL wanted every desktop it could get, even at a financial loss, so that it could deliver users to marketers. Even when it received lots of negative publicity for not having the capacity to accommodate the high numbers of users it attracted, executives smiled and thought of the big customer base it was building. The strategy worked: Today

AOL is the largest Internet hub, with 13 million users. Lots of money is pouring in as AOL makes deals with others who want access to those desktops.

Exhibit 4 - 4 PriceScan Search Results for Windows 98
Source: www.pricescan.com

PRICE LEADERSHIP

A price leader is the lowest-priced product entry in a particular category. In the offline world, Wal-Mart is a price leader, setting the pace for other retailers. With shopping agents on the Web, a price leader strategy is sweet indeed. In order to implement this strategy, however, marketers must shave costs to a minimum. This can be done through Internet marketing cost efficiencies described earlier, but a firm must do it better than the competition. Often the largest producer is able to be the price leader because of economies of scale, but on the Internet an entrepreneur operating out of a basement constantly challenges the large producer. This is a productive strategy on the Internet, but competition is fierce and price leadership is often fleeting. Of course, the second-lowest-priced item will also gain sales, especially if it offers advantages over the price leader's product entry. BuyComp, shown in Exhibit 4 - 4 follows a price leadership strategy.

PROMOTIONAL PRICING

Many online retailers have turned to promotional pricing to encourage a first purchase, to encourage repeat business, and to close a sale. Music Boulevard has been particularly adept at using promotional pricing. Exhibit 4 - 5 shows an e-mail promotion that Music Boulevard offers to Ticketmaster's customers in order to encourage *new* business. The consumer can redeem the $5 discount offer by following a link from the e-mail message to Music Boulevard's site. Fortunately for the author, Ticketmaster did not know that the author was already a Music Boulevard customer! Exhibit 4 - 6 shows an e-mail promotion which Music Boulevard sent to the author in order to encourage *repeat* business. Again, the customer follows the link in the message and the price discount is automatically credited. In both cases the promotion has an expiration date which helps to close the sale.

Subject: ** Save $5 on your favorite CDs courtesy of Ticketmaster
Resent-From: frost@CCSU.EDU
Date: Thu, 03 Sep 1998 12:06:38 -0400
From: Ticketmaster <Ticketmaster@music.ticketmaster.com>
To: "frost@ccsu.edu" <frost@ccsu.edu>

Dear Raymond Frost,

Ticketmaster is excited to announce a new free service that from time to time,
will notify you via email of special offers and promotions.

As a valued Ticketmaster consumer, we would like to offer you the chance to
save $5 on your next purchase at Music Boulevard – the world's #1 online music
store. Music Boulevard offers great prices on hundreds of thousands of titles,
plus reviews, sound samples and more.

Exhibit 4 - 5 Music Boulevard New-Customer Promotion

Subject:: $5 COUPON on Music Boulevard!
Resent-From: frost@CCSUA.CTSTATEU.EDU
Date: Thu, 13 Aug 1998 14:11:57 -0500
From: –Music Boulevard <manager@musicblvd.com>

Dear Music Fan,

We haven't heard from you in a while and thought you'd like to know
about some great new releases and special deals going on at Music
Boulevard - your online music store.

Plus, get a $5.00 COUPON HERE. See the bottom of this email for
details on redeeming your coupon!

Exhibit 4 - 6 Music Boulevard Repeat-Customer Promotion

Promotional pricing has at least three advantages. First, it can be highly targeted through e-mail messages as seen in Exhibit 4 - 5 and Exhibit 4 - 6. Second, research shows high customer satisfaction with Internet purchases. Doing everything possible to attract a customer is good business. Third, research shows that customers are more loyal online than offline. Customers would much prefer to remain loyal to an Internet store that has given them good service than to risk their credit information and bad service somewhere else.

S u m m a r y

A product is a bundle of benefits that satisfies the needs of organizations or consumers and for which they are willing to exchange money or other items of value. The word *product* includes items such as tangible goods, services, ideas, people, and places. The bundle of benefits often includes color, taste, style, product guarantee, service warrantee, and package design and size. In addition, the brand name and its image are often part of the benefits a user desires.

Some new products such as search engines are unique to the Internet while other products such as books simply use the Internet as a new distribution channel. The Internet is a new transactive medium, the fourth channel, after in-person, mail, and the telephone. Some new product opportunities are directly related to the technology itself. These include products for creating, delivering and reading messages. These roughly correspond to products used by content providers (creating), infrastructure companies (delivery), and endusers (reading).

Services have four characteristics that distinguish them from tangible products: inseparability, perishability, variability, and intangibility. Unlike most other services,

Internet services tend to be very low in variability since computer programs generally provide them.

Four new-product opportunity areas are communications and collaboration, networked applications, real-time multimedia, and electronic commerce. The Internet community is especially keen on the future of electronic commerce.

Six categories of new-product strategies are discontinuous innovations, new-product lines, additions to existing product lines, improvements or revisions of existing products, repositioned products, and lower-cost products. Examples of all six categories can be found online.

Branding online has become increasingly important. Some companies, such as Delta Airlines, were late to register their domain names and therefore were preempted by much smaller companies sharing the same name. Other firms intentionally choose different names for their online operations. As a rule names should describe the product, differentiate it from competitors, be easy to spell, and translate well into other languages. Co-branding often results from online business partnerships, such as Yahoo! and *TV Guide*.

The bases for online positioning include attribute, product user, competitor, scope, and price leadership. The goal of most firms is to build a strong, defensible position on one or more bases that are important to the consumers—and to do it better than competitors.

Products that are unable to differentiate themselves on the basis of benefits or perceptions of differences generally compete on price. Since it is very difficult to compete on price in the online world, most businesses would be better served through differentiation.

Products that sell well using the Internet as a distribution channel share four characteristics. They are nonperishable, have high relative value, are information intensive, and tend to be high tech.

There are many factors that drive prices down in the Internet channel. These include easy access to comparative pricing information, the Internet tax-free zone, and deficit financing. There are also factors that drive prices up in the channel. These include high distribution costs, syndicated selling, and auctions.

There are also factors that drive prices up in the Internet channel. These include high distribution costs, commissions paid on referrals, auctions, development and maintenance costs for Web sites, user demands for free products and samples, and high marketing and advertising costs.

Online pricing strategies include penetration pricing, price leadership, and promotional pricing. Promotional pricing is an especially effective strategy when directed at first-time buyers, who may then become loyal customers.

Key Concepts and Terms

1. The Internet is the fourth channel of communication after in-person, mail, and the telephone.
2. Many Internet products are a direct result of the technology itself—these include products to create (encode), deliver (transmit), and read (decode) messages.
3. Software companies often offer the decoding product for free to endusers in order to stimulate demand for the encoding product.
4. Products that are nonperishable, have a high relative value, are information intensive, and are high tech sell well on the Internet.
5. Services are inseparable, perishable, intangible, and variable, though Internet services tend to be homogeneous in quality since computers provide them.
6. Four new product opportunity areas are communications and collaboration, networked applications, real-time multimedia, and electronic commerce.
7. Six product mix strategies are discontinuous innovations, new product lines, additions to existing product lines, improvements or revisions of existing products, repositioned products, and lower-cost products.
8. Some major corporations were late to register their names online only to find their name taken by a company in a different product area—such as Delta Airlines.
9. Consumers report very high satisfaction with their online purchase experiences.
10. Promotional pricing is effective in the Internet channel, especially for first-time buyers.
11. Near perfect access to pricing information tends to drive prices down in the Internet channel.

- Additions to product lines
- Authoring tools
- Communications and collaboration
- Decoding
- Discontinuous innovations
- Electronic commerce
- Encoding
- Infrastructure
- Inseparability
- Intangibility
- Lower-cost products
- Networked applications
- New product lines
- Perishability
- Real-time multimedia
- Repositioned products
- Revisions to products
- Syndicated selling
- Transactive medium
- Variability

Exercises

REVIEW QUESTIONS FOR KNOWLEDGE TESTING

1. How were travel reservations made prior to the telephone?
2. List four reasons that innovation is so rapid on the Internet.
3. What are the top products purchased online?
4. What are four characteristics of services? Which one doesn't fit well in the Internet channel? Give an example.
5. List four areas of product opportunity online? Provide examples.
6. List six categories of new-product strategies. Provide Internet examples of each.
7. What characteristics do the top products purchased online tend to have in common?
8. List factors that keep prices low in the Internet channel.
9. List factors that increase prices in the Internet channel.

DISCUSSION QUESTIONS FOR CRITICAL THINKING

1. At what point will it become as important to have reliable Internet service as it is to have reliable phone service? What are the implications for business?
2. What do you think that the Yahoo! site could do to improve its product mix? What services are offered by other search engines that might be attractive?
3. Very few sites have been successful in charging consumers for online services or content. Exceptions include the *Wall Street Journal* and *Washington Post* online. Why do you suppose that these businesses can charge?
4. Is Ticketmaster/Music Boulevard a good match for promotional pricing? Why or why not? Can you think of three other pairs of companies that would be a good match?
5. Do you think that insurance should sell well online? Why or why not?
6. Near perfect access to pricing information is a problem that airlines have faced for years. How have airlines responded to this problem? Should Internet businesses adopt similar strategies?
7. Bucking the online trend, Gateway computer has recently begun setting up shops in communities. Consumers custom-order their Gateway computer at the store rather than online. Why might this strategy be successful?
8. Which of the online cost-saving factors do you think has the greatest effect on price? Why?

ACTIVITIES

1. Using a shopping agent such as PriceScan, what is the very lowest price that you can find for a bare-bones notebook computer sold online? How is it configured? What is the highest price for the same computer?

2. Survey 10 people that you know who have purchased online. Ask them why they purchased online, how brand loyal they are to the stores at which they purchased, and what it would take for them to try a different online store selling the same product mix.

3. Update chapter statistics about online spending. How much are consumers currently spending online? What products are enjoying the best sales?

INTERNET EXERCISE: ELASTICITY OF DEMAND

Most consumers view airline reservations as a commodity. Many will trade off nonstop flights, preferred travel times, and choice of airline to get the lowest possible price. Therefore, airlines offer advance purchase discounts to make sure they fill as many seats as possible. Demand tends to be very elastic, as evidenced by the heavy reservation activity that takes place during fare wars. One notable exception is the first-class traveler. First-class travelers will fly when they desire irrespective of price. In this exercise we are going to plan a vacation flight online. Sign onto the Expedia Web site at www.expedia.com or www.expedia.msn.com. Follow links to Expedia Travel Agent and register a new account; it's free. Price a round-trip flight from New York to Paris traveling coach class, departing tomorrow, and returning the following day. Record Expedia's response in the table below. Then press the Search Again button and vary the criteria to complete the rest of the table:

Class	Departing	Returning After	Airline & Departure Flight	Price
Coach	Tomorrow	1 day		
Coach	Tomorrow	1 week		
Coach	Next Month	1 day		
Coach	Next Month	1 week		
First	Tomorrow	1 day		
First	Tomorrow	1 week		
First	Next Month	1 day		
First	Next Month	1 week		

For Discussion

1. What can you conclude from this example about the elasticity of demand for coach fares? For first-class fares?

2. Do you think that it costs the airline the difference in price that they charge for the first-class seat?

3. How do the prices differ for one-day versus one-week trips? How can you explain this?

4. For first class, do the prices differ for trips departing tomorrow versus next month? Why or why not?

Practitioner Perspective

WHY DON'T THESE NUMBERS MATCH?

Bob Ivins, Senior Vice President of Media Metrix, Inc., is responsible for advanced analytics and application development, including e-commerce measurement initiatives, vertical sector services, and strategic business development.

At the Internet Advertising Bureau (IAB) meetings, I participated in a number of conversations that were essentially the same question: Why don't my audience measurement numbers match my log files? The simplest response to this line of questioning is that comparing audience measurement metrics (i.e., reach) to log files (i.e., hits, visits, and page views) is like comparing apples to oranges. However, most participants in these conversations wanted (and deserved) more. So here it is.

Both measurement methods focus on delivering accurate measures of activity; however, they do so from different perspectives. Log analysis approaches the problem from inside the Web site, or on the server side or site-centric, while audience measurement approaches the problem from outside the server, or on the client side or consumer centric. In doing so, these different methods deliver different data.

Site-Centric Measurement

Log data provide a record of all activity occurring at a server (a site or group of sites served by the same server). These data are entered into a log file as a record. Each record, or hit, stores the following information:

- Requesting IP address: the numeric code given to a specific computer as it is logged on to the Web

- Time stamp: the day and time the file was requested at the server (the server's time not the user's time

- File name: the file requested (could be an HTML page, a GIF [graphic file], a soundwave file, etc.)

To report total hits is simple, as it is a straightforward sum of all file requests. However, the challenge faced by site-centric measurement is to parse out hits and report in a more meaningful way—that is, calculate visitors, visits, and page requests. The catch is that each page is made up of multiple files, and many visitors visit a site simultaneously. The server, however, does not differentiate visitors or pages and simply serves and records file requests chronologically. In its doing so, different requesting IP addresses and files within pages are all intermingled. Therefore to calculate an individual visit, site-centric measurement must recognize, for example, that file requests (hits) 1, 15, 28, 49, and 104 are all files from one page and are all being requested by the same user.

Advantages and Disadvantages

The advantage of this measurement method is that it records all the activity at the server, allowing for in depth analysis. For example, if I was a marketer with a site and wanted to execute transactions, I could monitor "look to book" ratios by date/time, requesting IP address, by referral pages/URLs, and so on. This in-depth analysis would enable me to identify weaknesses in the site and make changes to improve its performance.

There are many advantages to site-centric measurement, but there are weaknesses too. Specifically, while the server is recording all activity occurring at the server, there is a significant amount of off-server activity that is never recorded. For example, server side measurement misses cache. Cache is simply material stored off the originating server by other computers, namely proxy servers or local cache. This material is cached to make the Web more efficient. Once your computer loads a page, rather than request that page from the original site, your computer can serve that page from your local cache. Site-centric measurement never sees the request and therefore never records this activity. Therefore if a visitor views a page multiple times and each time after the first view the page is served from cache, the server never sees the activity and consequently understates activity. The same is true, perhaps even more so, for large ISP or proprietary services like AOL.

Audience Measurement

Audience measurement takes a Web-user-centric approach and records activity as the end user receives and views content. The first step in collecting these data is building a sample, or panel, of users. The most important attribute of the panel is that it accurately represents the entire user population, or universe. As you might suspect, this is no easy task with the rapid growth of the Web in terms of both users and sites. Regardless, all audience measurement companies start with their sample.

Once a sample has been recruited, usage data must be collected. Reliable audience measurement uses a meter-based (versus recall) approach (note: some meters are better than others, but that is another topic). In general all meters collect the following information:

- Individual ID: linked to demographic profile
- Time stamp: Date and time of request (in the user's time zone)
- URL data: sequential URL data
- Other data: for example, some meters collect online service and PC application information

Once the data are collected, they are aggregated. Most audience measurement companies report the following metrics by site and by demographic variable:

- Reach: the percent of projected user universe visiting a particular site or group of sites
- Frequency: the number of times a visitor visits a site or group of sites in a reporting period
- Visit length: the time spent at a particular site or group of sites
- Session Length: the time the end user interacts with the computing device

The challenge here, however, is to recruit a large and representative sample of users so that the data are projectable and defensible in the market. If the sample is too small or not representative, the data provided will not reflect total Web usage.

Advantages and Disadvantages

The biggest advantage to these data is that we can take a broad view of the Web and know who is visiting which sites. That is, user-centric measurement enables us to measure activity across the entire Web, not limited to activity at an individual site. Audience measurement allows for extensive comparative analysis on an even scale. Additionally, since the Web usage data is linked to demographic profiles, one can drill down and compare usage data by demographic variable (i.e., age, gender, income, etc.). Lastly, these meters collect behavioral data and are therefore a very fertile (and as of yet unexplored) ground for understanding how behavior differs—for example, new users versus old users or men versus women. As an industry we are barely scratching the surface of this rich, robust data set.

Like site-centric measurement, audience measurement has its issues too. For example, if the sample is deemed not representative of the user universe, the measures are questioned. The biggest issue facing all audience measurement companies today is how to accurately sample, measure and report on "at work" activity. And as the Web usage grows outside the United States, the non-U.S. usage issue will be elevated.

Source:	Site-Centric Measurement	Audience Measurement
At Home	Yes	Yes
At Work	Yes	Yes
Other	Yes	No
Non U.S.	Yes	No
Local Cache	No	Yes
Proxy Cache	No	Yes

Exhibit 4 - 7 Inclusion Measurement Differences

So Why Are They Different?

These two measurement systems are different for two reasons: definitional issues and inclusion/exclusion issues. These two systems "measure" different metrics and therefore it is difficult to combine them. For example, the definition of a page view as recorded by site-centric methods differs from an impression as measured by the user-centric approach. Second, the two methods include/ignore certain traffic. For example, the server side collects traffic originating from EDU domains. However, to date, no client-side measurement company has recruited a school panel and therefore misses this traffic. Exhibit 4 - 7 summarizes some of the inclusion differences.

Conclusion

The mantra, "the medium is the measure," developed for server-side measurement, is not 100% accurate and a potentially damaging standard to be held to. As an industry we must thoroughly understand the data we are working with and use them appropriately. Site-centric measurement and audience measurement are two different measurement systems. They don't match because they are "apples and oranges." These two data sources are not substitutes but rather complements. Our job as researchers is to use the best data available and extract informational value. In some cases that means using log files exclusively. In other cases that means using audience measurement data. In most cases it means using both. If we as an industry describe all the data as suspect, as some have, we are, in essence, throwing the baby out with the bath water. We must leverage the strengths of each data source and be aware of weaknesses and advance our understanding of this medium.

Block of Definitions

- **Visit:** A series of page requests at a site by a visitor without 30 consecutive minutes of inactivity

- **Visitor:** An individual who interacts with a Web site. To calculate visitors, I/PRO for example uses Unique IP Addresses with heuristic statistical modeling to identify a visitor. This is one of the four methodologies approved by the IAB and the only one that can be applied to all Web sites.

- **Page:** All Web sites are collections of electronic pages. Each Web page is an HTML document that may contain text, images, or other media objects. A page can be either static or dynamically generated.

- **Page Request:** The opportunity for an HTML document to appear in a browser window as a direct result of a visitor's interaction with a Web site. Only one page can be counted per request. A click that is followed by a splash page (a page that precedes the requested page), an interstitial, and so on will count as only one page request.

- **Local (or Browser) Cache:** The storage of recently used documents on a user's disk to speed browsing. When a user revisits a page, his browser might display the document from the local disk rather than from the site's Web server. As a result, Web servers may undercount the number of times a page or advertisement has been viewed.

- **Proxy Cache:** The storing of downloads by a proxy server. The proxy server works as a receptacle of frequently requested files on the Internet so that several users may download the same object while using less bandwidth. As a result, Web servers many undercount the number of times a page or advertisement has been viewed.

Leveraging Technology

SHOPPING AGENTS

On May 13, 1997, Netbot Inc., a Seattle-based Internet software developer announced the availability of a beta (i.e., test) version of "the Internet's first intelligent shopping assistant," called Jango. The reaction from the Internet community was swift and enthusiastic. By June 25 the product had won two industry awards for its innovation. By July 22, 12,000 consumers had obtained and used the product for shopping. On September 8, AT&T WorldNet licensed a custom version of Jango for its 950,000 users. And on October 16, Excite Inc. acquired Netbot for $35 million of common stock. In the short course of five months a clever product with profound implications for electronic commerce had blossomed and been plucked. Such is the rate of change in the fast-paced world of the Internet.

What is an intelligent shopping assistant? An intelligent assistant helps consumers shop by eliminating the time-consuming drudgery of compiling all the information they need to complete a purchase. Such an assistant knows which stores to visit, provides accurate product and price information, helps people compare product features and prices, negotiates specials on their behalf, and finally completes the transaction with the click of a button. Science fiction? Hardly! Jango did all this and more, and it was quick and accurate. Unfortunately, at the time of this writing, Excite's implementation of Jango was not as comprehensive in its features as the original product.

The technology that shopping assistants, also known as agents, employ is called *parallel pull*. What appears to the user as one intelligent shopping assistant is actually multiple assistants that simultaneously (in parallel) collect (pull) information from relevant Web sites located worldwide. The entire process takes only minutes (in some cases seconds), during which time hundreds of pieces of relevant information are collected, categorized, and even sorted for the user. What makes this possible is that the agents quickly translate the query into the format required by each individual merchant. The merchants benefit since the agents attract customers to their sites. The agents benefit since they are able to sell advertising on their sites.

But not all is quite as rosy at it might seem. Some vendors refuse to honor inquiries from shopping agents, as they do not want to be forced to compete on the basis of price. These vendors actually monitor the originating IP address of each incoming search request. An IP (Internet Protocol) address is a unique number assigned to a computer connecting to the Internet. If the IP address is of a known shopping agent, then the vendor may block the request coming from that site. Nonetheless, many vendors do let the shopping agents through. The result is a downward pressure on prices.

PriceScan (www.pricescan.com) is a shopping agent that assists in sales of computer products. In addition to Web site pricing, PriceScan also gathers their pricing information from magazine ads and vendor catalogs. They do not charge vendors to be listed in their database. PriceScan makes money by selling advertising on its site. In the following example a search is performed for a notebook computer. The user has no brand preference and will make the decision based on the lowest price for the desired features. The user begins by selecting the desired features using pull-down menus (Exhibit 4 - 8). PriceScan then proceeds to find products that match those criteria and vendors that carry those products (Exhibit 4 - 9 and Exhibit 4 - 10). Note especially the final screen shot in the series (Exhibit 4 - 11), which shows a trend line for the product's price! This is information that would be extremely difficult, if not impossible, for a user to reconstruct.

Services such as PriceScan have tremendous marketing implications. First, they drive traffic to participating merchant Web sites. Second, they create a competitive edge for the Web as a shopping vehicle, because price-conscious consumers cannot easily perform price comparisons of this sort in the brick and mortar world. Finally, and most important, merchants are being forced to compete on the basis of price. When it is easy for consumers to price shop and when they perceive little product or merchant differentiation, then markets behave like commodity markets, with all prices reaching similar levels. Therefore, marketers must either compete on the basis of price or find other ways to add value that justify higher prices.

Exhibit 4 - 8 PriceScan Search Criteria
Source: www.pricescan.com

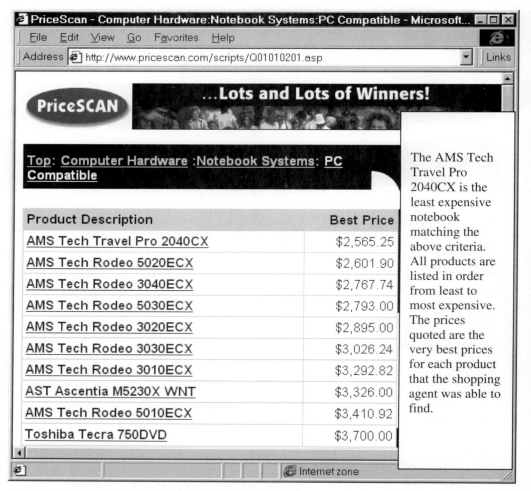

Exhibit 4 - 9 PriceScan Search Results
Source: www.pricescan.com

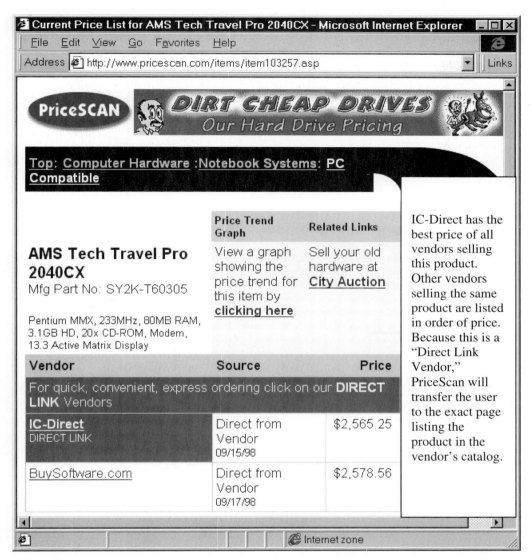

Exhibit 4 - 10 PriceScan List of Vendors
Source: www.pricescan.com

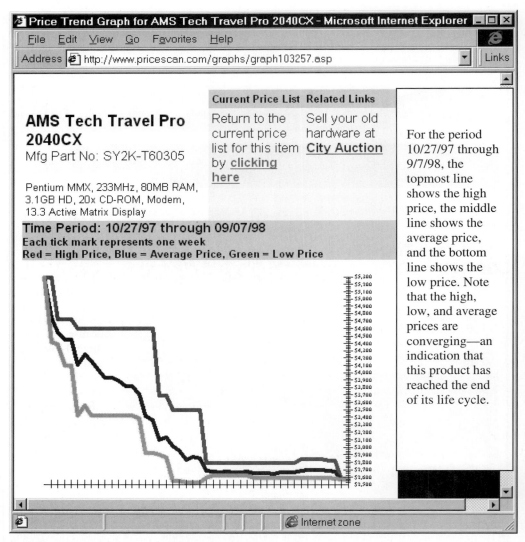

Exhibit 4 - 11 PriceScan Price Trend Graph
Source: www.pricescan.com

Ethics and Law

HYPERLINKS, META-TAGS, AND FRAMING

The World Wide Web has achieved remarkable popularity through its innovative methods of presentation. In addition to the combined modes of electronic text and graphics, perhaps the most attractive aspect of Web viewing is the ease with which pages of information may be navigated, giving rise to the popular term, "Web surfing." These features are made possible by digital applications which, like the Web itself, are new and challenging subjects for legal review.

Hyperlinks appear on most Web pages and enable users to connect to places within or without the site. In the case of linking to outside locations, it has been common practice for most Web authors simply to insert a link without asking the permission of the target site's owner. Often, the link points to the front page of the remote location, but it can also refer a user to more interior sections. This latter practice is known as *deep linking*.

In 1997, Microsoft's Seattle Sidewalk, a Web-based, informational guide to the city, was sued by Ticketmaster for creating an unauthorized, deep link into its events purchasing area. This path, it was alleged, avoided pages of Ticketmaster regulations, promotions, and other materials. It was charged that Microsoft's links, among other things, had diluted Ticketmaster's trademarks, caused deception as to the relationship between the two companies, constituted unfair competition, and depleted Ticketmaster's advertising revenues. The case is ongoing (*Ticketmaster Corp.* v. *Microsoft Corp.*, CV 97-3055 RAP (C.D. Cal., 1997).

In the Scottish matter of *Shetland Times Ltd.* v. *Dr. Jonathon Wills and Zetnews, Ltd.*, F.S.R. 604, 1997 S.L.T. 669 (Outer House Oct. 24, 1996), the plaintiff, a newspaper, was granted an injunction against the defendant, a news reporting service, which had been deep linking to its Web site without consent. Similar to Ticketmaster, the allegations stated a loss of profit and unfair benefit. The case was settled with the requirement that any linking to the Times be accompanied by clear attribution to the source and location of the article.

Meta-tags are essentially keywords which are placed within the coding of a Web page. This data is read by Web-based search engines which, upon finding tags matching an inquiry, will direct users to these sites through hyperlinks. In *Playboy Enterprises, Inc.* v. *Calvin Designer Label*, 44 U.S.P.Q.2d (BNA) 1156 (N.D. Cal. 1997), the defendant inserted the trademarks PLAYBOY and PLAYMATE into the meta-tag field of its own pages. In granting a preliminary injunction, the court held that *Playboy* had demonstrated that the defendant's use of these proprietary terms would likely be found at trial to be instances of unfair competition, trademark infringement, and dilution.

Framing involves the separation of a Web page into two or more independent sections or *frames*. While a new window is created by the click of a hyperlink, the material existing prior to that click need not be erased. This display status was the cause of a suit filed in 1997 in the matter of the *Washington Post Company* v. *Total News, Inc.,* No. 97 Civ. 1190 (PKL) (S.D.N.Y., 1997). Here it was alleged that the defendant had framed the Post's Web site in such a way that its unique Web site could no longer be distinguished from that of Total News and, in fact, was surrounded by the News's advertising and other information. This redesign resulted, according to the complaint, in unfair economic gain to the framer, as well as trademark dilution and infringement. The case was settled out of court.

In a more recent matter, a plaintiff was denied a preliminary injunction against a defendant framer who had incorporated to the plaintiff's site a framed link that held its copyrighted material. The court noted that the frame included a prominent border, identifying that within it to be the plaintiff's work. It noted that the law of framing is not established and that under the circumstances, copyright infringement had not been sufficiently demonstrated (*Futuredontics, Inc.* v. *Applied Anagramics, Inc., et al*, 45 U.S.P.Q.2D (BNA) 225 (C.D. Cal., 1998).

This necessarily brief survey of the current law suggests that Web navigational issues are yet to be fully or comprehensively considered by the courts. As with early tribunals determining the law of travel on the seas, the safety of informational cargo is being balanced against the benefits of unhindered passage.

Savvy Sites

Web Site and Address	Importance to Net Marketers
Egghead http://www.egghead.com/	Egghead operates an online auction called Surplus Auction. Here you can bid on computer products, jewelry, home appliances, camcorders, automotive electronics, and more. You can receive specialized bidding information via e-mail. Bidding closes at 2:00 P.M. on Wednesday.
Excite www.excite.com	Excite features a shopping agent called Product Finder. This Jango agent will process your request for a certain product by scouring the Web and reporting back with the lowest prices for that request.
Expedia www.expedia.com	Expedia is an online flight reservation system run by Microsoft that will search for the lowest possible airfare. Expedia also reports back to you via e-mail with updates on lowest fares. Expedia may make you never want to visit a travel agent again.
GTE SuperPages http://www.superpages.gte.net/	GTE SuperPages is a vast online directory that searches for businesses, Web pages, and products. The directory also provides maps and city guides.
Infospace www.infospace.com	Infospace is a loaded information repository with online yellow pages, classifieds, product search engine, and links to the Web's best shopping sites.
InterNIC www.internic.net	"The InterNIC provides domain name registration services for the top-level domains .com, .net , .org, and .edu"
Travelocity www.travelocity.com	Travelocity is an online airline ticket system that is very similar to Expedia.

UBid www.ubid.com	uBid is another online auction that offers bidding on computer software/hardware and various consumer electronics.
USALE AUCTION http://www.usale-auction.com/	USALE AUCTION is another online bidding system for computer hardware and software.

Chapter

5

The Net as Distribution Channel

"The art of getting rich consists not in industry, much less in saving, but in a better order, in timeliness, in being at the right spot."

—Ralph Waldo Emerson

Chapter Outline

- The Real Networks Story
- Introduction
- Distribution Channel Functions Online
- Length of Distribution Channels
- Power Relationships among Channel Players
- Online Retailing: "Click Till You *Drop*"

Practitioner Perspective
Electronic Commerce
—Peter Clemente, Vice President, Cyberdialogue

Leveraging Technology
Transaction Security

Ethics and Law
Expression on the Internet

Learning Objectives

- Marketing Review
  - Describe the functions of a distribution channel
  - Differentiate between an indirect and direct channel
- Describe the Internet's strengths in bringing buyers and sellers together
- Explain how the Internet has both shortened and lengthened distribution channels
- Discuss the advantages and disadvantages of electronic retailing from the retailer's perspective
- Tell how the Internet has added value to the consumer shopping experience
- Discuss the importance of shopping agents for Net retailers
- Explain the security risks for online shopping
- Understand how the Internet has changed the balance of power in distribution channels

The RealNetworks Story

Rob Glaser is founder and CEO of RealNetworks Inc. (www.real.com), a Yale graduate, and proud of his progressive political leanings (5% of profits go to charity—though so far there are none). He left a cushy vice president job at Microsoft to become an entrepreneur, founding a company that would pioneer an innovative distribution channel for online multimedia content. RealNetworks creates software to encode and deliver audio and video content over the Internet. It is the pioneer and market leader in this field, with over 85% of the market.

There are three key concepts behind RealNetworks' delivery of multimedia content: compression, streaming, and caching. Compression, streaming, and caching are designed to overcome the fundamental flaw of the Internet: lack of bandwidth—in other words the Internet is slow. Compression squeezes the signal into a smaller package; streaming allows that package to begin playing after only a piece of it has arrived; and caching allows frequently accessed content to be more quickly available to users. Compression uses mathematical routines to reduce the signal while maintaining fidelity. Streaming allows one piece to play while the next piece is loading (technical term: buffering) in the computer's memory. Caching stores the information at multiple points along the Internet so that it is closer to the user. Compression, streaming, and caching make it possible to deliver audio and video feeds from Web pages after only minimal delays. Prior to RealNetworks, users had to wait 30 minutes to download a 5-minute audio clip.

RealNetworks delivers audio and video either live or on demand. The Internet has played host to some live events. Most notable among them was the Voyager landing on Mars and the first Internet live birth. Unfortunately for the sponsors, in both cases the number of viewers exceeded the capacity of the servers. Other examples of Webcasting include hundreds of radio stations which reach new markets worldwide.

Delivering on demand allows users to time shift—listening and watching at their convenience rather than at preprogrammed times. This is analogous to flipping on the TV set at any hour of the day and then requesting the latest episode of *Spin City*. That's not possible in the world of broadcast television. It is, however, possible on the Internet. As an example, a user missing a basketball game on the radio could listen to the recorded broadcast from the NBA Web site.

One great example of a content provider with a good mix of live and on-demand offerings is Broadcast.com (www.broadcast.com). Its channels include:

- AudioBooks
- Business
- CD Jukebox
- Education
- Entertainment
- Live Radio
- Live TV
- Music
- News
- Public Affairs
- Special Interest
- Spiritual
- Sports
- Technology
- Video

How good is the quality? The audio has gotten quite good—FM radio quality with unfortunate dropouts when the Internet becomes congested. Of course audio quality is also dependent upon the sound system on the user's computer. The video, however, is still seriously lacking. Why? Because video requires many times more bandwidth than audio. Nonetheless, as bandwidth improves, video Webcasting will increase in usage, probably converging in some form with TV and radio broadcasting.

Corporate networks do not suffer from the bandwidth limitations of the Internet. Therefore video streaming over corporate intranets is a viable option. Corporations such as Boeing, 3Com, and MCI use RealNetworks' technology to deliver information and training videos to employee desktops. Other business opportunities for streaming technologies include:

- Multimedia ads such as banner ads and interstitials. RealNetworks claims click-through rates of about 5% on multimedia ads
- Video tours of remote locations
- Distance delivery of college courses

What challenges does RealNetworks face in the future? Ironically, the biggest challenge is from Glaser's former boss at Microsoft. Microsoft has developed competing software called NetShow Services, which it bundles with Windows NT for free. RealNetworks has no choice but to charge for at least the server portion of its G2 software. By most accounts G2 is superior to Microsoft NetShow Services. Glaser is banking that professionals will forgo the free offer from Microsoft and purchase the G2 server for the superior features. At the time of this writing, Wall Street disagreed. The value of RealNetworks' stock cooled off in the third quarter of 1998 as the competition with Microsoft came to light. Wall Street was particularly troubled by Glaser's claim in testimony before Congress that Microsoft's software actually disabled RealNetworks' G2 player.

Introduction

A distribution channel is a group of interdependent firms that work together to transfer product from the supplier to the consumer. The transfer may either be direct or employ a number of intermediaries. Intermediaries are firms that appear in the channel between the supplier and the consumer. By specializing, intermediaries are able to perform functions more efficiently than the supplier could.

For some digital products, such as software, the entire distribution channel may be Internet based. For example, the consumer purchases software online, which the supplier then delivers over the Internet to the user's computer. In most cases, however, only some of the firms in the channel are wholly or partially Internet enabled. For example, nondigital products such as flowers and wine may be purchased online but still must be delivered via truck. Nonetheless, it may be possible to track the exact location of that shipment using a Web-based interface.

This chapter will examine four major questions:

1. What are the functions of a distribution channel, and how does the value of those functions change when they become Internet based?
2. What is the effect of the Internet on the length of distribution channels?
3. How does the Internet alter the power relationships among channel players?
4. What are the obstacles and success factors for online retailing?

Distribution Channel Functions Online

The transfer of goods and services from the supplier to the consumer requires that a number of critical functions be performed. These include:

- Market research
- Marketing communications
- Contact with buyers
- Matching product to buyer's needs
- Physical distribution
- Financing
- Negotiating price

Each of the distribution channel functions will be examined in turn. Particular attention is placed on how the value of these functions changes when they become Internet based.

MARKET RESEARCH

Market research is a major function of the distribution channel. The benefits of market research include an accurate assessment of the size and characteristics of the target audience. Audience information helps to drive product development and marketing communications. Chapter 3 explored market research in some detail, and chapter 2 examined Internet user characteristics. Here comments will be limited to the costs and benefits of Internet-based market research.

The Internet affects the value of market research for five reasons. First, much of the information on the Internet, especially government reports, is available for free with no reproduction charges. Second, staff members can conduct research from their desks rather than making expensive trips to libraries and other resource sites. Third, the information obtained over the Internet tends to be timelier, a fact that increases its value. For example, some ad management firms allow their clients to monitor up-to-the-minute click-through rates for individual ad banners. Fourth, since Web-based information is already in digital form, loading the information into a spreadsheet or other data analysis package requires no further data entry. Finally, because so much consumer behavior data can be captured online, very rich reports can be obtained. For example, RelevantKnowledge (www.relevantknowledge.com) produces an individual site report which separates a given site into content sections (technical term: baskets) and then produces usage statistics for each section. These numbers help advertisers decide which page to buy.

Nonetheless, there is no free market research. Even free government reports require a significant investment of human resources to distill the material into a useful form for making decisions. Furthermore, many firms need access to costly commercial information. As an example, RelevantKnowledge sells its reports for about $50,000 each. The Internet not only assists with timely marketing research data collection, but it also can reduce research costs.

MARKETING COMMUNICATIONS

Marketing communications encompasses advertising and other types of product promotion, and it is the subject of chapter 6. Effective marketing communications requires resources to plan and implement. The marketing communications function is often shared among channel players. For example, a manufacturer may carry out ad campaigns while a retailer offers a coupon. Cooperative advertising is another example: In this case manufacturers share advertising costs with retailers. These communications are most effective when they represent a coordinated effort among channel players.

The Internet adds value to the marketing communications function in several ways. First, functions that previously required manual labor can be automated. For example, when Amazon sends out a promotional message to millions of its registered users, there are no papers to fold, no envelopes to stuff, no postage to imprint. A click of the Send button distributes the message to millions of users. As another example, promoting a Web site to the search engines can be automated by services such as Did-It (www.did-it.com). Did-It studies how the search engines rank Web sites and then optimizes their clients' Web sites to achieve a higher ranking. Second, communications can be closely monitored and altered minute by minute. For example, Flycast allows its clients to monitor the click-through rates of their banner ads in real time and make substitutions for poorly performing ads right from the customer's desktop. Thus, the firm can boost exposure of productive communications and remove unproductive communications. Third, software that can track a user's behavior can be used to direct highly targeted communications to that user. For example, Engage Technologies (www.engage.com) can anonymously track user behavior online and target ads down to the level of the individual user. Finally, promotional coordination among intermediaries is enhanced by the Internet. Firms send ads and other material to each other via e-mail, and all firms may view current promotions on a Web site at any time. This is a tremendous improvement because in the brick and mortar world companies often run ads and coupons while retailers remain in the dark until consumers show up asking for the special deal.

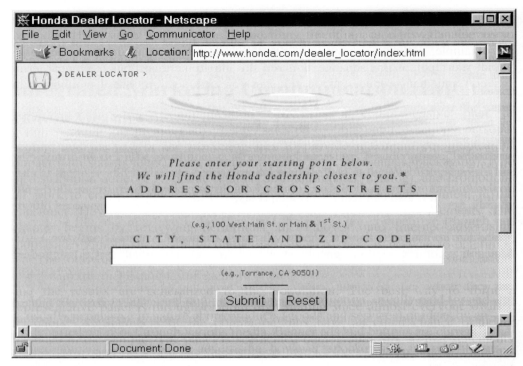

Exhibit 5 - 1 Honda Dealer Locator

CONTACT WITH BUYERS

The Internet provides a new channel for making contact with buyers. Forrester Research calls the Internet the fourth channel after personal selling, mail, and the telephone. The Internet channel adds value to the contact process for several reasons. First, the contact can be customized to the buyer's needs. For example, the Honda site (www.honda.com) allows customers to find a dealer in their area in order to complete the purchase. See Exhibit 5 - 1. Second, the Internet provides a wide range of referral sources. The sources of referral include search engines, shopping agents, newsgroups, chat rooms, e-mail, Web pages, and syndicated selling. Third, the Internet is always open for business. Buyers can contact a Web site 24 hours a day and seven days a week.

MATCHING PRODUCT TO BUYER'S NEEDS

Matching product to buyer's needs is an area where the Web has excelled. Given a generic description of the buyer's requirements, shopping agents can produce a list of products meeting the requirements. Shopping agents such as CompareNet (www.comparenet.com) and PriceScan (www.pricescan.com) allow the consumer to rapidly compare prices and features within product categories. Online retailers can also help consumers match product to needs. The Gap (www.gap.com) lets consumers mix and match clothes in order to select their wardrobe. Exhibit 5 - 2 shows the Land Rover site (www.landrover.com) which allows consumers to custom configure a Land Rover. Staples (www.staples.com) offers customized catalogs for its corporate clients. Of particular interest are collaborative filtering agents, which can predict consumer preferences based on past purchase behavior. Amazon uses a collaborative filtering agent to recommend books and music to its customers. Once the system is in place, there is very little incremental cost as it moves from handling hundreds to handling thousands of users. The effectiveness of the collaborative filtering agent actually increases as consumers are added to the database. Note that all of these services scale well because they are automated. By contrast, efforts to match product to buyer needs in the brick and mortar world tend to be very labor intensive and are quickly overwhelmed as volume increases. Salespeople in retail outlets attempt this chore, but the Internet improves on this function by being on call anytime and by matching buyers with products across retailers. Of course, doing this puts a burden on electronic retailers to compete on the basis of price or to differentiate their products in a way that is important to the market.

Exhibit 5 - 2 Outfit Your Land Rover

PHYSICAL DISTRIBUTION

One great hope for the Internet is to serve as a medium for the physical distribution of products and services. And while great strides are being made in this area, there is still a ways to go. Any content that can be digitized can be transmitted over the Internet: text, graphics, audio, and video content. The *New York Times* (www.nytimes.com) digitally distributes an online version of its newspaper. *Wired* magazine (www.hotwired.com) distributes an online version of its magazine. More than 1,100 radio stations broadcast live programming over the Internet 24 hours a day. Broadcast.com even distributes books, music, and video online. Computer software has a long history of online distribution. Companies such as WinFiles (www.winfiles.com) and CNET Download.com (www.download.com) serve as distribution intermediaries for much computer software. Exhibit 5 - 3 shows CNET Download.com's wide variety of software titles. In all the cases listed above, distribution costs are significantly lowered by online distribution. The alternative, physical distribution of digital product, is comparatively expensive. Physical distribution first requires the costly step of embedding the content in a medium such as newsprint, plastic coated paper, a CD, or a diskette. The medium must then be packaged and shipped to the consumer, thereby incurring further costs.

Exhibit 5 - 3 CNET Download.com

Nonetheless, many products sold online are still distributed through conventional channels. For example, most major record labels will not allow their music to be distributed online. The Internet consumer may make the purchase online but the CD will arrive via the Postal Service, UPS, FedEx, or some other carrier. Many products are distributed in a similar fashion. In one sense this type of distribution is rather inefficient. Rather than deliver a hundred copies of a CD to a record store in a single shipment, the UPS truck must make a hundred separate stops at consumers' homes. The consumer pays a premium for this service which in some cases outweighs the cost savings of purchasing online.

Furthermore, local regulations sometimes impede the direct distribution of product. For example, Virtual Vineyards (www.virtualvin.com), a wine distributor, has been forced by some state regulations to operate through local intermediaries—thus lengthening their distribution channel.

FINANCING

Most online consumer purchases are financed through credit cards or special financing plans. This system is not unlike that of many traditional store purchases. However, consumers have understandable concerns about divulging their card information online. The concerns are primarily fear of the unknown. Fortunately, great strides have been made to guarantee the security of online transactions. Curiously enough the safeguards now in place probably make online purchase in some ways the most secure channel for the consumer.

Concern over the security of online transactions is one of the greatest impediments to online retailing. Many consumers believe that their credit card numbers will be stolen if they engage in online commerce. While these concerns are real, the actual danger of credit card theft is greatly exaggerated. There are three places where the theft could take place: on the user's computer, in transit, and on the Web site to which the user is connecting.

The user's computer. Connecting to the Internet is a two-way proposition. Just as the user can browse other sites while connected, so too can others browse the user's computer if proper security is not in place. Nonetheless because of the logistical difficulties involved in hacking into great numbers of enduser computers, this is not a major problem.

In transit. Many consumers fear that their credit card numbers can be intercepted in transit by hackers eavesdropping on Internet communications. However, most electronic commerce transactions are encrypted. This means that even if a hacker was to intercept a credit card number, it would be completely unreadable. As a result, the card number is probably safer in transit than at any other point in the process.

The Web site. This is the most vulnerable stage in the process. Web sites may contain databases of thousands of card numbers—a tempting target for a hacker. There have in fact been instances of hackers breaking into Web sites to steal the database of card numbers. However, the situation is improving as the result of software programs that probe sites for security holes so that site administrators can fix them in advance of any problems.

There is also an additional problem with Web sites: namely, are they reputable? Con artists have been known to create false electronic storefronts in order to bilk consumers. The problem is made more acute because many Web-developed brands do not have the carry-over recognition from traditional media.

While consumers have a number of concerns over credit card transactions, online merchants have a major concern as well: How do they know that they are dealing with a valid consumer using a legitimate credit card?

It was in response to the above concerns that the major credit card companies banded together to form Secure Electronic Transactions (SET). SET is a vehicle for legitimizing both the merchant and the consumer as well as protecting the consumer's credit card number. Under SET the card number is never directly sent to the merchant. Rather a third party is introduced to the transaction with whom both the merchant and consumer communicate to validate one another as well as the transaction. The communication is initiated automatically in the background and thus places no further technical burdens upon the consumer. The problem with SET is that it is so technical that most consumers do not appreciate its subtleties. Furthermore, most merchants do not want to pay for costly upgrades to a SET system.

NEGOTIATING PRICE

Negotiating price is another area where the Internet has real potential to excel. Many businesses currently conduct bidding online. There are consumer market auctions such as those held by Onsale (www.onsale.com). See Exhibit 5 - 4. Businesses such as General Electric also solicit online bids from their suppliers. Online bidding has the effect of widening the supplier pool, thereby aggregating products and lowering prices. Shopping agents implicitly negotiate prices downward on behalf of the consumer by listing companies in order of best price first. But the future holds even more promise. Technology is now in development that would allow a buyer's shopping agent to interact with a supplier's shopping agent out in agent space. The agents could then negotiate and make deals on behalf of their respective clients.

AGGREGATING PRODUCT

Suppliers tend to operate more efficiently when they produce a high volume of a narrow range of products. Consumers, on the other hand, prefer to purchase small quantities of a wide range of products. Channel intermediaries perform the essential function of aggregating product from multiple suppliers so that the consumer can have more choices in one location. Examples of this traditional form of aggregation include online category killers such as Music Boulevard (www.Music Boulevard.com), which offers thousands of records from multiple suppliers. In other cases the Internet follows a model of virtual aggregation. Virtual aggregation brings together product from multiple independent firms and organizes the display on the user's computer. In the case of search engines the unit of aggregation is the online storefront. A search for a particular product will bring up a list of stores that carry the product. In the case of shopping agents, the unit of aggregation is the product page at the online store. A search for a particular product will produce a neatly arranged table with comparative product information and direct links to the vendor pages that carry the product. One way to understand this difference is to imagine a shopping mall in which the consumer can control which stores appear in the mall at any given time. For example, on a search for cellular phones the shopping mall would become loaded with Circuit City, Sprint PCS, Bernies, Best Buys, and so on. The user must still visit the individual stores to look for products. The shopping agent goes one step further by asking the store sales personnel to approach the consumer in the center of the mall and place their offerings before her. For the cellular phone search each store would neatly arrange its cellular phone offerings on a table in front of the consumer.

Exhibit 5 - 4 Onsale: Consumer Product Auction

Length of Distribution Channels

The length of a distribution channel refers to the number of intermediaries between the supplier and the consumer. The shortest distribution channel has no intermediaries—the supplier deals directly with the consumer. This is known as a direct distribution channel. Most distribution channels incorporate one or more intermediaries in an indirect channel. A generic indirect channel includes suppliers, a manufacturer, wholesalers, retailers, and end consumers. Intermediaries help to perform all of the functions listed in the previous section.

Disintermediation describes the process of eliminating traditional intermediaries. Eliminating intermediaries has the potential to reduce costs since each intermediary must add to the price of the product in order to make a living. Taken to its extreme, disintermediation allows the supplier to transfer goods and services directly to the consumer in a direct channel. Complete disintermediation tends to be the exception, because suppliers often find that intermediaries can provide services more efficiently than they can do themselves. The efficiency comes from specialization. An intermediary that specializes in one function, such as product promotion, tends to get very good at that function and can usually perform the function faster and more effectively than a newcomer to the field.

Much of the initial hype surrounding the Internet focused on disintermediation. It was thought that prices would plummet as the Internet eliminated costly intermediaries. This line of reasoning failed to recognize some important facts. First, the United States has the most efficient distribution system in the world. Second, intermediaries allow corporations to maintain focus on their core business. Third, many traditional intermediaries have simply been replaced with their Internet equivalents. Time will tell whether the online intermediaries are more efficient than their physical world counterparts. In at least one area the Internet is definitely more efficient—the online storefront. Online retailers do not have to rent, maintain, and staff expensive retail space in desirable shopping areas. An inexpensive warehouse provides an acceptable storage location for goods sold online. On the other hand, online stores do incur the costs of setting up and maintaining their commerce sites; while these charges can be significant, however, they do not outweigh the savings realized by eliminating the physical store.

Interestingly, the Internet has added new intermediaries that did not exist previously. For example, Broadcast.com is an aggregator of multimedia content. Broadcast.com is like a record store, audio bookstore, radio broadcaster, and TV broadcaster all rolled into one. As a record store, it provides something that record stores will not provide: the ability to sample a CD in its entirety prior to purchase. As a broadcaster, it allows users to listen to radio and TV programs from around the world. Other new intermediaries include shopping agents, search engines, and syndicated selling. Exhibit 5 - 5 shows CNET Shopper.com (www.shopper.com), a shopping agent specifically geared toward the purchase of computer products.

Power Relationships Among Channel Players

Whenever new information technology is introduced into a distribution channel, it has the potential of altering the power relationships among existing channel players. Nowhere has this effect been more evident than with the Internet. In many cases the power of the buyer has been significantly increased at the expense of the supplier. In other cases the power of the supplier has come out on top. Wal-Mart gained power over its channels when it introduced electronic systems to notify suppliers of needed product. This was a major power upheaval in channels where giant manufacturers such as Procter & Gamble had previously been in control.

The Internet has increased the power of buyers for two reasons. First, buyers have access to more information than ever before, including pricing information. Second, buyers have access to more suppliers than ever before. This power allows buyers to shop for price among suppliers. The power shows clearly with the advent of shopping agents. These agents automatically produce spreadsheets listing price and availability information from a wide variety of suppliers.

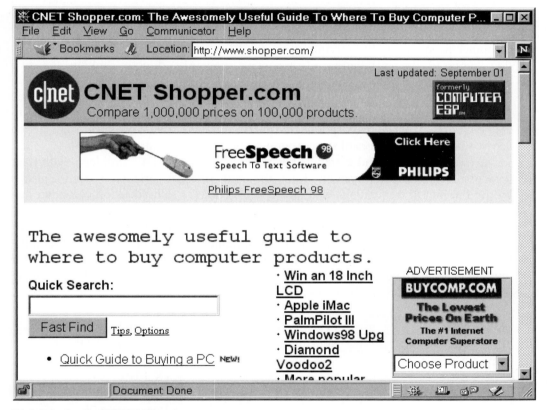

Exhibit 5 - 5 CNET Shopper.com

In other cases the Internet has increased the power of suppliers. Suppliers can gain power in two ways. First, the supplier that takes the early lead online will receive business from consumers and firms eager to shop in this channel. But even in cases where multiple firms are online, the power of suppliers can still be increased if they are able to establish structural relationships with buyers. For example, Amazon establishes structural relationships with its customers using its one-click ordering and collaborative filtering technologies. Amazon customers switching to another site would have to reenter their billing information and, more important, would lose the recommendations provided by Amazon.

A type of business-to-business commerce known as Electronic Data Interchange (EDI) is particularly effective for establishing structural relationships between businesses. Electronic Data Interchange (EDI) is the computerized exchange of information between organizations in order to avoid paper forms. The classic use of EDI is to eliminate purchase requisitions between firms. A buyer logs onto the supplier's computer system and types in her order. The order is instantly conveyed to the supplier, and the buyer receives an electronic bill. No paper changes hands. EDI has been available between organizations for quite some time. However, the old systems had two drawbacks. First they were proprietary, which meant that a different computer terminal might be required to order from each separate business. Second, they required the installation of expensive networks directly linking the two businesses sharing data.

The Internet has put a new face on EDI and given it a new name. EDI on the Internet is commonly referred to as an extranet. Technically, extranet refers to connecting two or more corporate intranets. Intranets are Web sites that can be accessed only by members of the corporation or its extranet partners.

Creating intranets and extranets has resolved some of EDI's problems with their legacy (older) computer systems. First, the expensive networks have been replaced by the Internet at tremendous cost savings. Second, the same desktop computer can be used to interface with multiple suppliers. Third, networks of suppliers and buyers are more easily able to exchange data using a Web-based interface.

The discussion above reveals three key variables: the openness of the system, the transport method (Internet or non-Internet), and the type of technology used for implementation. These variables yield in combination five flavors of EDI which are used in industry today as shown in the following table:

Openness	**Transport**	**Technology**
Proprietary	Non-Internet	Traditional EDI
Open system	Non-Internet	Standards-based EDI (X.12)
Proprietary	Internet	Application Program Interface (API)
Open system (nonstandard)	Internet	Extensible Markup Language (XML)
Open system (standards based)	Internet	Open Buying on the Internet (OBI)

The goal is to create a standards-based open system that runs over the Internet so that all suppliers and buyers can seamlessly and effortlessly integrate their systems. Open Buying on the Internet (OBI) is the technology that implements that goal. OBI requires that all suppliers and buyers use a standard electronic form for completing transactions. OBI empowers buyers since there is no additional work to ordering from a new supplier other than changing the name on the form. The industry has a long way to go before OBI is universally adopted, however. For now, the most successful extranets are proprietary systems that run over the Internet.

A great example of a proprietary extranet product is the Renascence System developed by Electronic Data Systems (EDS) (www.eds.com). EDS supplies computer services to hundreds of businesses and government organizations. It developed the Renascence System to link all of its suppliers with a common interface. The system was so successful that the company rolled it out to its customer desktops as well. Renascence allows customers to buy directly from suppliers at EDS-negotiated prices.

Another good example of EDI is found at the Cisco Corporation (www.cisco.com). Cisco is the world's largest manufacturer of networking hardware. Much of the Internet is powered by Cisco switches and routers. Cisco allows its largest buyers to tie directly into its order system and place orders in real time. The system has allowed Cisco to save millions of dollars a year while providing superior customer service.

Site	Product	Percent Reach from Home	Percent Reach from Work
Amazon	Books and music	8.1	11.3
Bluemountainarts	Greeting cards	7.4	5.6
Cnet Software Download Services	Software	5.4	3.9
Ebay	Auction	4.0	4.3
Barnes & Noble	Books	3.8	4.8
Columbiahouse	Music	3.6	3.5
Hotfiles	Software	3.0	N/A*
Coolsavings	Coupons	2.3	2.9
Valupage	Coupons, rebates, samples	2.1	N/A
Netmarket	Merchandise	2.1	3.0
Cdnow	Music	N/A	3.3
Bmgmusicservice	Music	N/A	2.9

Exhibit 5 - 6 MediaMetrix Ratings of Top Shopping Sites
*Items with an N/A designation did not make the top ten in their respective market (home or work)

Online Retailing: "Click Till You Drop"

Online retailing refers to electronic storefronts such as Music Boulevard (www.Music Boulevard.com) or Dell Computer (www.dell.com). Online retailing is a $17 billion industry with room for tremendous growth. By comparison, the traditional catalog industry garners revenues of $108 billion. The majority of products purchased online are high-involvement or information rich. Some of the top shopping sites in July 1998, according to Media Metrix are shown in Exhibit 5 - 6.

The data demonstrate slightly different demographics in the home and work markets. The differing demographics are just one of many factors that marketers must take into consideration when designing Web sites. This section will proceed by exploring who is purchasing online and reasons that consumers purchase online. Next the obstacles to online purchases will be explored.

ONLINE BENEFITS

Who is buying online? According to Cyberdialogue/findsvp, there were 11.2 million online purchasers in 1997. Seventy-one percent of these were men. Women, especially young single college students, do more online window-shopping. Another 15.8 million users researched a product online but made their purchase offline. The average age of all shoppers was 37.5 years. While this group represents many baby boomers, almost a third of the shoppers are GenXers under 29 years of age. Fifty-five percent were college graduates. Well-educated shoppers tend to prefer comprehensive product and price comparison information. The average income of online shoppers was $63,200 per year. Based on salary alone, this is an appealing demographic. Seventy percent of the shoppers were knowledge workers who use more brain than brawn to earn their living. Focus group research by Cyberdialogue/findsvp reveals the following reasons for purchasing online.

1. No travel required; shop at home/work/school
2. No travel expenses
3. Easy comparison shopping; even the offline purchasers do a lot of their comparison shopping online
4. Comprehensive product selection
5. One-on-one targeted ads
6. Information-rich medium
7. Instant interaction with seller
8. Seven-day/24-hour availability
9. Shopping privacy
10. No unknowledgeable salespeople

Cyberdialogue/findsvp also reports that an incredible 95% of online shoppers said that they were satisfied or very satisfied (48%) with their purchase experience. And consumers tend to become more satisfied as they make more purchases. The trick is to get consumers to make that first purchase. This would suggest that marketing strategies that heavily promote the first purchase would pay off in the long run. Interestingly, though women are more reluctant than men to purchase online, they also are more satisfied than men are once they do make a purchase. Women also tend to use the Internet more than men to reduce the number of trips that they make to retail stores.

Other research, conducted by Expedia (www.expedia.msn.com), lists the following reasons for purchasing online.

- Price
- Control over and objective display of information
- To dream and explore
- Convenience 24 x 7
- No hassle environment
- Comprehensiveness

Shopping agents can help users find the lowest *price* on any product online. Very often this price will be significantly lower than the equivalent price in a neighborhood retail outlet. The Internet retailers can charge less because they are not renting and staffing expensive retail space. In some cases they are not even carrying inventory with its associated financing costs. In addition, the Internet consumer does not have to leave the privacy of her home in order to make the purchase. The consumer saves time shopping; as a result, value is added to the product.

For products such as airline tickets, many consumers prefer to see exactly what is on the terminal screen rather than have that information relayed to them by a travel agent. *Control* over and objective display of information reassures consumers that they are not being steered to a particular product or service that the salesperson is trying to push.

Many consumers relish the experience of *dreaming and exploring* online. The computer has infinite patience for the consumer to spend hours exploring multiple vacation packages. A travel agent would soon tire of such a consumer.

Many people do not have the luxury of shopping during normal business hours. Night owls especially like the *convenience* of shopping 24 hours a day 7 days a week. Some research suggests that the peak time for many purchases is late at night. For certain purchases, such as stock trades, where timing is critical and trading occurs in different time zones, 24-hour access has become a major point of differentiation over the brick and mortar world.

One of the advantages of dealing with a computer interface is the *lack of pressure* to make a purchase. Some consumers appreciate the absence of a salesperson. Computer interfaces should be written so as to minimize the hassle that a user would experience online. Designing a good interface is a key driver of success. Why? Because consumers are being adventuresome by purchasing online. Retailers need to reward that adventuresome spirit with a pleasant shopping experience or risk losing business.

Search engines and shopping agents enable virtual aggregation, which produces a list of products and services that is far more *comprehensive* than any physical store could offer. In addition, online superstores such as Amazon can on their own provide a more comprehensive product offering than can a traditional bookstore.

ONLINE OBSTACLES

What are the obstacles to online purchases? In one research study consumers gave the following reasons for not buying online: fear of hackers (21%), lack of products (16%), can't see the products (15%), must reveal personal information (13%), poorly designed site (8%), company reputation (6%), and afraid of money or merchandise getting lost (6%) (Krantz 1998). Expedia researchers came up with the following "speed bumps" to shopping on the Information highway:

- Speed of Web
- Speed of buying process
- Concerns about service and support
- Security
- Overcoming existing relationships

The Internet is *slow*. Curiously enough it is slower in some parts of the country than in others. Boston, for example, has very good response times. In some areas users wait up to 30 seconds or more for a Web page to download. Since online purchases normally require navigating through multiple pages, the experience can be time-consuming and frustrating. The greatest speed bottleneck is the modem in the user's home computer. Many users would realize tremendous speed improvements by upgrading to a 56kpbs modem or, better yet, a cable modem or satellite dish. Nonetheless, until they do upgrade, their Internet experience will be less than optimal.

Rather than *speeding the buying process*, many sites require users to page through numerous screens to locate their item and then page through many screens again in order to complete the purchase. This is bad design. Sites improve their design by having a search facility to quickly locate the item of interest and then instituting a one-click payment system to complete the purchase.

Many users are concerned that *service and support* will not be forthcoming for their Internet purchases. This is a special concern when the company they are dealing with is not well known. These concerns will tend to drive traffic to the better-known sites—even more reason for sites to fight hard early on to establish brand equity.

Users are also concerned about the *security* of online transactions. They want reassurance that their credit card information will not be misappropriated. Most of the fear is more fiction than reality. As was previously discussed, the Internet may be the most secure medium ever devised to complete transactions.

Another barrier to online commerce are the *existing relationships* that consumers have with their retailers. Fortunately for Internet merchants, these relationships are comparatively weak compared with what they were twenty years ago. Nonetheless, users must be given compelling reasons, such as price and service incentives, to circumvent existing relationships.

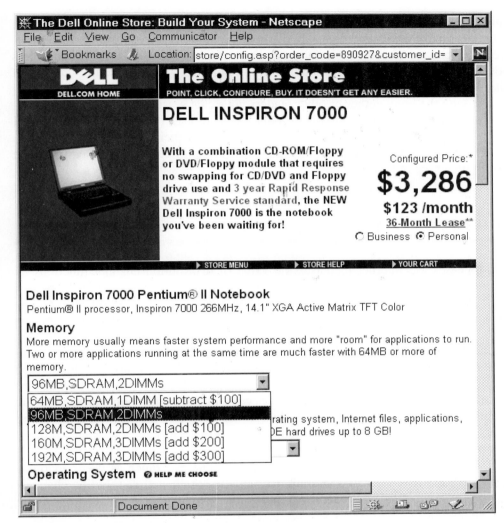

Exhibit 5 - 7 Dell Inspiron: Configuration Options

One lesson from this discussion is that the Web must provide a value-added experience in order to gain customers. This is one of the greatest points of differentiation for Web-based storefronts. There are two major opportunities to provide value-added experiences that would be impractical to deliver via traditional channels. The first is the delivery of innovative services and the second is customization.

In many cases the Internet can deliver a new service that is not otherwise available in any other channel. Some online record stores offer music sampling from thousands of CDs. Prospective shoppers can listen via RealAudio to 30-second clips from selected tracks. Additionally, music stores and bookstores often assist with selection of titles. Collaborative filtering technologies allow vendors to match user preferences with their existing database of users. The matching allows vendors to make informed recommendations about which titles would likely appeal to the user. Such services are not available in music stores and bookstores. Online bookstores provide a plethora of book review information both from national sources and from other readers. Furthermore, the bookstores sometimes give users an opportunity to interact with the book author or other readers via a chat session.

The Internet can also customize product to meet user needs. For example, Dell Computer (www.dell.com) allows customers to configure their machine over the Web. See Exhibit 5 - 7. Consumers can see the exact effect of each option change on the bottom line price of their computer.

S u m m a r y

In most cases the Internet increases the value of distribution channel functions by lowering costs while delivering more timely and customized information. Marketing communications are enhanced through individual targeting and coordination among channel players. Contact with buyers is improved through customizing to buyers needs, offering more sources of referral, and providing more hours of operation. Shopping agents, customized catalogs, collaborative filtering agents, and retail locators all assist in matching product to buyers' needs. Costs of physical distribution are lowered while speed of distribution is increased for any product that can be digitally distributed. Despite consumer concerns, online credit card transactions are probably safer in the Internet channel than in the brick and mortar world. Shopping agents assist in price negotiation. Finally the Internet virtually aggregates product from physically separate sources.

The Internet has not shortened distribution channels as much as was previously anticipated. In some cases the Internet has actually lengthened distribution channels and in other cases the physical-world intermediaries have been replaced by online equivalents.

The Internet has altered power relationships among channel players. In many cases the power of the buyer has been increased as a result of having much better pricing information and access to more suppliers. Conversely, the ability to establish structural relationships with buyers has increased the power of suppliers.

Online retailing is experiencing tremendous growth. Benefits include lower prices, user empowerment, convenience, a no-hassle environment, and comprehensive product offerings. On the other hand, the Web is slow, sites are poorly designed, users are concerned about service, support, and security, and it is difficult to overcome existing relationships with retailers. Fortunately, many of these concerns have remedies.

The Web must provide a value-added experience in order to gain customers. This is one of the greatest points of differentiation for Web-based storefronts. There are two major opportunities to provide value-added experiences that would be impractical to deliver via traditional channels. The first is the delivery of innovative services and the second is customization.

Key Concepts and Terms

1. The Internet may be the most secure distribution channel ever developed.
2. The Web increases the value of market research and lowers its cost.
3. The Internet increases the value of marketing communications primarily by monitoring ad effectiveness and targeting users.
4. In most cases the Internet increases the value of distribution channel functions by lowering costs while delivering more timely and customized information.
5. Disintermediation has not been as prevalent as was initially predicted.
6. Most digitally transacted products are still distributed through traditional channels.
7. The Web replaces many physical-world intermediaries with online equivalents.
8. In some cases the Internet can shorten distribution channels, especially when the product itself is digital.
9. The Web serves to virtually aggregate product to meet consumer needs.
10. In most cases the power of buyers has been increased by the Internet.
11. Suppliers can increase their power in the Internet channel by establishing structural relationships with buyers.
12. Shopping agents and collaborative filtering can efficiently match product to buyers' needs.
13. The goal of EDI is the creation of open systems which can seamlessly exchange information online. That goal has yet to be realized.

- Agent space
- Collaborative filtering agent
- Disintermediation
- Distribution channel
- Electronic Data Interchange (EDI)
- Extensible Markup Language (XML)
- Extranet
- Intermediary
- Intranet
- Open buying on Internet (OBI)
- Open system
- Proprietary system
- Secure Electronic Transactions (SET)
- Shopping agents
- Syndicated selling
- Virtual aggregation

Exercises

REVIEW QUESTIONS FOR KNOWLEDGE TESTING

1. What are the functions of a distribution channel?
2. List five ways in which the Internet increases the value of marketing research.
3. List three ways in which the Internet increases the value of marketing communications.
4. What is virtual aggregation? Give an example.
5. What is disintermediation? Give an example.
6. List six benefits of online retailing.
7. List five obstacles to online retailing.

DISCUSSION QUESTIONS FOR CRITICAL THINKING

1. How does the value of distribution channel functions change when they become Internet based?
2. What is the effect of the Internet on the length of distribution channels?
3. How does the Internet alter the power relationships among channel players?
4. What are the obstacles and success factors for online retailing?
5. What is the relationship between an intranet and an extranet?
6. What is the relationship between EDI and extranets?
7. Is it safe to shop online? Why or why not?

ACTIVITIES

1. Clip an ad for electronic products from the newspaper. Pick a specific computer product and look up the product online using a shopping agent such as www.shopper.com or www.pricescan.com. Complete a table showing how the online prices compare with the local ad.
2. Survey 20 people. Ask them to rate their online purchase experience on a scale of 1 to 10, with 10 as the best. If they have never purchased online, try to find out what stops them. Summarize the results.

INTERNET EXERCISE: HYBRID MARKETING CHANNELS

Many companies have adopted multichannel distribution systems or hybrid marketing channels. These allow companies to reach different customer segments simultaneously. One segment that publishers would like to reach is college students. Traditionally, students have been reached through the campus bookstore, which is probably where you bought this book. But what if the bookstore was out of stock and you needed the text right away? You have alternatives. For example, you can purchase the book directly from Prentice Hall by phone, or you can order it online from a Web bookstore. Visit Prentice Hall at www.prenhall.com/search.html to explore these options. Get price quotes from at least three of the online retailers listed.

Retailer	Price	Shipping Charge	Shipping Time
Campus Bookstore			
Prentice Hall by Phone			
Amazon			
Barnes and Noble (online)			
Borders (online)			

For Discussion

1. Which distribution channel offers the lowest prices (don't forget to include shipping charges)?
2. Is the shipping time for the off-campus channels substantial enough to present a hardship for the college student segment?
3. Are there advantages to the campus bookstore that the off-campus channels cannot provide?
4. What are the advantages to the publisher for maintaining a multichannel distribution system? Disadvantages?
5. Why doesn't Prentice Hall display the text on its site and simply charge users for using and printing it?

Practitioner Perspective

ELECTRONIC COMMERCE

Peter Clemente is vice president of Cyberdialogue/findsvp, a leader in providing Internet-related market research and analysis. He is also the author of State of the Net: The New Frontier. *Mr. Clemente is a graduate of Fordham University in New York, where he received a BA in Political Science and Philosophy in 1981.*

The Internet is rapidly emerging as the next great marketing Mecca, with the power to facilitate and increase sales of a growing range of consumer goods and services, both online and off, as well as to optimize customer relationships. Certainly, many brands and vendors now moving into the online environment see significant promise for extending the "lifetime" of their customers through use of interactive information and communications. In addition, some forward-thinking companies are utilizing direct consumer input via the Internet to accelerate product development. "Online commerce" ultimately is about all of these potentials - and their eventual impact on brand perceptions— resulting fundamentally from the ability to interact with prospects and customers online.

The year 1997 proved to be a watershed year for online commerce. Online sales of consumer goods and services exploded in the second half of the year as millions of consumers gained confidence in both their online skills and the quality of merchants and merchandise now available on the Internet. In a few short years consumer online commerce has become a multibillion-dollar market, already exceeding revenues derived from TV home shopping and infomercials.

Cyberdialogue/findsvp estimates that 11.2 million shoppers purchased $3.3 billion worth of goods online throughout 1997, up from $1.3 billion the prior year. Judging from aggressive growth in the total number of online users over the next five years, consumer online purchasing is expected to reach $34.7 billion by the year 2002.

The direct value of purchases made by consumers online in 1997 is only half the story. The number of adults who went online in search of product information jumped from 54% of total online users in mid-1997 to 71% by year-end. This translates to some 30 million consumers who sought prepurchase product information online. Clearly, online product information has the power to impact online sales, but our survey data show that it also has the power to significantly impact offline brand choices and channels, including local store traffic. In fact, an estimated 10.4 million consumers spent $4.2 billion purchasing products in retail stores after seeking product information online.

Though barely three years old in the eyes of the consumer, interactive shopping has had a profound effect on the traditional shopping behaviors of many Americans. Now that millions of consumers are using the Internet on a daily basis, online activities are beginning to measurably displace, replace, or otherwise fundamentally change the traditional consumer milieu.

Indeed, 23% of online purchasers indicated that Internet use decreases the time they spend shopping, 19% said they shop less at stores, and 14% said they use mail order catalogs less. Below are some additional highlights.

Women who shop online are more likely to shop less at stores or via direct mail than men who shop online. This finding bodes well for the online venue, given the well-documented shopping habits of women.

Shopping displacements of retail stores and direct mail also peak among midlife online shoppers. Since most shoppers are in this age category, this too bodes well for future growth of online shopping.

Not all online shopping leads shoppers away from stores. As was previously noted, one in four (25%) adults online said that after seeking product information online they went to local stores to complete their purchases. Following are some other highlights of Internet shoppers who purchased goods offline:

Some $4.2 billion, at a minimum, in offline purchases were affected by online shopping. This figure is derived by multiplying the 10.4 million shoppers who said they completed their online shopping by going to a local store by the median value of the offline purchases they said were influenced by their use of the Internet. The median reported value of offline spending was $400, while the average value was reported to be 2,838. We assumed the median is more representative, because of self-reporting biases and the impact of a few buyers of big-ticket items on the overall average. This means that the true impact of Internet product information on offline shopping is bound to be more than $4.2 billion because the median is surely lower than the "true" average impact on offline spending.

Shopping at stores after seeking product information is most common among 30- to 49-year-olds, and also increases as the income level rises. Strikingly, the ratio also rises among multiple online purchasers, to 37% who said they purchased at stores after seeking product information online.

Online product seekers who did not place an order, either online or offline, tend to be female, young, and single, and include many full-time students.

Leveraging Technology

TRANSACTION SECURITY

A study conducted for the Lycos corporation (www.lycos.com) by Cyberdialogue/findsvp (www.cyberdialogue.com) in the first quarter of 1998 revealed that transaction security is the number one concern of all users online—and a greater concern among women than it is among men. The other concerns are summarized in the following table.

Issue	Extremely Concerned or Very Concerned
Security of credit card transactions	86%
Protecting privacy	75%
Censorship	72%
Hate group Web sites	47%
Depiction of violence	38%
Pornography	30%

So why the great concern about transaction security? Is the concern legitimate? Is it fear of the unknown? Is it a result of media hype? The irony is that transactions are probably much more secure on the Internet than in the brick and mortar world. To understand why this is so requires exploring the technology behind transaction security.

There are three places that a credit card number could potentially be stolen on the Internet. It could be stolen from a user's home or business computer; it could be stolen in transit from the user's computer to the merchant's Web site; or it could be stolen once it reaches the merchant's site. So how likely are each of these scenarios?

1. **Stolen from the user's computer**: Very unlikely considering that most users do not store credit card numbers on their computers.

2. **Stolen in transit**: Almost impossible and in fact this has never been reported. Encryption algorithms to be described shortly make this possibility very remote.

3. **Stolen at the merchant's site**: Probably the most legitimate user concern. There are three possibilities:

   a. The merchant may be fraudulent.
   b. The merchant may be honest but have a dishonest employee.
   c. The merchant may be honest but fail to protect its database of credit card numbers from hackers.

Encryption algorithms

Encryption algorithms cannot stop dishonest merchants or employees, but they are designed to protect transaction information in transit. Try to read the following encrypted phrase:

   JCRRA JQNKFCAU

If you are clever you may have guessed that the key to decrypt this message is 2. All letters have been shifted two characters to the right in the alphabet.

   A-B-C-D-E-F-G-H-I-J-K-L-M-N-O-P-Q-R-S-T-U-V-W-X-Y-Z

To decrypt we shift back two letters to the left.

   J becomes **H**
   C becomes **A**
   R becomes **P**
   R becomes **P**
   A becomes **Y**

We continue in this fashion until we have the original message, "HAPPY HOLIDAYS." Encryption on the Internet works in a similar fashion except that the key is a very big number, which is almost impossible to guess, and the encryption scheme is a good deal more sophisticated than shifting along the alphabet. In fact the industry standard RSA (named after the inventors Rivest, Shamir, and Adleman) encryption scheme has never been broken outside of university laboratories, and then only with weeks of effort by high-speed computers. All of which means a user's information is quite secure in transit.

When two computers on the Internet communicate in secure mode, the messages are encrypted in both directions. Both Netscape and Internet Explorer have the ability to communicate with a Web site in secure mode. The user's browser encrypts her credit card number and then sends it to the merchant; the merchant in turn encrypts confidential information sent back to the user. Each side uses a key to decrypt the other's message.

But isn't there a problem here? How does the user get the merchant's key to start with? If the merchant sends the key unencrypted then it could be stolen in transit. As amazing as it may seem, this is not a problem. In fact, merchants willingly give out what is known as a public key. However, the encryption algorithms are so clever that while the public key can encrypt the message, the same key cannot decrypt it! Only a complementary private key, which the merchant does not distribute, can decrypt the message. How this is done is beyond the scope of this book. It involves complex polynomial calculations and very large prime numbers.

The software used to handle the encryption is part of the merchant's commerce server. A tiny lock, which appears in the browser window, indicates encrypted communication with the merchant. The design of this lock symbol may have limited the growth of electronic commerce: The consumer might be more reassured by a larger symbol, a change in screen color, or any other significant visual cue that the transaction is secure. Where browsers failed, merchants picked up the cue. Before entering secure mode, many merchants transfer the user to a page that explains the security of the transaction. See Exhibit 5 - 8. Exhibit 5 - 9 shows that the user has chosen to enter secure mode. Note how Amazon continues to reassure the user even on the secure mode screen!

Encryption protects the transaction while it is in transit between your computer and the retailer. Sometimes, however, the retailer does not adequately protect the records stored on its computer. In one security breach, the online storefronts of ESPN SportsZone and NBA.com were "broken into." The hacker stole the credit card numbers and e-mail addresses of hundreds of customers. As proof, he then sent each person e-mail containing his or her card number.

How does this happen? The fact is that most Web servers are very secure if properly installed and maintained. But in the rush to get things done, Information System professionals sometimes get sloppy. Passwords are set to easily guessed names, passwords are loosely shared, or some accounts are enabled without passwords. Hackers usually begin by obtaining access to an account with very limited access to protected computer resources. However, using that account they compromise an account with a bit more access. They continue to work their way up from account to account until they have sufficient access to compromise the system.

Merchants can protect themselves by trying to break into their own systems or hiring professionals to do so. Professionals are able to recognize flaws in the security system of the merchant's computer and suggest remedies to make it more secure. There are even computer programs such as Smurf, PingOdeath, and Satan Scan that merchants can use to attack their own sites. And of course there are corresponding intrusion detection systems, such as Real Secure and Entrust, that can notify the merchant of an actual attack by recognizing the digital signatures of these attack programs. These software systems experience short but sweet product life cycles: first a new attack program comes along, then a detection program is upgraded to counteract it, then a new attack program is designed and the cycle continues with increasing sophistication.

Exhibit 5 - 8   Amazon Explains Safety of Online Transacations

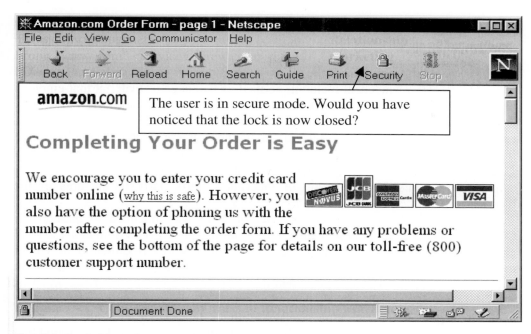

Exhibit 5 - 9 User Enters Secure Mode

Ethics and Law

EXPRESSION ON THE INTERNET

The Internet has been described as the public square of the digital era. Like its classical counterparts, the digital forum is a dynamic combination of voices which express opinions and interests as diverse as the users who populate its networks. At its best, this pluralism provides a positive resource for vigorous debate and the exchange of a wide variety of information. There are also negative aspects to this situation, highlighted by the transmission of such material as child pornography, false or misleading reports, or defamatory statements.

Since the Internet is a global entity, it is extremely difficult to make broad statements about how its content is regulated in various countries. In the future, treaties may provide some uniform standards, but currently, what is allowed is largely a question of national law. In American jurisprudence, any regulation of expression is considered within the context of the First Amendment to the U.S. Constitution. In addition to its unambiguous wording that no law shall be made abridging the freedom of speech or of the press, the Supreme Court has narrowly limited the ability of Congress to enact restrictive laws. As Justice Oliver Wendell Holmes stated in 1919, "the ultimate good desired is better reached by free trade in ideas."

Expression may be regulated under certain conditions. Such situations include the presence of obscenity, generally defined as that which a reasonable person would find appeals to prurient interest, describes patently offensive sexual conduct, and lacks serious literary, artistic, political, or scientific value (*Miller* v. *California*, 413 U. S. 15 [1973]), or indecent material, defined as language or material that employs patently offensive terms to describe sexual or excretory functions. While obscenity enjoys no constitutional protection, expression that is indecent is protected by the First Amendment and may be regulated only in the furtherance of a "compelling state interest" (*Sable Communications of California, Inc.* v. *Federal Communications Commission*, 492 U.S. 115 [1989]). The protection of minors stands as a prime example of permissible regulation of indecency, particularly in the area of the broadcast media.

In 1996, the Telecommunications Act of 1996 was amended to include the Computer Decency Act (CDA), which in relevant part, made it a criminal act to send an "obscene or indecent" communication to a recipient who was known to the sender to be under 18 years of age. An additional provision made it an offense to use an "interactive computer service" to present material that "depicts or describes, in terms patently offensive, as measured by contemporary community standards, sexual or excretory organs" in a context available to minors. In 1997, in the case of *Reno* v. *American Civil Liberties Union* (117 S. Ct. 2329), the U.S. Supreme Court found that these provisions were unconstitutionally vague, prohibiting, among other things, the exchange of information about such subjects as AIDS and reproductive decisionmaking. It further noted that the provisions would hinder or "chill" adult speech through the placement of undue burdens.

The *Reno* decision indicates that the Supreme Court will tolerate only narrowly defined constraints upon electronic speech. This, however, does not mean that all prohibitions will be struck down. Currently, a second CDA has been proposed in Congress (S.1482, introduced on November 8, 1997). This bill, drafted in terms that are more precise than in its predecessor, creates adult-only zones for sexually explicit material deemed harmful to minors. Unlike the CDA, this legislation is directed only toward commercial entities. The use of electronic zoning, requiring a form of identification, may become a legally accepted means of restricting access to sensitive material in the wake of the *Reno* decision.

Another popular means of restricting access, and thought by many to avoid the chilling effects outlined in the *Reno* decision, is known as the Platform for Internet Content Selection Rules (PICS). This application allows the filtering of sites that are deemed to be inappropriate for minors. Advocates claim that PICS will place control into the hands of parents and schools. Some civil rights groups are concerned that this device, which works behind the scenes, presents a subtle, but powerful means of censorship.

A separate issue which concerns expression on the Internet is the question of liability for defamatory statements. Often, the writer of such material is using an account obtained from an Online Service Provider. A question before the courts has been whether such providers may be held responsible for that which is published by their customers. Under conventional laws, persons deemed to be publishers of defamatory material can be held liable, whereas those who merely distribute published information are not deemed to be at fault. In *Cubby, Inc.* v. *CompuServe, Inc.* (776 S.D.N.Y. 1991), a court held that a provider would not be considered a publisher of defamatory material since it had no editorial control over its accused customer's activities nor had realistic means of review of its customer's expression. The *Cubby* court found that the function of online providers was similar to that of a public library, bookstore, or newsstand. To hold such entities accountable would, in the court's opinion, impose excessive burdens upon the free flow of information.

In contrast, the matter of *Stratton Oakmont, Inc. et al.* v. *Prodigy Services Co., et. al* (1995 Misc. Lexis 229 [N.Y. Sup. Ct. Nassau Co., 1995]), the court found that the provider could be held responsible for defamatory statements placed on its bulletin board. In this case, unlike that of *Cubby*, it was noted that the particular provider had held itself out as a stricter type of bulletin board system, making efforts to control user content and therefore exercising more power than that of a mere distributor.

These cases strongly suggest that the boundaries of expression will continue to be challenged by the Internet. While specific outcomes remain open to question, it appears that expression will be protected when the courts and the legislatures realize the purpose and importance of electronic communication. Education of all parties involved may prove to be the best security for the continued flourishing of online speech.

S a v v y   S i t e s

Web Site and Address	Importance to Net Marketers
Amazon Bookstore www.amazon.com	Amazon is "the world's largest bookstore." First-time visitors to the site should check out *About our Store* to get quickly familiarized with Amazon. To find a particular book, go to *Search* and enter a title, author, or words in the title. For best-selling business books, go to *Amazon Business 50*. And for books about computing and the Internet, visit the *Super Room*.

American Marketing Association www.ama.org/	The American Marketing Association is the biggest society of marketing professionals on the globe. This Web sites features industry news, marketing information, and professional development opportunities to the society's 45,000 members. To find the juiciest content on the site, click on the *Resources* icon. There are also links to the AMA's own publications, including *Marketing News* and the *Journal of Marketing Research.*
AudioNet www.audionet.com/	AudioNet is a site devoted to the phenomenon of broadcasting media over the Internet. The site features live and on-demand broadcasts of audio and visual media to Internet users. Online software to receive Internet broadcasts is available here. Some of the offerings include 24-hour Grateful Dead radio and Rush Limbaugh's greatest hits.
DigiCash www.digicash.com/	DigiCash is a software developer that offers an electronic money system called E-cash. E-cash acts as a common currency for transactions performed over the Internet. This is an alternative to using credit cards. This Web site provides a complete explanation of the E-cash concept and its advantages.
Internet Shopping Network www4.internet.net/	The Internet Shopping Network is one of the largest online malls. ISN allows you to advertise your own products at its site. The dominant themes of the site are computer and home electronic products.
INTERSHOP www.intershop.com	INTERSHOP Communications is a firm that develops and distributes eCommerce software, which is used to integrate storefront creation tools, business management tools, and hosting services. The software tools are designed for merchants, developers, Web designers, and hosts to exploit fully the business and creative potential of electronic commerce.
L.L. Bean www.llbean.com	If you want to see how clothes are sold online, visit L.L. Bean's Web site. However, if your modem is slow, you'll have to wait five minutes to download an opening graphic of a family canoeing.
Mastercard www.mastercard.com/	Mastercard's site allows you to apply for a card online. It also provides information about the firm's new secured Internet commerce services.
Music Boulevard www.musicblvd.com	Music Boulevard is like a music version of Amazon. Here you will find an extensive collection of music, along with downloadable samples and some interesting recommendation tools that match your music interests with those of others.

Network Frontiers www.netfrontiers.com	Network Frontiers site contains information and services related to Internet Commerce. You can find definitions of terms, online courses, books, consulting services, and other stuff related to Internet Commerce.
Pointcast www.pointcast.com	Pointcast was the first to implement "push" technology on the Internet. With this technology, your computer automatically goes out on the net and retrieves information as your computer sits idle. The software to operate this program is offered at this site and is easy to download.
The *Wall Street Journal* www.wsj.com	The *Wall Street Journal* online edition has been one of the more successful online subscription publications. A yearly subscription is $40 a year and includes many helpful supplements that don't come with the print edition.

Chapter 6

Marketing Communications on the Net

"Advertisers have every right to put all the ads on the Web they want and users have every right to try to block [the ads]."

–James Howard, former CEO of PrivNet

Chapter Outline

- The PrivNet Story
- Introduction
- Integrated Marketing Communication (IMC)
- The Net as a Medium

Practitioner Perspective

Exploding the Web CPM Myth
—Rick Boyce, Senior Vice President, Advertising and Commerce, Wired Digital

Leveraging Technology

Proxy Servers and Cache

Ethics and Law

Spam

Learning Objectives

- Marketing review
  - Define four promotion-mix tools
  - Explain the strengths and weaknesses of traditional media
  - Describe the importance of effectiveness and efficiency for media buying
- Differentiate brand and direct response advertising online
- Identify public relations stakeholders and common Net content directed to them
- Explain how the Net's interactive abilities are used to enhance customer service
- Discuss the power of online sales promotions to capture user attention
- Differentiate among broadcast, narrowcast, and pointcast electronic media
- Tell the strengths and weaknesses of the Web as an advertising medium
- Identify several ways to measure the Web audience, giving the strengths of each

The PrivNet Story

Removing banner ads is] a cute thing to do, but a lot of people find advertising is a key form of information. I think it's a prank, and I don't think it will be allowed to catch on. If advertising fails, content providers die, and people have no reason to go to the Internet."

— Kevin O'Connor, CEO of DoubleClick

Perhaps it is appropriate that a theater student would lead the high-profile drama of threatening Internet advertising. James Howard is 28 years old, retired, plays his guitar, travels, and as a hobby manages singer Suzanne Vega's Web site. Not many would guess that in December 1995 his company, PrivNet, created a product that threatened to bring Internet advertising—now a billion-dollar industry—to its knees.

At the time Howard was a senior at the University of North Carolina, Chapel Hill. One night while watching a *Nova* special on TV about the Internet and its pending heavy commercialization, he got the idea for a product to eliminate ads. On Halloween night of 1995 he floated his idea at a friend's house and PrivNet was born. Within a week the company was up and running. Howard financed the company with his trust fund savings and brought aboard four of his fellow classmates. The company made three main products. Its flagship product, and the one that received the most media attention, was called Internet Fast Forward (IFF). The inspiration for the product's name was the VCR. One major use of VCRs is to record TV shows and then watch them afterwards. Users often fast-forward through the commercials to save time. Howard's company extended this idea to the Internet by creating a product that would filter banner ads from Web pages. The users would see the entire Web page without the ad.

The motivation for Howard's product was the same as that for the VCR: to save time. IFF saves users time by eliminating the ad and with it the extra time it would have taken to load. Nonetheless, Howard estimates that only 30% of his market were interested in saving time. The other 70% were opposed to Internet ads on ideological grounds since they felt that ads represented the soiling of a heretofore noncommercial medium.

The PrivNet story created a media sensation. The company was featured on CNN, in *Wired*, on the *Pathfinder* site, and even in *Scientific American*. Howard found the *Scientific American* piece particularly amusing since there was very little science in the IFF product.

PrivNet quickly distributed an estimated 200,000 beta (test) copies. The ads were relatively easy to detect by IFF since many Web pages do not serve their own ads. Instead they rely on third parties such as DoubleClick to insert the ad into the content provider's Web page. The Web page and ad are seamlessly integrated so that most users have no idea that they originate from different sources (did you?). IFF stored the addresses of all the known ad servers and blocked the ads that they served to the user's computer. Pretty nifty, but one cannot expect Madison Avenue to take such a product lightly.

Two factors conspired to terminate IFF. First were lawsuits. Companies such as Starwave threatened PrivNet with legal action for tampering with their content. PrivNet might have eventually won these lawsuits. After all, by analogy would it make sense to sue VCR users for fast-forwarding through commercials or sue a scissors company because users cut out magazine ads with their product? Nonetheless, lawsuits are expensive and PrivNet did not have the resources to fight. Fortunately for them, they did not have to go to court. Another company, Pretty Good Privacy (PGP), bought PrivNet. PGP was after an e-mail product produced by PrivNet. PGP had no interest in IFF and it died on the vine. This was somewhat surprising considering the product's popularity and potential market. In fact the entire transaction is a bit murky. Perhaps PGP, already embroiled in lawsuits with the government for its own encryption product, was not anxious to step into yet another legal quagmire—and PGP had real assets to lose. However, this is not the rationale they gave at the time. When queried as to why PGP would discontinue IFF, a PGP spokesman replied, "It's really more of an issue of alienating the entire industry that relies on advertising for revenues and enables the Web to be free, basically." Said another spokesman, "We want commerce to thrive."

But the idea of blocking ads lives on. In 1998 two companies released products for ad filtering. One of these, CyberSitter (www.cybersitter.com), made ad filtering an add-on to their popular pornography-filtering software. The other company, Intermute (www.intermute.com), sells a stand-alone product which allows users to filter ads selectively —for example, filtering out only those ads containing animation. What is curious is that neither product has attracted much media attention—certainly nowhere near the attention that PrivNet received for IFF. One has to wonder why. Perhaps the change is a result of shifting user demographics. IFF was released at a time when the antiadvertising purists made up a sizable percentage of the Net population. And while their numbers may not have decreased, millions more mainstream users have come online. For these users ads are just a part of the landscape.

What are James Howard's plans for the future? For now he's content to be retired, play his guitar, and take pictures. He is also a closet fan of the Intermute product and wonders if it has made any money. But he occasionally receives offers from venture capitalists and would consider going back into business if he ever gets bored.

Introduction

In this chapter, we discuss the Net as a tool for marketing communication messages between marketers and their desired audiences (e.g., advertising). This, along with marketing research and distribution functions, are the major strengths and uses of the Internet for marketers. We examine the Net for marketing communications from two perspectives: first, each marketing communications tool is described in detail with respect to its full capability to carry messages over the Net, and second, the Net is considered as just another communications medium along with television, magazines, and others for media buyers purchasing promotional space.

Integrated Marketing Communication (IMC)

Integrated Marketing Communication (IMC) is a comprehensive plan of communication that includes advertising, sales promotion, public relations, personal selling, and the rest of the marketing mix to provide maximum communication impact with stakeholders. Price, product features (e.g., guarantees, packaging), type of distribution outlet (e.g., online retailer, discount retailer, catalog), and promotions all work to create product awareness, brand attitudes, and purchase intent in the consumer. However, the focus here will be on the promotion-mix elements. The chapter begins by reviewing definitions, then moves onto Internet advertising models.

The following is a brief review of definitions of the key promotion-mix elements along with Internet examples of each.

- *Advertising* is nonpersonal communication of information, usually paid for and usually persuasive in nature about products (goods and services) or ideas by an identified sponsor through various media. Banner ads and buttons are currently the predominant forms of online advertising; however, sponsorships and other forms are emerging.

- *Sales promotions* are short-term incentives of gifts or money that facilitate the movement of products from producer to enduser. Some firms e-mail sales promotions to customers and potential customers. Promotions may also appear in banner ads or on a site's Web page itself.

- *Public relations* consists of activities that influence public opinion and create goodwill for the organization. Many Web sites are designed to serve as public relations vehicles. The Rollerblade site is a great example of public relations (www.rollerblade.com). Comprehensive information is offered about all facets of the sport of inline skating.

- *Personal selling* is a direct face-to-face presentation to potential buyers. By definition, personal selling is not possible on the Internet, though the Internet can be used to generate sales leads.

Integration and consistency of message across all of the promotion pieces is important in order to create synergy with other marketing-mix tools.

INTERNET ADVERTISING

All paid-for space on a Web site or in an e-mail is considered advertising: conversely, the Web site itself is not advertising, even if it is sponsored by a commercial firm. This model parallels the traditional media model, in which companies create content and then sell space to advertisers. Advertising is used to create awareness, provide information, create positive attitudes about products (image), and remind users about product. Advertising can build brand equity and solicit direct response from the consumer. Internet advertising is projected to reach $1 billion in 1998. If the first quarter is any indication, this projection is low: the Internet Advertising Bureau (IAB) announced first quarter 1998 advertising revenues to be $351.3 million (www.iab.net). This is a 271% increase over the first quarter of 1997 and continues the upward growth pattern seen each quarter.

Exciting as this is for Web companies, advertiser spending on the Internet represents "half a cherry in a thousand," or "a few zeros to the right of the decimal" (Doyle et al. 1997, p. 6). To understand the context of the $1 billion spent on Net advertising, consider that total advertising expenditures in the United States during 1995 reached $162.7 billion (Meeker 1997), and over $400 billion worldwide in 1996. The market potential is tremendous. See Exhibit 6 - 1.

Medium	1995 Expenditures (in billions of dollars)	Medium	1995 Expenditures (in billions of dollars)
Television	38.1	Farm Publications	0.3
Radio	11.3	Direct Mail	32.8
Newspapers	36.3	Business Publications	3.6
Magazines	8.6	Outdoor	1.3
Yellow Pages	10.2	Other	20.2

Exhibit 6 - 1 U.S. Media Expenditures
Adapted from Meeker 1997

Which industries are advertising online? According to IAB, during the first quarter of 1998 most ad spending came from the following product categories:

- computing (27%)
- consumer-related (25%)
- telecom (14%)
- financial services (13%)
- new media (10%)

Brand versus Direct-Response Advertising

Advertising can be used either to build brands or to elicit a direct response in the form of a transaction or some other behavior. "Brand advertising creates a distinct favorable image that customers associate with a product at the moment they make buying decisions" (Doyle et al. 1997). Direct-response advertising seeks to create action such as inquiry or purchase from consumers as a result of seeing the ad. Brand advertising works at the attitude level of the hierarchy-of-effects model, while direct response works at the behavioral level (chapter 1).

Forrester qualitative research conducted in late 1997 shows that the Net is not particularly well suited for brand advertising at this time. The best media for brand advertising are TV and magazines, followed by radio and newspapers. As a branding medium, the Internet suffers as a result of low bandwidth and a relatively small audience. The lack of bandwidth is especially problematic for products requiring a strong emotional appeal. These products are better served by the high-bandwidth TV medium, which can provide the multimedia environment in which to showcase the product. While the Internet audience size continues to grow, its reach is still small compared with that of television. Specifically, in the United States there are approximately 60 million Internet users but about 260 million TV users. Nonetheless, dollars continue to pour into Internet branding strategies. Estimated spending on branding on Net for 1997 was $240 million, and in 1998 it was $450 million (Doyle et al. 1997). Exhibit 6 - 3 displays the actual and projected Internet advertising dollars spent on branding and direct response from 1997 through 2002, both in tabular and graphic format

The Net's big strength is direct-response advertising. Direct response leverages the Internet's unique opportunity for two-way communication with consumers. In one manifestation of this model, the consumer clicks through a banner ad to the sponsoring Web site. There she obtains further information about the product and has the opportunity to complete the transaction online. Direct response also allows for impulse buying. Estimated direct-response advertising spending on Net for 1998 was $550 million. This figure is projected to triple in 1999 (Doyle et al. 1997). See Exhibit 6 - 2 and Exhibit 6 - 3.

	Brand Advertising	Direct Response	Total
1997	$.24	$.24	**$.48**
1998	.45	.55	**1.00**
1999	.35	1.40	**1.75**
2000	1.00	3.10	**4.10**
2001	1.70	3.90	**5.60**
2002	3.20	4.90	**8.10**

Exhibit 6 - 2 Internet Ad Spend (billions of dollars)
Source: Forrester Research (Doyle et al. 1997)

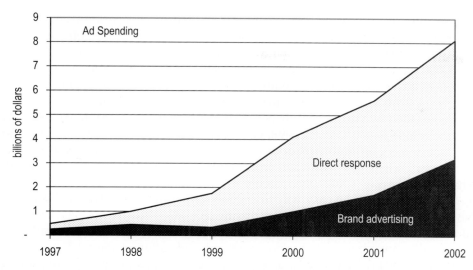

Exhibit 6 - 3 Ad Spending on the Internet: Actual and Projected
Source: Forrester Research (Doyle et al. 1997)

Internet Advertising Models

Two models for Internet advertising are text-based and multimedia-based advertising. Both models have useful applications. Text-based advertising operates through e-mail and bulletin boards. Multimedia advertising utilizes banners, buttons, interstitials, and sponsorships.

Text-Based Advertising Online

E-mail is the online equivalent of direct-mail advertising. However, e-mail has at least two advantages over direct mail. First, there are no postage charges. By contrast, direct mail costs average one dollar per household. Second, e-mail offers a convenient avenue for direct response. E-mail ads often direct users to Web sites using hyperlinks. At the Web site the user can obtain further information or complete a transaction.

E-mail distribution lists can be either generated or purchased. Lists are generated through Web site registrations, subscription registrations, or purchase records. Many sites require registration in order to access free information. At the time of registration, the site learns the user's e-mail address. The same is true for subscriptions or purchases. Harvesting addresses off of newsgroups or online e-mail directories can also generate lists, though this practice is questionable, for reasons to be mentioned shortly.

Lists can also be purchased from list brokers. These firms do not usually hand over the list but will send a company's e-mail message to massive distribution lists. Marketers should search for lists that are guaranteed to be 100% opt-in. This means that users have voluntarily agreed to receive commercial e-mail about topics that might be of interest to them. PostMaster Direct Response (www.postmasterdirect.com) has over a million opt-in names and e-mail addresses segmented by 9,000 categories. The cost is about $0.20 per 1,000 names. Compare this to a typical "snail mail" list at $20 per 1,000 names. BonusMail has 150,000 high-income consumers who agree to receive e-mail ads in exchange for credits that can be used for Web shopping.

Successful firms structure their e-mail advertisements so that they are welcomed rather than resented by the target audience. For example, when Amazon expanded its business to include music sales in 1998, company CEO Jeff Bezos sent a message to Amazon's customers informing them of the new product offering. Microsoft e-mails registered users when new software product patches are available for download. Even harmless messages like that should be judiciously distributed and should always offer the recipient an easy way to decline further messages. Doing this builds positive user relationships and minimizes dissatisfaction.

All of this caution serves notice that Netizens do not like unsolicited e-mail. The Net culture still views it as an unwelcome commercialization of the medium. Users have even developed the term *spam* as a pejorative reference to this type of e-mail. Furthermore, the Net is a community. Recipients of e-mail perceived as spam can vent their opposition to thousands of users in public newsgroup forums, thereby quickly generating negative publicity for the organization. The Nike Corporation is so sensitive to spam that it publishes an anti-spam policy right on their home page which reads as follows:

> OK, so you're on your computer minding your own business and you get an e-mail telling you about a special offer from Nike for free shoes, or some other golden opportunity. Don't believe it. It's not real.
>
> For the record, Nike doesn't send out unsolicited e-mails. From time to time we'll notify consumers who let us know they want to hear from us. Otherwise, any information on the Internet from Nike to the public comes on www.nike.com or www.nikebiz.com.

Spammers routinely harvest e-mail addresses from newsgroup postings and then spam all the newsgroup members. Spam lists can also be generated from public directories such as those provided by many universities in order to look up student e-mail addresses. Spammers often hide their return e-mail address so that the recipients cannot reply to the spammer. Other unscrupulous tactics include spamming through a legitimate organization's e-mail server so that the message appears to come from an employee of that organization.

Some measures have been put in place to limit spam. DejaNews filters spam postings from its Usenet archives (www.dejanews.com). Many moderated newsgroups also filter spam. Some e-mail programs offer users the option to filter spam as well. There have also been a number of suits filed by ISPs seeking to recover costs from spammers for the load put on their systems by the tremendous number of messages. It is important to remember that all unsolicited e-mail is considered spam, but just as with direct mail, when the e-mail is appropriate and useful to the recipient, it is welcomed, unsolicited or not.

A bulletin board or newsgroup is an area where users can post messages on selected topics for other users to read. The largest public newsgroup forum is the Usenet, which has 50,000 groups used by over 24 million people (source: www.dejanews.com). Two-thirds of the messages posted to Usenet are commercial in nature and normally are not welcomed by the newsgroup members. Many firms will also cross-post (post the same item under many different newsgroups), thus flooding multiple newsgroups with unwelcome advertisements. Such unsolicited postings are a form of spam. As a general rule users participate in newsgroups to obtain information and otherwise interact with other users, not to read ads. This is generally not a good forum in which to advertise. Many firms maintain private bulletin boards on their Web sites for this purpose, however. Expedia allows users to post travel information and Amazon maintains bulletin board-like book review postings from customers. Bulletin board ads are a good idea when users understand and accept that the forum is sponsored by commercial firms.

A LISTSERV is an e-mail discussion group with regular subscribers. Each message that members send to the LISTSERV is forwarded to all subscribed members. Advertisers can pay to sponsor the LISTSERV: For example, Apple Computer and Symantec sponsor the CyberSchool LISTSERV. LISTSERVs push content to subscribed users, sending it to individual desktops, whereas bulletin boards require users to visit the page and pull content.

Multimedia-Based Advertising Online

Multimedia based advertising is the primary model on the Web. Most advertising expenditures are for banner ads (55%) with sponsorships a close and growing second (40%), and interstitials (4%) and others (1%) following in use (www.iab.net). By the time this book is in print an entirely new form may have emerged: thus is the pace of Internet advertising. Each commonly used form is discussed in the following section.

Banners and Buttons

Banners and buttons occupy designated space for rent on Web pages. This is similar to the print advertising model used by magazines and newspapers, except on the Net there are video and audio capabilities in that few square inches of space. Buttons are square or round and banners are rectangular. The Internet Advertising Bureau (www.iab.net) and the Coalition for Advertising Supported Information and Entertainment (www.casie.com) proposed standard dimensions for buttons and banners. See Exhibit 6 - 4. The dimensions of buttons and banners are measured in pixels. A monitor set to standard VGA resolution has screen dimensions of 640 horizontal pixels by 480 vertical pixels.

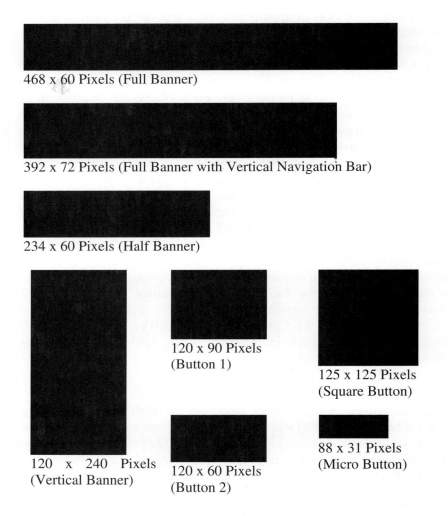

468 x 60 Pixels (Full Banner)

392 x 72 Pixels (Full Banner with Vertical Navigation Bar)

234 x 60 Pixels (Half Banner)

120 x 90 Pixels
(Button 1)

125 x 125 Pixels
(Square Button)

88 x 31 Pixels
(Micro Button)

120 x 240 Pixels
(Vertical Banner)

120 x 60 Pixels
(Button 2)

Exhibit 6 - 4 IAB/CASIE Ad Banner Sizes
Source: www.casie.com

Evolution of banners: Banner advertising has evolved substantially since the first banner ad on *HotWired* in 1994. The first stage featured banners that called out "click here," "free," and "download" in bright colors. This was to train users that banners were indeed interactive and that by clicking on them the user would be transported to another Web site. Most banners are hyperlinked to the advertiser's site. Users have since become savvy to the notion that banners have click-through capability, though some marketers still feel that the "click here" message is effective: See Exhibit 6 - 5. Like everything else on the Web, when the novelty wears off, content is what captures the user's attention. The same is true for banners. To distract a user from the site itself, the message in the banner must appeal to his needs.

The second stage of banner advertising featured banners with animation. Movement captures attention on an otherwise static page. Many banner ads today feature animation. A file called an animated GIF (Graphic Interchange Format) usually provides the animation. Animated GIF files consist of a series of frames each containing a separate picture. The animation results from rotating the frames with very short time delays between each one. The animation can be either continuous (which is somewhat annoying) or can loop through once, stopping on the final frame. Some animation is used to simulate movement while other animation is designed simply to expose the user to a sequence of messages. See Exhibit 6 - 6 for a five-frame animated banner ad from Mazda.

The third stage of banner advertising features the interactive banner. There are many varieties of interaction. Some banners sense the position of the mouse on the Web page and begin to animate faster and faster as the user approaches. Other banners have built-in games such as pong. Still other banners have drop-down menus, check boxes, and search boxes to engage and empower the user. Exhibit 6 - 7 displays a banner ad that allows users to interact in many ways.

Exhibit 6 - 5 Yahoo! Pager Banner

Exhibit 6 - 6 Mazda Protege Banner Ad

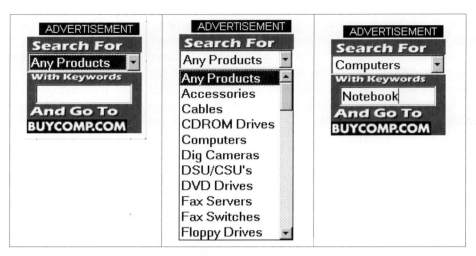

Exhibit 6 - 7 BuyComp Interactive Banner

Exhibit 6 - 8 Eddie Bauer Jeans Point-of-Sale Ad

All of the ads examined up to now have functioned via click-through. By clicking on the ad, the user is transported to the merchant's Web site, where the transaction or other objective is actually achieved. This means that the user must leave the site that he is browsing. Narrative.com has developed an alternative technology which allows the entire transaction to take place right in the banner, keeping the user on the original site! In other words the banner becomes an interactive point of sale. The software is called Enliven/Impulse. To see just how amazing this is, consider the screen shots taken from the Enliven/Impulse ad for Eddie Bauer jeans in Exhibit 6 - 8. Note the progression of frames in the ad to lead the user through the entire order process.

The ad is actually a Java applet (small program) which is downloaded to the user's computer. The user interacts with the applet to complete the order process. Everything that the user types is sent by the applet back to Eddie Bauer's site. Now as technologically amazing as this seems—is it really any better than the ads described earlier? Will interactive ads generate more user input? Narrative claims that they do. If true, Enliven/Impulse may herald in a new generation of interactive ads which capture the user's attention, imagination, and business. These transactional banners may become the fourth generation of banner advertising.

One downside of the movement toward interactive banners is that they tend to require more bandwidth. Keeping banner file sizes small reduces the time that they take to load. Ads under 9K in size tend to appear before most content on a given Web page. Therefore the ad is spotlighted on the user's screen if only for a split second. Users may not wait for large banner ads to download. The user may follow a hyperlink off of the page before the ad loads–effectively making the ad invisible.

Banner effectiveness: How effective is banner advertising? Some say not at all, yet the advertising dollars pour in. To shed light on this question, it is important to measure effectiveness against the banner's objective. Web banners help build brand awareness. IAB researchers tested twelve banner ads and found an average 5% increase in brand awareness with just one exposure (www.mbinteractive.com). Other researchers found from 9% to 23% increases in brand awareness from Web browser, ISP, and men's apparel banners (Briggs & Hollis 1997). Banners also help build brand images. IAB found Volvo banner ads increased brand perceptions 55%, and Briggs and Hollis conclude that banners cause people to change brand attitudes. The top banner ads are seen by as many as 5 million unique viewers a week.

The centerpiece of banner advertising, however, is behaviors such as click-through and transactions. We might conjecture that the Eddie Bauer ad in Exhibit 6 - 8 attempted to create transactions with brand-building as a secondary goal. So, how many users click on a banner? Click-through rates for banners vary, but the average is 2.6% (www.ipro.com). In the IAB study just mentioned, the click-through rate was 4%.

Millward Brown International summarizes Web advertising effectiveness with its FORCE score (First Opportunity to see Reaction Created by the Execution) (Briggs & Hollis 1997). This system allows the researchers to combine many effectiveness variables over time and use them to compare media. The Web received a score of 12, better than television's 10 score but not as effective as print advertising with a score of 18. Web banners score quite well compared with TV ads.

Banners are quite helpful for brand communication but do not drive much traffic to a site. To increase banner effectiveness, marketers use selective targeting as well as design factors. Just as in traditional advertising, the more relevant the ad, the better the chance that it will grab the viewer's attention and create attitude and behavior changes. To assist advertisers, many search engines (e.g., Yahoo!) allow advertisers to buy key words so that their banner appears only when a user enters those words. Naturally, keyword buys are higher cost since they reach a more highly targeted audience. Another way to increase relevance is to use an ad network. These firms store banner ads on their servers and distribute them to Web site users according to geographic location and psychographics. For example, users who visit a site about dogs may receive a pet food banner ad the next time they stop by one of the ad network's client Web sites. The largest ad network is Link Exchange, which reached 39.9% of Web users in June 1998 through its one million Web site network (www.linkexchange.com). Other ad networks include DoubleClick, Flycast, and Burst! Media.

Sponsorships

Sponsorships integrate editorial content and advertising—something traditional publishers abhor. Most traditional media clearly separate content from advertising; however, women's magazines are the exception. Food advertisers usually barter for recipes that include their products in these magazines, and fashion advertisers get mentions of their clothing in articles. This practice pleases advertisers because it both gives them additional exposure and creates the impression that the publication endorses their products. This blending of content by two firms is becoming increasingly adopted by Web sites: It now comprises 40% of all Web advertising expenditures. Two firms building Web content together is called co-branding, but when one charges the other for content space on the Web site, it is an advertising sponsorship.

Sponsorships are blooming on the Web as banner clutter rises and as more firms build synergistic partnerships to provide useful content. Sponsorships are particularly well suited for the Web because in many ways the commercial side of the Web is simply a series of firms clamoring after similar targets. Traditional publishers such as NBC (www.MSNBC.com) and *People* magazine (www.pathfinder.com) are only a small part of the companies doing business online. Another reason that sponsorships are an increasing source of advertising revenues for Web sites is the interactive possibilities. Examples of sponsorships include Dockers on *HotWired* Dream Jobs page and Microsoft's sponsorship of Hotmail. ServiceMaster sponsors the Handy Home Advisor on the HomeArts site (www.homearts.com). This sponsorship is displayed in Exhibit 6 - 9 and Exhibit 6 - 10.

Exhibit 6 - 9 ServiceMaster Sponsors Handy Home Advisor
Source: www.homearts.com

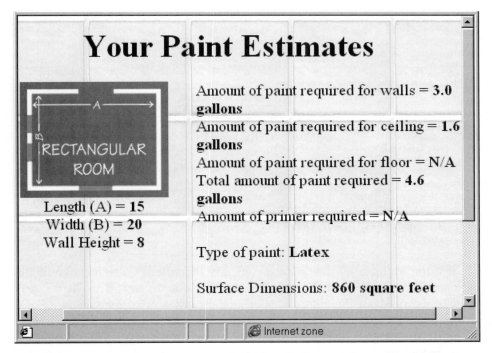

Exhibit 6 - 10 Handy Home Advisor Paint Estimator for a 15 x 20 Room
Source: www.homearts.com

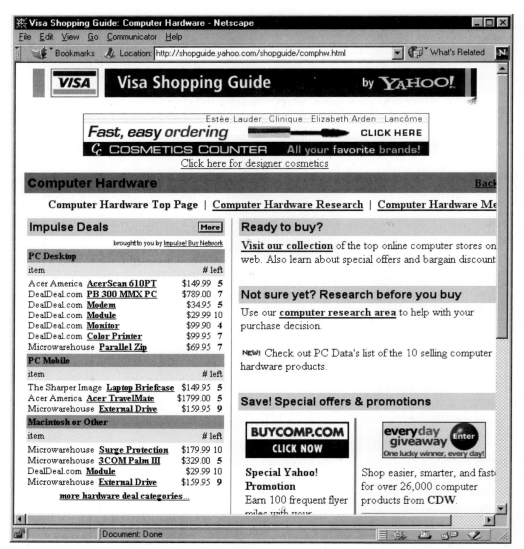

Exhibit 6 - 11 Sponsorships or Content?
Source: www.yahoo.com

Note that in Exhibit 6 - 9 the sponsor is clearly identified. Consumers know that this content is brought to them by ServiceMaster in conjunction with Home Arts. Some people worry about the ethics of sponsorships when consumers cannot easily identify the content author(s). Perhaps this is not a problem, because many users view the entire Web as one giant advertisement, but when advertising is passed off as locally generated content, it has the potential to lower trust in the Web site and thus hurt brand image. Examine Exhibit 6 - 11 from the Yahoo! site and see if you can tell what words Yahoo! authored and what words came from other firms. Most of the material on this page appears to be paid-for sponsorship or banner advertising and on quick glance looks like mostly Yahoo!-authored material. It would be interesting to determine whether or not users understand this fact and the accompanying bias in information content. Could this page hurt the fine Yahoo! image?

Interstitials

Interstitials or intermercials are Java-based ads which appear while the publisher's content is loading. They represent only 4% of all Web advertising expenditures. Interstitials held great promise when they were introduced, but they seem to be on the wane. One reason is that they are hard to execute properly, and another is that they give the impression of lengthening user waiting time: not good. The next iteration of interstitials is called *daughter windows*. These ads usually appear in a separate window which overlays the current browser window. Exhibit 6 - 12 shows a daughter window created by Adletts.com (www.adletts.com) for General Motors. The ad displays while the cover page for Upside (www.upside.com) is loading in the background. While most interstitials and daughter windows are visual, Broadcast.com (www.broadcast.com) uses audio interstitials which play before the selected CD or program begins to play. Video interstitials that will look very much like TV commercials are just around the corner–limited primarily by bandwidth.

PUBLIC RELATIONS ACTIVITIES ON THE NET

Public relations is one marketing communication tool that is appropriate for a diverse group of stakeholders. Whereas advertising, sales promotions, and personal selling are most commonly directed to buyers and prospects, public relations is used to create goodwill among a number of different publics. These include the company shareholders and employees, the media, suppliers, and the local community, as well as consumers, business buyers, and many other stakeholder groups. It is important to remember that many different stakeholders will view an organization's site: For example, prospective employees will check out a firm by viewing the site, and community members who may be displeased with local pollution caused by a firm may look for evidence at the Web site.

Exhibit 6 - 12 Final Frame of GM BuyPower Banner Ad Created by Catalyst Resources
Source: www.upside.com

Web content that is not advertising, sales promotion, or transactional is public relations: that is, most Web content. Most free online content published by corporations that is meant to inform, persuade, or entertain is public relations. By public relations we mean content that attempts to create a positive feeling about the company or its brands among various publics. Exhibit 6 - 13 displays six important stakeholders along with the type of public relations content that is wellsuited for the Web. Many of these will be discussed in subsequent paragraphs. The Web created an ideal vehicle for widely disseminating timely, inexpensive, and important public relations information. Two major differences between the Web and traditional public relations vehicles are that information can be quickly updated, and that data can be presented in interesting interactive multimedia formats. This is quite an improvement over the traditional annual report to shareholders or the brochure sent through the mail. E-mail is another important online public relation tool because it allows firms to communicate with stakeholders in an interactive format.

Stakeholder	Online Content	Stakeholder	Online Content
Shareholders	Financial reports SEC filings Management changes Company activities	Consumers and business buyers	Online events Brochureware / Product information Store locators Testimonials Customer service Activities
Employees	Employee accomplishments Employee benefits Employee directory Company information Training materials	Suppliers	New-product information Company news
Media	Press releases/news Media kit material Contact information	Community	Social programs Local news relating to firm Employment opportunities

Exhibit 6 - 13 Online Public Relations Content for Selected Stakeholders

Brochureware

Brochureware is used to describe sites that inform customers about products or services without providing interactive features. They are the equivalent of a product brochure placed online. Many of the early corporate sites featured brochureware. The greatest advantage of brochureware is that it is a low-budget method to establish a Web presence and thus serves as a public relations vehicle. In addition to product information targeted to consumers, brochureware sites can meet the needs of other stakeholders. Press releases can be provided for the news media, and corporate reports can be provided for investors. Employment information can be showcased for potential employees, and employee benefit information can be served out to current employees. Brochureware sites need routine maintenance in order to make sure that the information does not grow stale. Old information, like yesterday's news, has little value in the eyes of the public and may actually create an overall negative impression of the corporation.

Online Interactions with Stakeholders

An interactive Web site is a more extensive online public relations commitment. Interactive sites serve to inform and empower users. Interactive features can entertain (games and electronic postcards), build community (online events, chat rooms, and discussion groups), provide a communication channel with the customer (customer feedback and customer service), provide information (product selection, product recommendation, retailer referrals), and assist in site navigation (search buttons, drop-down menus, and check boxes). All of these features require some degree of programming and therefore are more expensive to implement. Some of the features such as customer service also require backend staffing to respond to customer inquiries and complaints.

Many users visit Web sites in search of information. Using interactive features, the site designer can shorten the user's path to the desired information. Such information includes product selection, product recommendation, and retailer referrals. For example, a site can implement a retail locator to assist users in finding a retailer in their area. Some retail locators operate by taking the customer's zip code as input while others have customers point to their town on a map of the country. Both options are superior to presenting the customer with a long list of every retail outlet in the country.

Another way to assist users is to speed their navigation through the Web site. Search buttons, drop-down menus, and check boxes all help users quickly locate the information that they seek on the site. Many sites offer multiple ways to locate information. A great example of this is the Microsoft site that on the same page allows users to search four different ways! Users can click on a product type from the navigation menu, search for keywords using the search button, select from an alphabetical list of products from a drop-down menu, or click on a popular product family. See Exhibit 6 - 14.

Sites that entertain the customer help to ensure repeat visits. Some sites provide free games. Yahoo! has a particularly extensive games offering on its site. At any given time it has thousands of users playing chess, checkers, bridge, poker, and many other games online. The free games create a favorable public image for Yahoo! at a relatively low cost. See Exhibit 6 - 15.

Online Community Building

Some sites build community through online chat rooms, discussion groups, and online events. Exhibit 6 - 15 displays the Yahoo! mini-chat room at the bottom of the chess board permitting users to converse while they play. More sophisticated chat rooms, such as Microsoft's Comic Chat, allow users to assume visual identities known as avatars. Discussion groups allow users to feel a part of the site by posting their own information and responding to other users. Amazon allows users to write their own book reviews and read the reviews of others. The PowerBar site (www.powerbar.com) lets users write in testimonials about PowerBars as well as post photos from their favorite hiking expeditions. See Exhibit 6 - 16.

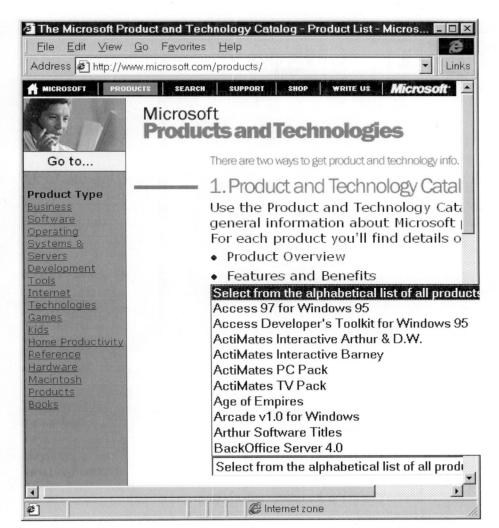

Exhibit 6 - 14 Microsoft Provides Multiple Ways to Search for Products
Source: www.microsoft.com

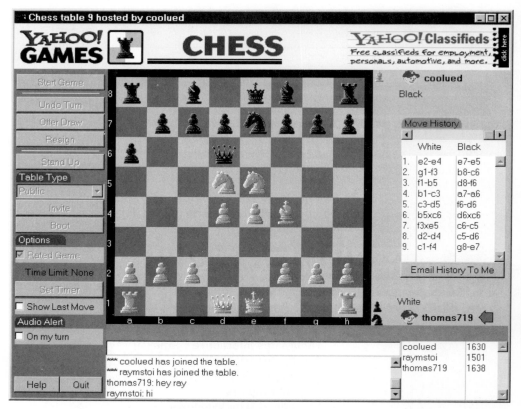

Exhibit 6 - 15 Yahoo! Games: Chess
Source: www.yahoo.com

Online Events

Online events also serve to generate user interest and draw them to a site. In a highly publicized event, Amazon let users contribute to a story started by the author John Updike. Each year Land Rover sponsors a race through exotic regions of the world called the Camel Trophy. Land Rover allows users to receive updates from the race at their Web site. See Exhibit 6 - 17.

Online Customer Service

Providing a communication channel for customers is an extremely important part of a customer service program. Normally the channel consists of a feedback button or form which delivers an e-mail message to the corporation. Often an automated backend program acknowledges the message via e-mail and indicates that a representative will be responding shortly to the message. And a representative must respond! Research shows that as many as half of the firms do not respond at all to consumer e-mails (Strauss & Pesce 1998). It is best to reply to customer inquires within 48 hours, though some firms will reply the same day. Not responding or responding after a long period of time decreases customer satisfaction (Strauss & Pesce 1998). L.L. Bean is particularly adept at customer e-mail communication, having committed a staff of nine to the task. The bottom line is to include feedback options on the Web site only if the company has the staff in place to respond.

Exhibit 6 - 16 PowerBar Testimonials
Source: www.powerbar.com

Exhibit 6 - 17 Land Rover Camel Trophy Photo Highlights

Similarly, a firm must be staffed to handle responses to mass e-mailings. Customer e-mail communication was previously discussed indepth as it relates to advertising; however, e-mail often serves to build relationships with various publics as well.

At the other end of the spectrum, the communications channel can be far more sophisticated than e-mail. Customers having a question about their Dell computer are able to enter a "Service Tag Number" which will bring up product and service information specific to their exact configuration. Mercedes-Benz takes customer service to a whole new level with its "teleweb" technology. The consumer types a question into his or her Web form and then receives an immediate phone call from a Mercedes representative. The consumer and representative can then discuss the consumer's questions while they each view the same Web pages.

SALES PROMOTIONS ON THE INTERNET

Sales promotion activities include coupons, rebates, product sampling, contests, sweepstakes, and premiums (free or low-cost gifts). Of these, coupons, sampling, and contests/sweepstakes are widely used on the Internet. While most offline sales promotion tactics are directed to businesses in the distribution channel, online tactics are directed primarily to consumers. As with offline consumer market sales promotions, many are used in combination with advertising. NetRatings announced the top three banner ad categories for August 1998: (1) Online/Internet services, (2) retail shopping, and (3) promotions (incentives, coupons, and sweepstakes). These three categories represented 60% of all banner advertising and reached 5% of all Web users according to their Banner Track study (www.netratings.com). Sales promotions are popular banner ad content and are also good for drawing users to a Web site, enticing them to stay, and compelling them to return.

Coupons

H.O.T! coupons (www.hotcoupons.com) and CouponsOnline (www.couponsonline.com) are among the many firms offering electronic coupons. They provide local coupons, allowing consumers to search the database by zip code (see Exhibit 6 - 18). They also send e-mail notification as new coupons become available, attempting to build brand loyalty. H.O.T! coupons is an interesting business, with roots in a 350-franchise direct mail distribution system. According to Jeff McIntosh of H.O.T! coupons, whereas most postal mailings result only in a 1% to 2% coupon redemption, H.O.T! coupons can add value by putting coupons on the Web site as well as in a traditional mail package. When retailers drive customers to the Web site through point-of-purchase or traditional advertising, coupon redemption increases substantially. H.O.T! coupons has 30,000 retail customers in the United States and is the price leader, charging only $100 for six months of coupon exposure on the site.

J. Crew, the retailer, sends electronic coupons to customers via e-mail. Exhibit 6 - 19 presents an e-mail written in response to a customer complaint sent by e-mail via a feedback button at the J. Crew Web site. The company sent an appropriate, customer-friendly e-mail in a timely manner and made the customer happy by providing a coupon for a later purchase. Interestingly, the customer does not have to clip the coupon, but merely has to give the number to a telephone staff member when placing an order. Music Boulevard has a frequent shopper's club and also sends out coupons periodically to registered customers.

Sampling

Some sites allow users to sample product prior to purchase. Many software companies will allow free download of fully functional demo versions of their software. The demo normally expires in 30 to 60 days, after which time the user can choose to purchase the software or remove it from her system. Online music stores similarly allow customers to sample music before ordering the CD. Market research firms often offer survey results as a sampling to entice businesses to purchase reports. For example, RelevantKnowledge posts the results of its monthly survey of top Web sites on the RelevantKnowledge Web site for prospects to see, use, and thus perhaps discover a need for more data.

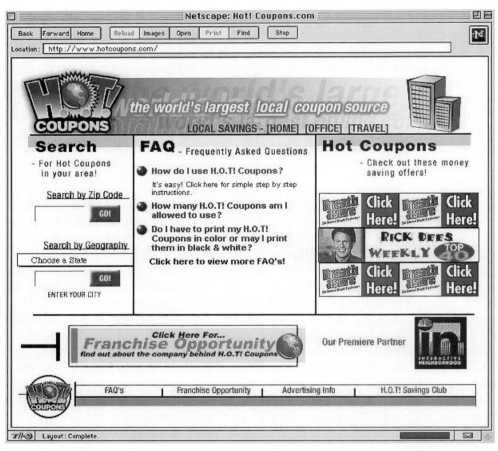

Exhibit 6 - 18 H.O.T! Coupons Distributes Coupons in Most Local Areas

Date: Mon, 09 Mar 1998 12:25:02 -0500
To: <johnson@ptd.net>
From: "jcrew.com" <service@jcrew.com>
Subject: Re: Italian Shoes
In-Reply-To: <199803090028.TAA22191@mail-ewr-2.pilot.net>

Dear Mr. Johnson:

J. Crew strives for complete customer satisfaction and service excellence. We sincerely apologize for the quality of the items you received. Your concerns are important to us and we appreciate you taking the time to write and bring this matter to our attention.

The strictest guidelines are followed when choosing vendors to make our merchandise and we guarantee it without reservation. Please return any items you are not pleased with and we will be happy to exchange them or refund your money. Please be sure to request return postage reimbursement at the time of your return.

As an expression of our sincere regret for the inconvenience you have experienced, we have attached a Merchandise Certificate for use with your next catalog order. We hope you will consider giving us another opportunity to serve you.

If you have questions or need further assistance, please feel free to contact our Customer Relations Department toll-free at 1-800-932-0043.

Sincerely,

Kim Williamson
J. Crew Customer Relations

MERCHANDISE CERTIFICATE $20.00
MERCHANDISE CERTIFICATE TOWARDS YOUR NEXT PURCHASE FROM THE J CREW CATALOG. BE SURE TO MENTION #J0298 TO YOUR ORDER CONSULTANT OR INCLUDE THIS CERTIFICATE WITH YOUR MAIL ORDER.
(certificate valid on your next catalog purchase only)

Exhibit 6 - 19 Electronic Coupon in Response to Customer E-mail Complaint

Exhibit 6 - 20 Playhere.com Consolidates Sales Promotions from Many Web Sites

Contests and Sweepstakes

Many sites hold contests and sweepstakes to draw traffic and keep users returning. Contests require skill (e.g., trivia answer) whereas sweepstakes involve only a pure chance drawing for the winners. Just as in the brick and mortar world, these sales promotion activities create excitement about brands and entice customers to stop by. If sweepstakes are changed regularly, users will return to the site to check out the latest chance to win product. Playhere (www.playhere.com) does an excellent job of consolidating sales promotions from many Web sites (see Exhibit 6 - 20).

Exhibit 6 - 6, the Mazda banner ad, contains a sweepstakes right on the banner itself. As was previously mentioned, this sales promotion delivery system is widely used online. According to the folks at Mazda, when users enter the sweepstakes, they are usually sent a surprise: a free CD of the cool Web Zine, *Launch* (technical term: premium). Through this sweepstakes, Mazda is able to add to its e-mail database while building relationships with potential and current customers.

PERSONAL SELLING ON AN IMPERSONAL MEDIUM

The Net is an impersonal medium, so it is not appropriate for this promotional tool except in ancillary role. E-mail solicitations are similar to outgoing telemarketing except that there is no opportunity for conversation unless the prospect sends a response. Like advertising and direct mail, the Web is very good for generating leads for the sales force. For example, Herman Miller office furniture has an online form for those wanting a salesperson to contact them.

The Net as a Medium

At this point we make a major transition from describing the way promotion tools can be put to work on the Internet to describing how marketers view the Internet as just one of many media to carry marketing communication messages. TV, radio, newspapers, magazines, outdoor (e.g., kiosks, bus cards, and billboards), and direct mail are all channels of communication as is the Internet. Because the Internet is often compared with traditional media, exploring the strengths and weaknesses of each of the major media helps to shed light on the Internet as a medium and thus helps marketers choose among them for buying promotional space. Later in this section audience measurement in the Internet medium is explored. Accurate audience measurement is a necessity in any advertising-supported medium, and Internet firms are still grappling with the solution to this problem. Successful media buys reach the target audience with the right message at the right place and time. Knowing the advantages and disadvantages of various Internet audience measures assists in making informed media buys. Finally, this section explores a few of the considerations media buyers use to select among media for advertising buys.

Marketers and lawmakers continue to search for the proper analogy with which to understand the Net. Some feel that banner ads are like interactive billboards. Others claim that the Net is like print media: Firms publish content and sell advertising. Still others feel that the Web and especially e-mail are like direct mail—only faster and cheaper. Multimedia technologies such as Real Player have even resulted in equating the Internet to TV and radio. With TV/Web convergence already a technical reality, and by the year 2008 a practical reality, the Web may indeed be most like TV. Stay tuned for the answer. The analogy that each marketer chooses influences how she approaches the buying of advertising space on the Internet. In the same manner, the analogy that lawmakers draw influences the laws that they pass.

ELECTRONIC MEDIA

Electronic media include network television, radio, cable television, the Internet, FAX machine, cellular phone, and pager. It is helpful to view these media as broadcast, narrowcast, and pointcast on the basis of their capability to reach mass audiences, smaller audiences, or even individuals. This categorization scheme also serves to underline the development of electronic media from broadcast in the 1940s to narrowcast in the 1990s. Important characteristics of each medium are discussed below as a prelude to comparison with the Internet for media buying.

Broadcast Media

Broadcast media (TV and radio) have a number of strengths and weaknesses. Television and radio allow only for passive attention: If the audience is distracted, they miss the message. TV penetration reaches over 98% of U.S. households, with one-third owning three or more sets. The strengths of network TV are that it reaches the masses, allows for multimedia, has good quality of production, is good for emotional appeals, adds status to a brand, has a low cost to reach a thousand viewers (CPM), allows for some demographic targeting, and has well-accepted audience measurement statistics (the Nielsen Ratings). TV remains the only medium for advertisers wanting to reach large numbers of consumers in one fell swoop, but the Internet is nipping at its heels. The weaknesses of network TV are that it is expensive ($70,000 to $550,000 for 30 seconds of prime time), encourages passive viewing, and has little flexibility over message length or geographic market coverage except in a broad sense.

Radio's penetration is also ubiquitous. Almost every household and car has a radio. The strengths of radio are that its advertising space is inexpensive ($20 to $200 for 60 seconds), has excellent local market coverage, has good merchandising tie-ins (e.g., contests tying to retail advertising buys), is immediate (hear ad, visit store), and has well-accepted audience measurement statistics (Arbitron). Weaknesses of radio are that it encourages passive listening, has little message-length flexibility, has low advertising recall by consumers, and has little emotional impact. Radio is often considered a "background friend" that does not command consumer attention.

Narrowcast Medium

Cable TV is a narrowcast medium. The reason it is called *narrowcast* is that cable channels contain very focused electronic content that appeals to special-interest markets. For example, cable channels such as CNN or ESPN are networks in that they reach extremely large audiences worldwide, but they still have very specialized programming. The strengths of cable TV are that it has good psychographic targeting, is low cost (especially for smaller audiences), allows for flexible message length (e.g., infomercials), and shares broadcast network TV's production quality and multimedia capability. Weaknesses of CATV are that its markets are fragmented and small (except for the most popular channels), it is a relatively low-status medium, and there are audience measurement difficulties. Nielsen measures CATV audiences, but the number of small audience channels precludes a cost-effective comprehensive measurement system: a problem shared with the Internet.

Pointcast Media

The term *pointcast* was coined by the folks at www.pointcast.com, who brought individualized news service to every computer desktop. Pointcast media include all electronic media with the capability of transmitting to an audience of just one person. These media are also used to transmit standardized messages in bulk to the entire audience who have the equipment to receive them (e.g., a computer), and these individuals can transmit a single message back to the sender using the same equipment: This is interactivity.

Pagers and cellular phones can now receive e-mail and are capable of receiving Web pages. FAX machines also receive marketing communications messages electronically, although the messages must be viewed in hard copy. The FAX medium is different in another important way: It is the only pointcast medium in which unsolicited marketing communications are illegal. This is due to the cost involved with receiving messages.

The Internet is the biggest pointcast medium. Strengths of the Net from a media buyer's perspective include selective targeting through e-mail databases, ability to track advertising effectiveness, flexibility of message length and delivery timing, and interactivity. The Internet is the first electronic medium to allow active, self-paced viewing (similar to print media) and the first and best medium for interactivity. In fact, many say that with the Internet, users create their own messages. This user control may be considered a weakness of the Net as medium, but it also means that if marketers can get the attention of audience members they will be more involved in marketing messages. Most of the weaknesses of the Net are in the process of being remedied. Audience measurement was initially a weakness, though companies such as RelevantKnowledge have made major improvements in this area. Nevertheless, it is still difficult to define Web audience member characteristics on an individual level. This problem must be solved in order for the Net to reach its full capability as a pointcast medium. More on this shortly. Lack of standards for items such as banner sizes was also a weakness which has been remedied by CASIE and IAB. On the Web it is possible to track advertising delivery, but Web sites name ad files differently, thus creating another standardizing problem. Audience tracking firms predict that this will be solved soon. Bandwidth is the one major weakness still outstanding, though even this is being tackled by infrastructure improvements and by clever compression techniques.

The Medium Is Not the Appliance

Now that we've described various electronic media as television, Internet, radio, and others, it is time to confuse, or perhaps clarify, the issue some by separating the medium from the receiving appliance. Messages are sent by content publishers in electronic form via satellite, telephone wires, or cable and received by the audience through appliances (also called receivers) such as a television, a computer, a radio, and so on. It is important to keep in mind that the receiving appliance is separate from the media transmission because this setup allows for flexibility. For example, computers can receive digital radio and television transmissions, and television can receive the Web. Some appliances, such as radio and FAX machine, have limited receiving capabilities while others are more flexible. At this point the computer is the only one to receive all types of digital electronic transmissions. Many appliances can also send messages. This idea is both quite mind boggling and exciting because of the business opportunities. Separating the medium from the appliance opens the door to new types of receiving appliances that are also "smart," allowing for saving, editing, and sending transmissions.

PRINT MEDIA

Many like to compare the Net to print media, because its content is so text and graphic heavy, and because Web pages allow everyone to be a publisher. Unlike television and radio, print media allow for active viewing. By this we mean that readers will stop to look at an ad that interests them, sometimes spending quite a bit of time reading the details. Readers can respond to print media offers either via snail mail or telephone, thus providing a low level of interactivity. Print media include newspapers (local and national) and magazines.

Strengths of local newspapers include good local coverage, good audience measurement statistics (ABC), a low cost to reach a thousand readers (CPM), and immediacy (see ad, visit store, buy product). Weaknesses of local papers include poor quality of reproduction, hasty reading (skim it, toss it), and few options for message creativity. National newspapers like *USA Today* do not have the high penetration of local papers but do have good pass-along readership and are good for national brands.

The Internet is similar to magazines in many ways. In fact many online publications are actually called e-zines. Strengths of magazines include good psychographic targeting, good quality of reproduction, good audience statistics (ABC), good pass-along readership, and good merchandising tie-ins. Weaknesses of magazines include high cost per thousand, low flexibility of timing (e.g., once a month), and low circulation numbers. Like cable TV, magazines reach many special-interest audiences.

DIRECT MAIL

Finally, the Net, especially e-mail, shares some of the characteristics of direct mail. Direct mail allows for more selective targeting than any other mass medium, can be personalized, gives good message and timing flexibility, can easily carry sales promotions, and is the best of the traditional media for measuring effectiveness because of response tracking capability. However, direct mail has a low image (junk mail) and high costs for production and postage. Conversely, e-mail has low costs but limited market coverage compared with snail mail. This is changing as companies build extensive e-mail databases. E-mail is increasingly being used to maintain a relationship with the consumer. Online travel agents offer to track fares and inform the consumer when there has been a major price change for a particular flight. Other uses include notification of software updates or promotional coupons.

AUDIENCE MEASUREMENT

No other medium provides as many audience measures as the Internet. This is so both because there are many things to measure and because the industry is still trying to find appropriate measures. The existence of good audience measures is critical to the success of the Web as an advertising medium. A major reason only $1 billion is being spent on Web advertising in 1998 is that advertisers are not able to figure out who they are reaching, demographically, geographically, and psychographically. Media buyers want to be sure the brand's target market is in the audience when they spend dollars on advertising space. Web companies cannot yet provide that assurance, but the situation improves daily.

When there are multiple ways to conduct audience measurement, then choosing a measure will be determined by marketing objectives. Marketers must ask what the goal is, define it carefully, and then seek the appropriate measure. For example, if the objective is to reach 5,000 Internet users who own dogs with an ad to build awareness about a new dog food, one appropriate statistic would be the number of impressions delivered for that ad, and the appropriate measure is the number of times that ad was served. One way to obtain that measure is to examine the site's log file to see how many hits were recorded for the ad. If doing this seems complicated, it is. Hang on and we'll explain a few popular audience measures.

Hits

The sophistication of Web audience measurement has advanced significantly since the early days of the Web. In the beginning, Web sites reported hits as a measure of audience traffic to the site. A hit is a record that a file was requested from a Web site. This measure failed since all but the simplest of Web pages contain multiple files. For example, the page in Exhibit 6 - 21 would generate seven hits while the page in Exhibit 6 - 22 would generate only one hit. Each graphic element including the bullets in Exhibit 6 - 21 is stored as a separate file and therefore registers a hit when requested. Hits tend to artificially inflate the popularity of a Web site.

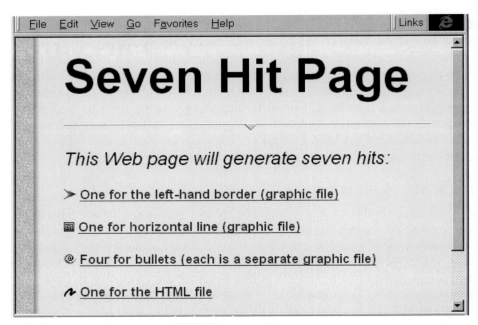

Exhibit 6 - 21 Seven-Hit Web Page

Exhibit 6 - 22 One-Hit Web Page

Page Views

One solution to the hit problem is to measure page views rather than hits. Page views describe how many Web pages a server sends out irrespective of the number of graphic elements that comprise that page. Exhibit 6 - 21 and Exhibit 6 - 22 would both register one page view. Clearly page views are preferable to hits. But page views have their own limitations. Some sites are organized into many short pages while other sites prefer fewer but longer pages. The site with many short pages will record more page views than the site with longer pages even when users access the same amount of content.

Visitors

A solution to the page view problem is to measure the number of visitors to a Web site. The measure of visitors avoids site design biases which plague hits and page views. But measuring number of visitors does not distinguish between one-time and repeat visitors. A site that receives visits from 15 separate people would record the same number of visits as a site visited 15 times by one person. An advertiser might be more interested in reaching multiple eyeballs than reaching one set of eyeballs multiple times. At any rate, the advertiser would like to know which scenario prevails.

Unique Visitors and More

The solution to the visitors problem is to measure unique visitors rather than just number of visitors. Firms such as RelevantKnowledge use the unique visitors measure in order to rank the most popular sites on the Web. Normally, the number of unique visitors is measured over a period of time, perhaps a month. This measure avoids all of the duplication present in the other measures described and for that reason has become a well-respected measure.

Another measure used in conjunction with unique visitors is length of stay. Sites that are able to hold the user's attention for a longer period of time may generate more ad sales. Site log files are excellent because they track users through a site, noting the time of day for every click.

Despite these new measures, the hits and page view measures are still very useful. One variation on hits, for example, is to measure the number of times a banner ad was served—that is, the number of impressions. This measure corresponds to the impressions measure from traditional media. Ad inventory is often sold on the basis of number of impressions. Page views are also important since some Web sites such as Yahoo! charge more for ads that appear on specialty pages—such as an automotive page. The reasoning behind the higher charge is that these pages deliver a more highly targeted audience.

Some companies, most notably Procter and Gamble, have even sought to purchase advertising based on click-throughs. A click-through is a user's clicking on a banner ad to visit the Web site to which it is linked. There are problems with this measure, however. First of all, the content of the banner itself will often determine whether the user chooses to click on it. A dull banner may not generate click-throughs—hardly the fault of the site providing the ad space. This is analogous to automobile advertiser paying CBS for advertising only if customers come to the dealership. Second, there is plenty of research to substantiate that user brand recognition and attitudes are enhanced whether or not they click on a banner.

How to Measure

Audience measurement on the Internet is emerging as either a consumer-centric or site-centric model. The consumer-centric model measures by recording clickstream data at the user's PC. The site-centric model records data at the Web site server's log file. Both measures provide useful information, and both have limitations which should be considered prior to use.

The Consumer-Centric Model

The consumer-centric model is similar to the Nielsen ratings for TV. A panel that is representative of the population is formed, their media viewing actions are recorded, and the results are generalized to the population. The best way to form a representative panel is through random digit dialing since almost everyone owns a telephone. All members of the population thus have an equal chance of being included in the sample. The panel is segmented demographically so that statements about the behavior of demographic groups can be inferred. This information is extremely important to advertisers because media buyers buy demographics.

Software installed on the panel member's computer is used to record clickstream data—every page that the user visits and the frequency with which the user returns to a page. This information not only provides information about traffic to a site but also provides traffic information about specific areas within a site. The clickstream data are automatically forwarded to a central location, where they are summarized in the aggregate in order to make inferences about the behavior of demographic groups.

The consumer-centric model has several advantages. First, if the panel is wellformed and large enough, then the data are statistically reliable. Second, the method differentiates the audience by demographics. Third, the model allows for comparisons among competing Web sites by revealing the audience share of each.

As attractive as the consumer-centric model is, it also has three disadvantages. First, as with cable television measurement, the results are statistically reliable only for the larger sites on the Internet. This is not as big a disadvantage as it may at first seem, since the larger sites also attract almost all of the media buy dollars. Second, business users are not as accurately counted as they should be. Many businesses are resistant to their employees' installing monitoring software on their computers. And it is precisely the businesses with the best demographics to deliver that may have the tightest controls. CNN and other popular Web sites for business use are underrepresented in these measures because of this bias (source: www.jupiter.com). Third, since the exact demographics of the Internet population are really not known, deficiencies in the panel composition cannot be corrected through weighting of results.

The Site-Centric Model

The Internet's site-centric model is unique for broadcast media. In this model user activity is tallied at the content provider's Web site to produce audience composition statistics, page views, and so on. Web servers keep a log of every single file that they send out, recording when and to whom it was sent. Analyzing this log file reveals the number of hits, page views, and visits that a site sustains in a given time period. These are actual numbers rather than inferred numbers, as in the case of the consumer-centric model. Some sites self-report the analysis of their log files–and there are software packages such as Marketwave which will perform the analysis automatically. However, media buyers tend to be more comfortable with analyses conducted by third-party auditing agencies. Auditing Web site logs improves accuracy, lends credibility, and helps to standardize reporting. ABC's ABVS and Nielsen-I/PRO are two firms that provide the log analysis service. They also take special care to make sure that the log file has not been tampered with to inflate usage statistics. It is no surprise that ABC (the Audit Bureau of Circulation) is in this game, because it is the premier measurement firm for magazine and newspaper media, which are measured in a similar fashion. That is, ABC audits print media numbers for total subscription and newsstand sales.

The site-centric model has three advantages. First, for sites with limited budgets it is less expensive than the consumer-centric model—especially if the site conducts its own auditing. Second, it is the only technique that can measure the number of times that an ad was served (impressions). Third, smaller sites that fall off the charts in consumer-centric measures can provide audience statistics through site-centric measures.

However, the site-centric model suffers from some disadvantages. One major disadvantage is proxy server caching. Proxy server caching describes the tendency of some corporations to make local copies of entire Web sites so that their users will enjoy faster access to those sites. Unfortunately, there is no way for the original site to capture usage data from the copied site. Thus thousands or even millions of visits could go uncounted. For more on proxy server caching see the Leveraging Technology section at the end of this chapter. Second, the site-centric model cannot reliably distinguish unique visits. The only identity information that the site can record is the IP address of the computer that visited. Most users get a new IP address from their ISP every time they sign on (technical term: dynamic IP addressing). Therefore, the same user might appear to be a different user on a repeat visit. Conversely, some organizations use the same IP address for all of their users, which again makes it difficult to distinguish users. Third, the model cannot reliably produce demographic information. The IP address contains no demographic information other than that which can be inferred. For example, IP addresses corresponding to the edu domain probably represent visits by students or faculty.

An additional problem created by proxy server caching is the inability to record the number of impressions delivered for a particular ad. The ad might be viewed thousands of times behind a corporate firewall while no record is made of these visits. ABC and MatchLogic joined forces to solve the proxy server caching problem for measuring ad impressions. They designed Web pages that would always request a new ad when viewed, even if viewed from a proxy server cache. The request goes out to an ad server which records the impression in its own log file.

WHICH MEDIA TO BUY?

Media planners want effective and efficient media buys. *Effectiveness* means reaching the target market, and *efficiency* means doing so at the lowest cost. In order to determine effective coverage, advertisers must have good audience statistics for a medium they are considering. Most media buyers do not feel that the Net provides good enough statistics to warrant large dollar commitments, at least not at the present time. However, advertisers were buying space to the tune of $1 billion in 1998 because they know that top sites draw eyeballs.

The other side of the equation is efficiency. To measure this, media buyers use a figure called CPM (cost per thousand). This is calculated by taking the ad's cost, dividing it by the audience size, and then multiplying by 1,000 (cost / audience * 1000). CPM is used because it allows for efficiency comparisons among various media and vehicles within the media (e.g., a particular magazine or Web site). If the audience for considered vehicles matches the firm's target, CPM calculations will reveal the most efficient buy. As an example, consider the average CPMs for major media in Exhibit 6 - 23. Magazines are usually the most expensive media to reach 1,000 readers, and radio the least expensive. Web CPM figures vary widely from $0.50 to over $100, depending on the site, but the average is about $20, down from $75 in early 1997. While CPM is still the dominant media buying model online, some advertisers recognize that the Web is different from other media and that perhaps CPM is not the best metric to use. For one thing, folks spend more quality time at a Web site than they do in front of the TV set. This means a better chance of a Web banner gaining viewer attention. Second, as was previously mentioned, there are many other fine ways of tracking online behavior that are not available in traditional media. The practitioner perspective at the end of this chapter explores this issue in more depth ("Exploding the Web CPM Myth").

For fiscal year 1998, Microsoft Corp allocated its $297.8 million media budget as follows: $41 million on the Web (14%), $149.8 million in print advertising (50%), and $107 million on TV (36%) (Johnson 1997). How did Microsoft decide on this allocation? There are many things to consider. First is the audience. Which vehicles will reach them effectively? Second is the CPM. Third are the products and messages themselves—certain media lend themselves better than others. For example, TV is best for a new product that needs to build large-scale awareness quickly. Similarly, if the message is emotional, TV works well. Conversely, if the product and message are technical and require lots of information, print and the Web are best. Fourth are the strengths and weaknesses of various media in delivering the required message.

Exhibit 6 - 24 summarizes the previous discussion. If an advertiser needs multimedia capability to show the product, she will use either TV or the Web. For global coverage, TV, magazines, and the Web do well. For broad reach, nothing beats TV, but for tracking message effectiveness direct mail and the Web prevail. It is also interesting to note that heavy Web users use of the Web at the expense of TV viewing time: Thus the allocation of media budget includes audience consumption patterns as well. There are many other criteria used by media buyers, but this brief summary builds understanding about the Web's relative strengths and weaknesses as a marketing communications medium.

Medium	Vehicle	Cost	Reach	CPM
TV	30-second spot on primetime	$120,000	10 million households	$12
Magazine	One page in Newsweek	$150,000	3.1 million readers	$48
Radio	60-second spot on local station	$75	10,000 listeners	$7.50
Web site	Banner on Infoseek	$10,000 per month	500,000 page views per month	$20

Exhibit 6 - 23 Ad Rate Comparison for Major Media
Adapted from Jupiter Communications (www.jup.com)

Criterion	TV	Radio	Magazine	Newspaper	Direct Mail	Web
Involvement	passive	passive	active	active	active	interactive
Media richness	multi-media	audio	text and graphic	text and graphic	text and graphic	multi-media
Geographic coverage	global	local	global	local	varies	global
CPM	low	lowest	high	medium	high	low
Reach	high	medium	low	medium	varies	medium
Targeting	good	good	excellent	good	excellent	fair
Track effectiveness	fair	fair	fair	fair	excellent	excellent
Message flexibility	poor	good	poor	good	excellent	excellent

Exhibit 6 - 24 Strengths and Weaknesses of Major Media

Summary

Integrated marketing communications (IMC) is a comprehensive plan of communication that includes advertising, sales promotion, public relations, personal selling, and the rest of the marketing mix to provide maximum communication impact with stakeholders.

Internet ad spending today exceeds $1 billion and is projected to increase dramatically. The product categories spending the most on advertising include computing, consumer related, telecom, financial services, and new media. In the near term direct-response advertising has a more favorable outlook than branding. Direct-response advertising leverages the Net's unique capability as an interactive medium.

Internet advertising may be either text based or multimedia based. Text-based advertising operates through e-mail and bulletin boards. Multimedia advertising utilizes banners, buttons, interstitials, and sponsorships. E-mail is most effective when sent to customers that have previously agreed to receive it. Unsolicited e-mail is often pejoratively viewed as spam.

Multimedia brand advertising is the primary model on the Web. Most advertising expenditures are for banner ads (55%), with sponsorships as a close and growing second (40%). Banners have evolved from static images to banners with animation to capture the user's attention. A third generation of banners is now appearing which provide interactivity. Banner effectiveness is a subject of debate, though research indicates that banners score well compared with TV ads. Sponsorships are growing in popularity, though some feel that the line between editorial content and advertising is becoming blurred.

Most Web content is public relations material. Public relations refers to content that attempts to create a positive feeling about a company or its brands among various publics. Marketers now design Web site content with multiple audiences in mind. Brochureware informs customers about products and services. Beyond this, interactive Web sites can entertain (games and electronic postcards), build community (online events, chat rooms, and discussion groups), provide a communication channel with the customer (customer feedback and customer service), provide information (product selection, product recommendation, retailer referrals), and assist in site navigation (search buttons, drop-down menus, and check boxes).

The Net may also be understood as just one of many media to carry marketing communication messages. TV, radio, newspapers, magazines, outdoor (e.g., kiosks, bus cards, and billboards), and direct mail are all channels of communication, as is the Internet. Because the Internet is often compared with traditional media, exploring the strengths and weaknesses of each of the major media helps to shed light on the Internet as a medium and thus helps marketers choose among them for buying promotional space.

Accurate audience measurement is a necessity in any advertising-supported medium, and Internet firms are still grappling with the solution to this problem. Successful media buys reach the target audience with the right message at the right place and time. Knowing the advantages and disadvantages of various Internet audience measures helps one to make informed media buys.

Various measures have been constructed to measure the Web audience. These may be broadly divided between consumer-centric and site-centric measures. Site centric measures include hits, page views, visitors, and unique visitors—items that are recorded by the site's log file. Consumer-centric measures observe the behavior of representative panels in order to make statements about the broader population.

Media planners want effective and efficient media buys. Factors to consider when making media buys include involvement (active or passive), media richness, geographic coverage, CPM, reach, targeting, track effectiveness, and message flexibility.

Key Concepts and Terms

1. Integration and consistency of message across all of the promotion pieces is important in order to create synergy with other marketing-mix tools.

2. Web ad spending is a very small but rapidly growing fraction of total media spending.

3. Because it is an interactive medium, the Web is particularly well suited to direct-response advertising.

4. Successful firms structure their e-mail advertisements so that they are welcomed rather than resented by the target audience.

5. Most online advertising expenditures are for banner ads (55%), with sponsorships a close and growing second (40%).

6. Selected targeting increases the effectiveness of banner ads.

7. Although personal selling is not possible in an online medium, the Net may be used to generate sales leads.

8. Marketers try to understand the Net by comparison with traditional media. These comparisons influence ad-buying decisions.

9. The Internet is the largest pointcast medium and allows for the most selective targeting.

10. The most commonly quoted measure of Web site popularity—hits—is also the most meaningless.

11. The consumer-centric measurement model is similar to the Nielsen ratings for TV.

12. The Net is the only medium allows for site-centric measurement.

- Animated GIF
- Banner
- Brochureware
- Button
- Clickstream data
- Consumer centric
- Daughter window
- Discussion group
- Hit
- Interstitial

- List broker
- LISTSERV
- Page view
- Pointcast
- Site centric
- Snail mail
- Spam
- Spam filter
- Unique visitor
- Visitor

Exercises

REVIEW QUESTIONS FOR KNOWLEDGE TESTING

1. Define four promotion-mix tools
2. What is the difference between effectiveness and efficiency? Use an example in your explanation.
3. What are the characteristics of each of the three generations of banner advertisements?
4. What is the difference between brand and direct-response advertising?
5. How is text-based advertising used on the Internet?
6. List the types of multimedia advertising used online.
7. How can the interactive capabilities of the Net enhance customer service? Give examples.
8. List examples of broadcast, narrowcast, and pointcast media.
9. What are the strengths and weaknesses of the Web as an advertising medium?
10. Identify several ways to measure the Web audience, giving the strengths of each.

DISCUSSION QUESTIONS FOR CRITICAL THINKING

1. Why is the third generation of banners very powerful for advertisers?
2. "The more successful list brokers are in selling their lists, the more they dilute the value of those lists." Do you agree or disagree and why?
3. How effective is banner advertising compared with other media?
4. Is there a danger in letting sponsorship blend with content? Defend your position.

5. If you were running an online ad campaign for Nike, how would you allocate your ad budget? Why?

6. Why would manufacturers make it possible to search for and print coupons online? Might this encourage customers who were prepared to pay full price simply to use the Net to lower their costs?

7. Why are hits a relatively meaningless measure of a Web site's popularity?

8. If you were running an ad campaign and could afford only consumer-centric or site-centric numbers, which would you buy? Why?

9. For some U.S. sites, a third of their viewers are from overseas. Do these users dilute the value of advertising at these sites? Why or why not?

10. What is meant by the expression, "The medium is not the appliance"? Do you agree or disagree and why?

ACTIVITIES

1. Find three banner ads that you think are particularly effective, and three more that are ineffective. Explain your reasons, telling how you might improve the ineffective ads.

2. Obtain an annual report for a large firm. Go to the firm's Web site and compare the printed and electronic version of content directed to shareholders. How do you explain the differences?

3. Identify a company, such as Microsoft, that advertises on TV, the Web, and one print medium. Make copies of ads from that firm and discuss the similarities and differences among them. Is the firm following the IMC concept? Why or why not?

4. Go to www.couponsonline.com or www.hotcoupons.com and print a coupon for a retailer in your area. Visit the retailer and interview him or her about the effectiveness of the electronic coupons. How many are redeemed? How long has the offer been running? How often do they change the offer?

INTERNET EXERCISE: ADVERTISING ON THE WEB

Athletic shoe companies such as Nike and Reebok may want to *pay* others to provide a link to its home page. These links are most often in the form of banner ads, which the user can clickthrough to visit the advertised site. In this exercise you will evaluate three sites that sell advertising space. You can use sites that maintain an inventory of advertising space on the Web, or you can go directly to the site itself (not all have advertising rates online). Visit Ad Home (www.adhome.com) and jump to its sports category, or go to any sports site (such as ESPN) and see if you can find its advertising rates. Select three sports Web sites that might be attractive for athletic shoe advertising. Complete the following table and calculate Cost Per Thousand (CPM), an important number used by media buyers for comparing ad costs:

Site	Monthly Cost	Guaranteed Impressions per Month	Cost per 1,000 impressions CPM = cost / impressions * 1000
1.			
2.			
3.			

For Discussion

1. Taking into account the cost of making 1,000 impressions (CPM) at each of the three Web sites, what is your recommendation for athletic shoe advertising and why?

2. According to what you learned about the costs of television advertising in this chapter, does the Web seem like a good buy for athletic shoe companies? Why or why not?

3. What advantages do athletic shoe firms realize for placing banner ads on sports-related Web sites? Disadvantages?

4. If Nike chose to place a banner ad on one of your sites, what would be an appropriate message for this medium?

Practitioner Perspective

EXPLODING THE WEB CPM MYTH

In his former life Rick Boyce (rick@wired.com) crunched numbers in a media department. He now battles the CPM myth daily as senior vice president, advertising and commerce, at Wired Digital. Rick also serves on the board of the IAB.

If you've read anything in the media or from Internet analyst reports recently, you've no doubt noticed all the chatter about Web cost-per-thousand (CPM) calculations. The common theme seems to be that Web CPMs are too high, particularly compared with television. Take for example this comment from Morgan Stanley's industry bible, "The Internet Advertising Report": "While CPM's on the Web vary widely, on average, they have been at higher levels than they are in most other media."

Much of what is published by the analyst community promulgates the Web CPM myth. As any media planner will tell you, it is impossible to compare CPM objectively across different media without accounting for the level of targeting the advertiser wants to reach.

Exhibit 6 - 25, from Jupiter Communications, appeared prominently in the Morgan Stanley Internet Advertising Report. It is often quoted but typical of many CPM analyses that are generated; some may feel this chart can only possibly intimate one conclusion: that Web CPMs are 66% higher than TV CPMs. But perhaps, since these two types of media are so diverse, a slightly different type of comparison would, in fact, be possible.

Medium	Vehicle	Cost	Reach	CPM
TV	30-second network primetime	$120,000	10 million households	$12
Consumer Magazine	Page, 4-color in *Cosmopolitan*	$86,155	2.5 million paid readers	$35
Online Service	Banner on CompuServe major topic page	$10,000 per month	750,000 visitors	$13
Web Site	Banner on Infoseek	$10,000 per month	500,000 page views per month	$20

Exhibit 6 - 25 Ad Rate Comparison Across Major Media
Source: Jupiter Communications

What is important to remember when looking at comparative CPMs is that TV is a mass reach medium. Even selective dayparts and programs reach giant cross-sections of the population. While the 30-second network primetime spot referenced in Exhibit 6 - 25 delivers a $12 CPM against all U.S. households, if the target audience is refined with the addition of income and education screens, the CPM jumps dramatically. The truth is that for reaching high-income, well-educated audiences, television CPMs are quite high, and Web advertising, in many cases, can actually deliver a lower CPM against the same demographics.

Using network primetime costs and ratings estimates from the fourth quarter of 1997, Exhibit 6 - 26 examines the reach and CPM of an average primetime when age, income, and education screens are added.

Target Definition	Audience (Estimate)	CPM (Gross)
U.S. TV Households	8,526,000	$12.52
A18-49	6,361,200	$16.78
A18-49 & $40k+ HHI	3,796,200	$28.12
A18-49 & $50k+ HHI & HOH 1+yr. College	2,171,700	$49.15
Key: HHI = Household Income HOH = Head of Household		

Exhibit 6 - 26 Network Primetime Reach and CPM vs. Select Demographics
Source: Netcosts Q4 1997 Primetime Scatter Estimates, Nielsen Nov. 1997 Audience Estimates

Now let's do the television/Web CPM comparison, and let's assume that our target audience is college educated and enjoys an above-average income. If we adjust the primetime CPM from $12 to $49 to account for the premium required to reach an upscale target audience with TV, the television/Web CPMs actually become far more comparable. As a single point of reference, consider that a banner schedule can be purchased on Quote.com—which delivers an audience with an average household income of $110,000 and 70% college graduates—for under a $50 CPM. Once television CPMs are adjusted to account for reaching a specific target audience, the economies of Web advertising—particularly for reaching discrete, affluent target audiences becomes clear.

It is worth noting that online media planners and buyers can target infinite demographic or psychographic audiences because the Web is home to more vertically targeted content than any other medium. This capability allows advertisers to purchase media schedules against nearly any target audience with a minimum amount of waste.

But even if Web CPMs aren't out of line relative to television, is Internet advertising really effective? The answer is yes, and here's why:

In a study conducted in 1997 for the IAB, MBinteractive (www.mbinteractive.com) concluded that "online advertising is more likely to be noticed than television advertising." The reasons that ad banners performed so favorably has to do with:

1. The lower ad-to-edit ratio on Web pages

2. The fact that Web users actively use the medium as opposed to passively receiving it

With regard to the proportion of advertising to editorial, think of it this way: The typical ad banner is 468 x 60 pixels, equaling a total of 28,080 square pixels. The commonly accepted default screen size is 640 x 480 pixels, for a total of 307,020 square pixels. This means that a typical Web page is 91% editorial and 9% advertising—dramatic compared with to magazines, which are typically in the 50/50 range, and with television, which is closer to 60% programming and 40% advertising.

To the point of passive vs. active viewing, television attention-level research is particularly interesting when contrasted with the online advertising effectiveness work done by MBinteractive. It's remarkable how few people are actually paying full attention to the television shows – not to mention the advertising. According to MRI, which measures television viewer attentiveness, not even two-thirds of the viewers of television's most popular shows – like *Seinfeld*, *60 Minutes* and *Mad About You* – report paying "full attention" to the programming.

And those actually watching the television commercials represent even a far smaller number. A 1993 study from The Roper Organization, Exhibit 6 - 27, found that just 22% of adults reported that they actually watch television commercials.

	Total	**Female**	**Male**
Watch commercials	22%	19%	24%
Turn down the sound	14	13	14
Change channels	27	31	24
Leave television	45	44	47
Get annoyed	51	51	50
Talk to others, ignoring commercials	35	36	34
Talk to others about commercials	14	13	16
Get amused by funny commercials	26	24	29
Pay attention to information on new products and services	10	8	11
Fast-forward through commercials when watching a taped program	35	38	32
Learn about products and services of interest	17	14	19

Exhibit 6 - 27 Percent of Adults Who Report They Often Respond to Television Commercials in Selected Ways
Source: The Roper Organization, 1993

To contrast, you simply can't navigate the Web without high concentration and high attention levels, and both are required for advertising to get noticed, remembered, and ultimately acted upon.

The lowly CPM has hit the big time and is no longer destined to an obscure existence like other media acronyms: GRP, CPP, RPC, and so on. But, if CPM is destined to become a mainstream term, we all need to work to understand how to use it to make accurate observations and smart analyses.

L e v e r a g i n g   T e c h n o l o g y

PROXY SERVERS AND CACHE

Banner ads are typically sold on a basis of Cost Per Thousand (CPM) impressions. This cost varies by site and even by page within site. Accurate counting of the number of impressions is critical to the revenue stream of a content site. Specifically, undercounting impressions robs the content provider of a major source of revenue. Undercounting has become a significant problem as a result of a technology that copies entire Web sites and then lets users view the copies: a technology that makes the Web seem faster for users. The device that makes the copies is called a *proxy server*. Clever solutions have been developed to count the number of times that a proxy server serves out a copy. Those solutions will be discussed here.

So how big is the problem of undercounting? According to a study by the Match Logic Corporation (www.matchlogic.com), which was independently audited by Ernst & Young, undercounting averages 76% and in some cases can be as high as 674%. That represents a tremendous loss of revenue for companies selling ad inventories. But the problem is even more serious. Most of the proxy servers are in corporations, and the demographics of users in those corporations represent precisely the affluent demographics that advertisers try to reach. This undercounting not only affects size counts but also biases user demographic descriptions.

Why Proxy Servers?

Proxy servers were developed primarily to solve one of the major problems of the Internet—lack of bandwidth. The more users within a corporation who access the Internet, the more bandwidth the company must purchase. Alternatively, the company can purchase a proxy server to squeeze more bandwidth out of the existing channel. The proxy server copies frequently accessed pages. Since the page is stored in a proxy server's memory, subsequent access does not use up bandwidth to resend the page from the Internet. Proxy servers work in the following way:

First Time Through

1. Employee John Doe browses the Web and types in www.espn.SportsZone.com to check out the latest sports scores.
2. The proxy server intercepts John's request.
3. The proxy server then forwards the request to www.espn.SportsZone.com.
4. www.espn.SportsZone.com delivers the Web page to the proxy server.
5. The proxy server saves the page in its memory. This part of a computer's memory is called cache since it tends to change often.
6. The proxy server then sends a copy of the page to John Doe.

Each Subsequent Time

7. Susan Smith types in www.espn.SportsZone.com to see the sports scores also.

8. The proxy server intercepts Susan's request.

9. Now before going out to www.espn.SportsZone.com the proxy server checks to see whether it has the ESPN page in memory.

10. Finding the page in memory, it checks to see whether the page is old (more on this later). If it determines that the page is still current, then it sends Susan Smith the copy from memory.

Therefore, ESPN never receives any notification that the second user, Susan Smith, has viewed its page. And other users viewing the same page are similarly not counted.

Several Problems Are Created by This Scenario

The above scenario creates problems for audience measurement techniques.

1. ESPN records one less impression for which it can charge the advertiser.

2. ESPN records one less page view that it can report to its investors.

3. The ads never rotate on the page. The same ad is seen over and over again, leading to ad burnout and potential loss of effectiveness.

4. The page will grow stale over time as the sports scores change.

How Does the Proxy Server Know When to Update a Page?

Pages growing stale over time are of particular concern to a proxy server. A proxy server really has little value if it is serving out old pages. Fortunately, there are solutions to avoid stale pages:

1. The proxy server can set an expiration date and time on all pages cached. For example, any page older than an hour or older than a day needs to be refreshed.

2. A Web site can set an expiration date on the cached page which the proxy server may or may not honor.

3. A Web site can record the Last-Modified-Date on every page. This date is accessible to the proxy server. The proxy server can compare the Last-Modified-Date that it has on the page in memory with the Last-Modified-Date for the page at the Web site. If the dates are the same, then the page has not changed and it is safe to send the user the cached copy. Checking with the Web site in this fashion is actually a very low bandwidth operation, since the only information being exchanged is a date—not an entire Web page.

Cache Busting

Because the problem of undercounting is so serious, many sites have developed techniques to prevent proxy servers from caching their pages. Such techniques are called *cache busting*. Here are examples of cache busting:

1. The Web site can set the expiration date of all of its pages to NOW. Such pages will not be cached.

2. The Web site can refuse to set a Last-Modified-Date on its pages. Pages without a Last-Modified-Date are normally not cached.

3. The Web site can update the Last-Modified-Date of all its pages every night even if the content does not change.

4. The Web site can set lots of cookies, since cookies are not usually cached (see explanation of cookies elsewhere in this text).

5. The Web site can use Common Gateway Interface (CGI) scripts, since these are not usually cached.

As may be expected, corporate IS managers attempt to bust the cache busters, leading to a vicious cycle in which the user ultimately loses.

The MatchLogic Solution

MatchLogic was the first company to develop a solution for the undercounting problem that both is proxy server friendly and at the same time ensures accurate counting. The MatchLogic solution is called TrueCount and works like this:

1. At the top of each Web page, MatchLogic includes a small piece of code which cannot be cached.

2. The rest of the Web page is cached normally.

3. When the user requests the Web page, the small piece of code, comes to life and sends a message to MatchLogic's ad server.

4. The ad server counts the new impression and then either sends a new ad to the page or allows the old one to be redisplayed.

It is important to note that this solution goes straight to the heart of the problem: How many eyeballs see an ad. When advertisers purchase impressions, this is the number they really want. In fact, this solution improves on TV and other traditional media audience measurement because Nielsen and others do not count the number of people who actually watch commercials during a show (versus go to the refrigerator). Screen space being small as it is, and consumer navigating behavior being focused and intense, adds up to good advertising exposure for banners on the Web. By the way, by watching the status line at the bottom of the browser window when surfing, one can see comments like "contacting ad server" in between comments about contacting the requested site.

Ethics and Law

SPAM

The transmission of unsolicited e-mail, known as *spam*, has received increasing attention in both ethical and legal discussions. The intensity of this interest has corresponded to the dramatic increase of spam over the past several years. Major Internet Service Providers (ISPs) state that spam can account for from 30% to 50% of all incoming e-mail. These rates have doubled from the volume reported only a year ago.

The prevalence of spam has caused negative reactions by both ISPs and users. Systems managers and some Internet experts have expressed the concern that mass electronic mailing may overload network capacity. Users complain of the annoyance of receiving unwanted solicitations. These complaints are often met with denials of hardware overload and the claim that bulk mail is routine and uncontroversial in conventional postal contexts and should be equally acceptable in the digital world.

On an ethical level, spam raises several issues. Although there may be some question as to the Internet's overall capacity to handle large quantities of e-mail, there appears to be substantial evidence to suggest spam can cause damage to network operation and thus constitutes a potential misuse of common resources. In addition to systemwide damage, the burdens placed upon individuals to sort and dispose of unrequested material is fast becoming significant in terms of time and effort. Finally, there is increasing evidence to confirm that spam is overwhelmingly found to be an annoyance within the general Internet community. The decision to engage in activities that are likely to be perceived in such negative ways may itself be ethically questioned.

Another related ethical as well as legal concern involves how target e-mail addresses are collected. In some instances, lists of addressees are obtained through the use of programs that record user names from Usenet postings, Web pages, and bulletin board messages. These lists are frequently sold, traded, or combined. Such activities may be problematic in the sense that they are accomplished without the knowledge or express permission of the user and may involve an impermissible intrusion upon an individual's privacy. It may be argued that, unlike a conventional postal address, the username carries with it information that is more personal and goes beyond simply designating a mailing location.

Spam has been addressed through both technical and legal means. In the former instance, some ISPs have implemented filters to block incoming mass mailings. Others have instituted and enforced policies prohibiting spamming activity within their systems. Legally, spam has met with a number of difficulties. In the case of *Cyber Promotions, Inc.* v. *America Online, Inc.* (948 F.Supp. 436 [E.D. Pa., 1996]), the court held that a spam producer had no First Amendment right to send its product to AOL subscribers and that consequently the ISP could block its messaging activity.

Similar actions have resulted in settlements which have limited the ways in which spamming activity can take place.

Legislation has been introduced to regulate spam through various means. Currently, the Telephone Consumer Protection Act of 1991 prohibits the sending of unsolicited Faxes on the reasoning that such communications present an unnecessary and unwelcome expense to the receiver. One 1997 congressional proposal would have attached spamming to this prohibition, effectively ending the activity. Another, more recent set of bills (S. 1618 and H.R. 3888) seek to require that spam be prominently identified as such in each mailing and that receivers be provided with an opportunity to remove themselves from future mailings. This approach has been criticized as being too weak, allowing spam to be sent to any individual at least once, before the option to leave future mailings is exercised.

Spam may also be a vehicle for deceptive or fraudulent advertising. Such activities may include the use of false return addresses or other information. Additionally, spam may be used to advertise sensitive or blatantly illegal services. The Federal Trade Commission (www.ftc.gov) has initiated an alert, which describes its interest in tracking and identifying such potential illegal behavior

In addition to individual ISP efforts and governmental regulation, a number of professional groups, such as the Direct Marketing Association, are working to enact professional guidelines which set forth standards in mass electronic mailing. Ideas include the use of incentives, such as reduced rates, to encourage users to accept these messages as well as the creation of a certification process which identifies reputable mass mailers.

Although spam likely will be found to merit increased regulation, it will be important to be mindful of the fact that a decision to curtail messaging should never be made lightly. Although commercial speech has been held to possess a lesser degree of First Amendment protection, it is still a form of expression. Similarly, the threat of any form of censorship must be seriously considered and carefully balanced against the ideals of a free society.

Savvy Sites

Web Site and Address	Importance to Net Marketers
American Association of Advertising Agencies www.commercepark.com/AAAA/	The AAAA is a national trade organization headquartered in New York and represents the advertising agency industry.
BrainBug www.brainbug.com	BrainBug is a marketing communications agency that specializes in online media services. The company also offers services in the traditional media of direct mail and P.R.

Fallon McElligott www.fallon.com/	This firm is one of the world's top advertising agencies. At its web site visitors can take a vividly defined guided tour of the company.
Federal Trade Commission www.ftc.gov/	The FTC is a government agency that regulates monopolistic trusts and protects customers from unscrupulous business practices, including deceptive advertising.
NetCreations, Inc. www.netcreations.com	NetCreations is an online firm that provides "opt-in" email marketing services allowing direct marketers to reach prospects in a cost-effective way that respects the culture of the Internet. Its PostMaster Direct Response service is a list manager and broker for more than 1 million e-mail addresses that encompass over 3,000 topical categories. NetCreations also offers Web site promotion and per-inquiry lead generation services.
Public Relations Society of America www.prsa.org/	With 17,000 members, the PSRA is the world's largest organization for public relations professionals. This site features news about public relations case studies, continuing education opportunities, and, of course, membership information.
Valupage www.valupage.com	This site features coupons for selective cities. Just enter your zip code, browse the selections, and print out what you like.
Playhere www.playhere.com	This infotainment-oriented site is a cool hangout where one can watch live Internet video, shop for post cards, download screensavers, test out arcade games, enter games and sweepstakes, track down celebrities, get advice on HTML, and more.

7

Relationship Marketing through Online Strategies

"The Internet may be the ultimate one-to-one marketing tool."

—Morgan Stanley Dean Witter

Chapter Outline

- The Amazon Story
- Building Customer Relationships, 1:1
- Relationship Marketing Defined
- Brand Loyalty Decline
- Relationship Marketing Benefits
- Internet Strategies Facilitating Relationship Marketing
- Guarding Consumer Privacy

Practitioner Perspective

The Dual-Value Proposition —Kathryn Creech, General Manager, HomeArts Online Network

Leveraging Technology

Cookies and Collaborative Filtering

Ethics and Law

Privacy

Learning Objectives

- Marketing review
  - Define relationship marketing
  - Explain six major differences between mass marketing and relationship marketing
  - Explain why consumer brand loyalty has declined in the United States
- Tell how the Internet can build relationship with four major stakeholders
- Differentiate and give examples of three levels of relationship building for Internet marketers
- Justify the value of relationship marketing to companies
- Explain the benefits of relationship marketing to consumers
- Describe how intranets and extranets are used to build relationship with stakeholders
- Discriminate between incoming and outgoing e-mail for relationship building
- Discuss several Web-based relationship marketing strategies
- Explain two facets of Internet privacy and their role in relationship marketing

<table>
<tr><td>

The

Amazon

Story

</td><td>

"Are we going to put physical bookstores out of business? No. TV didn't put movie theaters out of business. But physical bookstores will have to keep adding value to what they've got."

</td></tr>
</table>

—Jeff Bezos, founder and CEO, Amazon

Jeff Bezos, founder and CEO of Amazon (www.amazon.com) is 34 years old, is a Princeton graduate, and sits atop a company valued at $7 billion. Amazon opened its Internet storefront in July 1995 and has never looked back. The key to Amazon's success has been using technology to build relationships and brand loyalty both with its customers and with its partners: content sites that refer customers.

Bezos realized early on that purchasing on the Web was less than an idyllic experience for the average customer. While Net-heads may relish the experience, the general population finds purchasing online a bit scary, frustrating, and intimidating. Bezos is well aware that "the smallest amount of friction can stop people" from coming to a site, let alone buying from that site. To compensate for the inconvenience of purchasing online, Bezos had to add value to the shopping experience. He discovered that treating customers as individuals, anticipating their needs, and thus building relationships could add value.

Interestingly, the relationships that Bezos built were the ones that would be found in the smallest of bookstores—a personal greeting, recommendations based on past purchases, recommendations based on the mood of the consumer, notification of a new release by the customer's favorite author, and "conversations" with other customers about the book. To give just one example, Amazon's mood matcher includes the following categories:

- Fantastic Voyages
- Life's a Beach
- Serious Matters
- Summer Loving
- The Right Book for the Right Place
- Un-Put-Downable
- It Was a Dark and Stormy Night
- Love and Relationships
- Stargazing
- The Finer Things
- Transitions

One would not expect to develop such personal relationships in brick and mortar book superstores such as Borders or Barnes & Noble, let alone from the largest bookseller on the planet. The value of good customer relationships cannot be overstated. Forty-four percent of Amazon's 2.5 million customers are repeat purchasers. Furthermore, according to Forrester Research, consumers tend to be more loyal online than offline. In the offline world consumers will often choose to shop at the closest bookstore. However, in the online world all bookstores are equally distant. Customers will repeat purchase where the experience was satisfactory and where they received good value. Therefore, establishing the dominant online brand in a product category is critical. The message has not been lost on Bezos, who has repeatedly steered away from profitability in order to grow the business through increased advertising and acquisitions.

Amazon also builds relationships with content site partners. The driving force behind these relationships is financial. Amazon rewards the content sites with up to 15% in commissions for every customer referred to Amazon. Content sites need only display the Amazon logo with a link to the Amazon site. The content site receives a commission for each customer that follows the link and buys a book. Content sites even receive a monthly report itemizing exactly which books the customers purchased. An Amazon report is a valuable marketing resource for content providers because it informs them about their customer needs and behavior. This practice of referrals and commissions is called *syndicated selling*, since it distributes Amazon's points of sale throughout the Internet. Amazon startled the wired world by developing 15,000 points of sale in 15 months. The content sites become brand loyal to Amazon and are less likely to pursue similar arrangements with Borders or Barnes & Noble.

Amazon continues to leverage its customer base as it moves into new product offerings. The company now sells CDs and by the time this book is printed will even sell movies. In all these ventures it will apply the same tested formula—build relationships which add value to the purchase experience and foster brand loyalty. Perhaps the reader purchased this book from Amazon!

Building Customer Relationships, 1:1

Customers at Rina's Salon in Rocky Hill, Connecticut, are treated like friends. When a customer calls for a hair appointment a receptionist answers the phone and asks how the permanent wave is looking these days. This creates a discussion of whether or not it is time to redo the curls. When the customer arrives, Rina asks about the vacation the client was planning last month and about the kids. The customer might tell Rina that she wants a new look and ask for advice. Rina will honestly say what type of hairstyle will flatter the customer and what will not. What's unusual about the interaction between Rina and the customer is that Rina does not push product but instead suggests solutions based on her understanding of the client and her needs: "Are you ready to try that blonde streak, or do you want to work up to it for next summer?" Rina's Salon develops long-term relationships one at a time (1:1) not unlike those developed by retailers in the early 1900s. The customer trusts Rina and truly believes that Rina will make her look beautiful. A customer like this is brand loyal and will not easily be enticed by competition. In fact, we'd bet that none of Rina's customers would try another salon even if the haircut were offered free!

This example illustrates a major shift in marketing thought: from mass marketing to individualized marketing, and from focus on acquiring lots of new customers to retaining and building more business with fewer loyal customers. This way of doing business has been present in the industrial market for a long time, it has spread to the consumer market for services (e.g., Rina's), and now even marketers of tangible products are considering how to build long-term customer relationships. Internet technologies facilitate relationship marketing—the subject of this chapter.

Relationship Marketing Defined

The seemingly old-fashioned way of doing business practiced at Amazon and at Rina's returned to marketing practice in the 1980s and was dubbed *relationship marketing* (by practitioners as *1:1 marketing*.) In its original definition, relationship marketing is about establishing, maintaining, enhancing, and commercializing customer relationships through promise fulfillment (Grönroos 1990). Usually firms try to build profitable relationships in the long term (versus short term), and always the relationship is mutually beneficial. Promise fulfillment means that when firms make offers in their marketing communications programs, customer expectations will be met through product experiences. For example, if Domino's Pizza ads claim 30-minute delivery of delicious pizza, or if Amazon promises to send an ordered book in two days, a customer will be satisfied if the promise is fulfilled. Similarly, good relationships are built when the company operations personnel meet the promises of salespeople.

Relationship marketing involves more than promise fulfillment. It means two-way communication with individual stakeholders, one at a time (1:1). This includes listening as well as talking with both business and individual consumers. Amazon collaborates with other Web retailers, thus building its affiliate program. At Amazon, consumers visit the book finder and answer questions about the books they prefer, and then the firm returns a list of recommendations. Also, users may post reviews of books on Amazon's site for other shoppers to view. Amazon captures these data in an ongoing effort to tailor products and services to individual needs. Note that these "conversations" with customers are not entirely individualized but are rather exchanges of bits of automated information based on needs.

Another important tenet of relationship marketing involves customer development in the long term: "maintaining and enhancing." Firms that focus on discrete transactions are focusing on short-term market share goals. A firm using relationship marketing focuses on "share of mind," not share of market, and it differentiates individual customers based on need rather than differentiating products for target groups. It will be more profitable for Rina to identify her best customers, get to know them individually, and suggest additional products based on needs than to try to acquire new customers. If she is successful, clients will eventually buy all their beauty products and services at Rina's such as hair coloring, electrolysis, and perhaps even clothing. Rina saves on promotion and price discounting dollars: She spends time on customer retention versus money on customer acquisition. Exhibit 7 - 1 displays a summary of these ideas, comparing mass marketing to relationship marketing. It is important to remember that few firms fall on either end of the continuum but instead use varying strategies for different products and markets.

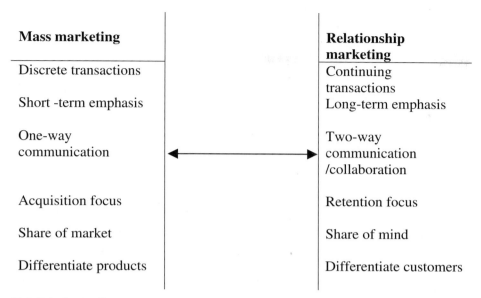

Mass marketing		Relationship marketing
Discrete transactions		Continuing transactions
Short -term emphasis		Long-term emphasis
One-way communication		Two-way communication /collaboration
Acquisition focus		Retention focus
Share of market		Share of mind
Differentiate products		Differentiate customers

Exhibit 7 - 1 Continuum from Mass to Relationship Marketing

STAKEHOLDERS

The core of relationship marketing is that creating customer support enhances a firm's profitability and loyalty by satisfying individual needs, one at a time. Most firms extend the early definition, however, and use relationship marketing techniques to build mutually supportive environments with stakeholders other than customers, such as employees and stockholders. It is possible for a firm to establish and maintain relationships with four different stakeholder groups (adapted from Varadarajan and Cunningham 1995). These relationships are listed below along with examples of how organizations use the Internet for relationship building.

1. **Internal stakeholders**: These are employees and stockholders. It is difficult for a firm to persuade buyers when employees are not happy. The University of Nevada at Reno features employee accomplishments on its Web site and also includes lots of information such as how to put an individual home page on the site from a remote location. Faculty and staff can apply for additional e-mail accounts through a form right on the Web site.

2. **Suppliers to the firm**: General Electric uses the Internet to receive bids from its suppliers. This system not only lowers transaction costs, but also enhances competition and speeds the order fulfillment process.

3. **Lateral partnerships**: These are competitors, not-for-profit organizations, or governments that join with the firm for some common goal. CargoNet Transportation Community Network, a consortium of 200,000 shippers, handles 250 million trade-related documents a year for Hong Kong shippers at the world's busiest port. The Internet facilitates document tracking and customer

service for manufacturers, ocean, rail, truck,, and air carriers as well as banks, insurance companies, and governments associated with CargoNet (www.eds.com).

4. **Customers of the firm**: These are businesses, other organizations, and individuals who are either distribution channel intermediaries or ultimate consumers. Amazon's 15,000 Web sites that refer customers through the affiliate program fall in this category, as do the consumers that patronize Amazon.

RELATIONSHIP LEVELS

Some marketers believe that relationship marketing is practiced on three levels (see Exhibit 7 - 2). The strongest relationships are formed if all three levels are used and if the product itself actually satisfies buyers. At level one marketers build a financial bond with customers by using pricing strategies. This is the lowest level of relationship because price promotions are easily imitated. Hotcoupons sends coupons via e-mail to users who have downloaded coupons at its site. One of the authors demonstrated this site to the class, printing a coupon for a local pizza restaurant, and subsequently received an e-mail containing a coupon for $1.00 off at a local dry cleaner.

Level	Primary Bond	Potential for Sustained Competitive Advantage	Main Element of Marketing Mix	Web Example
One	Financial	Low	Price	www.hotcoupons.com
Two	Social Build 1:1 relationships Build community	Medium	Personal communications	www.palmpilot.com
Three	Structural	High	Service delivery	my.yahoo.com

Exhibit 7 - 2 Three Levels of Relationship Marketing
Source: adapted from Berry and Parasuraman (1991)

At level two, marketers stimulate social interaction with customers. This involves ongoing personal communication with individual customers and may include aggressive pricing strategies as well. At level two there is more customer loyalty because of the social bond between customer and company or customer and salesperson. 3Com Corporation creates social bonding around its PalmPilot[tm]: the cool electronic hand-held personal organizer that is quickly gaining popularity. In one survey of business executives, 70% said they own a PalmPilot, using it primarily for personal information and e-mail. PalmPilot tries to build community with these buyers by linking to user groups (Exhibit 7 - 3). In addition, 3Com invites users to register for InSync Online, a service which sends one or two automated yet personalized e-mails a week giving tips on getting the most from the organizer.

Exhibit 7 - 4 displays an e-mail to one of the authors, personalized both by name ("Dear Judy") and by type of product owned (Pilot 5000). It is important to note that many of these e-mails have no selling message at all and thus serve to let customers know that 3Com cares about fulfilling its promise for its PDA products. An important feature of 3Com's e-mail program is the ability for consumers to be taken off the list ("unsubscribe"). This way, 3Com does not risk upsetting its valued customers. Further, 3Com has created a community of users who share software and tips on the Web site. There are hundreds of freeware and shareware applications created by users, and PalmPilot features the best on its Web site and in a newsletter. It also maintains a web ring of 150 independent Web sites to build community among PalmPilot users and the products that interest them. These examples show how 3Com maintains a community of users, software developers, and others interested in their products.

Level three relationship marketing relies on creating structural solutions to customer problems. Structural bonds are created when firms add value by making structural changes that facilitate the relationship. All of the major Web portals are seeking to create structural bonds with their users. Services like My Yahoo! allow consumers to customize their interface to Yahoo! so that it lists weather and movies in their area, their own stock portfolios, and news of interest to them. Once consumers invest the time and effort to customize this interface, they will be hard pressed to switch to another portal.

Brand Loyalty Decline

The move to relationship marketing was prompted primarily by the slow but sure decline in customer brand loyalty over the past twenty years. A 1975 study of 4,000 consumers found 74% of the women and 80% of the men agreeing with the statement, "I try to stick with well-known brand names" (Rapp and Collins 1996). In 1984 those numbers dropped to 58% for women and 52% for men. In 1993, Roper Starch Worldwide reported that in thirteen packaged good categories only 48% of consumers know what brand they want when they enter a store—down from 56% in 1988. There are two major factors contributing to this decline. First is the proliferation of products, and second is the increase in marketing use of sales promotions. These occurred in an environmental context magnifying their impact.

TOO MANY PRODUCTS

According to *New Product News,* there were 17,571 products introduced in 1993 (cited in Rapp and Collins 1996). There are over 200 brands of breakfast cereal alone in the United States. Most new products are line extensions, of course, because this is a lower-risk strategy for marketers. Kimberly Clark offers twenty types of Kleenex facial tissues, including lotion-impregnated tissues, unscented tissues, and different package sizes with designs for every taste (Shapiro 1994). Weilbacher notes that the explosion of new brands creates consumer drowning in "unfathomable and largely insignificant product differences" (Weilbacher 1993). Internet technologies gave marketers yet another venue for new products and line extensions, thus compounding the problem of product proliferation and subsequent need for differentiation. In this climate advertising cannot easily convince consumers to care about things such as Coca-Cola's secret formula or the fact that the Jolly Green Giant "personally" picks asparagus in the valley.

TOO MANY SALES PROMOTIONS

In order to combat declining loyalty, and to turn advertising into sales results, marketers increased use of sales promotion incentives such as coupons, rebates, and free giveaways (premiums). The overuse of these tactics trained consumers to watch for the sales and to evaluate products on price versus quality: value. Sales promotions that include price discounts are generally believed to create short-term sales at the expense of longer-term brand loyalty.

Exhibit 7 - 3 The Palm Computing Site Builds Community
Source: www.palm.com

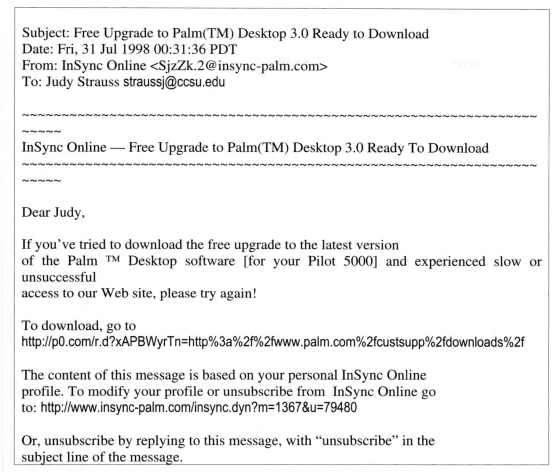

Subject: Free Upgrade to Palm(TM) Desktop 3.0 Ready to Download
Date: Fri, 31 Jul 1998 00:31:36 PDT
From: InSync Online <SjzZk.2@insync-palm.com>
To: Judy Strauss straussj@ccsu.edu

~~~~~~
~~~~~

InSync Online — Free Upgrade to Palm(TM) Desktop 3.0 Ready To Download
~~~~~~
~~~~~

Dear Judy,

If you've tried to download the free upgrade to the latest version
of the Palm ™ Desktop software [for your Pilot 5000] and experienced slow or unsuccessful
access to our Web site, please try again!

To download, go to
http://p0.com/r.d?xAPBWyrTn=http%3a%2f%2fwww.palm.com%2fcustsupp%2fdownloads%2f

The content of this message is based on your personal InSync Online
profile. To modify your profile or unsubscribe from InSync Online go
to: http://www.insync-palm.com/insync.dyn?m=1367&u=79480

Or, unsubscribe by replying to this message, with "unsubscribe" in the
subject line of the message.

Exhibit 7 - 4 PalmPilot^{tm} Personalized E-mail to Customer

MARKET ENVIRONMENT CHANGES

Finally, changes in the marketing environment facilitated the movement away from brand loyalty.

- High unemployment and the recession that ended in the mid-1980s created a climate for price shopping. During this time, consumers cut back on product spending and began watching for values (price/quality relationship). A sales promotion price incentive tips the balance toward value. Price shopping became a habit for many consumers that continues today.

- Social values have changed such that consumers are generally very sophisticated, distrusting advertising and demanding ethical behavior from firms. The proliferation of information brought about by the Internet gives consumers the ammunition they need to confront marketers, asking hard questions and demanding that their needs be met. In this climate, consumers evaluate brands more closely to see if they are doing business with a company they can believe in and trust.

Relationship Marketing Benefits

Relationship marketing is cost effective. This is true both because it is less expensive to retain one customer than to acquire one, and because it is easier and less costly to sell more products to one customer than to sell that same amount to two customers. Another benefit of relationship marketing is the positive word-of-mouth communication spread by satisfied customers. Finally, when two firms join forces and create a strong market relationship, synergy occurs.

INCREASED PROFITS

Most businesses spend more money acquiring new customers than they spend keeping current customers. Doing this is usually a mistake. It typically costs five times as much to acquire a new customer than to retain a current one, as is shown in Exhibit 7 - 5 (Peppers and Rogers 1996). In this example, if a firm allocates $3000 in its marketing budget to acquire six customers, the cost of each will be $500. Since it costs one-fifth less (on average) to retain customers, that same $500 would entice five customers to stay at a cost of $100 each. If instead of spending $3,000 on gaining six customers, a firm spent $1,500 on three new customers and $1,500 on customer retention, it would be twelve customers ahead.

Acquisition Emphasis		Retention Emphasis	
Gain 6 new customers ($500 each)	$3,000	Gain 3 new customers ($500 each)	$1,500
Retain 5 current customers ($100 each)	$ 500	Retain 20 current customers ($100 each)	$2,000
Total cost	$3,500	Total cost	$3,500
Total number of customers	11	Total number of customers	23

Exhibit 7 - 5 Maximizing Number of Customers
Adapted from Peppers and Rogers (1996)

More customers do equate to more sales. However, acquiring and retaining customers is only one half of the equation. A firm must also attempt to increase the amount purchased by each customer. Amazon recommends additional books and CDs to customers and will soon sell videos. Music Boulevard periodically e-mails special offers to its customers to encourage repeat business. Expedia[tm] and Travelocity e-mail customers when a fare of interest to them drops in price. 1-800-Flowers e-mails reminders to customers when their loved ones have special occasions.

Word-of-Mouth Communication

In addition to increased sales from satisfied customers, happy people make recommendations about Web sites, stores, and products to their friends. Word-of-mouth communication among customers has been called the heart of relationship marketing. Businesspeople commonly refer each other to bankers and other suppliers, just as consumers tell friends about product experiences. Positive word-of-mouth can bring many customers to the door, just as negative word-of-mouth can drive them away. And when one considers the lifetime value of one customer, those losses are heavy indeed. One research study reported that each dissatisfied customer tells nine or ten people about the unhappy experience, and 13% of dissatisfied customers each tell more than twenty people about how bad the company/products were (Sonnenberg 1993).

The Internet is especially well suited for word-of-mouth communication because of e-mail, newsgroups, chat, and personal Web pages. Users can easily forward e-mails to other people, adding positive or negative commentary. People send e-mails to other individuals or to groups of people on distribution lists. One of the hottest e-mail distributions occurred a few years ago when users distributed an animated audio/visual depiction of the Oscar Meyer Wiener song: a marketer's dream. E-mail sent to distribution lists is redistributed to the entire subscription list of the LISTSERV. Some companies maintain LISTSERVs for customers. Many other LISTSERVs are public forums typically organized around a topic or product. Users also employ word-of-mouth communication by posting to newsgroups such as Usenet. Like LISTSERVs, Usenet is also organized around topics or products. DejaNews archives the Usenet so that consumers can search for discussion on most products and learn what others have said about their experiences and perceptions. Chat rooms provide another venue to air product experiences. Finally personal Web pages, especially those that bash a company (e.g., www.ThisCompanySucks.com) are a very effective way to spread negative word of mouth. Many companies monitor these negative Web pages and often respond individually to consumer complaints.

The Travelzoo Company Giveaway

Travelzoo is a company that searches the Web for travel bargains and lists them on the site. As a new company, it wanted to generate traffic and build a site that met user needs. To do this the founders created an innovative word-of-mouth sales promotion: They offered to give the company away! Under the rules, any Web user could register for three free shares of stock in Travelzoo and receive additional shares for others they referred and who also registered for free shares. The following is their explanation:

> You are important to us...
> Of course the travelzoo "stock program" is quite innovative. "Why are they giving away shares for free" you ask. The answer is easy: We make you the offer to become a shareholder of travelzoo because YOU are important. As a participating co-owner you could tell

friends and colleagues about travelzoo, submit your ideas, participate in important company decisions, etc. You may already know that high site traffic (number of hits) is essential for successful sales of banner ads. An extraordinary Web site can attract a large number of visitors, but only if people know about it! When you tell others about the site, you create value for the company. That's why we are offering you the shares as a gift. It's our way of saying "thank you."

Users caught wind of this and rushed to get their free shares. See Exhibit 7 - 6 for an e-mail forwarded from one user to the next and finally to one of the authors. It reminds one of a chain letter! This is a good example of consumer word-of-mouth stimulated by a marketing promotion. How well did it work? On July 26, 1998, Travelzoo's home page announced, "Welcome to the Web site that is owned by 455,618 netsurfers!" At three shares each, imagine the online owner's meeting that will ensue! Travelzoo founders must be commended for their promotional savvy. In the end, however, the site must provide value to users, and the firm must be able to sell advertising or products to achieve profitability for its owners.

Partnership Synergy

When two or more firms join in a business relationship, the results often exceed what each firm might have accomplished alone. Amazon sells more books because of its additional 15,000 points of sale at partner Web sites. Through the Amazon relationship, each affiliate can offer added value to customers without incurring the expense of entering electronic commerce. Each partner also receives additional revenue from Amazon with virtually no expenses. This is a classic "win-win" situation.

The Internet spawned a large number of new business partnerships. An interesting example is the Microsoft-NBC (MSNBC) partnership. Each firm is investing an initial $200 million over a five-year period beginning in early 1996 to launch NBC's Internet operation. NBC brought its news gathering, reporting, and advertising space sales expertise to the table and Microsoft brought the Internet technology. Interestingly, the two different cultures made it difficult for communication: Microsoft executives in suits talked bytes and bandwidth in a formal business style, and NBC managers in polo shirts and khakis spoke of sound bites and camera angles in a creative and informal style. The NBC staff even had to become less "personal" and learn e-mail when the Microsoft folks entered the picture! MSNBC managers plan to make a profit for the venture at the end of the five-year period through advertising sales. NBC hopes to increase overall eyeballs by adding this third distribution channel as well as by drawing younger consumers to its network and cable news via the Internet. Microsoft adds content generation to its stable of products. Both firms benefit from potential profits and added skills.

Subject: [Fwd: Fwd: FW: Free Stock!!!!!!!!!!!!!!!!!!!!!!!!!!!!!!!!!!!!!!!]
Date: Thu, 18 Jun 1998 14:21:30 -0400
From: Jeff Jacobs <jacobs@xx.net>
To: dailey@xx.com, mp_word@xx.com, na@xx.com, Nicole@xx.com,
    SBailey@xx.com, m3raf@xx.com, M3ros@xx.com
CC: weidler@xx.net, herbr@xx.com, jack@xx.com, br01@xx.net,
Straussj@ccsu.edu,
    lchristen@xx.com, boyken@xx.com, leslie @xx.com

This appears to work, I tried just a couple of times and was able to get registered for my three shares of stock. When you register, please input my email address **"jacobs@xx.net"** so I can qualify for more shares!
Good luck!
Jeff

Subject: Fwd: FW: Free Stock!!!!!!!!!!!!!!!!!!!!!!!!!!!!!!!!!!!!
Date: Wed, 17 Jun 1998 18:23:24 EDT
From: <JBasin@xx.com>
To: Sutliff@xx.com, Hooper@xx.com, DEVADOBE@xx.com, s3cott@xx.net,
    steven@compuserve.com, jacobs@xx.net

This is really easy and if it works it could be fun. Remember to use my name **jbasin@xx.com** when you sign up. I had to try two or three times yesterday to sign up so keep trying.

Subject: Fwd: FW: Free Stock!!!!!!!!!!!!!!!!!!!!!!!!!!!!!!!!!!!!!
Date: Mon, 15 Jun 1998 21:49:08 EDT
From: Sheets@xx.com
To: EULYS@xx.com, JBasin@xx.com, NyrDreams@xx.com,
Ltllady@xx.com, Pozas@xx.com,
    ROBINSON@xx.com

Hi, try this if your interested, but be sure to use my email address: **sheets@xx.com**

Exhibit 7 - 6 Word-of-Mouth via E-mail

BENEFITS TO THE CUSTOMER

Most customers desire brand loyalty as much as do the firms they patronize. Sometimes it is tough being a consumer: One is constantly bombarded by marketing communications and unlimited product choices. Jagdish Sheth (1995) wrote that from a consumer's perspective the basic tenet of relationship marketing is choice reduction. This claim alludes to the idea that consumers want to patronize the same store, mall, and service providers simply because doing so is efficient. That is, consumers do not want to spend their days contemplating which brand of toothpaste to buy or how to find a good dentist. Many consumers are "loyalty prone," searching for the right product or service and then sticking with it as long as the promises are more or less fulfilled. For example, both of the authors buy online from Amazon books because they have had good past experiences, their preferences are already stored on file, the interface is familiar, and the prices are competitive (though not necessarily the lowest). Companies generally receive a positive return on marketing budget that is focused on the retention of loyalty-prone customers as long as it is used to build relationship and not purely to discount price.

Most customers like to patronize stores, services, and Web sites where they are treated like individuals with important needs and where they know those needs will be met, "satisfaction guaranteed." When 3Com sends an e-mail about nifty new uses of the PalmPilot that is addressed to the customer by name and refers to the exact product purchased, it seems like the company cares. When Amazon writes that it has a new book by an author a customer enjoys, this action builds brand loyalty. Of course, firms must learn to answer e-mails sent from customers as well. Listening to hundreds of thousands of customers, one at a time, can be difficult and expensive, but it satisfies customers.

Internet Strategies Facilitating Relationship Marketing

Incoming toll free numbers, fax-on-demand, voice mail, and automated telephone routing are examples of technology that assists in providing individual dialogue between customers and companies. The Internet, however, is the first fully interactive and individually addressable low cost multimedia channel. According to Berry (1995), information technology helps service marketers perform relationship marketing efficiently through these key tasks (p. 238):

- tracking the buying patterns and overall relationship of existing customers
- customizing services, promotions, and pricing to customers' specific requirements
- coordinating or integrating the delivery of multiple services to the same customer
- providing two-way communication channels—company to customer, customer to company
- minimizing the probability of service errors and breakdowns
- augmenting core service offerings with valued extras

- personalizing service encounters as appropriate

Peppers and Rogers (1996) agree, suggesting that information technology helps firms to understand and manage customers, to dialogue with customers, and to take products to customers. Through the Internet, companies can show customers the products they want, providing information and transactions right in the privacy of home or office. They suggest that "every time a consumer has to leave home to run an errand, a business opportunity is revealed" (p. vii).

The following sections focus on the strategic use of intranets, extranets, Web sites, and e-mail for relationship building.

INTRANET

In 1995 when Southern New England Telephone (SNET) decided to change its image from a stodgy, old-fashioned telephone company to a modern, high-technology company, it started with a communication campaign to employees. SNET reasoned that if it couldn't sell the employees on this idea, a consumer campaign would be wasted effort. Most corporate executives would agree that employee word-of-mouth influences a company's image in the marketplace. Naturally, companies want satisfied employees for other reasons as well. One way to build positive relationships with employees is through dissemination of timely information about the firm, its offerings, and the employees themselves. Many firms communicate with employees through hard copy newsletters and memos. Intranets are emerging as cost-effective and more timely alternatives to these vehicles. An intranet is a computer network, similar to the Internet, established within an organization to provide information internally to employees. The information on intranet Web pages can be quickly and easily changed: an advantage over paper publishing. SNET uses an intranet to convey the corporate identity shift to its employees while simultaneously building a relationship with those employees (see www.snet.com). It also puts the graphic standards manual online with password protection so that employees can download information about SNET logo usage.

Other uses of corporate networks include e-mail distribution lists (e.g., company announcements) and collaborative work environments. Many firms have adopted software such as Lotus Notes to facilitate collaborative work environments. Employees post documents to a Notes folder, where other employees can view and edit the material. All of these uses of intranets have the potential for a firm to build relationship with an important stakeholder: employees.

EXTRANET

Extranets are two or more networks that are joined for the purpose of sharing information. If two companies link their intranets, they would have an extranet. By definition, however, extranets are proprietary to the organizations involved. Companies participating in an extranet have formed a structural bond, the third and strongest level of relationship marketing.

Electronic Data Systems (EDS) is a Dallas-based firm that provides enterprise-wide computer desktop services from procurement to network management for large clients. The word *enterprise* means that they focus on all the computer desktops in an entire company, bringing them together in a network. They manage over 736,000 desktops, both internally to EDS and externally, in nineteen countries (Fernandes 1998). EDS created an innovative extranet called the Renasence Channel, which links desktops of their suppliers, clients, and employees in a 500,000-computer electronic marketplace. Forty suppliers selling over 2,000 software products fund the private network, paying $25,000 to $100,000 each to display their products and services in a catalog type format. The network is great for suppliers because they have access to and can build relationships with lots of potential buyers. These buyers trust the suppliers because EDS selected them. Suppliers are able to offer discounted prices to extranet users because their costs are low in this channel: one vendor reported a drop in order-processing expenses from $150 to $25 per item. Buyers benefit by having easy product information access, purchasing at the click of a mouse, product delivery tracking, online training, and expedited delivery directly to their offices. The Renasence Channel both creates a barrier to entry for suppliers not part of the network and presents switching costs for companies using the channel's services. The Renasence Channel is a good example of relationship building in the business-to-business market using Internet technology.

WEB SITE STRATEGIES

Listening to users and observing their Net behavior are two ways that organizations can learn more about customers and potential buyers. Armed with this information, firms can provide products and services that individuals desire. Firms can also use this information to personalize messages to users. Listening and observing is done either with or without the user's knowledge. When organizations ask users to complete information on a Web site, they are collecting information with the user's full knowledge and implicit permission. When firms observe consumers in chat rooms or track user behavior at Web sites, it is done behind the scenes. Tracking user behavior is useful to both users and companies, but it has its critics because of privacy considerations. Privacy is the subject of Ethics and Law in another chapter. In this section we discuss the use of information gathered at Web sites and how it is used to build relationships.

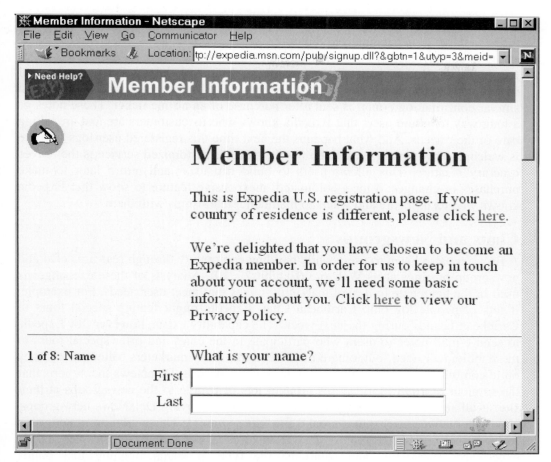

Exhibit 7 - 7 Expedia Registration Form
Source: www.expedia.msn.com

Web Forms

Web form is the technical term for a Web page that has designated places for the user
to type information. Many corporate Web sites sport Web forms, using them for a
multitude of purposes from site registration and survey research to product purchase.
Regardless of purpose, the information gathered serves to help the firm market its
products. Savvy firms also use the information to take advantage of the Internet's
ability to build relationships. One such firm is Expedia™: Microsoft Expedia Travel
Services, the online travel agency. After entering Expedia's site, but before using its
travel agency, a user must register (Exhibit 7 - 7). To register at Expedia, a user must
provide personal information such as name, physical address, and e-mail address, and
also product information such as the nearest airport. Once a user has provided

information, the site can build relationship by personalizing the page on subsequent visits or by sending personalized e-mail.

One author recently registered at Expedia and received the welcome e-mail in Exhibit 7 - 8. Note the list of services offered: this is an attempt to gain "share of mind," encouraging the user to use Expedia for all travel needs. Incidentally, a similar confirmation e-mail is sent after purchase of an airline ticket. These notes go a long way to assure users that Expedia knows who its customers are and are taking care of their needs. And what happens the next time this registered user logs on? She is welcomed by name! (see Exhibit 7 - 9). Another customized service is the "saved itinerary" feature. This allows users to build trip ideas and return later to make purchases or changes: a nice, automated, inexpensive feature to show that Expedia knows who its users are and wants to maintain relationships with them.

Chats and Newsgroups

A firm may also listen to users while building community through real-time chat and newsgroup postings at its Web site (Exhibit 7 - 10). Analysis of these exchanges is used in the aggregate to design marketing mixes that meet user needs. For example, if lots of people log onto Caribbean Chat, Expedia might feature special tours to Caribbean Islands during the next week. The capability exists, however, for Expedia to send e-mail notes to users who participate in the chats and offer special tours to these individuals (see "outgoing e-mail" section). Many marketers believe that if they build community at a site, users will return. Greg Wyse at DejaNews Inc. reports that the summer of 1998 Florida fires brought lots of people to the newsgroups at their site. It all started when a journalist sent an e-mail, copying DejaNews newsgroups, about alternative travel routes around fire-infested areas. This action prompted users to post their preferred routes. The result was a community of people sharing experiences, problems, and solutions: the type of social bonding that builds relationship between DejaNews and its users.

Subject: Expedia New Member Information
Date: 22 Jun 1998 21:32:01 -0700
From: accthelp@expedia.com
To: straussj@ccsu.edu

Welcome to Microsoft Expedia Travel Services!

Below is your new membership information. Please keep this
confirmation mail as a record of your Member ID.
Your Member ID is: 12345. The Expedia Internet address is: http://expedia.msn.com/

Expedia is a free service. To use the Expedia Travel Agent,
you will have to type your Member ID and Password on the
Sign In page.

Whether for business or pleasure, Microsoft Expedia makes it
easy for you to plan and purchase travel arrangements that best
meet your budget and personal preferences. Expedia is on the job
24 hours a day, 7 days a week. With a click of your mouse, you can:

* Reserve and purchase airline tickets
* Reserve hotel rooms
* Reserve rental cars
* Subscribe to Fare Tracker for the lowest airfares to your favorite destinations
* Research over 300 destinations in the World Guide
* Chart your course with over 200 city maps
* Check out the world of adventure in the Mungo Park online magazine
* Catch up on the latest travel news, weather and more

We look forward to fulfilling all of your travel needs.

Expedia Travel Services
Start your travel here.
http://expedia.msn.com/

Exhibit 7 - 8 Expedia Welcome E-mail

Exhibit 7 - 9 Expedia Welcome Web Page
Source: www.expedia.msn.com

Incoming E-mail

E-mail feedback from customers is another story. Most firms have feedback options at their Web sites yet many are not staffed to handle it in a timely and appropriate fashion. In research for his *Wall Street Journal* article, Weber (1996) sent e-mail questions to 24 major companies. Of the 62% percent responding, only three firms answered appropriately within one day. Two firms took three weeks to reply, and the others sent automated responses that were unrelated to the original inquiry. In a 1997 study, 62% of the firms responded to e-mail complaints (Strauss & Pesce 1997), and that figure increased to 70% response in a 1998 follow-up study. E-mail takes a lot of staff time to handle, and while it can help to build social bonds with users, it must be responded to in a timely manner in order to be effective at relationship building. Some firms, like Apple Computer, decide not to provide e-mail feedback from their Web sites, opting instead for automated telephone routing. This may be a good strategy if a firm cannot staff properly for e-mail communication. In the 1997 study, one major clothing retailer sent an automated reply to a complaining consumer stating, "While we cannot get back to you personally, we do appreciate your input." Companies with e-mail addresses on their Web sites must manage them well or risk negative responses from consumers.

Personalized Web Pages

The Expedia page welcoming Judy Strauss, and the Amazon page welcoming Raymond D. Frost in the Leveraging Technology section at the end of this chapter, are examples of personalized Web pages. They were created with cookies that were put on the user's hard disk by the Web site. Cookies are small data files which are written while a user browses or when a user completes a Web form. Cookies help companies to personalize Web pages by applying the user's name or by listing previous purchases, thus building relationship with users, one at a time.

Exhibit 7 - 10 Caribbean Bulletin Boards, Chat and Guest Book
Source: www.expedia.msn.com

Through collaborative filtering software, Web sites can make recommendations to users based on purchases of other similar customers. This is how Amazon is able to recommend books to users: They gather information on one user's tastes and compare it with aggregated data on similar users. One company, Net Perceptions, sells software called the GroupLens Recommendation Engine to companies such as Amazon. In its brochure, Net Perceptions claims that recommendation engines

> harness the collective knowledge of all your customers to make predictions for an individual. It is based on collaborative filtering technology, which automates word-of-mouth recommendations. . . . The recommendation engine lets you generate online recommendations in real-time, and dynamically tailor content and advertising to [the user's] preferences. With every visit, the recommendation engine learns more and gets smarter.

The Leveraging Technology section describes both cookies and collaborative filtering in more detail. These techniques automate personalized communication, thus cutting costs and making possible the Internet's big promise of mass customization.

Users can also create personalized Web pages by using Web forms. One example of this is My Yahoo! After registering at Yahoo!, users will get a standard Web page with their name on it. The page contains lots of information such as news headlines, sports scores, weather, stock quotes, TV listings, and favorite links. Users edit each category, selecting things such as in which cities they want to see weather, and for which teams they want scores, and for which stocks they want quotes. After putting favorite Web site links on the page, each user has a completely individual information source: all on a personal Web page. This is a value to users, and so they often visit the page. This is good for Yahoo! because they can sell advertising that is targeted to a user with very specific interests, and because it builds traffic at the Yahoo! site. My Yahoo! creates a structural bond with individual consumers, thereby boosting customer loyalty: something that was unheard of prior to the Internet.

OUTGOING E-MAIL

One outcome of Web-based information gathering is an electronic database of e-mail addresses. In fact, anytime a user interacts electronically with a firm, an e-mail address and other information might be added to a computer database. Most good marketing databases also include the names, physical addresses, phone numbers, and purchase behavior of customers or potential buyers. In addition to gathering user information from primary sources, firms may buy lists of e-mail address or gather them from the Internet. For example, some marketers "harvest" e-mail addresses of the posters to particular newsgroups in the Usenet or use a robot to gather webmaster addresses from Web sites in a particular industry. This practice has its critics, who call the robots "scavenger-bots." Their objection due to concerns about privacy and commercialization of the Usenet: topics discussed elsewhere in this book.

How do marketers use e-mail databases to build relationship? By keeping in touch with information that is useful to users. Earlier in this chapter we described 3Com's mailings to PalmPilot users and Expedia's mailings to registered users. Both

Expedia and its competitor, Travelocity, manage fare-watch services for their customers. Users simply enter their itinerary at the site, and receive e-mail alerts when the fare drops in price. HotWired and Amazon both send e-mails when new services of interest are offered at the Web site. These types of mass e-mailings are the stuff of mass customization. The user name and special product information can easily and automatically be inserted into an e-mail. Alternatively, a company might send special messages to smaller targets within a larger database. For example, Hotcoupons sends coupons to users who are targeted by local dry cleaners and restaurants. Users receiving information that is appropriate, timely, valuable, and nonintrusive will most likely be appreciative and return to the Web site, thus building relationship, one at a time.

Most companies maintain some type of e-mail database, even if it is limited to a distribution list of employees or retail partners. Commercial user databases are also available for purchase. Intellipost offers an e-mail direct marketing service targeting 300,000 consumers. Intellipost's product, BonusMail, rewards consumers with frequent flyer miles and gift certificates, all for reading targeted e-mail ads (Exhibit 7 - 11). Intellipost's client companies pay a fee for these e-mails. This system is analogous to an advertiser paying a third-party firm to send direct mail packages to residents at their homes. One difference, however, is that Intellipost has detailed profiles of its panel members, making demographic, geographic, and other targeting easy. Another difference is that because consumers are "paid" to read the e-mails, advertisers are sure to have their messages seen. This is an interesting strategy for advertisers: Instead of simply paying the publisher for advertising space, they are paying the consumer for reading the ad. Relevant to this discussion, however, is the effective relationship building that Intellipost has with its panel of 300,000: Without them there would be no BonusMail.

BonusMail advertises "responsible" e-mail messaging. By responsible, they mean that consumers agree to receive commercial messages within their e-mails. When consumers receive unsolicited e-mail that has been sent en masse, it is known as spam. The Internet provides the technology for marketers to send 500,000 or more e-mails at the click of a mouse, and all for less than the cost of one postage stamp. Spam has been the topic of much controversy because a few fly-by-night firms have sent a lot of questionable e-mail to ungrateful users. Most legitimate marketers understand that to build relationships over time, they must please customers and not upset them. This means sending e-mails that are valuable to users, sending them as often as users require, and offering users the chance to be taken off the list at any time. It means talking and listening to consumers as if they were friends.

Exhibit 7 - 11 BonusMail® Pays Users to Read Ads
Source: www.bonusmail.com

Guarding Consumer Privacy

Marketers have access to lots of information about every consumer and business, and that information can be easily stored in a database and used for direct marketing communications. "Big brother is almost here. His sister is the telemarketing operator who called you during dinner last night" (Peppers and Rogers 1996). All this information is very tempting to marketers, yet it is balanced by the need to satisfy customers and not anger them. The burden rests on marketers to use customer and prospect information responsibly, both for their own business health and for the image of the profession.

Relationship marketing is based on trust. Customers must believe that the information they give companies on Web forms, in e-mails, or in other ways will be used responsibly. This means using the information to improve the relationship by tailoring goods, services, and marketing communications to meet individual needs. It means allowing consumers to request removal of their information from databases, and not sharing information with other companies unless permission is granted.

Another important privacy issue concerns intrusions into people's lives. Junk mail, spam, repeated telephone calls requesting a switch of long distance provider—these are all examples of marketing messages that can be upsetting to consumers. Even the community classified ad newspaper that is thrown on the doorstep each week is an assault on the privacy of some residents. What's a marketer to do? On the one hand, marketers want to send offers to consumers and businesses that may find them useful, and on the other hand, these intrusions often serve to anger receivers. The answer is twofold: relationship building through dialogue and better target profiling. Firms must listen to customers and prospects and give them what they want. If a consumer wants to receive e-mail from PalmPilot, great. If not, 3Com should remove that customer from the list, perhaps writing back once a year to see if the status has changed. Why? This chapter has shown that retention and commercialization of customer relationships is more profitable than focus on one-time customer transactions. Second, marketers can use consumer information to build more precise target profiles. Instead of sending that mass e-mailing to all folks who visit the site, how about sending individual or small group e-mails to people who might really need a car for that flight they just booked at your site? Individuals are not upset with firms who send valuable and timely information to them.

To assist consumers and Web sites in developing trust, an independent, nonprofit, privacy initiative was created. TRUSTe provides its seal and logo to any Web site meeting its standards (Exhibit 7 - 12). It audits sites through a well-respected firm, Coopers & Lybrand. Sites must publish the following information right on the Web site to gain the TRUSTe seal (source: www.truste.org):

- What type of information your site gathers
- How the information will be used
- Who the information will be shared with (if anyone)

Further, the site must agree to:

- disclose information management practices in privacy statements
- display the trustmark
- adhere to stated privacy practices
- cooperate with all reviews

Other organizations also provide guidelines for Internet privacy. The American Institute of Certified Public Accountants offers a seal of approval for firms passing its business practices review. The certification program is called CPA WebTrust and is currently offered by several of the big U.S. accounting firms. The American Marketing Association recently drafted a code of ethics for Internet marketing (see Appendix D). This code deals primarily with privacy and intellectual property. The Ethics and Law section at chapter end illuminates legal perspectives on privacy.

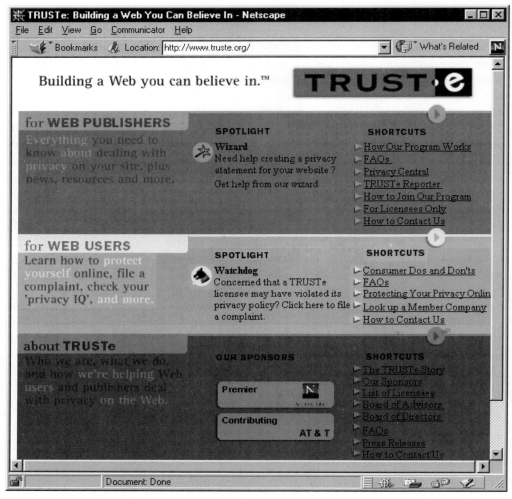

Exhibit 7 - 12 TRUSTe Builds User Trust

Summary

This chapter describes the benefits of relationship marketing and explains how Internet technologies can help to realize those benefits.

Relationship marketing means developing long-term relationships with customers in order to encourage repeat business. Companies develop relationships by carefully listening to customers and working to fulfill their needs. Fortunately, consumers prefer to be brand loyal—even more so online than offline. Relationship marketing gives consumers a reason to remain loyal. Nonetheless, the company must fulfill its promises to the consumer or risk souring the relationship. Companies enter into relationships with all of their stakeholders. These include employees, suppliers, and lateral partners. Satisfying the needs of each of these groups fosters loyalty and is good for business.

Relationship marketing is practiced at three levels: financial, social, and structural. The financial relationship is the weakest while the structural relationship is the strongest. Once a structural relationship is established, it is difficult for the consumer to switch.

The move to relationship marketing is at least in part a response to the decline in brand loyalty since the 1970s. Consumers who are pinched financially will tend to shop for value. Further, consumers are enticed away from brand loyalty by the many products and promotions in the marketplace.

Relationship marketing is cost effective. This is true both because it is less expensive to retain one customer than to acquire one, and because it is easier and less costly to sell more products to one customer than to sell that same amount to two customers. Another benefit of relationship marketing is the positive word-of-mouth communication spread by satisfied customers.

Internet technologies can further relationship marketing include intranets, extranets, Web sites, e-mail, chat, and newsgroups. Companies build relationships with internal stakeholders, primarily employees, using intranets. Extranets allow companies to share data with each other, thereby building structural bonds—the strongest level of relationship marketing. Web forms can be used to solicit consumer information and feedback. Feedback may also arrive via e-mail. Chats and newsgroups provide forums for building community. Personalized Web pages such as My Yahoo! build a structural relationship between the Web site and the consumer. Firms use outgoing e-mail to send promotions, updates, and other information of interest to their consumers.

There are no universally adopted standards regarding online privacy. One movement in the industry advocates disclosure—letting consumers know in advance what will and will not be done with information collected on them.

Key Concepts and Terms

1. Technology allows for mass customization—automating the process of building old-fashioned relationships with consumers.

2. Consumers prefer to be brand loyal since that is a more efficient use of their time.

3. Relationships can be developed with all stakeholders (internal, suppliers, and lateral partners), not just with consumers.

4. It is more cost effective to work to retain customers than to acquire new customers.

5. Relationship marketing requires promise fulfillment, two-way communication with stakeholders, and long-term customer development.

6. The decline in brand loyalty since the 1970s has created the need for relationship marketing.

7. Benefits of relationship marketing include increased profits, word-of-mouth recommendations, synergy with partners, and satisfied customers.

8. There are no universally adopted standards regarding online privacy. Surfer beware.

- Acquisition focus
- Affiliate
- Brand loyalty
- Chat room
- Competitive advantage
- Differentiate customers
- Extranet
- Intranet
- Lateral partnership
- Line extension
- LISTSERV
- Newsgroup

- Online community
- Personalized Web page
- Relationship marketing
- Share of mind
- Social bond
- Stakeholder
- Structural bond
- Syndicated selling
- Synergy
- Web form
- Web ring
-

Exercises

REVIEW QUESTIONS FOR KNOWLEDGE TESTING

1. Define relationship marketing.
2. List six major differences between mass marketing and relationship marketing.
3. Explain why consumer brand loyalty has declined in the United States.
4. What are the three levels of relationship building?
5. What is an acquisition focus?
6. How do extranets create structural bonds between companies?
7. Why do consumers tend to be more loyal online than offline?

DISCUSSION QUESTIONS FOR CRITICAL THINKING

1. Compare and contrast the concept of differentiating customers with that of differentiating products.

2. Using rough figures, prepare an argument that it is in your favorite restaurant's interest to nurture a long-term relationship with you. Include in your argument the dollar value of any negative publicity that you could generate.

3. If relationship marketing is such a good idea, then why do so many businesses give it merely lip service?

4. How does privacy enter into relationship marketing?

5. The big buzzword in the industry is "building community." From what you've read, should Net firms be building structural bonds? Are the strategies complementary?

6. Should Internet privacy standards be legislated or should the industry self-regulate? Defend your answer.

ACTIVITIES

1. Working in small groups, discuss online shopping experiences and what companies did to meet group members' needs, including follow-up e-mail.

2. Have each group member visit an online store and describe how that store could improve its relationship marketing.

3. Register at two Web sites and see if you get e-mail. Identify the ways in which those sites attempt to build relationship with you: Evaluate the sites as well as the incoming e-mail.

INTERNET EXERCISE: CUSTOMER SATISFACTION

In the highly competitive world of Internet content providers, customer satisfaction is key. Therefore, content providers must continuously innovate to meet or exceed customer expectations. The core content of search engines has always been to serve as an index to the rest of the Web. Recently, search engines have branched out to include other customized services. One of the more innovative services provided by Yahoo! (www.yahoo.com) allows users to customize content. Click on the My Yahoo! link, build your custom content, and then estimate the frequency with which you would return to check out each of the categories you selected.

Category	Number of times you would check out in a week

For Discussion

1. There is no charge for the My Yahoo! service. What benefits does Yahoo! realize from providing the service?

2. How could Yahoo! marketers use aggregate information about the categories selected and frequency of visits to redesign their service?

3. What other services does Yahoo! provide on its site? How would these other services encourage repeat visits?

Practitioner Perspective

THE DUAL-VALUE PROPOSITION

Kathryn Creech is General Manager of Hearst's HomeArts Online Network, the number 1 lifestyle site for women on the Web.

When Hearst launched the HomeArts Network (www.homearts.com) in 1995, we set out to give women the information they wanted and needed on the Web. So what do women want in this time-starved modern era? We define our value proposition as "what you want, when you want it: quick and easy access to information, communication, and entertainment that meets your needs." Jupiter Communications reports that women make up 45% of today's Web population and that women will outnumber men on the Web within four years. The Internet isn't your little brother's medium anymore! Every day at HomeArts we try to figure out how to deliver content for women that is relevant and satisfying, whether it is a quick supper idea from our recipe finder, a mortgage calculator from our financial toolkit, or a rainy-day project to keep the kids occupied.

Our focus on women creates a valuable audience for advertisers. Women come to our network for great interactive content in a context relevant to their lives. Advertisers buy space on HomeArts to reach these important consumers, who make some 60% of all purchasing decisions. Better still, they're reaching them effectively—in an environment where women are actively seeking information. For example:

Consumer Perspective: Linda is searching the HomeArts food channel for a chicken recipe for tonight's dinner. In the Recipe Finder she can indicate her preferences for preparation time, calories, and ingredients. With just one click, Linda has a selection of chicken recipes that fit her personal criteria: quick to prepare, low in calories, cooked in a wine sauce. She chooses one, prints it out, and takes it to the grocery store.

Advertiser Perspective: Kraft Foods advertises on the HomeArts food channel because it recognizes the value of our quality content. Visitors to our food channel are the perfect audience for Kraft—they are pre-qualified consumers, interested in food, ready to purchase. They search our recipe database for what they need and—presto!—they get a Kraft banner and often even a Kraft recipe.

Dual-Value Proposition: The consumer and the advertiser are in synch: Linda has a recipe personalized for her, and Kraft has positioned its branded products in front of a targeted consumer.

Key Concepts to Keep in Mind

- Who is the audience, what are their needs?
- How can I best satisfy the consumer's need? Better navigation? A new application? Make it obvious!
- Personalization is king (or queen, in our case!).
- Offer the user something different.
- Advertiser value comes from a pre-qualified customer.

Leveraging Technology

COOKIES AND COLLABORATIVE FILTERING

An advertiser's dream is to be able to efficiently target products and ads to a market segment of one. A Web technology called cookies makes that dream at least partially possible today. Cookies are files which Web sites are permitted to store on a user's computer. The contents of those files can contain information about a user's preferences—and that information is a valuable resource for marketers.

Two forms of relationship marketing using cookies will be examined. The first form establishes a relationship between a user and a single site. As an example, consider Amazon, which uses cookies to identify repeat visitors, greet them by name and call up their billing and shipping information. The second form establishes relationships across multiple sites. The sites share information about the user in order to be able to target ads wherever the user goes.

Note that in the descriptions that follow, much of the material is deduced from known characteristics of how databases operate and may contain minor inaccuracies. For obvious reasons, the Web sites do not publish trade secrets of how their backend systems function.

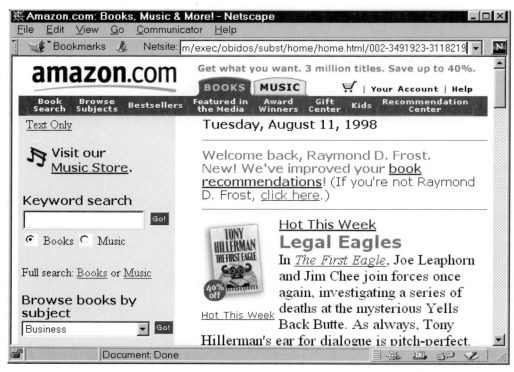

Exhibit 7 - 13 Amazon Welcome Screen

Relationship Marketing with a Single Site

Exhibit 7 - 13 shows relationship marketing in action at Amazon. The process begins when the user first registers with Amazon. Amazon records information about the user in its user database file, a simplified form of which looks like Exhibit 7 - 14.

Userid	Last	First	Street	City	Zip	Credit Card #
12345	Frost	Raymond	8 Web Way	New Britain	06050	4444 5555 6666 7777
76543	Strauss	Judy	10 Net Lane	Reno	89557	3333 2222 9999 8888

Exhibit 7 - 14 User Database File

```
.amazon.com  Userid = 12345
my.yahoo.com  Userid = 88875
.hotwired.com  Userid = 55235
```

Exhibit 7 - 15 Cookie File

Amazon then stores the user's Userid in a cookie file on the *user's* computer. A simplified form of the cookie file appears in Exhibit 7 - 15.

On a return trip to the Amazon site, the user's computer sends the Userid value (12345) from the cookie file to Amazon's server. Amazon's server uses that number to look up the user's record (12345, Frost, Raymond D., 8 Web Way, New Britain, 06050, 4444 5555 6666 7777) in its database. The server then merges the user's name with its home page, inserting the personalized greeting ("Welcome Back, Raymond D. Frost") in the appropriate spot. The process is not unlike a mail merge in a word processor except that only one document is created.

But Amazon doesn't stop there. Note the line after the greeting: "We've improved your book recommendations." Clicking on this link brings up Exhibit 7 - 16. The exhibit shows recommendations in three areas in which the author has recently ordered books: graphic design, the Internet, and pedagogy.

So how did Amazon identify the author's last book ordered? It maintains a separate file containing all the orders for its users. A simplified form of the file looks like Exhibit 7 - 17.

Using the Userid (12345) it is able to look up the last title ordered. The same file contains books that other users have ordered. Note how in this example two users who ordered *Light and Color in the Outdoors* also ordered *Interaction of Color*. Assume that there are a hundred users following the same pattern. The pattern would then be enough to place *Interaction of Color* on the recommendation list.

TO REVIEW THE PROCESS ONCE AGAIN:
First Purchase

1. The user makes a purchase with Amazon.
2. Amazon stores the user's full information in its user file.
3. Amazon stores the purchase record in its orders file.
4. Amazon stores the user's Userid (not the full user record) in a cookie file on the user's computer.

Subsequent Visits

1. Amazon pulls the cookie record from the user's computer to find the Userid.
2. The Userid is used to look up the user's record.
3. The name is extracted from the user's record and merged with the Web page to produce a personal greeting.
4. The Userid is used to look up the user's last order from the orders file.
5. Collaborative filtering software is used to find patterns among other users' orders which can help to recommend book titles.

One-Click Ordering

One additional feature that Amazon has on its site is called One-Click Ordering. If the user accepts the recommendation to purchase *Interaction of Color*, the following screen appears. A single click here will order and ship the item, since the shipping address and credit card number are already in the user file. Exhibit 7 - 18 shows the One-Click Order option.

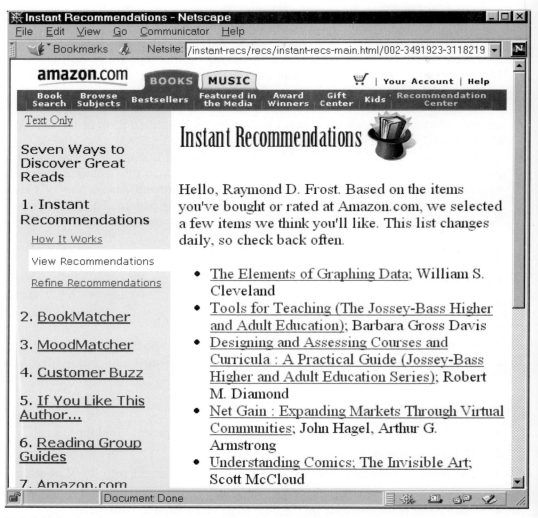

Exhibit 7 - 16 Amazon's Customized Recommendations

Userid	Title
12345	Light and Color in the Outdoors
12345	Food for Life
76543	Light and Color in the Outdoors
76543	Interaction of Color
22233	Light and Color in the Outdoors
22233	Interaction of Color

Exhibit 7 - 17 Amazon Orders File

Exhibit 7 - 18 Amazon's One-Click Order Screen

Clicking on the One-Click button produces the order confirmation screen shown in Exhibit 7 - 19.

RELATIONSHIP MARKETING ACROSS MULTIPLE SITES

In the previous example, Amazon was able to garner information about the user because the user purchased an item. But what about a user just visiting a Web site without making a purchase or divulging any personal information? What can marketers do to target this user with an ad campaign?

As an example, consider the following scenario. A user visits a Web site about dogs. The Web site shares with an advertising agency the information that the user is a dog lover. The agency can now target dog product ads for that consumer even when he visits a different Web site! What is truly amazing is that this can all take place without the consumer ever divulging her name, address, and so on. So how is this possible?

Exhibit 7 - 19 1-Click Order Confirmation

1. The user browses the Web and types in www.familydog.com (fictional).
2. The FamilyDog site sends its Web page with a placeholder for an ad but *without* the ad itself.
3. The Web page contains code which requests the ad from the ad agency's computer.
4. The ad agency delivers the ad.
5. The ad is seamlessly inserted into the Web page as it appears on the user's screen.
6. The ad agency takes the opportunity to write also a cookie in the user's cookie file. The cookie entry appears in Exhibit 7 - 20.

So now the user has a cookie on his computer from an ad agency's site that he has never visited! Though technically he did visit the site by requesting (indirectly and unknown to him) that the ad be delivered from the ad agency's site.

1. Now the user goes to another site whose ads are served by the same ad agency. Assume that it is a site for home and garden.
2. The Web page from the home and garden site makes a request to the ad agency for an ad to be delivered.
3. The ad agency reviews the cookie on the user's computer (UserPetPreference=DOG).
4. Armed with this information the ad agency sends an ad for dog food.

This type of relationship marketing across multiple sites raises some ethical issues concerning the user's privacy. Specifically, is it ethical to record information about the user without her knowledge or consent? This debate will be investigated elsewhere in this text.

However, a technical solution has been proposed that would give sites needed information to serve customers without compromising user privacy. It is called the Platform for Privacy Preferences (P3P). The model for the standard is software developed by FireFly (now purchased by Microsoft) called Passport. The standard is supported by a number of companies including Netscape, Microsoft, and Verisign. The idea behind P3P is that all of the user's information would be stored on an encrypted file on the user's computer. The file might look like Exhibit 7 - 21.

```
.amazon.com  Userid = 12345
my.yahoo.com  Userid = 88875
.hotwired.com  Userid = 55235
.adagency.com  UserPetPreference = DOG
```

Exhibit 7 - 20 Cookie File

```
[Identification]
Last = Frost
First = Raymond
MI = D.
Phone = 860-555-1234
E-mail = frost@ccsu.edu
Street = 8 Web Way
City = New Britain
Zip = 06050

[Demographics]
Sex = M
Age = 37
Marital Status = M

[Interests Section]
Tennis
Travel

[Userid Section]
.amazon.com = 12345
my.yahoo.com = 88875
.hotwired.com = 55235
```

Exhibit 7 - 21 P3P File

The existence of such a file would greatly simplify the process of registering at different sites. Any site that supported the standard could request permission from the user to transfer information to the site's server. Part of the standard specifies that information could be extracted from the file only with the user's expressed consent. Alternatively the user could choose settings to always release demographic information while withholding identifying information. At the time of this writing no site had implemented the standard.

Ethics and Law

PRIVACY

Perhaps more than any other legal or ethical concept, privacy is a product of the twentieth century. While many cultures have possessed customs establishing social boundaries, detailed consideration of this subject did not come about until 1890, when Samuel Warren and future Supreme Court Justice Louis Brandeis published an article that urged the recognition of a right to privacy within American law. This protection was defined as the "right to be left alone"(Warren and Brandeis 1890, 193). Significantly, many of the justifications of this new idea were reactions to the phenomena of a maturing industrial and technological age, including the mass distribution of newspapers, the development of listening devices, and the widespread use of photography. In essence, privacy's young tradition has always been about information and the means of its delivery.

Although it has been the subject of constant debate since the Warren and Brandeis article, privacy has proven to be an elusive concept, both ethically and legally. One reason for legal confusion is the lack of any specific privacy provision within the Constitution. This situation was recognized in the U.S. Supreme Court's 1965 decision of *Griswold* v. *Connecticut* (381 U.S. 479), which held that privacy in the use of contraceptives could be inferred from a number of elaborated constitutional rights, including those of association, freedom from illegal searches and seizures, self-incrimination, and the quartering of soldiers. Later, in the 1973 opinion of *Roe* v. *Wade* (410 U.S. 113), the Court found a privacy right in a woman's reproductive decisionmaking. Through the Fourth Amendment to the U.S. Constitution, the privacy of the home has been established against governmental agencies, who are required to obtain warrants before entering upon and searching a dwelling. This provision is, however, applicable only to officials or those acting on their behalf and not against private individuals.

In addition to constitutional developments, privacy has been addressed in the common law. This term refers to decisions, presumptions, and practices that have traditionally been embraced by Anglo-American courts. The common law has established a series of privacy violations which, individually and together, form the basis of invasion of privacy lawsuits. They are arranged into four categories: unreasonable intrusion into the seclusion of another, unreasonable publicity of another's private life, the appropriation of another's name or likeness, and the publication of another's personal information in a false light. These elements are codified in many state statutes and appear in the influential Restatement of Torts (1977, sec. 652).

Despite these developments, much disagreement remains as to what privacy entails. Attributes that have been identified as central fall into three general areas. The first is the Warren and Brandeis concept of a right to be left alone, often referred to as the "seclusion" theory. Privacy within this perspective is the ability to remain isolated from society. This model encourages laws and ethical standards that are oriented toward maintaining personal distance and punishing those who cross the limits set by individuals. An intermediate viewpoint, known as "access-control", does not presume isolation as a norm, but places its emphasis upon laws and standards that enable persons reasonably to regulate the information they are giving up. Expressions of this model can be found in laws and standards that empower individuals to protect personal material from unauthorized release.

While both seclusion and access-control models provide measures of protection, their focus is concerned more with how information is released than with what actually constitutes private data. A third theory, known as the "autonomy" model, attempts to provide such a definition. It does so by identifying private matters as those that are necessary for a person to make life decisions. This entails freedom from the coercive use of personal information as well as the ability to be alone when reflection is necessary.

In addition to difficulties in definition and scope, privacy exists as one value among many. Within society, privacy interests routinely compete against concerns of personal and public safety, economics, and even the social and psychological need for association with others—a process that can require the divulging of sensitive information. The ways in which these interests are coordinated involve complex balances which can result in difficult choices. Often, people are willing to give up personal information for benefits that they perceive to be worthwhile—credit cards, frequent flyer mileage, and security precautions in airports are but a few of these situations. In such cases, ethics and law attempt to provide guidelines in the final decision by critically examining definitions, priorities, and implications.

S a v v y   S i t e s

Web Site and Address	Importance to Net Marketers
Bonus Mail www.bonusmail.com	Visitors at this site can fill out a profile and receive e-mail offers about things that are of interest to them. Those who fill out the profile will receive Rew@rd credits that can redeemed for free stuff at stores such as Barnes & Noble, Disney, Tower Records, GAP, Target, and more.
Cisco Connection online cio.cisco.com/	Cisco is one of the most rapidly growing companies in the United States. The firm dominates the market for switching applications that provide the backbone of the Internet and Intranets.
Dell Computer www.us.dell.com/	Dell Computer is a leading manufacturer and direct marketer of computers. The site enables visitors to access their annual report and updated stock quotes, in addition to product descriptions, a list of vendors, and technical support.
Mail Jail www.mailjail.com	Mail Jail offers anti-spam programs on this site. Visitors who use Outlook can download a free lite version of Mail Jail.

Net Perceptions www.netperceptions.com	Net Perceptions offers online business customized tools to make the shopping experience of its customers more personalized. GroupLens is a software product that employs collaborative filtering technology to offer customers product and service suggestions.
Telecom Information Resources china.si.umich.edu/telecom	This site contains links to information resources regarding intranets and telecommunications. It is a great academic resource.
Zero Junk Mail www.zerojunkmail.com	Zero Junk Mail offers a variety of software products that are designed to block spam.

Chapter **8**

The Internet Marketing Plan

"It must be considered that there is nothing more difficult to carry out, nor more doubtful of success, nor more dangerous to handle, than to initiate a new order of things. For the reformer has enemies in all those who profit by the old order, and only lukewarm defenders in those who would profit by the new order. . . . This arises partly from the incredulity of mankind who do not truly believe in anything new until they have an actual experience of it."

—Niccolo Machiavelli, *The Prince*

Chapter Outline

- The Adjacency Story
- Introduction
- Creating an Internet Marketing Plan
- Situation Analysis
- Identify Target Stakeholders
- Set Objectives
- Design Marketing-Mix Strategies to Meet the Objectives
- Action Plan
- Budgeting
- Evaluation Plan

Practitioner Perspective
The Web Development Process
—Matt Straznitskas, Founder and President, BrainBug

Leveraging Technology
Building a Web Site

Ethics and Law
Privacy in Digital Contexts

Learning Objectives

- Marketing review
  - Explain the stages in the marketing planning process
  - Understand why marketing strategies flow from the situation analysis
  - Compare and contrast marketing objectives, strategies, and tactics
- Describe several important environmental factors for Internet marketing
- List several objectives that are appropriate for Internet marketing plans
- Identify several Internet strategies for brand awareness building and positioning
- Explain several Internet strategies used to build sales revenues
- Tell how the Internet can be used to lower marketing costs
- Discuss several important decisions in an Internet action plan
- Explain the importance of tracking user surfing behavior

Adjacency

Story

"It's easier to teach a great print designer interactivity than it is to teach a Web designer good taste."
—Andrew Sather, Creative Director and CEO, Adjacency

How does a former third shift Kinko's employee rise to head one of the premier Web design firms? How does this happen in Wisconsin (in the cheddar belt!) rather than on one of the coasts? How is it financed without venture capital or an Initial Public Offering (IPO)?

Andrew Sather is 26 years old, an art history/graphic design/creative writing major and the Creative Director and CEO of Adjacency. He is more articulate in speech than most people are in writing. Adjacency is an award-winning design firm that creates and maintains sites for some of the Web's highest profile clients. Sather formed the firm in 1995 because he saw a gaping need for good Web design. "The corporate sites I visited said nothing about the brands that they were built to represent, and they didn't aesthetically or editorially serve those companies' identities. Quite simply, I couldn't find much effective branding on the Web." Unlike some Web design firms, Adjacency operates with a clear marketing focus, which integrates all aspects of design and implementation.

Sather and friends began the firm from a basement in Wisconsin with a Macintosh that he purchased on a student loan. His first client was Patagonia. He called the company in California with a pitch to design its Web page. Within two minutes, he had to admit that he was a student operating out of a basement. Nonetheless, he managed to convince them to give him a chance. Over the weekend the basement crew worked up some sample Web pages. Patagonia signed onto Sather's site from California and liked what it saw. It awarded Sather the job though he never met with a Patagonia employee until the first site was finished!

Designing Web pages is Adjacency's only business. It eschews design for other media in order to maintain focus. As a result Adjacency has invented proprietary software including tools to compress images and a 360-degree virtual reality viewer. Adjacency creates these new tools when off-the-shelf software does not meet its high-quality standards. The tools it creates then form its part of competitive advantage.

There are hundreds of Web design firms on the Internet. With 45 employees, Adjacency is a modest size firm. Yet it is able to command top dollar (from $100,000 per site) because of its award-winning designs. Its Web sites have won numerous awards, including two of the most prestigious industry awards: Gold at the One Show Interactive and Gold at the Clio Awards. It also won the High Five Web site Award and was named one of the 20 best Internet consulting firms by Internet Computing. With all this success, Sather moved his shop to San Francisco in search of an even larger design talent pool.

Adjacency designed the Land Rover site (www.landrover.com), which is hailed as one of the best examples of user empowerment by using new media to move beyond brochureware. At the site users can outfit their Land Rover interactively and see immediate visual results. Users can choose from menus of colors, wheels, running boards, roof racks, mud flaps, and brush bars. The on-screen Land Rover changes instantly to reflect the options selected. Users can then print a list of the options selected along with a picture of their configured vehicle. Many take these specs to the dealership to complete the transaction. Other high-profile clients include Patagonia (www.patagonia.com),   Apple   Computer   (www.apple.com),   Rollerblade (www.rollerblade.com),   Lufthansa   (www.lufthansa-usa.com),   Tag   Heuer (www.tagheuer.com) Motorola (www.motorola.com), Specialized (www.specialized.com), PowerBar   (www.powerbar.com),   Nordstrom   (www.nordstrom-pta.com),   Pixar (www.pixar.com), and Esprit (www.esprit.com). The Adjacency home page features its high-power clients: an excellent way to impress prospective customers (Exhibit 8 - 1).

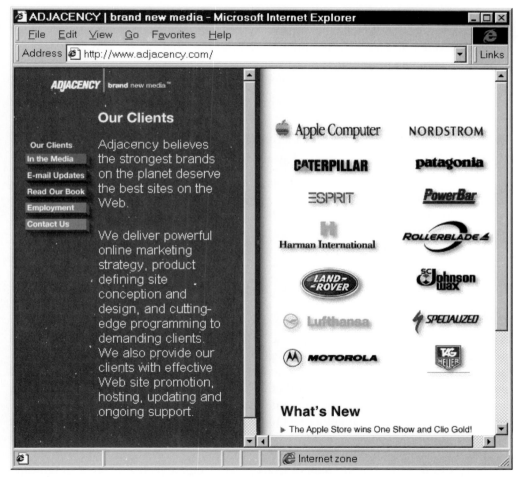

Exhibit 8 - 1 Adjacency Home Page Features Clients

Adjacency's goals include creating sites "that inform, entertain and empower users." Interestingly, they insist on maintaining the site once designed, thus incorporating any new changes. This control ensures that new material is consistent with the overall site design.

Adjacency's design process consists of five steps:

1. Distill the client's brand
2. Determine objectives
3. Design site structure and interactivity
4. Design site aesthetics
5. Build

Distilling the client's brand may be the most critical step. In this step Adjacency staff exhaustively question the client company so they can learn everything possible about the brand. Without successfully completing this step, there is no way to determine objectives, let alone design the site.

Adjacency structures its business into three areas:

1. Creative: Graphic and information design, content, marketing, and advertising
2. Production: HTML and JavaScript
3. Technical: Programming and system administration

Unlike in many other advertising firms, these divisions do not work in a linear fashion, passing off work from creative to production to technical. Rather the three groups work together: Sather feels that this system is one of the strengths of his shop. Given the acclaim that Adjacency has garnered, few would disagree.

Introduction

Why would a company pay Adjacency $500,000 to design and build its Web presence? Why not buy an off-the-shelf package and have the IT department produce the site in an afternoon? An obvious answer is to protect the corporate and brand identities. One tenet of integrated marketing communications is that every aspect of a consumer's interaction with the company reflects back on the firm and its brands. Therefore, throwing a site together just to be online could actually do more harm than good.

The not-so-obvious answer lies in the complexity of designing Web strategies and tactics to meet marketing plan objectives. How can a Web site assist in building market share or lowering marketing costs? The best Web sites have clearly established marketing goals and a well-executed site design to attain those goals. There is a tremendous amount of work that goes into this process. The marketing process entails three steps: marketing plan creation, plan implementation, and plan evaluation/corrective action. This chapter will examine the first of these steps: how to develop an Internet marketing plan.

Creating an Internet Marketing Plan

Creating an Internet marketing plan requires at least seven steps.

1. Conduct a situation analysis.
   - Review the existing marketing plan and any other information that can be obtained about the company and its brands.
   - Examine environmental factors related to online marketing.
   - Develop a market opportunity analysis (includes a SWOT analysis).
2. Identify target stakeholders.
3. Set objectives. Some objectives are global while others apply to specific targets.
4. Design marketing-mix strategies to meet the objectives.
5. Design an action plan (tactics to implement the strategies).
6. Develop a budget.
7. Develop an evaluation plan.

One way to understand the process is by analogy and example.

The marketing plan can be understood by analogy with preparing for a football game. While reviewing game films, a situation analysis reveals each team's strengths and weaknesses (e.g., the home team has a tremendous passing game, the visitors have an excellent run defense). A likely objective would then be to win the game by throwing the ball. Strategies are developed to meet this objective (e.g., use play action to draw in the coverage; throw deep). Finally, tactics implement the strategies (e.g., use a play action pass on first down; run on second down to keep them honest, pass on third down).

The following is a marketing example which tackles planning for expanding in a geographic region. While scanning the firm's environment, a situation analysis reveals the firm's strengths and weaknesses (e.g., the firm performs strongly in Connecticut, where it has partnerships with retail outlets, but performs weakly in New York, where it enjoys no such partnerships). A likely objective would be to increase sales in New York by developing partnerships. Strategies are developed to meet this objective (e.g., provide pricing and rebate incentives to prospective partners). Finally, tactics implement the strategies (e.g., offer chain X a 20% rebate on each product sold).

Situation Analysis

REVIEW THE EXISTING MARKETING PLAN

Some people feel that planning a Web site means starting from scratch. Nothing could be further from the truth. While it may be the case that an organization wishes to launch a product line extension just for the Web, or to establish a different image online (perhaps a bit more high-tech), the online communication will be consistent with the overall marketing goals and current marketing efforts of the organization. What are those marketing goals? Who are the selected target markets? What competition has already been identified? What marketing materials has the organization already produced?

Working with existing materials is an excellent place to start. The current marketing plan will be loaded with information of vital importance to an Internet planner. For example, the demographics and geographics of target markets may have already been identified. Using this information, the marketer can work to determine whether these target markets utilize the Internet. For example, J. Crew (www.jcrew.com) has an excellent opportunity to reach an Internet audience since its trendy yuppy target demographic fits perfectly with a major online demographic group. Other corporations similarly blessed include the Sharper Image (www.sharperimage.com) and Brookstone (www.brookstoneonline.com). But the Internet population is large enough to support less dominant populations as well. For example, while Australia is not one of the highest-access countries, www.sidewalk.com features local sites for both Sydney and Melbourne.

Furthermore, there will already be established marketing-mix strategies designed to reach those targets. The firm's pricing philosophy may dictate online pricing strategies for electronic commerce. The distribution plan will identify areas where promotion is needed and suggest whether online product distribution fits. Promotion plan information will give clues about how the Internet fits with the firm's advertising, sales promotion, and other marketing communications. Also in the plan is information about the firm and brand positioning in the marketplace. Net planners must decide how closely the site will follow current positioning strategies.

CONDUCT AN ENVIRONMENTAL SCAN

An important step in any marketing plan, Internet or otherwise, is to perform an environmental scan. While the results of an environmental scan may appear in the existing marketing plan, the Web should be treated as a unique environment to be reviewed. For example, while many like to think of the Web as moving toward a mainstream audience, it is not there yet. A review of Net user characteristics is critical. The environmental scan helps to set the context within which to plan marketing strategies. The following sections illuminate some environmental factors that are particularly important for Net marketing.

Legal/Political Environment

The online legal and political environments greatly influence marketing strategies. Chief among these are laws regarding taxation, access, copyright, and encryption. The Internet tax-free zone advocated by the Clinton administration opens up enormous opportunities for commerce by positioning Web retailers with a competitive advantage over their brick and mortar counterparts. There is a continuing struggle to get states and other countries to go along with the tax-free zone. The Federal Communications Commission (FCC) affects access to the Internet. At the time of this writing the FCC was very concerned that minorities were underrepresented in the online community. Also, designers producing sites for content providers will need to stay abreast of the latest rulings regarding copyright for online materials. If copyright can be safeguarded internationally, then other businesses such as music labels might be encouraged to distribute their product online. Finally, encryption allows for the security of online transactions. The U.S. government has so far fought encryption standards that did not include giving the government a copy of the encryption key, which would be kept in escrow for law enforcement officials.

Technological Environment

Technology developments alter the composition of the Internet audience as well as the quality of material that can be delivered to them. For example, there is an anticipated explosion in the installed base of cable modems. Cable modems allow for high-speed access and multimedia content. Some Web sites are beginning to create two forms of content: a high speed multimedia form for cable modem subscribers and regular form for telephone modem subscribers. Cable modems tend to be rolled out first in highly affluent neighborhoods—a very attractive demographic. At the low end, Web TV allows less affluent households to go online. Since a TV screen is lower resolution and differently shaped than a computer monitor, Web sites targeting this segment need to be designed accordingly. Also important are technology concerns in developing countries. As communication infrastructures improve, new geographic markets develop. Software developments should also be monitored. For example, technologies that target consumers according to their online behavior are becoming increasingly sophisticated. Incorporating these technologies into a Web site design may provide a distinct competitive advantage.

User Trends

Chapter 2 contains lots of information about user demographics, geographics, psychographics, and online behavior. Changing online demographics present marketing opportunities. For example, children are coming online at an increasing rate. This trend poses new marketing opportunities in this segment, as is evidenced by many new Web sites targeted to kids. Also important are adoption rates in various geographic areas. Countries such as Taiwan and Spain had the largest host growth from 1997 to 1998, again presenting huge marketing opportunities (see chapter 2). Part of the design process must consider these diverse cultural audiences. Should the site be duplicated in multiple languages and designs or should a multinational corporation standardize the site in English? Should the content be tailored for each country to fit with its mores and customs? These are questions asked by every global marketer.

Net marketers constantly monitor online behavior. An understanding of surfing habits and time spent online helps Net planners design effective communications. Online usage patterns provide critical information for Net retailers. For example, recent data show less window shopping and more purchasing online. Other data show that consumers are increasingly willing to buy big-ticket items such as automobiles online.

Rather than take a simple snapshot of who is using the Net today, a planner needs to take a more longitudinal approach. How has the Net audience changed within the last six months, the last year, the last two years? How does this change correspond with changes in the underlying population? What are the trends? Is there an important target segment coming online? User trends spotlight future opportunities which may not be fully developed today.

World Economies

The Internet is a global market with opportunities existing in unimagined locations. A Net marketing planner must consider economic conditions in potential geographic segments. For example, with an annual average income of U.S.$300, Vietnamese citizens who opt to spend 28% of their salary on online services do not have much purchasing power. As of this writing the Russian economy was in a free fall, as situation impacting Internet marketing in that country. Many countries charge by the minute for local phone access. This is a tremendous deterrent to the kind of casual surfing practiced by the U.S. audience. In addition, the infrastructure in some countries does not support the high-speed modems currently on the market. Content delivered to these countries may therefore have to be light on bandwidth.

DEVELOP A MARKET OPPORTUNITY ANALYSIS

After reviewing the marketing environment, a firm conducts several additional analyses all focused on finding and selecting from among many market opportunities. A traditional market opportunity analysis includes both demand and supply analyses. The demand portion reviews various market segments in terms of their potential profitability. For example, in the early days of the Net, *the New York Times* found a highly educated, global online population, closely resembling its readership base. In a demand analysis the *New York Times* would estimate the size and potential sales from the online segment, perhaps also estimating the percent of cannibalism to its hard copy edition that might result from an online edition. Conversely, the supply analysis reviews competition in selected segments that are under consideration. How well is this highly educated online segment being served by other news services? The *New York Times* must evaluate other news products serving this online segment and do a thorough analysis of their comparative strengths and weaknesses. This process will lead the newspaper to broaden its idea of competition: MSNBC and other broadcast media as well as strictly online services such as Pointcast suddenly become competitors in this new market. On the other hand, local community newspapers that compete in the *New York Times*'s hard copy market may not be contenders in the online market. The purpose of this supply analysis is to assist in forecasting segment profitability as well as to find competitive advantages to exploit in the online market. In general, many Web sites lack imagination in design, so there may be real opportunities to gain a competitive advantage, especially while the Web is still in its infancy. Another competitive opportunity exists in 1:1 marketing. For example, most firms are not prepared to communicate quickly and appropriately with individual customers via e-mail.

The next step, sometimes included in the market opportunity analysis, is a Strengths, Weaknesses, Opportunities, and Threats (SWOT) analysis. The SWOT analysis objectively evaluates the company's strengths and weaknesses with respect to the environment and the competition. Strengths can be used to take advantage of opportunities or to combat threats, whereas weaknesses may exaggerate threats or prohibit jumping on opportunities found in the firm's environment. The opportunities may help to define a target market; the threats reveal areas of exposure. For example, when Amazon (www.amazon.com) seized the opportunity to sell online it had no competition. The biggest threat that it faced was a full-scale push by one of the large offline bookstore chains to claim the online market. Fortunately for Amazon, the big stores were caught napping. The delay by the bookstore chains gave Amazon the opportunity to establish its brand online. Barnes & Noble (www.barnesandnoble.com) did not fight back until Amazon was on the eve of a stock offering. By then it was too late. The stock was very successful and Amazon's worth in the stock market (technical term: market capitalization) quickly rose to exceed that of Barnes & Noble. The enormous infusion of cash helped Amazon to further its competitive position. Keep in mind that a company's strengths and weaknesses in the online world may be somewhat different from its strengths and weaknesses in the brick and mortar world. Barnes & Noble has enormous strengths in the brick and mortar world but these do not necessarily translate into strengths in the online world. For example, Barnes & Noble can easily find itself in the unfortunate position of channel conflict —having to explain to customers why they can purchase cheaper online than in the store. Selling only online, Amazon has no potential channel conflict.

Identify Target Stakeholders

While the market opportunity analysis focuses on target markets for the firm's wares, Net marketing plans are targeted to many additional stakeholders. McDonald's Inc, for example, has Web pages for investors and employees as well as customers. In this stage, then, a firm decides with which stakeholders it wants to communicate. With buyers, it decides whether to pursue the entire Net population or to select one or more target market(s). When multiple targets are identified, they should be ranked in order of importance so that resources can be allocated to priorities. Obviously, each target will be well described by its characteristics and desires in this product category. HomeArts (www.homearts.com) has been very successful at appealing to the women's market with recipes and home decoration tips. It is evident that it focuses all its efforts on this target and it knows its visitors well.

Set Objectives

While sales are an exciting dimension of an online presence, there are other worthwhile objectives as well, especially when the site goal is stakeholder communication. In fact, many Web sites aim to accomplish multiple online objectives. An organization will be more effective if it uses carefully worded objectives that flow from plan analyses. In general, a well-worded objective will have a task, contain a specific measurement device, and have a time frame for accomplishment. For example, Amazon might set the following objective: increase the number of associates from 15,000 to 30,000 within one year. The task is to increase the number of associates, and this objective both is measurable and has an identified time frame. Amazon will know if it meets this goal or not. Below are examples of appropriate tasks for Internet marketing programs grouped by Internet Hierarchy of Effects categories (see chapter 1), plus additional operational objective examples that affect marketing budgets.

Cognitive and Attitude Goals
- Increase awareness of a new brand
- Position a brand as high tech
- Make employees aware of an incentive program
- Increase knowledge of the company's many brands
- Disseminate information about a particular topic (e.g., risks of smoking)
- Build relationships with users as evidenced by return visits to a Web site
- Build positive attitudes through more effective customer service

Transactive Behavior Goals
- Build sales of a product distributed over the Internet
- Increase the amount or frequency of sales from current customers
- Increase advertising space sales on the Web site
- Sell content to regular subscribers
- Increase the number of points of sale for a product by building the associate program

Internal Efficiencies That May Affect Marketing Budgets
- Decrease advertising costs

- Provide timely communication to various stakeholders
- Decrease distribution costs, thus lowering prices
- Lower coupon distribution costs

Design Marketing-Mix Strategies to Meet the Objectives

Now comes the part everyone enjoys: deciding how to accomplish the objectives through the Internet. Chapters 4-7 outlined many marketing-mix strategies for online marketing. In this section we present major strategies as a review, focusing on those that are currently being discussed as potentially profitable business models (see chapter 1 for discussion). Marketing-mix strategies are organized as they help to achieve the three general objectives previously outlined:

- Cognitive and attitude objectives: stakeholder communication strategies
- Transactive behavior goals: selling product and services over the Internet
- Internal efficiencies: gaining internal efficiencies through online strategies

STAKEHOLDER COMMUNICATION

Having identified the stakeholders in the planning process, the Web provides an excellent opportunity to communicate with them. There are many possible avenues for stakeholder communication. These include advertising, public relations, sales promotion incentives, and lead generation. These strategies can build awareness and knowledge about firms and their products, aid in brand positioning and other brand-building objectives, enhance stakeholder relationship building, and assist in increasing e-mail stakeholder databases. In addition, the Internet is currently a low-cost alternative to stakeholder communication in other media such as direct mail and television. In short, stakeholder communication strategies can help marketers to accomplish cognitive and attitude objectives, often at substantial cost savings over traditional methods.

Advertising and Sponsorships

One way to communicate with stakeholders is by purchasing advertising on other Web sites. The ads can be used to create brand awareness or to position a brand. Firms may also pay to send ads with e-mail. This strategy is better for awareness building than branding because a significant number of users cannot receive multimedia content in their e-mail. Companies can also sponsor content on other sites. For example, Bloomberg sponsors investor information on the Women's Wire site. Microsoft sponsors Hotmail, the largest free e-mail service in the world. The Microsoft sponsorship allows Microsoft to cross-promote — directing users back to the Microsoft site when they log out of their Hotmail accounts. Obviously, firms can advertise on Web sites even if they do not have their own online presence.

Public Relations and Brochureware

A site that provides information about the company's products and services is called *brochureware*. Brochureware provides an excellent opportunity to build a brand as well as to develop relationships with consumers and other stakeholders. Public relations (PR) communication is the most likely to target stakeholders other than customers and potential customers. Traditional PR publications such as the employee newsletter and stockholder annual report are ideal for online distribution. Many firms, such as MediaMetrix, provide press releases for the media on their Web sites.

Sales Promotion Incentives

Promotional activities on the Web are limited only by the marketer's imagination. These can include sweepstakes, coupons, and even free samples of digital products (e.g., software). Companies use sweepstakes to encourage repeat visits as customers check back to see if they have won. Users can print coupons from Web sites and in exchange provide sponsoring firms with very valuable demographic information for databases.

Lead Generation

A Web site can generate sales leads by offering consumers the option of a follow-up sales call. Auto-By-Tel uses this technique to match automobile consumers with a dealership in their area that offers the exact vehicle and options desired by the consumer.

Relationship Building

All marketing communication strategies have the potential to build relationships with stakeholders. To take advantage of this potential, however, organizations must personalize communications, 1:1. Advertisers following a traditional model will create one-way standardized messages and put them on Web pages or send them via e-mail. Conversely, firms desiring to build relationships will allow users to set up personal pages at their sites (e.g., MyYahoo!), serve banner ads to individuals based on surfing patterns, or create a personalized e-mail campaign. In addition, firms will use feedback buttons on Web sites to communicate with customers individually. For example, L.L. Bean, the Maine catalog marketer, maintains a staff of employees dedicated to answering consumer e-mail in a timely and appropriate manner.

Branding and Corporate Image Building

Corporate and brand images are the result of all stakeholder contacts with an organization as well as word-of-mouth communication among individuals. For example, consumers form opinions about Nike products based on the Web page design as well as on their experiences with the products. Although advertising for the sole purpose of building brand awareness and image consists of only one-half of all Web advertising expenditures (versus transactions), it is important to remember that all marketing communications must be coordinated to create a consistent, positive, and desired image among target stakeholders.

One image-building strategy used by many firms online is to provide useful and free services to Netizens. This strategy is consistent with the "gift culture" of the Net which permeates its existence. It also taps into a social trend in the United States: Many consumers are skeptical of the self-serving nature of big business and often patronize companies such as Ben & Jerry's because they "give back" to the system and care about the environment. On the Web, it is quite common to see sites that offer free news services or other valuable information. This practice not only draws users to the site, but makes them feel good about the firm. For example, Nike provides news on sporting events and gives tips for amateur athletes.

SELLING PRODUCTS AND SERVICES OVER THE INTERNET

Strategies in this area help firms achieve sales and market share objectives by soliciting online transactions. Strategies range from introducing new products and services that capitalize on new technologies to using the Internet as a distribution channel for current products. New-product introductions carry more risk than opening an electronic storefront for existing products, yet the Internet landscape is heavily populated with success stories. Below are a few common strategies.

New Products and Services

New technology provided the springboard for a plethora of new products and services (see chapter 4). In addition to discontinuous innovations such as Internet shopping services, the Net creates an opportunity for product line extensions. The *New York Times*, for example, formulated an online edition. The biggest future opportunities are in communications and collaboration, networked applications, real-time multimedia, and electronic commerce.

New technologies created new product opportunities for creating, delivering, and reading Internet messages. There are products to help content providers develop Web sites, infrastructure products to run the Internet itself, and end user products to connect to the Internet. Many service firms sprang into existence just to assist content providers in building and maintaining their Web sites: Ad agencies such as Adjacency and BrainBug; research firms to help measure Web traffic such as RelevantKnowledge and NetRatings, are just a few. Also in this category are site promotion services and firms that build databases. Infrastructure services exist to maintain satellites, switches, and other equipment that keeps messages moving over the Net.

Product differentiation is an important strategy for online sales, especially because there is tremendous downward pressure on Internet prices. Vendors can differentiate either by product offerings—such as hard-to-find or specialty items—or by other dimensions such as the buying experience, product information, service, or after-sales support. When a firm differentiates its products in a way that is both unique and important to the target, it has found a market niche. The Web is ideal for niche marketing, and firms that find and defend their niches can command higher product prices. A good example of product differentiation is the Baby Jogger site (www.babyjogger.com), which carries a line of baby strollers geared toward active parents, as shown in Exhibit 8 - 2. Baby Jogger targets affluent active parents and provides a rich selection of strollers in this product category.

Advertising Sales

An important Internet business model involves selling advertising space on a Web site to other firms. Banners ads and content sponsorships both help an organization reach revenue objectives. Other forms of advertising include sending ads with e-mail, and sponsoring bulletin boards and other discussion formats. The media have traditionally derived their primary revenue from advertising and thus are attempting to repeat this success with their electronic publishing. *HotWired*, the online version of *Wired* magazine, sold the first banner ad on the Internet in 1994 and continues to support its Web site through advertising.

While publishers attempt to set the standards for Internet advertising, others sites are hot on their trail. If a Web site can draw traffic, advertisers will follow. Ghosh (1998) dubbed this strategy *customer magnet*. A customer magnet attempts to meet all of a customer's needs so that she does not have cause to go elsewhere, and thus draws lots of users. The major Web portals such as Yahoo! AOL, and Excite have added a tremendous number of services such as shopping, movie reviews, weather, news, chat rooms, and yellow pages. Users rarely need to stray off of the portal to have their information, entertainment, and social needs met. However, it is also possible to create a magnet within a particular segment. Tripod, for example, serves as a magnet for Generation Xers, Women's Wire serves as a magnet for women online. It is also possible to create a magnet within a particular industry. A good example of an industry magnet is InsWeb for insurance sales. InsWeb shops the customer's data with multiple insurance agencies to obtain the best price. These companies deliver very specific target markets to advertisers.

Agent Services

Agents normally do not take possession of the product or service but rather link buyers and sellers in a distribution channel. For their efforts, agents normally extract a commission from the exchange. Examples of such agents include stockbrokers, travel agents, insurance agents, real estate agents, and auction houses. The online equivalents of these agents have enjoyed tremendous success. Online commissions are often lower and the product offerings are often greater than offline. Additionally, many consumers enjoy the power of being the one "behind the terminal," as well as the convenience of 24 x 7 access. Business-to-business agent services such as natural gas auctions generate tremendous amounts of revenue since the transactions are often in the millions of dollars.

Syndicated selling is an exciting form of agent service. A good example is the Amazon Associates program. In this program Web sites place links on their pages back to the Amazon site and receive a commission for every consumer who follows the link and makes a purchase. The link can be either to the Amazon home page or to a page listing a particular book or group of books. Exhibit 8 - 3 shows a page from one of Amazon's associates, the Dogtoys site (www.dogtoys.com). Amazon has over 15,000 authors, publishers, e-zines, nonprofit organizations, and other sites all linking back to its site, thereby creating an enormous number of points of sale for its products.

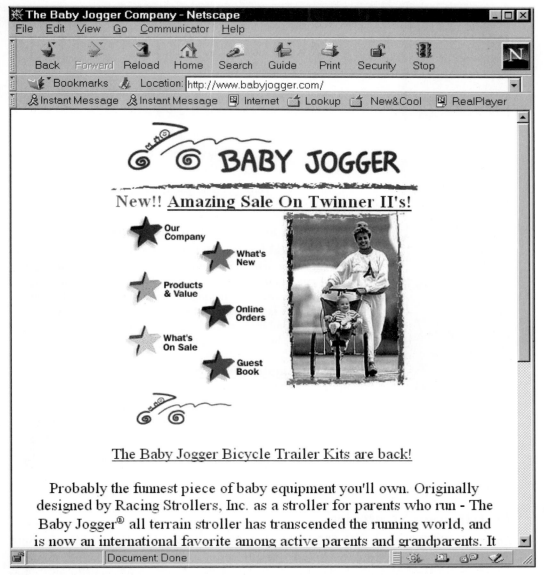

Exhibit 8 - 2 Baby Jogger

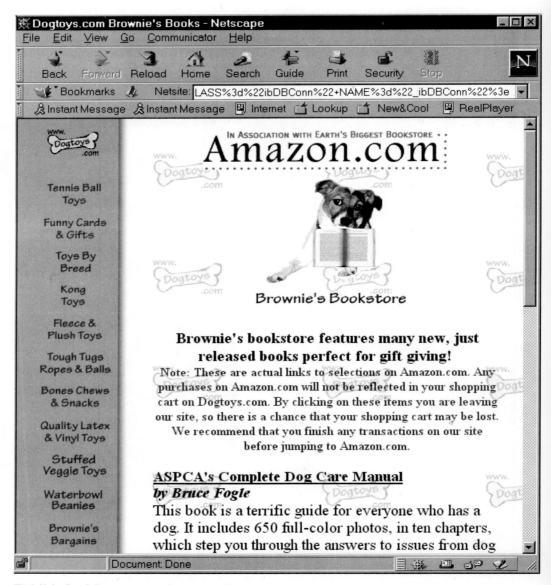

Exhibit 8 - 3 Dogtoys as Amazon Agent

Distribution Strategies

Online retailing has brought $17 billion in sales to firms with electronic storefronts. This strategy involves putting a firm's products on a Web site and taking online or telephone orders. It is much more complex than that, because of security and other concerns, but nevertheless, if a firm's target markets use the Internet, its current products might sell well in this new channel. Obviously, the Internet can be a viable distribution channel for discontinuous innovations and product line extensions (discussed above) as well as for a firm's current products. Catalog retailers such as Land's End find online selling an easier transition than do firms who do not have experience with mail order techniques.

Pirating the value chain is an interesting distribution strategy that is well suited to the Internet (Ghosh 1998).   Value chain pirates extend vertically into either a supplier's or buyer's existing business. For example, some companies that distribute through retail outlets may decide to sell direct to consumers online. Such arrangements are risky, however, since they may offend displaced members of the value chain, creating channel conflict. By selling online Barnes & Noble runs the risk of upsetting its retail outlets. A more extreme example of pirating the value chain would be if Barnes & Noble began publishing books rather than just distributing them.

Another distribution strategy involves delivery of digital products directly over the Internet. Digital products that can be sent electronically from producer to consumer consist of audio, video, graphics, and text content. For example, electronic publishing has grown into a major Web industry. While most content is currently free and ad supported, there are some subscription services, including the *Washington Post* and the *Wall Street Journal*. Other content publishers such as the *New York Times* offer their current issue for free but charge users to retrieve documents from the archives. Still other services such as Forrester Research offer a short teaser introduction to an article and then charge users to read the remainder.

Pricing Strategies

Online pricing strategies are similar to offline strategies. Two important online pricing strategies are penetration pricing and price leadership. Penetration pricing is the practice of charging a low price for a product for the purpose of gaining market share. This strategy is particularly effective in a price-sensitive market like the Internet. Many firms, such as Netscape and Eudora, give their products away for free just to gain customers to whom they can then sell other products. The best examples of low-price leadership are found in the highly competitive markets for computer components. However, a vendor competing on price had better be among the lowest price or risk going unnoticed. This is so because services such as CNET Shopper.com are able to aggregate and compare prices for computer systems across vendors, as is shown in Exhibit 8 - 4. Consumers are likely to gravitate toward the low price vendors at the top of the list.

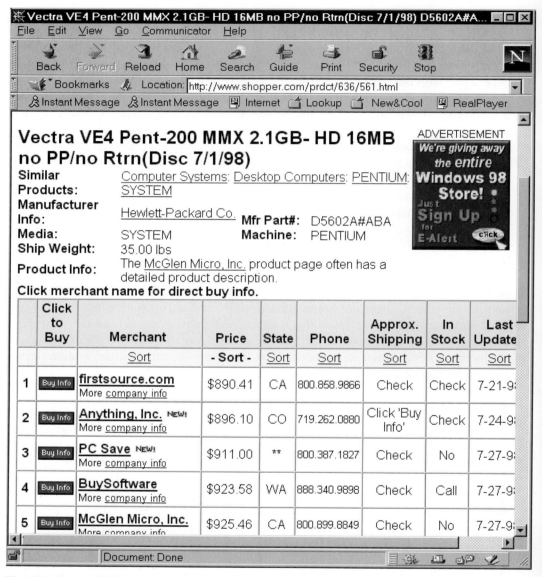

Exhibit 8 - 4 CNET Shopper.com

GAINING INTERNAL EFFICIENCIES

One of the best reasons to go online is to reduce the cost of doing business by gaining internal efficiencies (Ghosh 1998). Organizations can reduce marketing expenditures through electronic marketing communication. For example, the University of Nevada Web site home page changes nearly daily to reflect current and positive news about grants received and faculty research discoveries. This updating saves the cost of printing and distributing an employee newsletter while creating a positive image among many stakeholder groups. Similarly, J. Crew's electronic distribution of coupons and PalmPilot Computing's e-mail communication with customers not only provide timely information, but will save marketing funds. An additional benefit is the ease with which electronic communication can be changed. By contrast, a firm is stuck with an error or misguided tactic in print.

Many firms gain internal efficiencies by cutting distribution costs through online strategies. In the case of business-to-business sales these savings can be very dramatic. Cisco Systems, the world's largest manufacturer of networking equipment, allows Web-based orders from their customers. The paperwork reduction it reaps from this saves $270 million each year. General Electric saved $500 to $700 million over three years by linking its suppliers, and in addition reduced the time required to complete orders by up to 50%. In the consumer channel, Dell computer sells $3 million in computers daily from its Web site. The Web site tremendously reduces the load on and staffing cost of its call center. Additional savings are realized since Dell does not support retail outlets. Lack of retail outlets gives Dell a competitive advantage over manufacturers, such as Compaq, which have to finance retail channels. Furthermore, Dell does not carry stale inventory since all Dell computers are built to order.

Action Plan

In this phase of the Internet marketing plan, the marketer identifies specific tactics to implement selected strategies. These are the daily action plans. For example, a firm wanting to sell its products online will build a very specific plan involving necessary product adaptations, the site design, technical aspects of electronic commerce, and the pricing, distribution, and marketing communications tactics to make it all work. Specific Internet tactics are beyond the scope of this book; however, we suggest several important and general points to consider when a company is building an Internet action plan.

PROJECT SCOPE

How big of an Internet commitment does the firm want to make? A small Web site (technical term: microsite) is quickly developed, inexpensive to build, and easy to manage. Starting small takes less commitment and can be quite effective for certain objectives but necessarily limits the firm's Internet exposure. Larger sites need much more planning and resources but allow for extensive content and electronic commerce. If the plan includes an e-mail communication program, the firm will need database software as well as procedures and staff to write and respond to stakeholder e-mail.

SITE DEVELOPMENT

Who will build the Web site? Internal developers understand the business and are easier to control but are less likely to know the technology and unique aspects of the

Net. Unless the firm is experienced with Web development, in-house production can result in trial-and-error, which may be more expensive in the long run.

There are at least seven reasons to outsource Web development. First, outsourcing speeds completion of the project. The design firm has no learning curve to slow down progress. It knows the technology and how to use it. Second, because the project is completed faster, personnel cost savings often more than compensate for the design firm's fee. This is a surprising result until one adds up all the person hours really involved in site development and maintenance. Third, outsourcing is likely to result in a site that loads faster. There are a number of technical tricks to speed the load times of Web sites which are known to outsourcers. Many sites developed in-house tend to be heavy on graphics with correspondingly intolerable download times. Fourth, design firms tend to produce a more user-friendly product. Design firms are aware of the navigation standards that users have come to expect, and they are able to meet these needs. Fifth, graphic and information design on the site tends to be more polished and professional. Sites developed in the firm tend to be sloppy in terms of unity of design. Sixth, outsourcers are aware of copyright rules. Many sites designed in-house tend to borrow generously from copyrighted material. Seventh, you don't get a second chance to make a first impression. Users who are totally put off by a home-grown site may not return.

Nonetheless, outsourcing may be expensive. Forrester research estimates the cost for a "conservative" site to be $10,000 to $100,000, while an "aggressive" site costs $1 million or more. There are many fine Web development firms such as Adjacency and many large ad agencies offering this service. BrainBug, a Connecticut interactive agency, reports on the Web site development process in the Practitioner Perspective at the end of this chapter.

SITE MAINTENANCE

Part of the action plan should include a section on Internet program maintenance. It is estimated that Web sites change on average every 75 days, and many change daily. The Internet offers an opportunity (and burden) to update content frequently. For example, the firm may want to disseminate new information about products or personnel, or announce new promotional campaigns. In addition, a site that constantly adds interesting material, promotions, or information will entice its users to return often. Content maintenance takes human resources that should be planned in advance for an effective Internet program. Technology maintenance also takes planning, especially if the Internet program will expand over time. The Internet marketer will want to take advantage of new technologies that are introduced if they fit the marketing plan goals. Web site maintenance may be more difficult and costly if outsourced than if done in-house.

Budgeting

A key part of any marketing plan is to identify the expected returns from a Web site investment. These can then be matched against costs to develop a cost/benefit analysis which will ultimately help to determine whether the effort is worthwhile. This process is difficult because sometimes the Internet investment produces intangible results which will bring long-term returns, such as recognition in the industry, brand building, or favorable stakeholder images.

REVENUE STREAMS

Initial funds to support a Web site can come from investors, loans, and the firm's operating budget. Revenue streams that produce Internet profits come mainly from Web site product sales, advertising sales, and agent commissions. Soft revenue comes from cost savings such as distribution channel efficiencies. Some of the largest Web sites, such as Amazon and MSNBC, are not profitable ventures. These Web sites are so focused on establishing their brands that they and their investors are willing to sustain losses for years. The conventional wisdom is that when the shakeout comes, there will be room only at the top. Therefore, the fight to be the number one Web site in each product category is rather fierce.

So who is financing this bleeding of capital? Some of it is debt financed through bank loans, though much of it is equity financed. Startup companies often tap private funds (friends and family) and venture capital. There are a number of firms that specialize in providing venture capital to startup firms, although in the classic Catch-22, the venture capitalists prefer to infuse money once they have seen some evidence of success. Continued success allows the company to issue stock (technical term: initial public offering [IPO]). The stock market runs hot and cold on Internet IPOs, though when they are hot they are white hot! Of particular interest to investors are projects that involve business-to-business commerce, since the dollar amounts transacted in these ventures are enormous.

PRODUCT AND SERVICE SALES

Not all Web sites sell online. Those that do, however, are able to track this important revenue stream and use it for break-even and other budgeting analyses. At the current time the most popular form of payment is via a credit card. This is fine for larger purchases, but what about purchasing an article that costs 50 cents? New schemes are being devised that would allow for micropayments of pennies in these situations. Online subscription sales have not been a very successful business model. However, there are notable exceptions such as the *Wall Street Journal*.

ADVERTISING SPACE SALES

Many content providers sell advertising in the form of banners, buttons, and sponsorships. This model is so successful that it often allows the content to be delivered for free. Nonetheless, a major portion of ad inventory often goes unsold. Even big name sites such as Yahoo! sell only about 30% of their ad inventory. This helps explain why so many ads on Yahoo! are for Yahoo! products and services. Many feel that advertising dollars will continue to grow as marketers realize the effectiveness of the Web media. Unfortunately, 90% of the advertising dollars go to the top 100 Web sites, leaving little money for the smaller sites. Because advertising sales on all but the top sites are so unpredictable, they are very difficult to use in the budgeting process.

AGENT FEES

A final source of hard revenue is through syndicated selling. In this model a Web site, serving as agent, receives a commission for each customer referred to another site who purchases on that other Web site. Syndicated selling may be particularly effective for small Web sites that are unable to attract advertising dollars. Amazon, Netscape, and CD Now all run syndicated selling programs.

COST SAVINGS

Money saved through Internet efficiencies are considered soft revenue for a firm. For example, if a distribution channel contains a wholesaler, distributor, and retailer between the producer and consumer, each intermediary will take a profit. A typical markup scheme is 10% from manufacturer to the wholesaler, 10% to the distributor, 100% to the retailer, and 50% to the consumer. If a producer sells the product to a wholesaler for $50, it will sell to the consumer for $165. If the producer cuts the intermediaries (disintermediation) and sells this product online directly to the consumer, it can price the product at $85 and increase revenue by $35. Whether or not this translates to profits depends on the cost of getting the product to the consumer. Other examples include the $5,000 a marketer saves in printing and postage for a direct mail piece costing $1.00 per piece to 5,000 consumers or the $270 million Cisco saved in one year on handling costs for its online computer system sales.

INTANGIBLE BENEFITS

The intangible benefits of an Internet program are much more difficult to establish but this is no different from the case in traditional media. How much is the goodwill worth that is incurred through PalmPilot Computing's e-mail program that gives users tips to enhance product usage? How much goodwill does a Web site create? Marketers are challenged to come up with answers to these questions.

When the Internet program seeks cognitive or attitude objectives, the benefits are difficult to measure. Advertising strategies to build brand awareness or image and Web sites that serve public relations purposes fall in this category. Even more difficult is the value of customers with whom a firm uses an Internet based relationship-building program. Complicating matters are difficulties with audience measurement at Web sites: This makes benefit extrapolation a wild guess. The cable TV industry experienced these problems in its infancy, but as the industry matures the numbers are becoming more reliable. Nevertheless, intangible benefits of advertising and public relations remain slippery measures. In spite of these difficulties, the advertising dollars continue to pour into the Web.

COST/BENEFIT ANALYSIS

Investment benefits derived from a Web site typically involve either an increase in revenue (e.g., sales) or a decrease in costs (e.g., lower coupon delivery costs). Additional and intangible benefits include goodwill, brand/image building, and relationship building. Against these benefits are the costs of an Internet program. These include some of the following: connecting to the Internet (e.g., the ISP), hardware and software, Web site and advertising designers, and staff to maintain Web site content and manage e-mail with stakeholders. If the firm sells products online, there will be distribution and product costs to consider, as well as other costs that are similar to those of offline product sales. If the company sells advertising on the site, there are space salespeople to fund, or fees to pay to advertising aggregators (the space reps).

A detailed list of costs is impractical here, but the point is that a firm must attempt a cost/benefit analysis for its Internet marketing program. We say "attempt" because break-even and other analyses are very difficult and unreliable in this new frontier called the Internet. MSNBC plans to break-even within five years of introduction, but when it made this prediction Web/TV convergence was just an idea. It will be reality during the five-year break-even period, thereby throwing a huge new variable into the equation. At this time, most firms focus on the cost side of the equation and try to build the Net business, assuming revenues will catch up.

Evaluation Plan

Once the site is created, its success needs continuous evaluation. This involves tracking systems that must be in place before the electronic doors are opened. What should be measured? The answer is that it depends on the Internet plan objectives.

For cognitive objectives of awareness building, a common measure of success is the number of unique visits to a site. If users stopped by, they probably gained some degree of awareness about the firm and its messages or products. For example, if a company puts a sales contest on the Intranet, it will want to track the number of salespeople who visited. The same is true for advertising: Page views and number of impressions are commonly used statistics prepared by Web sites for their advertisers.

If a firm's objectives are to build brands or reach other attitudinal objectives, evaluation is more difficult. As with other media, firms must conduct surveys to see if attitudes changed. Fortunately this is easier to do with Web forms and e-mail, but, as was discussed in chapter 3, not necessarily too reliable.

Transactive behavior is the easiest to measure, because users must physically do something like enter an online order and use a credit card. Marketing managers want to track not only number of purchases, but what path users took through the site prior to purchase. Also important is what sites users viewed immediately prior to purchasing. For example, a user might have seen your ad on a related site, clicked on it, and immediately bought: This process generates a statistic known as click-through rate. Many statistics are emerging to measure transactive behavior such as dollars purchased per pages viewed, or amount of time spent at the site per dollars spent.

Tracking user behavior at a firm's site is extremely important. The Internet offers the technology to do this tracking easily and then to make quick tactical changes, but the measurement systems must be in place first. For example, an especially poorly performing ad can be yanked in real time and replaced by another. Such flexibility is not possible in other media such as magazines. There is no way to yank the Marlboro Man once the magazine has hit the newsstand!

S u m m a r y

Because of the volume of detail in this chapter, the summary is presented in outline form. Creating an Internet marketing plan requires at least seven steps.

1. Conduct a situation analysis
   - Review the existing marketing plan and any other information that can be obtained about the company and its brands. Existing materials help to give direction and set boundaries on the Internet marketing plan.
   - Examine environmental factors related to online marketing
     - Legal/political environment
     - Technological changes
     - User trends
     - World economies
   - Develop a market opportunity analysis (includes a SWOT analysis)
2. Identify target stakeholders
3. Set objectives. Some objectives are global while others apply to specific targets.
   - Cognitive and attitude goals
   - Transactive behavior goals
   - Internal efficiencies that may affect marketing budgets
4. Design marketing-mix strategies to meet the objectives
   - Stakeholder communication helps achieve cognitive and attitude goals
     - Advertising and sponsorships
     - Public relations and brochureware
     - Sales promotion incentives
     - Lead generation
     - Relationship building
     - Branding and corporate image building
   - Selling products and services over the Internet helps meet transactive behavior goals

- New products and services
- Advertising sales
- Agent services
- Distribution strategies
- Pricing strategies
  - Penetration pricing
  - Price leadership
- Gain internal efficiencies to help marketing budgets

5. Design an action plan (tactics to implement the strategies)
   - Project scope
   - Site development
   - Site maintenance

6. Develop a budget
   - Revenue streams
     - Product and service sales
     - Advertising space sales
     - Agent fees
   - Cost savings
   - Intangible benefits
   - Cost-benefit analysis

7. Develop an evaluation plan

The plan follows the lines of a military campaign. In a military campaign, a situation analysis shows an army's strengths and weaknesses (e.g., we have air and sea superiority; their army is busy on the Russian front). A thorough assessment of the situation allows development of objectives (e.g., we can probably occupy France). Strategies are developed to meet the objectives (e.g., establish a beachhead at Normandy). Finally, tactics implement the strategies (e.g., land 50,000 troops at Omaha Beach).

Selling products and services over the Internet helps meet transactive behavior goals

Key Concepts and Terms

1. The traditional marketing planning process adapts smoothly to the Web environment.

2. Serious planning efforts should precede any online initiatives.

3. The environmental scan should reference the online environment.

4. Online objectives include cognitive, attitude, transaction, and internal efficiencies.

5. Primary marketing-mix strategies for online marketing include marketing communication, selling products online, and lowering marketing costs through online strategies.

6. For many sites not engaged in sales, the benefits of an online presence are much more difficult to measure. This difficulty unfortunately leads some managers to conclude that the online efforts are a waste of resources.

- Action plan
- Agent services
- Brochureware
- Environmental factors
- Evaluation plan
- Internal efficiencies

- Market opportunity analysis
- Revenue streams
- Situation analysis
- Stakeholder communication
- SWOT
- Outsource

Exercises

REVIEW QUESTIONS FOR KNOWLEDGE TESTING

1. What are the steps in an Internet marketing plan?
2. What is a SWOT analysis?
3. List some Internet-based marketing-mix strategies; use examples.
4. List reasons that a company may wish to outsource Web site development

DISCUSSION QUESTIONS FOR CRITICAL THINKING

1. If an insurance company were to go online, what stakeholders should it consider?
2. If an automobile manufacturer were to go online, what stakeholders should it consider?
3. In which of the marketing-mix strategies do you think the Internet adds the greatest value? Why?
4. Make the case for developing a Web site in-house rather than outsourcing. Which would you choose?

ACTIVITIES

1. Visit the Web sites of several automobile manufacturers. Write down the top-level links from their home page. For each link, try to identify the stakeholders who are being targeted.

2. Visit the McDonald's Corp. Web site. List each stakeholder it reaches and tell what basic content is targeted to each stakeholder.

3. Consider a local business that you know about and sketch a bare-bones Internet marketing plan for it.

4. Find the Web site for a firm that offers Web site building services. What steps does it recommend? What does it charge to develop a Web site?

5. Go to the Web site for your university and describe how well you think the site fulfills the marketing objectives of the university. Suggest improvements.

INTERNET EXERCISE: ONLINE MARKETING

Online book selling is big business. The first successful online bookseller was Amazon.com, an exclusively online retailer. The company quickly established itself as the market leader. Attracted by the profit potential, Barnes & Noble, the giant book retailer, expanded online in early 1997. In fact, the Web is such an excellent place to sell books that perhaps you'd like to jump in and compete. Before you do, however, you need a strategic plan. This exercise will get you started. Review www.amazon.com and www.barnesandnoble.com. Then complete the table by speculating on parts of their business plans.

	Amazon	**Barnes & Noble**
Mission statement		
Target customers		
Market position		
Product: number of books		
Product: anything other than books offered?		
Distribution: geographic areas		
Price: general strategy		
Price: shipping price strategy		

For Discussion

How will your new company compete? Begin to form your strategic plan by answering the following questions:

1. What will be the cool and catchy name for your online book company?
2. What are your company's marketing objectives?
3. Who are your target customers? Will you compete head-on with the big guys or select a special target market?
4. What will be your market position?
5. What products will you carry: for example, more books, specialized books, other products?
6. What geographic areas will you service with your books?
7. What will be your general pricing strategy: above, below, or the same as the competition?

Practitioner Perspective

THE WEB DEVELOPMENT PROCESS

Matt Straznitskas is founder and president of BrainBug, an award-winning interactive agency headquartered in Hartford, Connecticut

As founder of BrainBug, a pioneering Web development agency, I've learned that the most valuable tool for creating Web sites is the process by which a site is delivered on time, on budget, and bug free. Most clients understand that the Web is a new medium and everyone is learning as they go, but if an agency bungles the development process enough times, it won't be in business very long. Here are the steps I've established for successful Web development:

Initial Consultation: This first step is the accumulation of key information about the project. Facts to be gathered include the target audience for the site, the primary message to be communicated, and the overall business goals of the organization. Initial consultation typically concludes with the draft of a logic diagram that notes all of the pages in the site — commonly referred to as a site map.

During initial consultation, BrainBug will also work with the client to determine where the Web site will be hosted — either internally on a corporate Web server or externally with an Internet service provider (ISP). With this issue resolved, the client is required to select an available domain name for the Web site.

Content Development: With the parameters of the project laid out, we work with the client to develop the main text of the Web site. Writing for the Web is much different than for print, so it is important for an interactive agency to have experienced Web copywriters on staff.

Another part of the content development phase is the selection of keywords that will be used to ensure a high standing in search engines. Since many search engines base their results on how often keywords are repeated in the main text of the Web site, it is critical for a client to settle on a specific list of keywords early on in the process.

Concept Development: While the content is being developed, BrainBug's creative staff will sketch out visual ideas for the site. Often, these ideas are presented to the client as loose pencil sketches that provide a range of different layout, design, and navigation choices.

Digital Comps: Upon the client's selection of a preferred concept, the creative staff moves ahead with the production of digital color comps (short for "comprehensives"). The static images, typically no more than 600 pixels wide by 300 pixels tall (the viewing area of a small monitor), are printed in color and put on black matte board for presentation.

Layout and Navigation: Once the comps are approved, we'll create a few functioning Web pages. Navigation is programmed into the page, providing the client with the first real taste of how users will interact with the site.

Production: With all of the major elements of the site approved, we'll proceed to build the entire site. The written content and graphics are brought together and each section of the site is systematically assembled.

Testing: Before the site is delivered to the client, every Web page and link is tested on a variety of browsers and computer platforms. With a written list of problems in hand, the technical staff will make each repair and cross it off the list.

Delivery: Upon receipt, clients will often conduct their own testing, with a special focus on sensitive content like financial figures and news releases. After any changes are made, the site is officially launched.

This whole process can take anywhere from one to twelve months to complete, with the average being about four months. Following the launch of a site, measurements are conducted to determine how people are using the site. Over the course of three to six months, data are gathered, site improvements are initiated, and the Web design process will likely start again to reflect the client's evolving online business goals.

Leveraging Technology

BUILDING A WEB SITE

The process of building and publishing a Web page has become greatly simplified over the last few years. Originally all Web pages were constructed using a language called HyperText Markup Language (HTML). While HTML is not much of a challenge for a MIS or computer science student, it is quite a challenge for a user who is not accustomed to programming. Furthermore, the HTML language has become more complex over the years as more and more features are added. Fortunately, a number of companies have come to the rescue with authoring tools that automatically generate HTML. The authoring tools allow the user to design the Web page in a WYSIWYG (What You See Is What You Get) fashion as though they were composing a document on a word processor. The authoring software then translates the page into HTML. As good as these tools are today, they still do not compare with a talented team of HTML programmers. Why? First, because these software programs are not able to keep up quickly enough with advances in HTML capabilities. That situation may change over the next several years as the authoring tools become even more sophisticated. Second, menu-driven products are limited by the preprogrammed menu options. Straying from the menu options sometimes creates unstable code.

All Web pages rely on the HyperText Markup Language (HTML). HTML uses beginning and end tags to identify which words appear as <B>**Bold**</B>, <I>*Italicized*</I>, <U>Underlined</U>, etc. The tags are placed on either side of the item to be formatted. The end tag begins with a forward slash. The browser (Netscape or Internet Explorer) reads the tags as page formatting instructions. The user doesn't see the tags — only the formatted item. As an example, consider the following HTML code created in the Notepad editor and how it looks through the browser (Exhibit 8 - 5).

The <HTML> at the beginning identifies this as an HTML file. The <BODY> tag indicates that what follows should be displayed on the page. The </BODY> tag indicates that the display is finished and the </HTML> tag indicates that the HTML is finished. The <P> between lines indicates a paragraph break. It is used to skip a line. You can try this yourself by typing the sample in Notepad (or in any word processor if saved as plain text), then opening the file in Netscape or Internet Explorer.

To view the HTML tags of any page on the Web, choose View→HTML Source when surfing the page. Programmers actually memorize these tags and use them to construct Web pages. Exhibit 8 - 6 is another example showing the HTML to display a click-through banner ad.

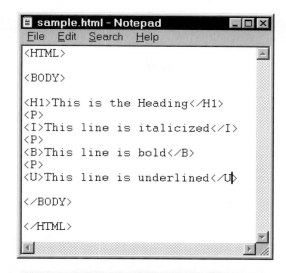

Exhibit 8 - 5 HTML Code and How It Displays in Browser

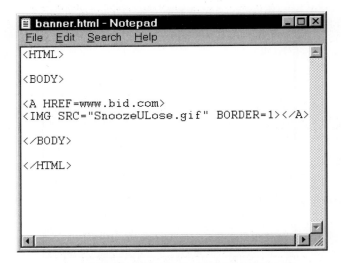

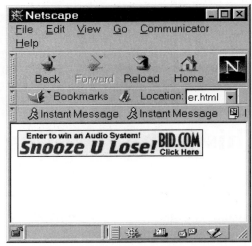

Exhibit 8 - 6 HTML for Banner Ad

IMG SRC stands for image source, that is, the name of the file that contains the banner ad. In this case the name of the file is SnoozeULose.gif. Many web graphics files have a .GIF extension to indicate that they follow the Graphics Interchange Format (GIF) standard. The BORDER=1 puts a thin border (one pixel wide) around the banner ad. This is a standard so that the user does not confuse the ad with the page content. Most of the time the merchant wants the user to be able to click through the banner ad to reach the merchant's Web site. Linking the graphic with an actual Web site (www.bid.com) enables click-through. The <A> and </A> are the start and finish of the HTML anchor or link. Note that the IMG SRC is contained within the anchor—this makes the banner a hyperlink. HREF stands for Hypertext Reference, that is, where to go when the user clicks on the banner. Got all that?

Luckily, many tools generate the tags automatically. For example, each product in the Microsoft Office Suite incorporates a "Save as HTML" feature. For even more sophisticated Web page design, use a product such as Microsoft FrontPage 98, Page Mill, or NetObjects Fusion. These tools allow nontechnical users to design fairly complex Web sites.

Even publishing the pages has become simplified. Transferring files from the designer's computer to the Web server using a procedure called File Transfer Protocol (FTP) publishes web pages. Originally rather cumbersome to use, FTP is now a menu button on many authoring tools. This means that a marketer can develop a Web page almost as easily as typing a text document and then can send it electronically to the Web server for addition to the company Web site—instant Web page development and maintenance!

These tools are great for designing brochureware, a Web site that will contain information. Most businesses begin with brochureware since it is safe and relatively inexpensive to launch. Brochureware may contain text, graphics, an e-mail feedback button, and perhaps a guest book. The design tools are not nearly as good at implementing a Web site capable of electronic commerce. The problem is that electronic commerce requires that the Web page interact with a database that contains at a minimum the pricing and transaction information as well as a way to verify credit card purchases. And this is hard to program. As a result most businesses rely on professional programmers to design and implement electronic commerce sites.

Nonetheless, commerce site design tools that are especially targeted to small businesses are beginning to appear. Recently, some very clever products have automated the design of electronic commerce sites. Two of these products are iCat Commerce Online (www.icat.com) and Yahoo! Store (store.yahoo.com). These products allow small and medium-sized businesses to set up an electronic commerce site without hiring a programmer. Both products allow construction of a Web site online in a step-by-step fashion. Furthermore, they require no installation of additional software on the user's computer! They both utilize a point-and-click interface for Web site construction. They claim that a user with a registered business and a merchant account with their bank could literally be taking transactions on the Web in 30 minutes!

The pricing model for the iCat and Yahoo! Store products is a monthly charge that typically depends on the number of products offered in the online store. At the time of this writing iCat even offered a *free* online store for merchants selling 10 products or fewer! So how do they make money? Well, as the client's business succeeds, they succeed. Once the business exceeds a 10-item product offering, then it begins to incur a monthly charge. Furthermore, iCat markets services to help publicize the online store.

The effect of all these design tools has been to spawn a proliferation of Web sites, and the tide will continue as they become progressively easier to implement. In the future the points of differentiation between sites will rely on quality content. Sites based on a solid marketing plan which are well implemented have the greatest chance for success.

Ethics and Law

PRIVACY IN DIGITAL CONTEXTS

In 1990, Lotus Development Corporation, a software concern, and Equifax, Inc., a consumer data analysis firm, announced a joint venture. The result was to be a computer-based application to be known as *Lotus Marketplace: Households*. Targeted to small businesses, it would contain the cross-referable information of 80 million households, including names, addresses, ages, income, and lifestyle patterns. Reaction to the news was virtually instantaneous. Privacy advocates—among them, a number of computer professionals—argued that in terms of consumer notification, access to data, and ability to correct errors, the new system presented dangerous threats which were clearly accentuated by the employment of digital technology. Congressional hearings were conducted and the developers were inundated by negative phone calls and letters. Ultimately, the product was withdrawn, but not before the problem of digital privacy had received a first, and powerful introduction.

The events precipitated by *Households* serve as a stark reminder that privacy concerns must play an active role in the formation of any information-driven system. It is important to note that privacy implications are inherent in the dissemination as well as the collection of information. Methods of transmission that include the unwanted sending of data, such as mass electronic mailings, known as *spam* (see chapter 6) are the subject of legislative consideration, chiefly because of a perceived unreasonable intrusion upon the seclusion of Internet users.

A primary field of attention is the means and the manner of data collection. A starting point for this discussion is the AMA Code of Ethics for Marketing on the Internet. This states that "information collected from customers should be confidential and used only for expressed purposes." This principle is concise and straightforward in general terms, but it must be applied to the Internet's many information-gathering mechanisms.

A "cookie" is a packet of data which is normally created within the hard drive of a user as a result of a contact with a Web page. Once stored, it can be retransmitted from user's computer to the pertinent Web site. Cookies serve many purposes. They may handle online shopping information, such as multiple purchases. They may remind the user of links already visited on a page. While having many conveniences, cookies can also pose privacy concerns. Information that the user has offered during a site visit can be recorded, along with the sequence of links selected (known as "click stream" data). It can also store the site from which the page was accessed. Such data can then be configured into a user profile which may direct tailored advertising, special options, or other information to be sent to the user's screen. Data obtained from cookies can also be sold to outside entities.

Java is a Web-friendly programming language which allows the downloading and running of programs or *applets* on individual computers. These applications are increasingly used to provide dynamic animation, Web-based simulations, and other useful additions to plain hypertext. Java programs known as *hostile applets* may also be used to access and transmit data on hard drives, including e-mail addresses.

Intelligent agents are a current topic of interest within Web marketing. The products of artificial intelligence research, agents are programs which, once released by a user, can function autonomously within the Web to make electronic decisions. Some potential tasks include the searching of sites or the buying of products that conform to an individual's tastes or interests. Critics of agents worry that the preferences they entail may be chosen or controlled by entities other than their "owner." Such a situation would limit the individual's privacy-linked ability to make autonomous decisions and could create an incentive to distribute personal information contained in the agent applications.

Cookies, Java applets, and intelligent agents are *ubiquitous* applications; that is, they are able to function in the course of nearly any online session, without a user's knowledge or control. The ease of their operation can be a persuasive factor in favor of failing to inform a user that data are being collected. This attitude is objectionable when it favors technological ease above ethical principles. Similarly, since much of the information is not of an explicitly confidential character, it may be tempting to ignore privacy implications. This argument ignores the fact that even innocent data may, when combined, result in very specific information.

In addition to application-based collection, sites often elicit information from users through forms and electronic mail. Often, this is done in exchange for browsing privileges or other benefits and with the full disclosure of the terms of use. However, information may also be gathered through explicitly fraudulent methods—an approach that has unambiguous ethical and legal implications.

Another concern involves the mishandling of sensitive data. In a recently publicized matter, America Online (AOL) allowed information concerning a user's sexual preference to be displayed in a public profile area. This revelation initiated an official investigation of the user, a member of the U.S. Navy. In the end, AOL acknowledged its error and issued an apology. The incident stands to enforce the fact that protocols for information storage and retrieval are strongly relevant to users.

A particularly active area of study involves the collection of material from children. A 1998 report of the Federal Trade Commission (FTC) indicates that 89 percent of the children's sites surveyed collected identifiable user data and 46 percent of these sites did not reveal their policies of collection or use. Merely 10 percent of the surveyed sites contained provisions for parental control ("Privacy Online," p. 12). Currently, Congress has considered, but not passed, laws specifically directed to Internet data collection. As was suggested above, conventional criminal statutes can address explicit offenses such as fraud. Additionally, sanctions for misuse of consumer data are present in the Fair Credit Reporting Act (15 U.S.C. 1681). The

FTC and other agencies are also capable of developing regulations but have chosen to delay these efforts in favor of promoting self-regulation. Organizations such as the Direct Marketing Association have developed comprehensive guidelines for Web privacy (The Direct Marketing Association guidelines are available at www.the-dma.org/policy.html). Critics argue that despite these efforts, most professional organizations lack the ability to meaningfully enforce such codes.

Legislation that may encourage the swift development of American law is directive 95/46/EC of the European Parliament and of the Council of 24 October 1995 on the protection of individuals with regard to the processing of personal data and on the free movement of such data (Article 25). This enactment, scheduled to take effect in October 1998, contains strict rules concerning the collection and transfer of European citizens' personal information. It specifically prohibits transactions with entities possessing inadequate protections.

As legislation and professional endeavors progress, the following norms have been identified in the FTC report as widely accepted in the industry and essential to the ethical use of consumer information:

1. **Notice:** Users should be aware of a site's information policy *before* data are collected.

2. **Consent:** Users should be allowed to choose participation or exclusion from the collection.

3. **Access:** Users should have the ability to access their data and correct them if erroneous.

4. **Security:** Policies to ensure the integrity of data and the prevention of misuse should be in place.

5. **Enforcement:** Users should have effective means to hold data collectors to their policies.

Savvy Sites

Web Site and Address	Importance to Net Marketers
DoubleClick www.doubleclick.com	DoubleClick is a firm that specializes in putting banner ads on Web sites. Right now DoubleClick produces over 430 million impressions every month for the company's clients.
Internet Advertising Bureau www.iab.net	The Internet Advertising Bureau is an association entirely devoted to the coverage of advertising on the Internet. The site provides news, research materials, and membership information.
MatchLogic www.matchlogic.com	"MatchLogic is a full-service, centralized ad management company supporting the entire Internet advertising community. We've built our reputation on the rapid delivery and management of all forms of Web advertising—GIF, JPEG, HTML and Java ad banners."
MediaMetrix www.mediametrix.com	MediaMetrix is a leader in marketing information services. The company designs tools that online marketers can use to measure activity on their Web sites. Their renowned program is called PC Meter, which provides real-time analysis of usage patterns.
RelevantKnowledge www.relevantknowledge.com	RelevantKnowledge provides online audience demographic measurement reports for the Web. Marketers who are interested in advertising on top Web sites will find detailed charts available regarding the demographic profile of each site's audience.

Appendices

The History and Technology of the Net

(And Why Marketers Should Care About It)

A

The Internet ("Net") is a network of computers reaching every country in the world. It is similar in some ways to the telephone system. Just as calls can be made anywhere in the world, so too can a computer contact any other computer connected to the Net.

The Internet has been around since the 1960s, when the Defense Department conceived it as a fail-safe way of messaging in case of a nuclear attack. As a result the Internet is quite robust—communications almost always go through—albeit rather slowly at times. From the 1960s until the early 1990s the Internet was used primarily by the Defense Department and by researchers in industry and education. It was used to grant shared access to distant supercomputers and as a means of sending electronic mail. In those days, the Net was fairly hard to use and it was difficult to find one's way around. Outside of a fairly small community, not that many people knew of or cared much about the Internet. All that changed in the mid-1990s.

This decade has been witness to a revolution created by three major developments: the birth of the World Wide Web (WWW or Web), hyperlinks, and graphical browsers. The Web and hyperlinks are two pieces of the same puzzle. The Web began as a standard that defined how to travel from computer to computer throughout the world by following embedded links in a screen display of written words (text). A click on the link instantly transported the user to another computer as directed by the embedded instruction. Such clickable text was called *hypertext*. The Web and hypertext made it easy to get around; they formed a basis for navigation in cyberspace. What was missing, however, were pictures, icons, and color. People like a graphical interface since it is intuitive and easy to master. The graphics problem was solved by the development of graphical browsers, the most prominent of which are Netscape Navigator and Microsoft Internet Explorer. Graphical browsers allow users to click on images as well as text links to navigate in a multimedia world. Not only can sites contain text and graphics, but they can also contain sound, video, and even 3D video. Graphical browsers have brought visual appeal and entertainment value to the Web. The Web, hyperlinks, and graphical browsers have made cyberspace a very friendly place and have spawned the rush to get connected.

BITS ARE BITS

One way to understand the Internet is to look at the technology that supports it. The details of that technology are incredibly complex but the concepts behind it are quite simple. To paraphrase Negroponte (1995), the Internet is all about moving bits from one place to another. Bits are the essential building blocks of digital information much as atoms are the building blocks of molecules. A bit can be either a zero or a one. Grouping bits forms more complex information such as letters, words, graphics, sound, or video. From the Internet's perspective, a bit is a bit is a bit. The Internet does not distinguish between bits that carry text, graphics, sound, or video. From this humble beginning comes a new marketing landscape: things such as electronic commerce and banner advertising.

MAKE IT FAST AND EASY

If the major task is to move bits from one location to another, then two key subtasks are critical to the Internet's success. First, the infrastructure must move those bits as quickly as possible. Speed is important and has been a repeated theme throughout this text. The Internet is currently too slow (see the leveraging technology side bar at the end of chapter 1 to find out why). Slow speeds mean loss of business opportunities. For example, reliably carrying phone calls and music over the Internet requires lots of speed. The Holy Grail of the Internet architecture is video on demand, and for that the speed is nowhere near adequate.

Second, making it easy for users to exchange bits is the basis for the World Wide Web. The Web was created to link all the bits together with a point-and-click graphical interface. In addition to pictures and sound, users want tools such as search engines to find the bits they need quickly. Tomorrow's users may well demand an intelligent interface which understands speech. For their part, marketers can reach target markets more effectively with tools that track which bits the users are viewing.

So how do these bits move, really? What is the process by which the bits beam around the world as though they were out of an episode of *Star Trek*? The answer is one node at a time. Nodes are computer systems on the Internet which agree to serve as a relay point for passing traffic in exchange for joining the Net. Bits move (technical term: hop) from node to node until they reach their final destination. The amazing thing is that all the nodes are independently owned and operated. Yet all the nodes seamlessly link together to interconnect the world. In fact that's where the Internet gets its name—it is the greatest INTER-NETwork (interconnection among networks) of all time.

But if the Internet lacks central organization, then why does it work so well? It works well precisely because it was designed to work in a world of unreliable nodes. The Internet was designed by the Defense Department to work in time of war, when it was expected that some nodes would fail or disappear. The assumption was that bits would be lost or garbled in transit. Detecting and *correcting* loss and corruption of bits is a cornerstone of the Internet's infrastructure.

The infrastructure follows rules of communication (technical term: protocols) which all the computers on the Net agree to follow. The most important of these protocols is called TCP/IP (Transmission Control Protocol/Internet Protocol). This protocol groups the bits into packets and then sends the packets through the network. Each packet acts like an envelope for its bits. And like an envelope in the brick and mortar world, each packet has the address of the recipient as well as a return address. Furthermore, each packet has a crucial sequence number. The sequence number identifies the packet as, for example, packet 22 of 50 packets which comprise, say, a Web page. These sequence numbers are part of what makes the Internet so reliable, because as long as even one packet gets through, then the receiving node knows how many packets there are in total (50 in this example) and by counting can determine the ones it has not received. After waiting a short period of time for the laggard packets to arrive, the receiving node will send a message back through the network requesting a resend of the missing packets!

Why do marketers care about all this talk of bits, nodes, and protocols? How valuable is it to know some of the technical details? Here are some reasons that savvy marketers find it valuable:

- Electronic commerce cannot be successful unless the packets get through. If it takes five attempts to order an item, the consumer may just give up. Furthermore, the packets must get through intact. Billions of dollars are managed daily through electronic commerce, online stock trading, and banking. Accidentally dropping or adding a zero to a transaction is not acceptable.

- Customers care about the security of their credit card information. They don't want the packet containing their credit card number to be stolen in transit as it hops from node to node. Understanding how the process works helps marketers design campaigns to reassure consumers.

- The Internet is slow. The packets just don't move fast enough from node to node. This problem actually presents some interesting marketing opportunities for those who can deliver more speed.

- One way to speed up the Internet is to prioritize packets. The technology now exists that would allow some packets to get preferential treatment in transit. These packets would move to the head of the line at each of the hops from node to node. Is this a good idea from a marketing perspective? The answer is maybe, but it also raises an ethical issue. For if some packets receive priority then others will be delayed even more than they are today, making Internet use almost intolerable for the poorest Netizens (Net citizens). Other ethical issues are examined at the end of each chapter of this text.

- Some online stock trading services will not charge users a commission if their trade takes longer than 60 seconds to execute. This is a marketing opportunity that leverages the high-speed computers and connections these companies provision in order to expedite the trade.

- A faster Internet would allow 3D imaging of products with views from many different angles. This would allow online stores to deliver more look and feel of the product than mail order catalogs. A consumer could view a supermarket shelf, click on a cereal package, and rotate it to read the nutrition label. The possibility even exists to clothe a simulated mannequin which represents the customer.

- As was mentioned previously, if packets move fast enough, then they can carry real-time data like voice and video. In fact there are those who believe that Internet telephone will eventually pose a threat to long-distance phone companies—

especially in the lucrative international market. Many believe that real-time video on demand will threaten video rental stores. Will consumers drive to pick up and return videos if they can browse an online video rental store and have the movie delivered over their Internet connection?

Basic Online Search Procedures

B

Once marketers have defined their information needs, there are several steps to finding the data: first identify potential sites that might contain the information, second find the sites, third find the page within the site, and fourth find the text on the page.

The most difficult step is the first—identifying sites that contain the needed information. This is where careful planning is critical. The type of information must be precisely defined in order to save time. Do you want to know which country has the greatest market potential for your product? This problem is not well defined, and a search at this point will result in wasted time and much frustration. Do you want to see if competitor X distributes automobiles to Argentina? Do you want to know how many college students there are in France? Do you want to know what the current dollar/Mexican peso exchange rate is? These are examples of specific information needs that will enhance search effectiveness. The researcher must next figure out who would gain from publishing this type of information online. This entails an understanding of the domain of various government agencies and other not-for-profit organizations. Sometimes corporate sites contain general data, but not typically—except for media firms. Search engines are very helpful, but only to the extent that researchers begin with a well-defined problem and stay focused.

Armed with a list of potential organizations that might publish the needed information, the researcher can then use the search engines to find site addresses, or can deduce the addresses. The Web domain naming system specifies an organization system for Web sites. U.S. company site addresses end in .com, government in .gov, educational institution sites in .edu, Japanese sites in .jp, and so forth. Therefore, if the marketer wants to find the U.S. Food and Drug Administration for information on package labeling regulations, he might attempt www.fda.gov (and be right). If this doesn't work, head for the search engine.

Once at an appropriate site, find the page at the site containing the desired information. Some sites have thousands of pages. A researcher could roam around for hours. Most sites have some type of index to help locate information. Increasingly, however, the larger sites include a search feature right on their home page. The search feature indexes all pages at the site and can help locate the desired information.

Finally, find the text on the page and hit the bull's-eye. Some pages are very long and can scroll many computer screens. For a very long page use the "find" feature on the browser to jump right to the text in the page that contains the target information.

SEARCH TOOLS

Most search tools offer two types of searches: open text and subject tree. An open text search is like using the index in a book, whereas subject tree search is like using the table of contents. Open text searches are also called key word searches. These searches scan the Web looking for a word or group of words that were entered as a search string. The search engine then lists links to pages that it determines are most relevant to the search string. A page with more matches is considered more likely to be relevant.

A subject tree search takes a different approach. A subject tree is a catalog of a great number of pages on the Web, neatly organized by category, subcategory, sub-subcategory, and so on. For example, <u>Recreation⇒Automotive⇒Makes and Models⇒ Porsche</u>. Users navigate down through the subject tree until they reach a link pointing to a page that looks relevant. There is more work involved in a subject tree search but the results are often much more relevant to the information needs. We generally recommend beginning with a subject tree search, especially if the information need is not clearly defined. First, people, not robot programs, compile subject trees. The people provide some filtering by simply not listing sites that they deem useless. Second, subject trees will help orient the search by showing which sites fall into the same category. Third, the premier subject tree index, Yahoo! is very good.

SEARCHING TIPS

Following are just a few important tips to make using the search tools more effective. Using the search tool "help" button is the most important thing to remember. Also, in general do not use capital letters; lowercase matches both lower and uppercase whereas uppercase matches uppercase only. However, if you are looking for the country "Turkey," do use a capital letter to exclude the bird "turkey" from search results. For open text searches:

- Use quotation marks (e.g., "Internet course") to indicate words that must be right next to each other—otherwise the search engine will turn up pages where the two words appear separated on the page.

- Be careful in selecting words and be as specific as possible. The word "butterfly" will retrieve sites about the insect as well as swimming. AltaVista has a feature called Way-Cool Topics Map that assists researchers in finding related meanings to help narrow a search.

- If a search reveals too many unrelated listings, simply use additional words to qualify the original term—get increasingly specific.

- Use a plus when the word should appear in the text and a minus when you want text without that word appearing (e.g., + "internet course" – university).

It is also useful to understand how the people at Yahoo! create their directory. Their home page lists many general categories, under which all their catalogued Web sites are listed. A search begins with a general topic and "drills down" to increasingly specific topics. When assigning sites to categories, Yahoo! considers:

- Commercial versus noncommercial. All sites that sell something or are about companies that sell something are listed under <u>Business and Economy</u>⇒<u>Companies.</u> These same sites are probably cross-listed somewhere else as well, just to make things easier. For example, a company selling music CDs will also be listed under <u>Entertainment</u>⇒<u>Music.</u>

- Regional versus nonregional. An increasing number of Web sites are targeted to local audiences. Yahoo! lists all local sites under <u>Regional</u> so if users are looking for hotels in San Francisco they know where to begin searching. If a company is truly global, such as Coca-Cola, it will not be in the regional listings.

- Finally, Yahoo! assigns particular codes immediately after each category listing. The number in parentheses indicates how many listings are in that category. The @ sign in <u>Advertising on Web and Internet@.</u> means that this category is cross-listed, and clicking on it leads to listings under the general category <u>Computers and Internet.</u> It is not especially important to know which category one is in at any particular time, but it is helpful to understand that sites are cross-listed and that in a good directory several different approaches will lead to the same result.

ESOMAR® Guideline on Conducting Marketing and Opinion Research Using the Internet 1998

Note: Because online research is rapidly changing, we suggest visiting the ESOMAR® site for the latest edition of these guidelines (www.esomar.nl).

BASIC PRINCIPLES

All marketing and opinion research carried out on the Internet must conform to the rules and spirit of the main ICC/ESOMAR International Code of Marketing and Social Research Practice and also to Data Protection and other relevant legislation (both international and national).

Such research must always respect the rights of respondents and other Internet users. It must be carried out in ways which are acceptable to them, to the general public and in accordance with national and international self regulation. Researchers must avoid any actions which might bring Internet research into disrepute or reduce confidence in its findings.

INTRODUCTION

The rapid growth of the Internet has opened dramatic new opportunities for collecting and disseminating research information worldwide. At the same time it raises a number of ethical and technical issues which must be addressed if the medium is to be used effectively and responsibly for marketing and opinion research purposes.

The fact that the Internet is inexpensive to use and difficult to regulate means that it can be open to misuse by less experienced or less scrupulous organisations, often based outside the research industry. Any Internet surveys which fall seriously below the high standards promoted by ESOMAR and other leading professional bodies will make it more difficult to use the medium for genuine research and could seriously damage the credibility of such research, as well as being an abuse of the goodwill of Internet users generally.

ESOMAR has issued this Guideline to protect the interests both of Internet respondents and of the users of Internet research findings. Because information technology and the Internet are evolving and changing so rapidly it is not practicable to discuss in detail all the technical features of Internet research in such a Guideline. This therefore concentrates on the main principles which must be followed in carrying out research on (or about) the Internet and in reporting the findings of such research.

REQUIREMENTS

Cooperation Is Voluntary

1. Researchers must avoid intruding unnecessarily on the privacy of Internet respondents. As with all forms of marketing and opinion research, respondents' co-operation must at all times be voluntary. No personal information should be sought from, or about, respondents without their prior knowledge and agreement.

2. In obtaining the necessary agreement from respondents the researcher must not in any way mislead them about the nature of the research or the uses which will be made of the findings. They should also be alerted to any costs that they may incur (e.g., of on-line time) if they co-operate in the survey. Respondents are entitled at any stage of the interview, or subsequently, to ask that part or all of the record of their interview be destroyed or deleted and the researcher must conform to any such request where reasonable.

The Researcher's Identity Must Be Disclosed

3. Respondents must be told the identity of the researcher carrying out the project and the address at which they can without difficulty re-contact the latter should they wish to do so.

Respondents' Rights to Anonymity Must Be Safeguarded

4. The anonymity of respondents must always be preserved unless they have given their informed consent to the contrary. If respondents have given permission for data to be passed on in a form which allows them to be personally identified, the researcher must ensure that the information will be used for research purposes only. No such information may be used for subsequent non-research purposes such as direct marketing, list-building, credit rating, fund-raising or other marketing activities.

Data Security

5. Researchers should be prepared to offer respondents adequate security in transmission of sensitive data. Researchers must also reasonably ensure that any confidential information provided to them by clients or others is protected (e.g. by firewall) against unauthorised access.

Reliability and Validity

6. Users of research and the general public must not be in any way misled about the reliability and validity of Internet research findings. It is therefore essential that the researcher:

    (a)   follows scientifically sound sampling methods within the constraints of the medium

    (b)   publishes a clear statement of the sample universe definition used in a given survey, the research approach adopted, the response rate achieved and the method of calculating this where possible

    (c)   publishes any appropriate reservations about the possible lack of projectability or other limitations of the research findings resulting from non-response and other factors.

    It is equally important that any research *about* the Internet (e.g. to measure penetration, usership etc.) which employs other data collection methods, such as telephone or mail, also clearly refers to any sampling, or other, limitations on the data collected.

Interviewing Minors

7. It is incumbent on the researcher to observe all relevant laws specifically relating to minors. ESOMAR requirements about the precautions to be taken are set out in the ESOMAR Guideline on Interviewing Minors. According to the ESOMAR Guideline, permission of a responsible adult must be obtained before interviewing a minor aged under 14, and asking questions on topics generally regarded as sensitive should be avoided wherever possible and in any case handled with extreme care. Researchers must use their best endeavours to ensure that they conform to the requirements of the Guideline referred to, for example by introducing special contacting procedures to secure the permission of a parent before carrying out an interview with a child. Where necessary, researchers should consult ESOMAR or their national society for advice.

Unsolicited E-mail

8. Researchers will keep unsolicited E-mail to a minimum, and reduce any inconvenience or irritation such E-mail might cause to the recipient by clearly stating its purpose in the first sentence and keeping the total message as brief as possible. An option to exclude the respondent from further mailings relating to this research project, or to any follow-up research resulting directly from it, should also be provided wherever practicable.

This guideline was first published in 1998. The present edition is copyright August 1998.

Permission for using this material has been granted by ESOMAR® *(European Society for Opinion and Marketing Research), J.J. Viottastraat 29, 1071 JP Amsterdam, The Netherlands. Telephone: +31 20 664 21 41. FAX: +31 20 664 29 22. E-mail:* email@esomar.nl

American Marketing Association Code of Ethics for Marketing on the Internet

Note: See www.ama.org *for the latest copy of these guidelines.*

PREAMBLE

The Internet, including online computer communications, has become increasingly important to marketers' activities, as they provide exchanges and access to markets worldwide. The ability to interact with stakeholders has created new marketing opportunities and risks that are not currently specifically addressed in the American Marketing Association Code of Ethics. The American Marketing Association Code of Ethics for Internet marketing provides additional guidance and direction for ethical responsibility in this dynamic area of marketing. The American Marketing Association is committed to ethical professional conduct and has adopted these principles for using the Internet, including on-line marketing activities utilizing network computers.

GENERAL RESPONSIBILITIES

Internet marketers must assess the risks and take responsibility for the consequences of their activities. Internet marketers' professional conduct must be guided by:

1. Support of professional ethics to avoid harm by protecting the rights of privacy, ownership and access.
2. Adherence to all applicable laws and regulations with no use of Internet marketing that would be illegal, if conducted by mail, telephone, fax or other media.
3. Awareness of changes in regulations related to Internet marketing.
4. Effective communication to organizational members on risks and policies related to Internet marketing, when appropriate.
5. Organizational commitment to ethical Internet practices communicated to employees, customers and relevant stakeholders.

PRIVACY

Information collected from customers should be confidential and used only for expressed purposes. All data, especially confidential customer data, should be safeguarded against unauthorized access. The expressed wishes of others should be respected with regard to the receipt of unsolicited e-mail messages.

OWNERSHIP

Information obtained from the Internet sources should be properly authorized and documented. Information ownership should be safeguarded and respected. Marketers should respect the integrity and ownership of computer and network systems.

ACCESS

Marketers should treat access to accounts, passwords, and other information as confidential, and only examine or disclose content when authorized by a responsible party. The integrity of others' information systems should be respected with regard to placement of information, advertising or messages.

Source: www.ama.org
Reprinted by permission.

Glossary

achievers Successful career and work-oriented people who like to, and generally do, feel in control of their lives. They value consensus, predictability, and stability over risk, intimacy and self-discovery. They are deeply committed to work and family. [*]

action plan One of the phases of the Internet marketing plan, where the marketer identifies specific tactics to implement selected strategies.

actualizers Successful, sophisticated, active, "take-charge" people with high self-esteem and abundant resources. They are interested in growth and seek to develop, explore, and express themselves in a variety of ways—sometimes guided by principle, and sometimes by a desire to have an effect, to make a change. [*]

ad click rate The number of ad clicks as a percentage of ad views, or, the number of times an ad is clicked on by users as a percentage of the number of times an ad was downloaded and viewed by users. [**]

ad clicks The number of times a user "clicks" on an online ad, often measured as a function of time ("ad clicks per day"). [**]

ad views On the Internet, the number of times an online ad was downloaded by users, often measured as a function of time ("ad views per day"). The actual number of times the ad was seen by users may differ because of "caching" (which increases the real number of ad views) and browsers that view documents as text-only (which decreases the number of ad views). [**]

additions to product lines Organizations' addition of a new flavor, size, or other variation to a current product line.

adoption curve Representation of the adoption process, consisting of five decision-making steps consumers go through before buying a good or services: (1) unawareness, (2) awareness, (3) interest, (4) evaluation, and (5) trial.

advertorial A print advertisement styled to resemble the editorial format and typeface of the publication in which it runs. [**]

affiliate A broadcast station bound to a contractual relationship with one or more networks to carry network-originated programs and commercial announcements. [**]

affinity group People with a common interest. On the Internet, typically a subject-oriented mailing list, a newsgroup, or a conference on a Web site. [**]

agent services Services in which firms serve as middlemen but do not take possession of the product.

AIO Activities, interests, and opinions of consumers.

attitudes Internal thoughts about people, products, and other objects. They can be either positive or negative, but the whole thing happens inside a person's head.

audience accumulation The net number of people (or homes) exposed to a medium during its duration—e.g., a half hour broadcast program, or magazine issue. [**]

audience composition The demographic profile of a media audience. [**]

audience turnover The average ratio of cumulative audience listening/viewing to the average audience listening/viewing. [**]

automatic customization Tailoring of the content presented to the user based upon information known about the user and the user's historical surfing behavior. See *mass customization.*

average audience (AA) In broadcast, the average number of homes (or individuals) tuned to a given time segment of a program. In print media, the number of individuals who looked into an average issue of a publication and are considered "readers." [**]

bandwidth The data transferring capacity of a system—how much information can be sent from one place to another in a given period of time. There are many ways to measure this—for example, the number of megabytes transferred per second.

banner ad A rectangular space appearing on a Web site, paid for by an advertiser, which allows the user to click-through to the advertiser's Web site.

barter The exchange of goods and services without the use of cash. Usually, the acquisition of media time or space by a media company in exchange for similar time/space in return. [**]

basic cable A "basic" service agreement in which a subscriber pays a cable TV operator or system a monthly fee. Does not include "pay" services that might be offered by the cable operator. [**]

believers Conservative, conventional people with concrete beliefs based on traditional, established codes: family, church, community, and the nation. They follow established routines, organized in large part around home, family, and social or religious organizations to which they belong. [*]

brand advertising Advertising that creates a distinct favorable image that customers associate with a product at the moment they make buying decisions. [†]

brand loyalty Level of commitment customers feel toward a certain brand, expressed by their continued purchase of that brand.

brochureware A site that provides information about the company's products and services. Brochureware provides an excellent opportunity to brand as well as to develop a relationship with the consumer and other stakeholders.

cable TV Reception of TV signals via cable (wires) rather than over the air (i.e., via a TV antenna). **

caching Phenomenon that occurs when access providers or browsers store or buffer Web page data in a temporary location on their networks or in their disk space to speed access and reduce traffic. Reduces the number of measured page views at the original content site. **

chat room "Virtual space" where Internet users can communicate in real time using special software.

circulation In print media, the number of copies sold or distributed by a publication. In broadcast, the number of homes owning a TV/radio set within a station's coverage area. Or, in cable TV, the number of households that subscribe to cable services for a given network. In out-of-home media, the number of people passing an advertisement who have an opportunity to see it. **

click-throughs same as **ad clicks**.

collaborative filtering agents Software programs able to predict consumer preferences based on past purchase behavior.

communications and collaboration A part of Net commercialization, which includes gathering and processing information, communicating, collaborating, and publishing. All media that place their content online for subscription or as advertising fall into this category.

concentrated targeting Also called *niche marketing*, a firm's selecting one segment and developing one or more marketing mixes to meet the needs of that segment.

consumer centric A Web audience measurement model similar to the Nielsen ratings for TV. A panel representative of the population is formed, their Web viewing actions are recorded, and the results are generalized to the population.

cookie A persistent piece of information, stored on the user's local hard drive, that is keyed to a specific server (and even a file pathway or directory location at the server) and is passed back to the server as part of the transaction that takes place when the user's browser again crosses the specific server/path combination. **

cost per rating point (CPP) The cost of an advertising unit (e.g., a 30-second commercial) divided by the average rating of a specific demographic group (e.g., women, 1849). **

cost per thousand (CPM) The cost to deliver 1,000 impressions (associated with delivery of ad views on the Internet, and delivery to people or homes in traditional media). **

coverage The percentage of a population group covered by a medium. Commonly used with print media to describe an average issue's audience within defined demographic or purchasing groups. Akin to rating. **

creative The name given the art/design within an advertisement. [**]

cume (cumulative) Rating the reach of a radio or TV program or station, as opposed to the "average." [**]

daughter window Separate window that overlays the current browser window and contains content or advertisements.

decoding Reading; receiving of the message transferred over the Internet.

demographics The characteristics of populations.

demography The study of the characteristics of population groups in terms of size, distribution, and vital statistics. [**]

differentiated targeting Also called *multisegment targeting*, exists when a firm carefully selects two or more segments and designs marketing mix strategies for each. Most firms today use a multisegment strategy.

diffusion of innovations The process by which new products are spread to members of the target market over time.

discontinuous innovations New-to-the-world products never seen before, such as were music CDs and the television at their introductions.

disintermediation The process of eliminating traditional intermediaries. Eliminating intermediaries has the potential to reduce costs since each intermediary must add to the price of the product in order to make a living.

distribution channel A group of interdependent firms that work together to transfer product from the supplier to the consumer. The transfer may either be direct or employ a number of intermediaries.

domain name The unique name that identifies an Internet site, such as "microsoft.com." A domain name always has two or more parts, separated by periods. A given server may have more than one domain name, but a given domain name points to only one machine. [**]

duration time The length of time between two events, such as successive requests to one or more Web pages (page duration) or visits to a given Web site (intervisit duration). [**]

early adopters The next 13.5% to purchase the product, after the innovators, who comprise the first 2.5%. Early adopters are eager to buy new products, but they are more community minded than innovators and tend to communicate with others about new products. For this reason, early adopters are often opinion leaders: people whom others seek for advice about products and other things.

early majority Consumers comprising the next 34% after innovators and early adopters. These consumers do not rush to try new products but collect information first, perhaps talking to opinion leaders, and purchasing only after thoughtful consideration. For new products that are low involvement (i.e., low financial, social, technological risk and low emotional appeal and importance), the early majority may not give much thought before purchase, but they do watch to see others using the product before they purchase it. The consumers who are just beginning to surf the Net as of this writing may be in this group.

EDI (Electronic Data Interchange)   The computerized exchange of information between organizations in order to avoid paper forms. The classic use of EDI is to eliminate purchase requisitions between firms.

effective frequency   The level of exposure frequency at which reach is deemed "effectively" delivered. [**]

effective reach   The percentage of a population group reached by a media schedule at a given level of frequency. [**]

effectiveness   Refers to choosing the right thing to do in order to maximize a company's competitive advantage.

efficiency   Generally refers to the relative costs of delivering media audiences. [**] See *Cost per rating point* and *Cost per thousand*

electronic commerce   Includes buying/selling online, digital value creation, virtual marketplaces and storefronts, and new distribution channel intermediaries.

encoding   Creating messages or documents to be transmitted via the Internet.

environmental factors   The online legal, political, and technological environments that can greatly influence marketing strategies, alter the composition of the Internet audience, and affect the quality of material that can be delivered to them. These factors also affect laws regarding taxation, access, copyright, and encryption on the Internet.

environmental scan   Continual task that includes economic analysis as well social and demographic trends.

evaluation plan   System whereby the site is continually evaluated after it is created and published. This requires tracking systems that must be in place before the site is launched.

experiencers   Young, vital, enthusiastic, impulsive, and rebellious people. They seek variety and excitement, savoring the new, the offbeat, and the risky. Experiencers combine an abstract disdain for conformity with an outsider's awe of others' wealth, prestige, and power. [*]

extranet   Two or more networks that are joined for the purpose of sharing information. If two companies link their intranets, they would have an extranet. Extranets are proprietary to the organizations involved.

flow   The state occurring during network navigation that is (1) characterized by a seamless sequence of responses facilitated by machine interactivity, (2) intrinsically enjoyable, (3) accompanied by a loss of self-consciousness, and (4) self-reinforcing. ‡

frequency   The number of times people (or homes) are exposed to an advertising message, an advertising campaign, or a specific media vehicle. Also, the period of issuance of a publication, e.g., daily, monthly. **

frequency discount   A rate discount allowed an advertiser that purchases a specific schedule within a specific period of time, e.g., six ads within one year. **

frequency distribution   The array of reach according to the level of frequency delivered to each group. **

fulfilleds   Mature, satisfied, comfortable, reflective people who value order, knowledge, and responsibility. Most are well educated and in (or recently retired from) professional occupations. *

geodemographics   Combination of geography and demographics of consumer market segmentation designed to identify and reach the right people at the right time.

geographics   Separation of large markets into smaller groupings according to country, region, state, city, community, or block divisions.

gross rating points (GRPs)   The sum of all ratings delivered by a given list of media vehicles. Although synonymous with TRPs, GRPs generally refer to a "household" base. In out-of-home media, GRPs are synonymous with a *showing.* **

GUI   Graphical user interface lets users interact with their computer via icons and a pointer instead of by typing in text at a command line.

hierarchy of effects model   Device that attempts to explain the impact of marketing communication. It assumes that consumers go through a series of stages when making product decisions and that communication messages are designed to assist that movement.

hit   Web-speak for any request for data from a Web page or file. Often used to compare popularity/traffic of a site in the context of getting so many "hits" during a given period. A common mistake is to equate hits with visits or page views. A single visit or page view is usually recorded as several hits and, depending on the browser, the page size, and other factors, the number of hits per page can vary widely. **

homes using TV (HUT)   The percentage of homes using (tuned in to) TV at a particular time. **

hop   Movement of a digital packet of information from one node to the next. In general the fewer the number of hops, the faster the packet arrives at its destination.

HTML (hypertext markup language)   A simple coding system used to format documents for viewing by Web clients. Web pages are written in this standard specification. **

hyperlink See link.

hypertext Generally, any text on a Web page that contains links to other documents—words or phrases in a document that can be chosen by a user and which cause another document to be retrieved or displayed. [**]

impressions The gross sum of all media exposures (number of people or homes) without regard to duplication. [**]

information publishing Marketing communication with the goal of disseminating persuasive information to create awareness, knowledge (cognitive step), and positive attitudes (attitude step).

infrastructure The equipment and communication lines that allow data to travel through a network.

innovators The first 2.5% of consumers to purchase a product. They tend to be risk takers, eager to try new products (especially high-tech products), and with higher levels of education and income. They are very self-reliant, gaining information from experts and the press rather than from peers.

inseparability Characteristics of intangible products or services whereby they must be consumed where they are produced.

intangibility Characteristic of a service that is a performance, which cannot be seen, felt, or touched. The service provided by a dentist is a good example of intangibility.

intermediary A firm that appears in the channel between the supplier and the consumer. By specializing, intermediaries are able to perform functions more efficiently than the supplier could.

internal efficiencies Reductions in marketing and operations costs. A company going online usually realizes internal efficiencies.

interstitials Java-based ads which appear while the publisher's content is loading.

intranet Computer network, similar to the Internet, established within an organization to provide information internally to employees and other internal stakeholders. The information on Intranet Web pages can be quickly and easily changed—an advantage over paper publishing.

inventory Normally defined as the quantity of goods or materials on hand. On the Internet, a site's inventory is the number of page views it will deliver in a given period of time, and is thus the amount of product that can be sold to advertisers. [**]

ISP (Internet Service Provider) Company that has a network of servers (mail, news, Web, and the like), routers, and modems attached to a permanent, high-speed Internet "backbone" connection. Subscribers can then dial into the local network to gain Internet access.

laggards The last 16% of buyers of new products. They are very traditional and generally of lower socioeconomic status. Often they adopt a product when newer products have already been introduced. For example, laggards might use the Internet via the telephone through an Internet Service Provider when most of the market has already moved to cable modems or some other new fast information delivery technology.

late majority Consumers comprising the next 34% to adopt new products, after innovators, early adopters, and early majority. These folks are skeptical and generally purchase a product only after their friends already have done so. They adopt because of the desire to conform to group norms. These consumers rely more on word-of-mouth communication than on media advertising. These are the people who are cybercritics, calling the Internet a fad and saying it is a waste of time.

lateral partnerships Competitors, not-for-profit organizations, or governments that join with the firm for some common goal.

line extensions A lower-risk strategy for marketers introducing a new product line.

link The path between two documents, which associates an object, such as a button or hypertext, on a Web page with another Web address. The hyperlink allows a user to point and click on an object and thereby move to the location associated with that object by loading the Web page at that address. [**]

LISTSERV A program that provides automatic processing of many functions involved with mailing lists. E-mailing appropriate messages to it will automatically subscribe the e-mailer to a discussion list or unsubscribe the person. A LISTSERV will also answer requests for indexes, FAQs, archives of the previous discussions, and other files.

log file In Internet server software, a feature that records every file sent by the server along with the destination address and time sent.

lower-cost products Products introduced to compete with existing brands by offering a price advantage. The Internet spawned a series of free products with the idea of building market share so the firm would have a customer base for marketing other products owned by the firm. For example, Eudora Light, the e-mail reader software, was an early entry with this strategy.

macroenvironment Consists of all stakeholders, organizations, and forces external to the organization.

makers Practical people who have constructive skills and value self-sufficiency. They live within a traditional context of family, practical work, and physical recreation and have little interest in what lies outside that context. Makers experience the world by working on it—building a house, raising children, fixing a car, or canning vegetables—and have enough skill, income, and energy to carry out their projects successfully. [*]

manual customization Creating systems according to explicit *a priori* instructions from the user regarding preferred content categories. See *mass customization.*

market opportunity analysis Analysis, conducted by a firm upon reviewing the marketing environment, focusing on finding and selecting among market opportunities. A traditional market opportunity analysis includes both demand and supply analyses. The demand portion reviews various market segments in terms of their potential profitability. Conversely, the supply analysis reviews competition in selected segments that are under consideration.

marketing concept The idea that an organization exists to satisfy customer wants and needs while meeting organizational objectives.

mass customization Creating systems that can personalize messages to a target audience of one. There are two forms of mass customization—automatic and manual. See *automatic customization, manual customization.*

microenvironment Consists of stakeholders and forces internal to the organization.

micromarketing Individualized targeting. Amazon.com, for example, builds a profile of each user who buys books at its site. It keeps track of the books that its customers read and makes recommendations based on past purchases. Amazon also sends e-mail notification about products that might interest particular individuals. This is the marketing concept at its finest: giving individual consumers exactly what they want at the right time and place.

MIS (Marketing Information System) The system of assessing information needs, gathering information, analyzing it, and disseminating it to marketing decision makers. In a separate context MIS also refers to Management Information Systems—a field of study in many business schools.

multisegment targeting See *differentiated targeting.*

narrowcast An electronic media term referring primarily to cable channels because they contain very focused electronic content that appeals to special-interest markets.

network A broadcast entity that provides programming and sells commercial time in programs aired nationally via affiliated or licensed local stations—e.g., ABC television network, ESPN cable network. On the Internet, an aggregator/broker of advertising inventory from many sites. [**]

networked applications Include distributed Internet applications, linked corporate and legacy data, Web-enabled and live applications, and object-oriented applications. These are database applications and methods for sharing information within an organization.

new product lines Lines introduced when firms take an existing brand name and create new products in a completely different category. For example, General Foods applied the Jell-O brand name to pudding pops and other frozen delights.

open text search   Open text searches are also called keyword searches. These searches scan the Web looking for a word or group of words that were entered as a search string. The search engine then lists links to pages that it determines are most relevant to the search string. A page with more matches is considered more likely to be relevant.

out-of-home media   Those media meant to be consumed only outside of one's home—e.g., outdoor, transit, in-store media.[**]

outsource   To contract services from external firms in order to accomplish internal tasks.

page   An HTML (hypertext markup language) document that may contain text, images, and other online elements, such as Java applets and multimedia files. It may be statically or dynamically generated.[**]

page view   The number of times a page was downloaded by users, often measured as a function of time ("page views per day"). The actual number of times the page was seen by users may be higher because of caching.[**]

paid circulation   Reported by the Audit Bureau of Circulation, a classification of subscriptions or purchases of a magazine or newspaper, based upon payment in accordance with standards set by the ABC.[**]

penetration   The percentage of people (or homes) within a defined universe that are physically able to be exposed to a medium.

perishability   Characteristic whereby if service is not consumed when it is produced, it goes to waste.

personal interest consumers   The 46% of all Internet users who pay for their own access and go online for personal reasons such as entertainment, sports, and local information. This has been the largest and fastest-growing segment since 1995, with 16.7 million current users. Their average age is 40, their income $54,300, and most tend to be married with children under 18.

personalized web page   Web Page created with cookies that were put on the user's hard disk by the Web site. Cookies help companies to personalize Web pages by greeting the user by name or by listing previous purchases, thus building relationship with users.

pointcast   Electronic media with the capability of transmitting to an audience of just one person.

primary data   Information gathered for the first time to solve a particular problem. It is usually more expensive and time-consuming to gather than secondary data, but conversely, the data are current and they are generally more relevant to the marketer's specific problem. In addition, primary data have the benefit of being proprietary and thus unavailable to competitors.

probability sample A sample selected in such a way that each item or person in the population being studied has an equal likelihood of being included in the sample.

Product Life Cycle (PLC) A model that describes the stages that a product or a product category passes through, from its production to its removal from the market.

protocol A formal, standardized set of operating rules governing the format, timing, and error control of data transmissions and other activities on a network.

proxy server A system that stores frequently used information closer to the end user to provide faster access or to reduce the load on another server; it also serves as the gateway to the Internet.

proxy server caching The process that occurs when users access copies of Web sites rather than the site itself. Users accessing Web sites from proxy servers are not counted as new visitors.

psychographics Pertains to the identification of personality characteristics and attitudes that affect a person's lifestyle and purchasing behavior.[**]

random digit dialing Telephone survey technique of calling people at random and asking specific questions.

rating The percentage of a given population group consuming a medium at a particular moment. Generally used for broadcast media but can by applied to any medium. One rating point equals one percent of the potential viewing population.[**]

reach The number of different homes/people exposed at least once to an impression (ad view, program, commercial, print page, etc.) across a stated period of time. Also called the cumulative or unduplicated audience.[**]

real-time multimedia Technology that offers opportunities like distance learning and education, virtual reality, entertainment, and video/audio conferencing through live broadcasting from radio stations or online chatting and other real-time broadcasts.

relationship marketing Establishing, maintaining, enhancing, and commercializing customer relationships through promise fulfillment, two-way communication with individual stakeholders, one at a time. This includes listening as well as talking with both business and individual consumers.

repositioned products Current products that are either targeted to different markets or promoted for new uses.

revenue streams Cash flows which may come from Web site product sales, advertising sales, and agent commissions.

revisions of existing products Products that are introduced as "new and improved" and thus replace the old product. On the Internet, firms are continually improving their brands to add value and remain competitive.

secondary data Information that has been gathered for some other purpose but is useful for the current problem; it can be collected more quickly and less expensively than primary data.

session A series of consecutive visits made by a visitor to a series of Web sites. [**]

SET (Secure Electronic Transaction) A vehicle for legitimizing both the merchant and the consumer as well as protecting the consumer's credit card number. Under SET the card number is never directly sent to the merchant. Rather a third party is introduced to the transaction with whom both the merchant and consumer communicate to validate one another as well as the transaction.

share "Share of audience" is the percentage of homes using TV (HUT) tuned to a particular program or station. "Share of market" is the percentage of total category volume (dollars, unit, etc.) accounted for by a brand. "Share of voice" is the percentage of advertising impressions generated by all brands in a category accounted for by a particular brand, but often also refers to share of media spending. [**]

share of mind Refers to relationship marketing focusing on customer development in the long term: "maintaining and enhancing." A firm using this kind of relationship marketing differentiates individual customers based on need rather than differentiating products for target groups.

shopping agents Programs that allow the consumer to rapidly compare prices and features within product categories. Shopping agents implicitly negotiate prices downward on behalf of the consumer by listing companies in order of best price first.

site centric Audience measurement model in which user activity is tallied at the content provider's Web site to produce audience composition statistics, page views, and other statistics.

situation analysis Review of the existing marketing plan and any other information that can be obtained about the company and its brands, examination of environmental factors related to online marketing, and development of a market opportunity analysis.

social bonding Stimulated social interaction between companies and customers resulting in a more personalized communication and brand loyalty.

spam Unsolicited e-mail, either sent to users or posted on an electronic bulletin board.

sponsorship Sponsorships integrate editorial content and advertising on a Web site. The sponsor pays for space and creates content that appeals to the publisher's audience.

spot Refers to the purchase of TV or radio commercial time on a market-by-market basis, as opposed to network (national) purchases. Also the term is scommonly used in lieu of "commercial announcement." [**]

stakeholder   Entity with a specific interest in a company—for example, an employee, a stockholder, supplier, a lateral partnership, and a customer.

stakeholder communication   Interaction with a stakeholder involving strategies, such as advertising, public relations, sales promotion incentives, and lead generation, that can help marketers to accomplish cognitive and attitude objectives, often at substantial cost savings over traditional methods.

strivers   People who seek motivation, self-definition, and approval from the world around them. They are striving to find a secure place in life. Unsure of themselves and low on economic, social, and psychological resources, strivers are concerned about the opinions and approval of others. *

structural bonds   Bonds created when firms add value by making structural changes that facilitate the relationship with customers and suppliers. All of the major Web portals are seeking to create structural bonds with their users. Services allow consumers to customize their interface so that it lists weather and movies in their area, their own stock portfolios, and news of interest to them. Once a consumer invests the time and effort to customize this interface, she will be hard pressed to switch to another portal.

strugglers   People who are chronically poor, ill educated, low skilled, without strong social bonds, elderly, and concerned about their health, they are often resigned and passive. Their chief concerns are for security and safety. *

SUG   Selling Under the Guise of surveys. Marketing promotion disguised as marketing research through "surveys" conducted for the purpose of building a database of contacts for later solicitation.

superstation   An independent TV station whose signal is transmitted throughout the United States via satellite. **

switchers   Consumers who do not care which brand they use—in other words, do not show any specific brand loyalty but go for the best price.

SWOT   Strengths, Weaknesses, Opportunities, and Threats analysis. The SWOT analysis objectively evaluates the company's strengths and weaknesses with respect to the environment and the competition.

syndicated selling   Web sites paying a commission on referrals. Syndicated selling rewards the referring Web site by paying a 7% to 15% commission on the sale. Paying the commission, like all channel intermediary costs, has the effect of inflating the price of the item or lowering company profits.

syndication   In broadcasting, a program carrying on selected stations which may or may not air at the same time in all markets. In newspapers, an independently written column or feature is carried by many newspapers (e.g., "Dear Abby"). In magazines, a centrally written or published section being carried by newspapers, generally in the Sunday edition (e.g., *Parade).* **

synergy   Result that occurs when two or more firms join in a business relationship where the results often exceed what each firm might have accomplished alone.

TCP/IP   Transmission Control Protocol/Internet Protocol, the most widely used protocol on the Internet. TCP/IP is a set of rules that each computer follows in order to enable communication. Only computers using the same protocol are able to communicate.

trailblazer page   Also called an index page, helps marketers find relevant Web sites quickly. Trailblazer sites are those that contain long lists of links to outside sites on a particular topic.

Transaction-based online systems   Systems that allow organizations not only to communicate with the consumer but to sell online as well.

transactive media   Interactive channels of communication that are capable of carrying out product transactions.

undifferentiated targeting   Another terms for mass marketing. In this case the firm offers one marketing mix for the entire market.

unique users   The number of unique individuals who visit a site within a specific period of time. With today's technology, this number can be calculated only with some form of user registration or identification. **

universe   The total population within a defined demographic, psychographic, or product consumption segment against which media audiences are calculated to determine ratings, coverage, reach, etc.

URL (uniform [or universal] resource locator)   The URL provides information on the protocol, the system, and the file name, so that the user's system can find a particular document on the Internet. An example of a URL is http://www.sholink.com/, which indicates that "hypertext transfer protocol" is the protocol and that the information is located on a system named "www.sholink.com," which is the Sholink Corporation's Web server. This example does not show a particular file name (such as index.htm), since most Web servers are set up to point to a home page if no file name is used. **

usenet   Worldwide network of thousands of computer systems with a decentralized administration. The usenet systems exist to transmit postings to special-interest newsgroups.

variability   Means that the quality is changeable from one use of the service to another. Variability occurs because people, not machines, deliver services.

viewers per 1,000 households   The number of people within a specific population group tuned to a TV program in each 1,000 viewing households. **

virtual aggregation   Bringing together product from multiple independent firms and organizing the display on the user's computer.

visit A sequence of hits made by one user at a site. It is important to understand that Internet technology does not maintain a continuous "connection" (like a radio signal) to a site. The data is sent in packets. If a user makes no request for data from the site during a predetermined (and discretionary) period of time, the user's next hit would constitute a new visit. This length of time is known as the "time-out" period. While this interval is different for each site, I/PRO currently uses 30 minutes for all sites for purposes of comparability. [**]

volume discount The price discount offered advertisers who purchase a certain amount of volume from the medium —e.g., pages or dollar amount in magazines. [**]

wearout A level of frequency, or a point in time, when an advertising message loses its ability to effectively communicate. [**]

Web form Technical term for a Web page that has designated places for the user to type information. Many corporate Web sites sport Web forms, using them for a multitude of purposes from site registration and survey research to product purchase.

Web page An HTML (hypertext markup language) document on the Web, usually one of many that together make up a Web site. [**]

Web ring A number of independent Web sites that together build community among users and the products that interest them.

Web server A system capable of continuous access to the Internet (or an internal network) through retrieving and displaying documents and files via hypertext transfer protocol (http). [**]

Web site The virtual location for an organization's presence on the Worldwide Web, usually made up of several Web pages and a single home page designated by a unique URL. [**]

worldwide Web The mechanism originally developed by Tim Berners-Lee for CERN physicists to be able to share documents via the Internet. The Web allows computer users to access information across systems around the world using URLs (uniform resource locators) to identify files and systems and hypertext links to move between files on the same or different systems. [**]

Notes
[**] Reprinted with permission from Dean Witter Morgan Stanley
[*] Reprinted with permission from SRI
‡ Quoted from Hoffman/Novak Project 2000
† Quoted from Forrester Research

References

- "1998 Internet World Industry Awards" (1998), *InternetNews* (September). Internet: www.internetnews.com/iwlive/iwindustry/index.html.

- "1998 StudioONE Award Recipients" (1998), IPPA StudioONE (September). Internet: www.ippa.org/studio/studio-content.html.

- "About Amazon.com" (1998), Amazon (September). Internet: www.amazon.com.

- "About BizRate" (1998), Binary Compass Enterprises (July). Internet: www.bizrate.com/display.pl?b=about.

- "About Net Nanny" (1998), NetNanny (July). Internet: www.netnanny.com/allabout/allabout_bottom.htm.

- "Amazon.com Talks to Andrew Sather" (1998), Amazon (July). Internet: www.amazon.com/exec/obidos/show-interview/s-a-atherndrew/002-5327610-3567040.

- American Marketing Association (1996). *Code of Ethics.* Chicago: American Marketing Association.

- "Aptex Announces SelectCast for Commerce Servers" (1997), *ZdNet* (May 2). Internet: www.zdnet.com/icom/news/199705/02/news5.html.

- "Aptex Customer Quotes" (1998), Aptex (October). Internet: www.aptex.com/news-quotes.htm.

- "Aptex Fact Sheet" (1998), Aptex (October). Internet: www.aptex.com/about-factsheet.htm.

- "Aptex Products" (1998), Aptex (October). Internet: www.aptex.com/products-index.htm.

- "Aptex Technology" (1998), Aptex (October). Internet: www.aptex.com/about-technology.htm.

- "Background of Datek Online Holdings Corporation" (1998), Datek (August). Internet: www.datek.com/marketing/about/abouthome.html.

- Barboza, David (1998), "Golden Boy? He's Dazzled Wall Street, but the Ghosts of His Company May Haunt His Future," *The New York Times On The Web* (May 10). Internet: www.nyt.com.

- Barboza, David (1998), "The Markets: Market Place: Some Clouds Dim a Star of On-Line Trading," *The New York Times On The Web* (July 8). Internet: www.nyt.com.

- Barrett, Randy (1998), "Webcasting: Still A Way To Go," *Inter@ctive Week* (June 29). Internet: www.zdnet.com/intweek/print/980629/334494.html.

- Berinato, Scott (1998), "RealNetwork's Glaser Sings Praises of Streaming Media for Enterprises," *PC Week Online* (May 7). Internet: www.zdnet.com/zdnn/content/pcwo/0507/314557.html.

- Berry, Leonard (1995), "Relationship Marketing of Services—Growing Interest, Emerging Perspectives," *Journal of the Academy of Marketing Science,* 23 (4), 236–245.

- Berry, Leonard, and A. l. Parasuraman (1991). *Marketing Services—Competing Through Quality.* New York: Free Press.

- Berst, Jesse (1998), "Bill G's Bandwidth Secrets," *ZDNet AnchorDesk* (March 31). Internet: www.zdnet.com/anchordesk/story/story_1925.html.

- "Beyond Cool: Online Trading Goes Mainstream as Quality Rises and Commissions Plunge" (1998), *Barron's* (March 16). Internet: www.datek.com/marketing/about/in_news/bar031698.html.

- Booker, Ellis (1997), "Microsoft Buys Stake in Progressive Networks," *WEBWEEK* (July 28). Internet: www.internetworld.com.

- Briggs, Rex and Nigel Hollis (1997), "Advertising on the Web: Is There Response Before Clickthrough?" *Journal of Advertising Research* (March/April), 33–45.

- Broersma, Matthew (1998), "Yahoo!'s Yang: Web Is Now a 'Lifestyle Medium,'" *ZDNN* (March 12). Internet: www.zdnet.com/zdnn/content/zdnn/0312/293987.html.

- "Broker Ratings: The Best and Worst Online Brokers" (1998), *SmartMoney* (February). Internet: www.datek.com/marketing/about/in_news/sma0298.html.

- Brown, Millward (1998), "Methodology of Online Advertising Effectiveness Study" (October). Internet: www.mbinteractive.com/site/iab/ad_01.html.

- "Bust the Junk Out of Your Web Browsing" & "The Top Ten Questions" (1998), *JUNKBUSTERS* (September). Internet: www.junkbusters.com/ht/en/ijb.html.

- Carl, Jeremy (1995), "Bookseller's Online Ambitions," *Web Week* (October: Vol. 1, Issue 6). Internet: www.internetworld.com/print/ww-back.html.

- Casimir, Jon (1998), "The Net: Driftnet," *The Sydney Morning Herald* (April 11). Internet: www.smh.com.au/icon/content/980411/net.html.

- Caulfield, Brian (1998), "RealNetworks' Newest Ally Is Affront to One of Its Oldest," *INTERNETWORLD News* (February 2). Internet: www.internetworld.com.

- Caulfield, Brian (1998), "Streaming Media Platform Updated," *INTERNETWORLD News* (May 4). Internet: www.internetworld.com.

- Caulfield, Brian (1998), "When Good Web-Page Design Comes Before the Customer," *InternetWorld* (January 12). Internet: www.internetworld.com/print/1998/01/12/index.html.

- "Checking For Online Security On The Lycos Shopping Network Stores" (1998), Lycos (August). Internet: www.lycos.com/emarket/shopping/secureshop.html.

- Chum (1997), "Exposing the Hubris, the Hype, the Humor, and the Dark Side of Comdex," *The Red Herring Magazine* (February). Internet: www.redherring.com/mag/issue39/chum.html.

- Clemente, Peter (1998). *The State of the Net: The New Frontier*. New York: McGraw-Hill.

- Clemente, Peter, Thomas Miller, Andrew Richardson, and Craig Gugel (1998), "Consumer Online Commerce," Private Report. New York: Cyber Dialogue and Organic.

- "Company Information" (1998), @Home Network (July). Internet: www.home.net/corp/.

- "Company Profiles 'Pretty Good Privacy'" (1997), *The Red Herring Magazine* (February). Internet: www.redherring.com/profiles/0297/pretty.html.

- Cooper, Charles (1998), "The Guys Running Yahoo! Are Far from Yahoos," *ZDNN* (April 30). Internet: www.zdnet.com/zdnn/content/zdnn/0429/311279.html.

- Coopers & Lybrand L.L.P (1997), "2nd New York New Media Industry Survey: Opportunities and Challenges of New York's Emerging Cyber-Industry," Industry report sponsored by New York New Media Association and NYC Economic Development Corporation.

- "Creating Killer Interactive Web Sites" (1997). Adjacency's Web Design Book. New York: Hayden Press/Macmillan.

- "CYBERsitter Now Blocks Web Site Advertising" (1998), *BUSINESS WIRE* (February 12). Internet: www.solidoak.com/pr298.txt.

- Dawson, Fred (1998), "Smaller Cable Operators Also Cash In On Data," *Inter@ctive Week* (June 11). Internet: www.zdnet.com/zdnn/content/inwk/0522/324826.html.

- Dodge, John (1998), "Traffic Leaders Emerge as the Web Matures," *PC Week Online* (May 11). Internet: www.zdnet.com/pcweek/opinion/0511/11week.html.

- "DoubleClick Privacy Statement" (1998), DoubleClick (October). Internet: www.doubleclick.com/advertisers/privacy/.

- Doyle, Bill, Bill Bass, Ben Abbott, and Kerry Moyer (1997), "Branding on the Web," *Forrester Report: Media & Technology Strategies* (August).

- Dreier, Troy (1997), "Safeguarding the Web," *ZDNet* (October 2). Internet: www.zdnet.com/products/special/filter2.html.

- Eisenstadt, Steven (1996), "Students' Software Blocks Ads on Web," *The News & Observer* (May 21). Internet: www1.nando.net/newsroom/nao/top/052196/topstory_8069.html.

- "Excite Shopping Channel" (1998), Excite (August). Internet: www.excite.com/shopping/guarantee/.

- "Fast Forward Through the Ads?" (1996), *Netday News* (May 9). Internet: www.internetnews.com/96May/0509-ads.html.

- Fernandes, Gary (1998), "IT on the Frontlines of Commerce." Speech at Forrester Research IT Forum, Chicago, April 21.

- "For Panel Members" (1998), Cyber Dialogue, Inc. (October). Internet: www.cyberdialogue.com/panel.html.

- Foust, Dean (1998), "New Kids on the Street," *Yahoo! Internet Life* (January: Vol. 4. No.1). Internet: www.zdnet.com/yil/filters/toc/tocv4n1.html

- "Free Enterprise Comes to Wall Street " (1998), *Forbes* as cited in Datek (April 6). Internet: www.datek.com/marketing/about/in_news/forbes0498.html.

- "Frequently Asked Questions" (1998), NetNanny (July). Internet: www.netnanny.com/support/faq.htm.

- Gardner, Elizabeth (1998), "Amazon Buys Three Companies To Move Into European Market and Video Sales," *InternetWorld News* (May 4). Internet: www.internetworld.com/print/1998/05/04/news/19980504-amazon.html?InternetWorld+3808+Amazon.

- Gardner, Elizabeth (1998), "Slower Pace, Cheaper Living Entices Net Workers to Midwest," *InternetWorld* (July 13). Internet: www.internetworld.com/.

- Ghosh, Shikhar (1998), "Making Business Sense of the Internet," *Harvard Business Review* (March-April), 126–135.

- Glave, James (1998), "InterMute Cleans Up Web-Site Clutter," *Wired News* (March 18). Internet: www.wired.com/news/technology/story/11012.html.

- Gomez Advisors, Inc. (1998), "69 Internet Brokers for Q2 '98'," Internet Broker Scorecard (August). Internet: www.datek.com/marketing/about/in_news/gomez.html and www.gomez.com/Brokers/Scorecard/.

- Grönroos, Christian (1990), "Relationship Approach to Marketing in Service Contexts: The Marketing and Organizational Behavior Interface," *Journal of Business Research*, 20 (January), 3–11.

- Guglielmo, Connie (1997), "No Sacred Trust: Personal Data Up For Grabs," *Inter@ctive Week* (December 8). Internet: www.zdnet.com/intweek/printhigh/120897/cov1208.html.

- Guglielmo, Connie (1998), "Audio Gives The Web An Earful," *Inter@ctive Week* (February 9). Internet: www.zdnet.com/intweek/print/980209/283997.html.

- Guglielmo, Connie (1998), "Stream Market Splits Into Two Camps," *Inter@ctive Week* (February 4). Internet: www.zdnet.com/zdnn/content/inwk/0504/281720.html.

- Gussow, Mel (1997), "John Updike, Impressario of Fictional Relay Race," *The New York Times* (August 2).

- "The Guys Running Yahoo! Are Far from Yahoos" (1998), *ZDNN* (April 30). Internet: www.zdnet.com.

- Haney, Clare (1998), "Streaming Media Market Gets Small as RealNetworks Buys Rival Vivo," *COMPUTERWORLD Computer Industry News* (February 23). Internet: www.computerworld.com/home/online9697.nsf/all/980223streaming1D066.

- Hertzberg, Robert (1996), "RealAudio's Convictions Lead It to Top of Charts," *Web Week* (January: Volume 2, Issue 1). Internet: www.internetworld.com.

- Heyman, Karen, Paul Hoffman, Tom Negrino, Richard Raucci, Anne Ryder, Charles Seiter, Dave Taylor, and Karen Wickre (1996), *Yahoo! Unplugged.* Internet: www.idgbooks.com/yp/yahoounplugged/history/wbhist1.htm). (Also at www.idgbooks.com.)

- Hoffman, D.L., T.P. Novak, and M.A. Peralta (1997), Discussion Paper prepared for the Conference, "Anonymous Communications on the Internet: Uses and Abuses," University of California Irvine, (November 21-23)

- "High Access Charges = Lower Net Use?" (1997), *Wall Street Journal* (March 14).

- "How to Get Customers Inside Your Online Store—and Back Again" (1998), *PC Week* (February 2). Internet: www.zdnet.com/pcweek/sr/0202/02cust.html.

- "How to Join TRUSTe" (1998), TRUSTe (September). Internet: www.etrust.org/webpublishers/howtojoin.html.

- "Internet History Highlights" (1998), ETRG (July). Internet: http://etrg.findsvp.com/timeline/history.html.)

- Johnson, Bradley (1997), "Microsoft Web Ad Spending to Explode," *Advertising Age* (August 11), 1.

- Krantz, Michael (1998), "Click till You Drop," *Time* (July 20), 34–49.

- Lamb, Charles W., Jr., Joseph Hair, and Carl McDaniel (1994), *Principles of Marketing.* Cincinnati: South-Western Publishing Co.

- Lawrence, Steve, and C. Lee Giles (1998), "Searching the World Wide Web," *Science,* 280 (5360), 98.

- Machlis, Sharon (1998), "Warning: Web Selling Isn't Cheap," *Computerworld* (October 12: Vol. 32, No. 41).

- Marlatt, Andrew (1998), "Newsmaker - Rob Glaser: RealNetworks," *INTERNETWORLD News* (April 27). Internet: www.internetworld.com.

- Meeker, Mary (1997), "The Internet Advertising Report," *Internet Quarterly: Technology: Internet/New Media* (January). Internet: www.ms.com.

- Moeller, Michael, and Scott Berinato (1998), "NT 5.0: Justice's Next Target?" *PC Week* (May 8). Internet: www.zdnet.com/zdnn/content/pcwk/1519/315003.html.

- Moran, Susan (1996), "Amazon.com Forges New Sales Channel," Web Week (August 19: Vol. 2, Issue 12). Internet: www.internetworld.com/print/ww-back.html.

- Mougayar, Walid (1997), *Opening Digital Markets.* New York: McGraw-Hill.

- Murphy, Kathleen (1996), "Plug-in Weeds Out Advertising," *Web Week* (May 20: Vol. 2, Issue 6). Internet: www.internetworld.com/print/1996/05/20/webweek.html.

- Murphy, Kathleen (1997), "Vendors Hope Privacy Worries Lead to Profits," *Web Week* (April 28: Volume 3, Issue 12). Internet: www.internetworld.com/print/1997/04/28/markcomm/profits.html.

- Negroponte, Nicholas (1995), *Being Digital.* New York: Vintage Books.

- "Net Nanny Homepage" (1998), Net Nanny (July). Internet: www.netnanny.com.

- "The New Stock Traders: They're gusty, they're savvy, and they don't need a broker" (1998), *BusinessWeek* as cited on Datek (May 4). Internet: www.datek.com/marketing/about/in_news/bw050498.html

- Newbery, Michael (1998), "How to Upset a Web Cache" (October). Internet: www.vuw.ac.nz/~newbery/rant.html.

- Nolan, Godfrey (1998), "Context Sensitive Search Engines," *Deja News* (May 26). Internet: http://x6.dejanews.com/.

- "Online Advertising: Simple Truths" (1998), *AdKnowledge* (September). Internet: www.adknowledge.com/cgi-bin/show?Reference/online_ad.html.

- "The on-line elite" (1997), *Institutional Investor* (September). Internet: www.datek.com/marketing/about/in_news/ii0997.html.

- "On-line Investing: 'Datek Online: A Haven for the Hyperactive'" (1998), *Forbes* as cited in Datek (May 4). Internet: www.datek.com/marketing/about/in_news/forbes0598.html.

- "Online Trading: Datek Hits the Top of the Heap" (1998), *The Street.com* (May 13). Internet: www.datek.com/marketing/about/in_news/street0598.html.

- "Open Your Own Online Store Today! Amazon Associates Program" (1998), Amazon (September). Internet: www.amazon.com.

- Ozer, Jan (1998), "Microsoft Netshow 3.0," *PC Magazine* (July 7). Internet: www.zdnet.com/products/content/reviews/199807/net.netshow/2.html.

- Peppers, Don, and Martha Rogers (1996), *The One to One Future*, New York: Doubleday.

- "PGP Acquires PrivNet" (1996), *Netday News* (November 15). Internet: www.internetnews.com/96Nov/1501-pgp.html.

- Piquet, Lori (1998), "The Twenty Best Internet Consulting Firms," *Internet Computing MegaSite* (April 6). Internet: www.zdnet.com/icom/content/anchors/199804/06/best.202/index.html.

- "Pretty Good Deal" (1996), Suck (November). Internet: www.suck.com/daily/96/11/18/daily.html.

- "Products of RelevantKnowledge" (1998), RelevantKnowledge (October). Internet: www.relevantknowledge.com/Products/index.html.

- "Profile of Andrew Sather" (1998), Highfive Profile (Issue 9). Internet: www.highfive.com/profile/past/profile_07.97.html.

- "The Questions of Cookies" (1998), *AdKnowledge* (September). Internet: www.adknowledge.com/cgi-bin/show?Reference/ques_cookies.html.

- Randall, Neil (1997), "The New Cookie Monster," *PC Magazine* (April 22). Internet: www.zdnet.com/pcmag/issues/1608/pcmg0035.htm.

- Rapp, Stan, and Thomas Collins (1996), *The New Maximarketing.* New York: McGraw Hill.

- Ray, Michael L. (1973), "Communication and the Hierarchy of Effects," in *New Models for Mass Communication Research,* P. Clarke. ed., Beverly Hills, CA: Sage Publications, 147–175.

- Reid, Robert H. (1997), *Architects of the Web.* New York: John Wiley & Sons (also on Internet: www.architectsoftheweb.com/jw).

- Rogers, Everett M. (1962), *Diffusion of Innovations.* New York: Free Press.

- Rupley, Sebastian (1998), "Different Feeds for Different Speeds," *PC MAGAZINE Online* (April 29). Internet: www.zdnet.com/pcmag/news/trends/t980429a.htm.

- "Safeguarding the Web" (1998), *ZDNet Special Reports: Products* (February 5). Internet: www.zdnet.com.

- "Sellers List" (1998), Flycast (September). Internet: www.flycast.com/flycast/CPsellerslist.html.

- Shapiro, Eben (1994), "Consumers Leaving New Twists on Old Products on the Shelves," *The Wall Street Journal* (February 1), B1.

- Sheth, Jagdish N. (1995), "Relationship Marketing in Consumer Markets: Antecedents and Consequences," *Journal of the Academy of Marketing Science,* 23 (4), 255–271.

- Siegel, David (1998), "High Five Redesign Contest," High Five (July). Internet: www.highfive.com/past/high_five_7.3.96.html.

- Sonnenberg, Frank (1993), "If I Had Only One Client," *Sales and Marketing Management,* 56 (November), 4.

- Stamper, Chris (1996), "A Horrible Mistake," *Netly News* (May 8). Internet: http://cgi.pathfinder.com/netly/article/0,2334,11561,00.html.

- Strauss, Judy, and Anna Pesce (1998), "Corporate Responses to Consumer E-mail Complaints: A Pilot Study," *Marketing Management Association 1998 Proceedings, ed.* D. Varble, J. Young, and K. Glynn. Chicago: Marketing Management Association, 46–50.

- "Survey: Lycos Users Most Concerned About Credit Card Security" (1998), *InternetNews* (March 5). Internet: www.internetnews.com/bus-news/1998/03/0501-lycos.html.

- Toffler, Alvin (1980), *The Third Wave.* New York: William Morrow and Co.

- "Traffic Leaders Emerge as the Web Matures" (1998), *PC Week Online* (May 11). Internet: www.zdnet.com/pcweek.

- Varadarajan, P. Rajan, and Margaret Cunningham (1995), "Strategic Alliances: A Synthesis of Conceptual Foundations," *Journal of the Academy of Marketing Science,* 23 (4), 282–296.

- "Vital Statistics on 124 Web Design Shops" (1997), *InternetWorld* (December 1). Internet: www.internetworld.com/print/1997/12/01/undercon/19971201-webdesign.html.

- Vonder Haar, Steven (1996), "Amazon Tries Amway-Style Book Selling," *Inter@ctive Week* (July 19). Internet: www.zdnet.com/intweek/daily/960719a.html.

- Vonder Haar, Steven (1997), "DoubleClick Brings Darwin To Web" *Inter@ctive Week* (September 8). Internet: www.zdnet.com/intweek/print/970908/inwk0057.html.

- Vonder Haar, Steven (1997), "Nielsen, I/Pro Turn Tables On Web Traffic Measurement," *Inter@ctive Week* (November 21). Internet: www.zdnet.com/intweek/daily/971121d.html.

- Vonder Haar, Steven (1998), "Can Yahoo! Stay The Meteoric Course?" *Inter@ctive Week* (April 29). Internet: www.zdnet.com/zdnn/content/inwk/0516/310746.html.

- Vonder Haar, Steven (1998), "Roll 'Em: Bringing Video To The Net," *Inter@ctive Week* (June 15). Internet: www.zdnet.com/intweek/print/980615/327251.html.

- Vonder Haar, Steven (1998), "Web Firms To Track Individual Ads" *Inter@ctive Week* (January 12). Internet: www.zdnet.com/intweek/print/980112/270968.html.

- Wang, Nelson (1997), "Startup Offers Service To Fix Undercounting Of Page Views," *WebWeek* (October 13). Internet: www.internetworld.com/print/1997/10/13/news/19971013-startup.html.

- Wang, Nelson (1997), "Wall St. Buys Into Amazon," *Web Week* (May 19: Volume 3, Issue 15). Internet: www.internetworld.com/print/news-index.html.

- Warren, S. & Brandeis, L. (1890), "The Right to Privacy," 4 Harvard Law Review 193.

- Weber, Thomas (1996), "Simplest E-Mail Queries Confound Companies," *Wall Street Journal* (October 21), B1.

- Weilbacher, William (1993), *Brand Marketing*. Lincolnwood, IL: NTC Business Books.

- Weisul, Kimberly (1998), "Online Brokerages Target Niches" *Inter@ctive_Week* (May 4). Internet: www.zdnet.com/intweek/print/980504/314056.html.

- Weisul, Kimberly (1998), "Online Trades Jump 25 Percent," *Inter@ctive_Week* (June 1). Internet: www.zdnet.com/intweek/daily/980601n.html.

- Weisul, Kimberly (1998), "Web Alters Stock Quote Market" *Inter@ctive_Week* (June 8). Internet: www.zdnet.com/intweek/print/980608/325654.html.

- Wingfield, Nick (1998), "Start-Up Vignette Makes Life Easier for Web Publishers," *Wall Street Journal* (September 24), B4.

- "Yahoo! and AT&T to Offer Web Users Expanded Access to Communication Services" (1998), Yahoo! (May 18). Internet: www.yahoo.com/info/pr/releases.html.

- "Yahoo! and MCI Unveil New Internet Online Service; Yahoo! Online Powered by MCI Internet" (1998), Yahoo! (January 12). Internet: www.yahoo.com/info/pr/releases.html.

- "Yahoo! and Ticketmaster Give Users Easier Access to Live Event Information and Ticket Purchasing Online" (1998), Yahoo! (June 1). Internet: www.yahoo.com/info/pr/releases.html.

- "Yahoo! to Acquire Viaweb" (1998), Yahoo! (June 8). Internet: www.yahoo.com/info/pr/releases.html.

- "Yahoo!'s Yang: Web Is Now a 'Lifestyle Medium'" (1998), *ZDNN* (March 12). Internet: www.zdnet.com.

- ZDNet (1998), "MS, Compaq, Cable Firms Eye High-Speed Web," *Reuters*, June 15 (cited on Internet: www.zdnet.com/zdnn/stories/zdnn_display/0,3440,2112446,00.html).

Index

Page numbers in italics refer to tables and figures.